THE
TRANSFORMING
DRAUGHT

THE TRANSFORMING DRAUGHT

Jekyll and Hyde,
Robert Louis Stevenson
and the Victorian Alcohol Debate

THOMAS L. REED, JR.

McFarland & Company, Inc., Publishers
Jefferson, North Carolina, and London

LIBRARY OF CONGRESS CATALOGUING-IN-PUBLICATION DATA

Reed, Thomas L.
  The transforming draught : *Jekyll and Hyde*, Robert Lewis Stevenson and the Victorian alcohol debate / Thomas L. Reed, Jr.
    p.   cm.
  Includes bibliographical references and index.

  ISBN-13: 978-0-7864-2648-5
  ISBN-10: 0-7864-2648-9
  (softcover : 50# alkaline paper) ∞

  1. Stevenson, Robert Louis, 1850–1894. Strange case of Dr. Jekyll and Mr. Hyde.   2. Horror tales, Scottish — History and criticism.   3. Alcoholism in literature.   4. Symbolism in literature.   5. Multiple personality in literature.   6. Split self in literature.   7. Stevenson, Robert Louis, 1850–1894 — Language.   I. Title.
PR5485.R45   2006
823'.8--dc22   2006020670

British Library cataloguing data are available

©2006 Thomas L. Reed, Jr. All rights reserved

No part of this book may be reproduced or transmitted in any form or by any means, electronic or mechanical, including photocopying or recording, or by any information storage and retrieval system, without permission in writing from the publisher.

Cover image © 2006 PhotoSpin

Manufactured in the United States of America

McFarland & Company, Inc., Publishers
  Box 611, Jefferson, North Carolina 28640
  www.mcfarlandpub.com

For Daniel

Acknowledgments

Many people have been instrumental in the development of this argument. My students at Dickinson College have for years taken to *Jekyll and Hyde* with the enthusiasm and insight that brilliant texts invariably elicit from them. Pre-eminent among them is Nicole Slagle — now a teacher exploring the novella with her own classes — whose engagement with Stevenson in an upper-level English course led to our collaborating on a research project and ultimately to a jointly-authored paper on RLS and Drink which she read at the Modern Language Association Convention in December of 1999.

The organizer of that Chicago session was Martin Danahay, whose support and advice have been constant boons over the last half decade as this study moved towards its final form. Antje Andersson and Ellen Rosenman also read substantial portions of the manuscript and offered invaluable advice.

To the staff at the Waidner-Spahr Library at Dickinson College, the Sterling and Beinecke Libraries at Yale University, the University of Canterbury Library in Christchurch, New Zealand, the University of Lancashire Library (and their Joseph Livesey Collection), the Library of Congress, and the British Library, I owe great thanks for consistent helpfulness, resourcefulness, and wisdom. Concetta Maresco of the Interlibrary Loan Department at Dickinson has been especially saintly in her ministrations — as indeed has Jean Weaver of our Information Technology staff, who scanned (and doctored) many of the Illustrations.

Among the numerous colleagues who have offered gracious support, both psychological and scholarly, I would like especially to mention Ash Nichols and Bob Winston of Dickinson's English Department. I was fortunate enough to meet Gareth Cordery during the sabbatical leave that yielded the bulk of the research and writing for the book, and I am abidingly grateful not only for the guidance and assistance he afforded me as I explored the representation of alcohol in Victorian fiction but also for countless recommendations of stunning mountain walks and equally countless insights into the finer points of rugby and cricket. Thanks as well to his department at the University of Canterbury, for the generous provision of office space and other forms of Kiwi hospitality. I should also say that Sir Brian Harrison, author of the indispensable *Drink and the Victorians,* not only paved the scholarly way for my earliest explorations of the context in which I've read Stevenson's novella but also — towards the very end of this undertaking — helped me track down an image which is central to Chapter Seven.

Finally, I owe my family an immeasurable lot — for freeing me to pursue what must have seemed to them to be a terribly arcane interest; for welcoming me back into the fold at the end of long days when my energies and patience were sorely spent; and ultimately for professing sustained and sincere interest in how it was all going. So thank you, Dottie, Abby, and Dan, for the understanding and for the love. If I can somehow, some day, coerce you into reading this, I hope your sacrifices will seem to have resulted in some tangible good.

Carlisle, Pennsylvania
July 2006

Contents

Acknowledgments vii
List of Illustrations x
Introduction 1

ONE. Jekyll the Addict   9
TWO. Alcohol in the Text: The Letter   19
THREE. Alcohol in the Text: The Spirit   32
FOUR. RLS and the Drinking World   47
FIVE. The Literary Contexts of Stevenson's Tale of Alcohol   63
SIX. "Self" and "The Other Fellow"   79
SEVEN. The Temperance Agenda   96
EIGHT. Dream Scenes: Neighborhoods of Nightmare   114
NINE. "Street Crime"   131
TEN. Jekyll and Hyde: Beginnings and Endings   161
ELEVEN. Stevenson's "Allegory" and Its Reception   186
TWELVE. Conclusion: Finding the Balance   198

Appendix: The Language of the Times   215
Chapter Notes   231
Bibliography   243
Index   251

List of Illustrations

Figure 1. George Cruikshank, "The Gin Juggarnath" 42

Figure 2. "The Influence of Morality or Immorality on the Countenance" 104

Figure 3. "Essence of Parliament" 106

Figure 4. "Which Way Shall I Turn Me?" 107

Figure 5. "The Savings' Bank and the Losings' Bank" 109

Figure 6. "Pot and Kettle" 111

Figure 7. "Publican-Barrel and Pharisee-Pump" 112

Figure 8. "The English Juggernaut" 137

Figure 9. "Our Once Facetious Contemporary Is By No Means Funny This Week" 147

Introduction

Early in 1874, when he was in his mid-twenties, Robert Louis Stevenson confessed to his friend and sometime mentor Sidney Colvin, "Curious how, wherever I go, I come trailing clouds of dipsomania" (*Letters* 1.467). Stevenson was writing to Colvin from Menton, on just the first leg of what evolved into a life-long global quest for tolerable health. Yet, as the following pages will consistently reveal, the author's entire journey from cradle to grave was undertaken in the penumbra—if not the full shadow—of Bacchus. Fanny Stevenson's preface to *A Child's Garden of Verses* notes of her ever-ailing husband's early years in rheumy Edinburgh, "When the child ... took cold after cold, antimonial wine [sherry with tartaric antimony] was administered continuously for a period extending into months; 'enough' said Dr George Balfour, 'to ruin his constitution for life'"(*Letters* 3.197n.). Four decades later, Stevenson's last trip in that life was down to his Samoan wine cellar to fetch a bottle of burgundy for his supper. When he collapsed shortly afterwards, struck down by a fatal cerebral embolism, Fanny ironically embraced the enduring if contested medical wisdom of the age as she administered a dose of brandy in a fruitless attempt to restore that long-ruined constitution (McLynn 504).

The cloud of alcohol shadows *Strange Case of Dr. Jekyll and Mr. Hyde* (*J&H*) as thoroughly as it did its author, albeit in ways that have been only spottily acknowledged and never until now been fully explored. To state the case most simply—and in the novella's own terms—Stevenson's best-known tale documents the fate of a man who regularly escapes from an over-burdening respectability into an addictive world of recreational excess by drinking a "blood-red *liquor*" whose effects "braced and delighted [him] like *wine*"—but which ultimately reduce him to the same crushing self-recrimination that is suffered when "a *drunkard* reasons with himself upon his vice" (*J&H* 76, 84, 90; emphases added). If *J&H* is not actually an allegory of alcoholism, of the disruptive "Hyde" that strong drink can release in any human being, then it is everything but that— especially if one reads the work against the twin backdrops of Stevenson's life and of the century-long debate over drink that split Britain into what Thomas Whitaker called two "distinct races," two "nations" whose sometimes lethal wrangling figured so strongly in the making and breaking of parliamentary governments (*Brighter England* 161). In the process of grounding his unquestionably fantastic story of "man's double being" ("A Chapter on Dreams" 208) in a widely-apprehensible social reality, Stevenson turns for his most potent metaphors to the almost universally experienced form of social self-abandon that is drink, crafting a fiction that consistently evinces mid– and late–Victorian ambivalence towards intoxicating beverages.

As the following pages reveal, that collective ambivalence was one that Stevenson himself deeply shared, embodying his conflicted feelings in this particular case in a fictional "life" that he hinted could perfectly well be his own. The month the novella appeared, in January of 1886, he wrote to his cousin Katherine de Mattos about the little poem in which he dedicates the work to her: "I only wish the verses were better, but at least you like the story; and it is sent to you by the one that loves you— Jekyll, and not Hyde" (*Letters* 5.168). A month earlier, Stevenson's letter to American painter William Low had suggested that the writer saw an even broader topical applicability in the text. He was sending the artist a pre-publication copy of the tale at which he'd been laboring, something he whimsically dubbed his "gothic gnome." The covering message confides that "the gnome's name is *Jekyll and Hyde*; I believe you will find he is likewise quite willing to answer to the name of Low or Stevenson" (*Letters* 5.163). And ultimately, John Addington Symonds, the consumptive, oenophile friend who tellingly dedicated to Stevenson his own bacchanalian *Wine, Women and Song*, registered what he himself saw as an almost universal applicability in the novella—significantly couching his remarks in the very language of drink. "Viewed as an allegory," he writes to the author in March of 1886, "it touches one too closely. Most of us at some epoch of our lives have been upon the verge of developing a Mr Hyde";

Symonds then goes on to observe of another nineteenth-century Bard of Bacchus that, when compared to his old Davos drinking partner Stevenson as a scribe of horrid duality, "Poe is as water" (Maixner 210–11).

When other commentators have discerned an Everyman experience limned allegorically in *Jekyll and Hyde*, they have customarily explained the work's universality in Freudian or neo-Freudian terms—along predictably general lines that need no further rehearsal here. More recently, assessments of the work's broad relevance have often focused on issues of late-Victorian sexuality and gender, making explicit the kinds of concerns that may indeed lie behind Symond's troubled response to Stevenson's tale. William Veeder, Elaine Showalter, and Wayne Koestenbaum, for example, have all written persuasively on the homo-social or homosexual resonances that a closeted gay like Symonds could have found so exercising.[1] Other recent and illuminating strains of cultural analysis have situated the text in the evolving world of publishing in which Stevenson struggled to find his distinctive niche and "level"—and, in related ways, amidst the welter of social angst spawned by Darwin's revolutionary ideas on human evolution and by the ancillary theories of "degeneration" offered by B. A. Morel, Cesare Lombroso, Max Nordau, and others. One thinks most notably of three rich arguments by Patrick Brantlinger and Richard Boyle, by Stephen Arata, and by Robert Mighall, all of whom read the novella as a kind of nightmare of biological and moral atavism.[2] Long appreciated as a work of multiple points of view, then, *J&H* is also a work of multiple *bona fide* subtexts. Nevertheless, for all of the insight and usefulness of these prior studies, if one stands comfortably back from the novella and looks for its most consistent patterns of language, plot, characterization, and imagery, no subtext emerges any more strongly or any more consequentially than the subtext of alcoholism.

As to where those patterns might have emerged from, some of the prime responsibility for the story's distinct content and form must go to Stevenson's "Brownies," those pre-conscious creative forces to which the writer charmingly but revealingly attributed the basic impetus for his work ("A Chapter on Dreams" 208). To some extent, then, this study will emulate the method of John Livingston Lowes in *The Road to Xanadu*, exploring numerous potential wellsprings of creative imagination, some of which may have remained hidden from Stevenson's conscious mind and intention. Yet it will also emerge from what follows—and especially from a consideration of the author's textual revisions of *J&H*—that a full dozen years after that confessional letter to Sidney Colvin, Stevenson could well have known that he was still the chronicler of a haunting "dipsomania." In any case, if we can trust its author when he claimed the novella derived from his longstanding wish to document "man's double being," we will need to acknowledge that the sense of "doubleness" that Stevenson knew best—both personally and through the marked and sometimes tragic examples of his closest friends—was the one provoked by strong drink. As a result, it should come as no surprise that Jekyll's addiction to the liberties of Hyde should smack so consistently of the language and lore of alcoholism. The surprise is more that this crucial vein of Stevenson's invention should have waited this long to be uncovered.

It will be useful to map here at the outset the various tracks that this first real look at Stevenson's alcoholic sub-text will take. Chapter One, "Jekyll the Addict," simply establishes *Jekyll and Hyde's* prime concern with addictive behavior, quickly reviewing the relevant extant criticism in the process. Chapter Two, "Alcohol in the Text: The Letter," introduces Stevenson's specific concern with the social impact of alcohol via a detailed, formalist look at the work's many literal references to strong drink—and at the way those references not only introduce the clash of "High" and "Low" principles that Stevenson extends into his broad explorations of psyche and social class but also reflect, in their own topical microcosm, the work's consistent ambivalence towards the opposed values of restraint and free expression. Chapter Three, "Alcohol in the Text: The Spirit," expands the careful analysis of language to the work's metaphors, further revealing the novella's overriding concern with alcohol and, indeed, with alcoholism as it was defined by Stevenson's predecessors and contemporaries.

Chapter Four, "RLS and the Drinking World," shifts the primary attention from text to social context. It elaborates on the sociology of drink in Victorian Britain (as introduced in Chapter Two), surveys Stevenson's life-long patterns of drinking, defines his borderline alcoholism, and treats the marked frequency with which his correspondence deals with other drinkers and with the virtues and dangers of drink. "The Literary Contexts of Stevenson's Tale of Alcohol" (Chapter Five) subsequently explores a range of Low and High nineteenth-century literary treatments of the alcohol problem in comparison to which one may assess *J&H* and its "seriousness" and success as a novel of drink and addiction. The chapter also considers other, more explicit treatments of alcohol as they are laced throughout Stevenson's fiction and poetry. The sixth chapter, "'Self' and 'The Other Fellow,'" takes Stevenson at his word when he claims that the novella spoke directly to the lives of those he knew well. It identifies a number of possible fictional and real-life models for the duality of Jekyll and Hyde, including James Hogg's *Justified Sinner*, Stevenson himself, and the writer's fatally alcoholic friend, Walter Ferrier — whose death the man's mother, with incalculable consequence, blamed on Stevenson and his pernicious bacchanalian influence.

Chapter Seven, "The Temperance Agenda," shifts the contextual focus from people to politics. It traces the history of the temperance movement in nineteenth-century Britain, reviews the popular temperance imagery with which Stevenson was familiar and which he incorporates into his text, and surveys his intermittent commentary on the temperance debate in his other fiction and in his letters as well. Chapter Eight, "Dream Scenes: Neighborhoods of Nightmare," discusses the two central episodes of *J&H* that Stevenson claimed were delivered to him by his "Brownies" via a dream — thereby affording him what he called the long-awaited "vehicle" for "the tale of man's duality" he had for years been eager to write ("A Chapter on Dreams" 208). This section returns to the close, textual scrutiny which characterizes the opening chapters, demonstrating the extent to which the two seminal scenes that finally loosed Stevenson's creativity were driven in thoroughgoing, if subtle, ways by traditional temperance imagery and ideology. The novella grew, in sum, out of a dream that was partially "scripted" by the contemporary politics of the drink question.

The next two chapters continue to probe the specifics of Stevenson's language, plot, and imagery with an eye to their trenchant topical allusiveness. "'Street Crime'" (Chapter Nine) documents the extent to which the three acts of violence that we see Hyde commit are also specifically informed by the ideas and images of the temperance movement. Proposed in this section are possible historical models for the murdered Member of Parliament, Sir Danvers Carew, together with a new hypothesis for Stevenson's choice of Hyde's name. "Jekyll and Hyde: Beginnings and Endings" (Chapter Ten) in turn relates the novella's action and language to the substantial impact of Britain's industrial development on the patterns and oversight of working-class recreation — most particularly recreational *drinking*— as well as on housing patterns and evolving challenges to social control. This chapter also explores the rich topicality of the tale's interest in "adulterated" chemicals and in tea.

Chapter Eleven, "Stevenson's 'Allegory' and Its Reception," begins a process of stepping back from the main argument in order to assess its ultimate strength and utility. It explores just how plausible it is to read *J&H* as, in large part, an allegory of alcoholism—first by looking at the representational modes that were common to the most influential spokespersons of temperance and, in turn, by assessing Stevenson's own occasional bent for allegorical (as opposed to realistic) narratives.[3] The chapter then surveys the novella's contemporary reception, suggesting that Stevenson's text was indeed read by some of his contemporaries as "about alcohol," while modern readers have been blinded to the text's most potent topicalities by inevitable social and cultural change—and, perhaps even more consequentially, by the irony that the work is now simply too well-known. That is to say, one can hardly read *J&H* any longer in the naïve ways that should lead one initially to hypothesize "realistic" reasons why Hyde looks and behaves the way he does—among those possible realistic reasons being alcoholic excess and the bestial violence it could so commonly entail. Finally, the "Conclusion: Finding the Balance," confirms that the novella's varied representations of alcohol reflect the profound ambivalence of Stevenson and his Age to temperance and the drink trade—but that, for all of its evident warnings against mind-altering draughts, the work ultimately advocates and models the "balanced" approach to drink that Stevenson fought hard to achieve in his own life.

In the end, temperance chronicler A. E. Dingle is very much in line with other social historians when he concludes that, "Victorians were obsessed with alcohol. Among the literate and the articulate, the proper place of drink in society was debated with an intensity and an exhaustiveness which is now difficult for us to comprehend" (*Campaign for Prohibition* 8). Among the more literate and articulate men of his age, Stevenson was no stranger to that debate, and he regularly explored in his texts and in his correspondence alike the social and psychological impacts of alcohol. Yet, as students of his work and times have been distanced by passing decades from the potent controversy that swirled around temperance reform, they have understandably lost a substantial measure of their ability to appreciate strong drink's greater and lesser effects on the literary output of the age. As a case in point, Richard Altick's voluminous *Presence of the Present* (1991), although its sub-title promises to offer comprehensive coverage of the manifold "Topics of the Day in the Victorian Novel," boasts no index entry at all for "alcohol," "drink," "prohibition," *or* "temperance." More than addressing a rather serious and unaccountable oversight in Stevenson criticism, then, the current study should also go some ways towards re-establishing the crucial role played by the drink question in a broader range of mid– to late–Victorian texts as well. Of what social historians have long acknowledged, literary scholars can profitably be reminded. What follows will, one hopes, make a reasonable start towards that end.

ONE

Jekyll the Addict

We'll do well to begin by establishing the clear but under-appreciated fact that Henry Jekyll is an addict. Hyde is most simply the persona Jekyll assumes when he pursues an obsessive gratification: the doctor accordingly confesses that "men have before hired bravos to transact their crimes, while their own person and reputation sat under shelter. I was the first that ever did so for his *pleasures*" (86; emphasis added). Beyond associating the doctor's Hyde-self with the "pleasure" that drives most addictive behavior, the passage also hints at the hedging against social censure that addiction commonly involves. Jekyll has earlier located the youthful seed of Hyde in "a certain impatient gaiety of disposition, such as has made the happiness of many, but such as I found it hard to reconcile with my imperious desire to carry my head high.... Hence it came about that I concealed my pleasures"—which leads both to the "profound duplicity of life" that is the tale's chief subject and, in turn, to that revealing "morbid sense of shame" (81).

Hyde, then, is the altered state of being in which Jekyll feels comfortable indulging his morally troublesome appetites. Significantly, the potion that enables his metamorphosis and his subsequent access to gratification also answers Jekyll's need for relief from the moral tension that "base" desires may call forth in the self-respecting man. "If each [of my conflicting desires]," he told himself before beginning his fatal course of experimentation, "could but be housed in separate identities, life would be relieved of all that was unbearable; the unjust might go his way, delivered from the aspirations and remorse of his more upright twin; and the just could walk steadfastly and securely on his upright path, doing the good things in which he found his pleasure, and no longer exposed to disgrace and penitence at the hands of this extraneous evil" (82). Thus, becoming Hyde not only gives Jekyll unencumbered *future* access to his "shameful" satisfactions but it also represents one of those classic "behaviors of addiction [that] ... attempt to palliate *pre-existing* severe psychic stress" (Lilienfeld 229; italics added) — in this case, the moral anxiety of wanting something that is out of line with social proprieties. That Jekyll turns to his potion to anaesthetize "the agonized womb of consciousness" (82) is established by Stevenson in two ways. On the one hand, he writes, when Hyde was empowered and "virtue slumbered" (85), then "conscience slumbered" as well (87). And on the other, he makes Jekyll fantasize hypocritically that his addictive personality is "separate" from his true nature, a trait that addiction specialist Patrick Carnes deems absolutely central to the psychic strategies of the addict (Wright 7). "It was Hyde, after all, and Hyde alone, that was guilty," claims the doctor (87), nicely overlooking his own enabling responsibility for Hyde's murderous liberties. Subsequently, as the eventually drugless Jekyll contemplates the finality of his "own" consciousness giving way to Hyde's, he similarly claims "what is to follow concerns another than myself" (97).

Hyde's behavior intensifies in the classic pattern of a deepening addiction. While Jekyll's "low" gratifications had at first involved nothing more grave than "an impatient gaiety of disposition" (81) — flippant "pleasures" which strike the doctor as "undignified" and little more than that (86) — "in the hands of Edward Hyde they soon began to turn towards the monstrous" (86). We'll come back to the significance of Hyde's pleasure turning to sadistic violence, but for now let it simply be said that, like the stereotypical addict, he craves over the course of his habit increasingly extreme forms of stimulation and gratification in order to get his "fix" — a fact that Stevenson reflects not only in Hyde's growth in "stature" relative to Jekyll (88) but also in the increase in chemical dosage that is required to subdue him (89). And once Hyde's lust for inflicting pain drives him to the murder of Sir Danvers Carew, Jekyll accordingly displays the repentant addict's stereotypical determination to free himself from his vice and amend his ways. "I resolved in my future conduct to redeem the past," he writes, "and I can say with honesty that my resolve was fruitful of some good" (92).

Yet the old cravings inevitably return, and "as the first edge of my penitence wore off," Jekyll confesses, "the lower side of me, so long indulged, so recently chained down, began to growl for license" (92). He had much earlier assured his solicitous friend Utterson, after the lawyer had warned him of the potential shame of "associating" with Hyde, "the moment I choose, I can be rid of Mr Hyde. I give you my hand upon that" (44). Yet Jekyll's ability to control his addictive metamorphoses instead begins to slip away, and he is soon alarmed lest "the balance of [his] nature be permanently overthrown, the power of voluntary change be forfeited, and the character of Edward Hyde become irrevocably [his]"; "I was slowly losing hold of my original and better self," he laments, "and becoming slowly incorporated with my second and worse" (89). And once the reversion to Hyde has gone beyond Jekyll's conscious choice and he begins regularly to awake, willy-nilly, in his "inebriated" form, he observes that "between these two [identities] I now felt I had to choose" (89). Nevertheless, like many an addict, he continues in the midst of his re-imposed discipline to suffer in "fires of abstinence" (89) and is finally obliged to admit that "it fell out with me, as it falls out with so vast a majority of my fellows, that I chose the better part and was found wanting in the strength to keep it" (89). "I began to be tortured with throes and longings," he observes, "as of Hyde struggling after freedom; and at last, in an hour of moral weakness, I at once compounded and swallowed the transforming draught" (90). The addictive self is simply too strong for him, as each of these multiple attempts to regain control of his life proves to be fruitless. In sum, if its villain's crimes suggest that the title of *Strange Case of Dr. Jekyll and Mr. Hyde* relates primarily to a *legal* or an *investigative* "case" (as with the varied "cases" of Sherlock Holmes), the protagonist's struggles to control the addictive "pleasures and adventures of Hyde" (89) suggest instead a medical or psychiatric or (to use the Victorian term) *alienist's* "case."

Other commentators have admittedly touched on *Jekyll and Hyde*'s concern with the psychology of addiction. Rarely, though, have they done so in any depth — and even less frequently in ways that acknowledge what it might mean that Jekyll characterizes his tragic dependence on his "transforming draught" as exactly like the short-sighted indulgence of a "*drunkard*" (90; italics added.) Daniel Wright's brief article on *J&H*—"'The Prisonhouse of My Disposition': A Study of the Psychology of Addiction in *Dr. Jekyll and Mr. Hyde*"(1994) — is the most compelling work to date on Jekyll's fatal dependency on both his potion and his dark "other." Wright nicely documents Jekyll's entrapment in the four-step cycle of preoccupation, ritualization, compulsive behavior, and despair that Patrick Carnes associates with classic addiction. He notes that Jekyll displays, as we've seen, the addict's stereotypical denial of dependency, his fantasy that the addictive personality is "separate" from his true nature, his cyclical shame and resolution to break the habit and amend his ways, and his ultimate failure to maintain his fine resolve — such that he loses his life to his uncontrollable "other self." Yet Wright narrowly and literalistically treats Jekyll's use of an "undisclosed psychoactive substance that turns him into Edward Hyde" and concludes that, for all of Stevenson's profound insights into drug dependency, the question of whether the author "could have been himself an addict of some kind ... will ever only be speculative in its conclusions" (263) — a judgment which the current study should go a ways towards modifying.

Gerald Dollar's "Addiction and the 'Other Self' in Three Late Victorian Novels" (1994) in turn treats *J&H* in relation to Wilde's *Picture of Dorian Gray* and Hardy's *The Mayor of Casterbridge*, but, despite his attention to Michael Henchard's tragic tale, Dollar explains Jekyll's addictive "dependency on the Hyde self" as the result only of a "magic potion" (268), never catching a whiff of the strong spirits that, through both their literal and their metaphorical presence, consequentially link Stevenson's text to Hardy's, as we'll see. Finally, Katherine Linehan, in her Norton Critical Edition of *J&H* (2003), suggests that Jekyll's life may represent "a symbolic enactment of the loss of self-control that can come with regression, addiction, madness, or sleep" (xii). Furthermore, Linehan appends to the text a brief selection from Norman Kerr's *Inebriety, Its Etiology, Pathology, Treatment and Jurisprudence* (1882), which she entitles "Abject Slaves to the Narcotic" (136–38) — and in glossing Jekyll's allusion to the "impatient gaiety of disposition" that becomes Hyde notes that one of the available Victorian meanings of "gay" was "addicted to social pleasures and dissipations" (47, n.2). Yet, in keeping with the critical restraint required of an editor, she goes no further than that in uncovering the novella's concern with addiction.

Given that Jekyll's enslaving drug is specifically dubbed a "transforming *draught*" that he "*swallowed*" in order to obtain its effects (90; emphases added), interpreters should think of this addictive agent as necessarily more like alcohol or laudanum, among the handful of intoxicants favored by late–Victorians, than like either pure opium (which was customarily smoked) or cocaine (which the Sherlock Holmes's of the world injected in their seven-percent solutions). Interestingly, the thing that actually came to Stevenson's own mind *directly* after he hit on the phrase that epitomizes both the tale's action and its prime catalyst (the "transforming draught") — that thing was in fact *alcohol* and a ruinous dependence on the stuff. "I do not suppose," Jekyll confesses, "that, *when a drunkard reasons with himself upon his vice*, he is once out of five hundred times affected by the dangers that he runs through his brutish, physical insensibility; neither had I, long as I had considered my position, made enough allowance for the complete moral insensibility and insensate readiness to evil which were the leading characters of Edward Hyde" (90; emphasis added). This is of course not explicitly to say that Jekyll "drank himself" into being Hyde in the commonest sense of that expression. But it does clearly imply that, if we want to understand the doctor and his addiction, the best and most accessible behavioral analogy is alcoholism — a point very much in line with Norman Kerr's observation four years before *J&H* was published that alcohol was indeed the archetypal addictive substance of the time (30). Whether Stevenson's words offer a simple analogy to Jekyll's fatal short-sightedness or in fact signal a consistent sub-textual concern with strong drink is something for the following pages to resolve. Yet those suggestively linked passages surely invite at least a passing look at alcohol's role in the text.

Inspired by Stephen Gwynn's fleeting observation in 1939 that "there is no other of all [Stevenson's] books where his kindly feeling for vintages makes itself so often felt" (130), Vladimir Nabokov did memorably extol *J&H*'s "delightful winey taste" (180). Yet neither he nor Andrew Jefford, in his dedicated commentary on Nabokov's analysis of the text, read the work as in any sustained way about alcohol, let alone addiction. And when they do treat drink, both Nabokov and Jefford contrast the "warmth" that Mr. Utterson feels and radiates when drinking wine with the "icy pangs" that Jekyll feels in quaffing his blood-red liquor — thereby overlooking the complicating but crucial fact that (as we'll see) the potion essentially thrills and delights Jekyll exactly "*like* wine" (84; italics added.) Jefford goes on to suggest that, "when [wine] is possible or present, or even drinkable, we are among the positive image clusters [of the text]," again paying inadequate attention to the implications of Utterson finding an impressive stash of vintages in the villainous Hyde's Soho digs (52). As a result, both Nabokov and Jefford overlook the striking but revealing ambivalence that both the writer and his age displayed towards his favorite drug — an ambivalence that it is one of this study's prime goals to explain.

Other modern commentators have treated Jekyll as an addict and have at least *mentioned* alcohol as one of the substances that can lead to such dependency. Daniel Fraustino (1984) notes that "wine ... is probably used in connection with Hyde because of its liberating effect in reducing inhibitions," and goes on to discuss two or three examples of that "connection," including the vicious little man's suggestively "*drinking* pleasure with bestial avidity" (207) when he inflicts pain on others. As he scans the tale for evidence of the universal hypocrisy that he declares its prime theme, however, Fraustino is obliged to conclude that "moral culpability ... attends all who indulge their appetite for wine" (208), basically reversing Jefford's error by overlooking the overwhelmingly positive associations of wine that we shall find to apply when Utterson is involved with it. And Ian Bell, in his very readable 1992 biography of Stevenson, touches on *J&H* as a "parable of those 'not themselves' because of vice, drugs, or alcohol." He in fact mentions the writer's unfortunate university chum Walter Ferrier as one "victim" of "the alluring toxins, drink or drugs, [that] made men bestial" (179), a biographical fact whose striking implications we shall explore in a subsequent chapter. As suggestive as Bell's remarks are, however, they are developed no further than this.

In sum, the role played by alcohol in Stevenson's psychological tour de force remains to be fully documented and explained. The rest of this chapter briefly aligns some of the observations on Jekyll's addiction offered above with more specific hallmarks of alcoholism as understood both by Stevenson's contemporaries and by twentieth-century social science. Thereafter, we will immerse ourselves even more deeply in the revealing language of the text.

When Jekyll explicitly likens himself to a drunkard, he's speaking in the realm of metaphor. Stevenson's protagonist does, nonetheless, show a significant number of the traits of the problem drinker, as understood by his own age as well as our own. Some of those traits are physical. Hyde sometimes speaks with the "husky, whispering and somewhat broken voice" of the habitual over-indulger (40).[1] Moreover, the broadly disquieting (but somehow indescribable) "strangeness" of his appearance (e.g. 34 and 77) may hint at some of the subtle but undeniable physiognomic effects of alcohol that, for example, render snap-shots of abandoned partiers both amusing and distressing to their subjects once they've sobered up. Among Hyde's revealing behavioral traits, however, the "impatient gaiety of disposition" which Jekyll sees as the germ of his problem (81)—a trait which yields such disastrous consequences for Sir Danvers Carew when Hyde's "ill-contained impatience" (46) with the old man's long-winded civilities explodes into a "tempest of impatience" (90) and "insensate cruelty" (47) — is a version not only of the alcoholic Michael Henchard's "restless impatience" in *The Mayor of Casterbridge* (156) but also of the distinctive intolerance for frustration that recent clinicians consistently link with alcoholism (Levin 129–33).[2] One accordingly sees the same peevish violence in the drunkard Billy Bones early in *Treasure Island*. Jim Hawkins testifies that, "in these [drunken] fits, he was the most overriding companion ever known; he would slap his hand on the table for silence all round; he would fly up in a passion of anger at a question, or sometimes because none was put, as so he judged the company was not following his story" (5–6).

Torn apart by the "perennial war among [his] members" (82) — by the ill fit between his "honourable" (81) and his "undignified" (85) urges — Jekyll turns (as we've seen) to a potion that allows him to externalize his "brutish, physical insensibility" so that "life would be relieved of all that was unbearable" (82). In the same vein, Samuel Johnson had in the century before Stevenson's explained the special allure of drink by saying that "he who makes a *beast* of himself gets rid of the pain of being a man" (Crouch 20–1). Equally to the point, and in Stevenson's own era, social analyst Charles Booth famously cited one sympathetic cleric who said of London's poor, "Worry is what they suffer from, rest and hope what they want. Drunkenness dulls the sense of present evil" (201). This *is*, in the end, a novel about the mitigation of psychic stress, about a doomed attempt to banish an all-too-present evil. That it should adumbrate alcohol's most commonplace role in those adaptive strategies makes perfectly good sense, as both Dr. Johnson and Booth would have been quick to acknowledge.

Jekyll's confessed failure to "make allowance" either for the extent of Hyde's depravities or for his own inability to control his alter-ego in turn directly mirrors the modern alcoholic's "inability to assess long-range consequences of actions or to control impulsive behavior" (Lilienfeld 228–229). Closer to Stevenson's day, both George Eliot and William Booth also captured the alcoholic's classic loss of control. *Janet's Repentance* turns upon "that evil habit, which [Janet] loathed in retrospect and yet was powerless to resist" (280), while Booth's *In Darkest England* laments of the drunkard, "The insatiable drive controls him. He cannot get away from it. It compels him to drink, whether he will or not" (180–1). As Hyde first appears "a little man" (31) but ultimately seems to Jekyll to have "grown in stature" (88), so Janet's tyrannical craving for drink "got stronger and stronger" (286). And in turn, just as Janet laments her apparently irreversible spiral downwards towards damnation, Jekyll decries his gradual but inevitable "losing hold of [his] original and better self" (89). Of the typical repentant inebriate, Norman Kerr had aptly written in 1882, "again and again does he resolve to drink no more, but his resolution is overborne by the dominating drink impulse" (208).

In his watershed 1960 definition of "gamma alcoholism," E. M. Jellinek explicitly coupled the problem drinker's powerlessness with the kind of "withdrawal symptoms and 'craving'" (37) that Jekyll also experiences: "I began to be tortured with throes and longings," he confesses, "as of Hyde struggling after freedom" (90). Once she has sworn off liquor, George Eliot's Janet is equally and representatively hard pressed to overcome the "impetuous desire [that] shook ... through all her members" (319). Jellinek's study predictably cites this frightening loss of control as "impair[ing] interpersonal relations to the highest degree. The damage to health in general and to financial and social standing are also more prominent than in other species of alcoholism" (37). Jekyll is accordingly estranged from friends (Lanyon, for example, seeing "devilish little" of him once his experiments begin [36]), he terminates an obviously lucrative medical practice in order to devote his finances not only to chemical research but also to the wanton expenditures of Hyde (the costs of separate accommodations in Soho, of profligate recreation, and of blackmail payments included), and falls to the level of a man whom Poole declares unfit to "dine" with Jekyll and his cronies (41). Although such radical alterations in the patterns of daily life could then, as they can now, characterize virtually any powerful addiction, we'll discover that this kind of social isolation and decline is for temperance pundits from George Cruikshank and James Greenwood to William and Charles Booth most commonly — and almost invariably — the sign of *alcoholic* ruin. Furthermore, Jekyll's psyche fragments into two disparate components to the extent that, late in his account, he refers to Hyde as a completely separate being: "He, I say — I cannot say, I" (94). Jekyll's "Strange Case" could thus be an archetypal if relatively early case study of the "weak ego structure" that is seen to characterize many modern alcoholics (Lilienfeld 228) and, indeed, that also characterized Samuel Taylor Coleridge's addictive son Hartley, who consistently referred to himself only in the third person (Taylor 154).[3]

As we observed above, the garden variety addict may feel shame for what he has done but he still paradoxically seeks to displace onto some other person or agency any final responsibility for his fate and actions. Modern alcoholics, we are told, conform to type (Lilienfeld 233); and Hardy's tragic mayor affords classic conformation from Stevenson's own era, largely blaming Fate for the sweeping misfortunes that devolve from his early dipsomania. Jekyll is cut from the same cloth. "It was the curse of mankind," he claims of the dark causes that he sees driving his ruin, "that these incongruous faggots [of his 'warring members'] were bound together" (82). For him, the root of the problem lies either in genetics or in something like Original Sin — rather than in any individual weakness or failing or inclination. And once his radical program of Victorian self-help goes dreadfully wrong, he likewise blames Hyde: "It was Hyde, after all, and Hyde alone, that was guilty" (87). Although the root of an addiction to drink is, in essence, "at the core of the total personality," "in an alcoholic personality alcoholism is imagined to be outside the self, and threatening or invading the self" (Taylor 90). Thus, despite Jekyll's initial awareness of the key etiological role played by his own indigenous "impatient gaiety," he comes to see Hyde often enough as an "insurgent horror," coalesced out of "the slime of the pit" and resolved to "usurp the offices of life" (95). The "I," as the rightful captain of the Ship of Life, is displaced by the mutinous "he." "And thus," says Jekyll, "conscience slumbered" (87). Just so, claimed Norman Kerr of the late–Victorian inebriate's moral vagrancy, is "conscience ... impaired" and "enfeebled" by strong drink (30; 61).

One could go on and on in this vein, adding alcoholic particulars to the general sketch of addiction offered above. Like Utterson (as we'll soon see), Jekyll's moderate social drinking of wine with his professional cronies is augmented by a secretive habit for something much stronger, consumed at a discreet but dangerous remove from his customary "support group" — this kind of secretive solitary indulgence being a prime popular earmark of the alcoholic. Norman Kerr, for example, writes three years before Stevenson of the "double life" (48) of an English gentleman who could almost have been a model for Jekyll:

> S.J., male, 59.... A brilliant scholar and an elegant writer, a man of profound learning. A gentle and unselfish spirit, even on his deathbed devising a deed of munificent generosity. Originally a warm friend of temperance, he gradually fell into the habit of secret drinking, and for some ten years, unknown to the world, drank to intoxication every night. Only his servants knew of his failing. I discovered his secret accidentally,

on being called to him on one occasion during a sudden and alarming illness with which he was seized late at night [47].

When Utterson first approaches him about "the Hyde problem," Jekyll protests that "the moment I choose, I can be rid of Mr. Hyde" (44). The closest analogy in the Stevenson corpus is when the alcoholic Captain Davis swears to Herrick in *The Ebb-Tide* after he's almost lost his ship to his drunkenness: "There ain't nothing wrong but the drink — it's the old story, man! Let me get sober once and you'll see…. [I]f you see me put a glass to my lips again till we're ashore, I give you leave to put a bullet through me" (224). Curiously enough, even the "murderous mixture of timidity and boldness" that Utterson meets with in Hyde (40) might be likened to the over-determined facial expression that temperance doctor Kate Mitchell described in the typical drunk of 1880: "the glance is either indistinct and wavering, or endeavours to assume a very piercing and defiant regard" (198).[4] This much, however, should confirm that, whether one applies contemporary Victorian or more modern standards of diagnosis, the tale's likening of Jekyll/Hyde to the more and less sober states of a "drunkard" is both deep-seated and extensive. If the Jekyll-self models the measured social drinker safely in tune with societal and moral proprieties (as characterized by the congenial, gentlemanly tippling that we shall watch him indulge in the next chapter), Hyde is the abandoned binge drinker who relishes tasting all of those forbidden fruits that his "upright twin" denies himself. "Men have before hired bravos to transact their crimes," claims Jekyll, "while their own person and reputation sat under shelter. I was the first that ever did so for his pleasures" (86). This is true, perhaps, in a literal sense. But the more one looks at it, the more the tale seems a prime and calculated metaphor for the way men have timelessly, under the cover of drink, indulged *themselves* in passionate acts that, come the cool light of day, they variously rue or deny having willfully committed.[5]

TWO

Alcohol in the Text: The Letter

While no less acute a reader than Nabokov noted *Jeykll and Hyde*'s "delightful winey taste," his off-hand observation is, as we've begun to see, very much an odd-insight-out when it comes to characterizations of this tale of chemical transformation. No published critic, for example, has remarked on the simple fact that, of the novella's ten brief chapters, a full seven touch on some type of alcoholic drink and its consumption. In fact, if we allow Dr. Lanyon's suggestive reference to Jekyll's catalytic "blood-red liquor" to count, the tally is upped to a rather remarkable eight out of ten chapters. And although alcohol's *literal* agency in the tale never reaches the consummate level of narrative importance of, say, the spiked "furmity" that spawns Michael Henchard's miseries in another of 1886's most heralded fictions—or even of the rum that does so consequentially for minor characters like Captain Flint, Billy Bones, and Israel Hands in Stevenson's own *Treasure Island* (1883)—anyone who pays careful attention to our tale's many and varied nods towards intoxicating drink will be taken quickly and directly to the heart of the work's most pressing themes. In fact, *J&H* could almost be sub-titled "A Drinker's Mirror of Temperance." In the interests of making that case as carefully and judiciously as possible, we shall begin here with alcohol's literal role in the text, observing in the sections that follow the ways what might seem to be merely "cameo" appearances by strong drink nonetheless betoken its far deeper participation in this classic drama of human addiction and duality.

Stevenson himself was passionately and abidingly devoted to the grape. "I am interested in all wines," he confessed in his California memoir, *The Silverado Squatters* (1883), "and have been all my life, from the raisin wine that a school-fellow kept secreted in his play-box up to my last discovery" (188). Perhaps predictably, then, of all *Jekyll and Hyde*'s explicit references to alcohol, those to wine are easily the most frequent (and thus Nabokov's memorable assessment.) The first comes as early as the novella's second sentence, where one learns that, despite the lawyer Mr. Utterson's customarily "cold" reserve, "at friendly meetings, and when the wine was to his taste, something eminently human beaconed from his eye" (29). Stevenson wastes no time evincing not only alcohol's considerable potential for transforming human character (that theme being, of course, the whole text's prime business) but also its traditional capacity to foster good fellowship, a service that had been nicely articulated for the age by Charles Dickens' claim that drink inspires "kindness of feeling and openness of heart" (Cordery 2). One might think as well of Hardy's observation that "comforting beverages" dismantle the "iron grills" of social difference (*Casterbridge* 31–2); or Thomas Love Peacock's recommendation (as significantly endorsed by various members of the Disraeli family) that "political enemies are best reconciled by a 'jorum of claret'" (Merrett 109).

Jekyll's old friend Dr. Lanyon is introduced in much the same way as his lawyer. When Utterson visits the medical man in search of information on the newly bothersome Hyde, he is,

> ushered direct from the door to the dining-room, where Dr. Lanyon sat alone over his wine. This was a hearty, healthy, dapper, red-faced gentleman, with ... a boisterous and decided manner. At sight of Mr. Utterson, he sprang up from his chair and welcomed him with both hands. The geniality, as was the way of the man, was somewhat theatrical to the eye; but it reposed on genuine feeling [36].

One can safely assume that Lanyon's "genuine" geniality has only been enhanced by the wine the doctor is just imbibing: *in vino*, as ever, *veritas*— of character as well as utterance. A contemporary student of alcohol like Norman Kerr, in fact, might well have attributed directly to the drink's chemical action the facts that the doctor's "spirits are more buoyant" and that his "face appears flushed" (204). Also evident in the passage is the long-standing supposition, very much alive and kicking in Victorian England, that alcohol contributed immeasurably to sanguine good health. Dickens speaks eloquently if economically to the benign effects of the grape when he boasts that "Pure wine makes good blood" (Briggs 39). True enough, as we'll see below, more contemporary voices than Fanny Stevenson's Dr. Balfour questioned the physical salubriousness of alcohol, just as more than one warden of social order regularly complained about alcohol's fractious effects over and against its capacity to bring drinkers closer together. The novella itself outlines many of the physiological and sociological dangers of drink, as will duly be shown. It's important to note for now, however, that Stevenson opens his famous tale of drugs and altered psyches with what is predominantly a benevolent sketch of Bacchus, and one that accords with the author's own life-long drinking practice and taste.

Wine next surfaces as a marker of class. Some two weeks after Utterson's cousin and compatriot Enfield tells his inaugural "Story of the Door," Jekyll "gave one of his pleasant dinners to some five or six old cronies, all intelligent reputable men, and all judges of good wine" (43). The tacit assumption here that intellectual, moral, and aesthetic quality keep regular and invariable company is one that the story will in the end most assuredly challenge, but the explicit association between wine and society's upper crust was very much an ideological and economic given of Stevenson's century. *The British Critic* had asked in 1839, for example, "What is a peer without wine on his table?" (Harrison, *Drink* 143) Fifteen years later, Dickens' Mrs. Sparsit personally and symbolically embraces her own humbling "hard times" by renouncing both "made dishes and wines at dinner" (*Hard Times* 186), while her moral and social converse, Mr. Bounderby, betrays the hypocrisy of his own affected identification with the poor by persistently (and addictively) quaffing sherry with his lunch. Wine's demarcations of social standing could be quite precise indeed. Victorian social pundits traditionally construed a partiality to fortified Iberian wines as an earmark of Whigs, squires, merchants, and the professions—while French wines betokened Tories, Jacobites, and the aristocracy (Hewett 140). Robert J. Merrett, in fact, tellingly discovers these tried associations informing the literary invention of Trollope's Barsetshire novels.[1]

While this time-honored oenological sign system was certainly challenged once William Gladstone reduced wine excises in 1860 as part of his bid to encourage trade with France (thereby rendering claret and burgundy much more affordable for people like Stevenson and his fictive professional men alike), the working classes never really took to wine, thereby frustrating the Liberal Chancellor's hopes not only of stimulating cross–Channel trade but also of weaning the immoderate masses from their notoriously lethal favorite beverage, gin (Spiller 35). Reasoned estimates in the 1880s held that, although the working classes accounted for seventy-five percent of all insular beer and spirits sales, those same plebeians bought no more than ten percent of the wine sold in Britain (Briggs 72). Of some special interest in this regard is a *Punch* drawing from 11 August 1885, published only a month or so before Stevenson began penning *J&H*. Inside and outside Parliament, in the speeches of Lord Bramwell or in the columns of the various victualler's trade journals, widespread reformist pleas both for the right of local self-determination on licensing the sale of alcohol ("Local Option") and for the Sunday closing of pubs were vociferously condemned as elitist. Restrictive temperance proposals of this sort — or so went the outraged reactionary argument — threatened the recreational pleasures of the working classes but not of their professional and aristocratic betters; for while the limiting finances of the former obliged them to buy their ale and sprits "as needed" from licensed vendors during legal opening hours, the latter regularly drank at home (like Jekyll's circle of professional principals) from ample private stocks (Harrison, *Drink* 199). So when *Punch* treats the issue of "Sunday Equality" between patricians and plebes, it imagines "The Reunion of Champagne and Porter" in a drawing of personified bottles of wine and beer, caught up in amiable conviviality (57). As we shall see, Stevenson was a devoted and regular reader of the satirical weekly and, whether with full intention or not, worked a number of its wonted themes and images into the fabric of his narrative.

The next wine bottles turn up in Hyde's Soho digs, and thereby start to complicate the novella's vinous sub-text. It's not that Soho is an inappropriate haunt for a general type of the inveterate drinker, if that's what Hyde should ultimately be revealed to be. Contemporary tallies put the density of pubs in that section of London at a remarkable 798 per square mile (Gutzke 46). A decade after *J&H* appeared, the Fabian Society accordingly voiced its firm conviction that no "Permissive Bill" (a version of "Local Option" involving a direct plebiscite) would ever quash the licensing of premises in Whitechapel and Soho because the huge majority of tippling residents would never, ever, vote for local restrictions on drink (Harrison, *Drink* 201). If Hyde should be fundamentally constructed as a drinker, then, "the little room in Soho" (87) is a perfect lair for him, something that may have entered Stevenson's mind when he emended his Note Book Draft and its original reference (instead) to a *Holborn* residence for Hyde — his "dreary and exiguous rooms off Gray's Inn Road" (Veeder, "Manuscript" 45.) The new Soho locale is in some ways perfect for the argument being pursued here. The complication lies in what Utterson and Inspector Newcomen discover in the villain's digs.

The pair is shown by Hyde's landlady to "a couple of rooms ... furnished with luxury and good taste. A closet was *filled with wine*, the plate was of silver, the napery elegant: a good picture hung upon the walls, a gift (as Utterson supposed) from Henry Jekyll, who was much of a connoisseur" (49; italics added). By making wine the very first index of "good taste" in this passage, Stevenson again exploits the conventional signs of his culture.[2] And if one thinks of Hyde simply as the genteel Dr. Jekyll's appetitive alter-ego, it makes perfectly good sense that his place should be stocked with fine vintages. Yet, to this point in the narrative, as indeed through much of the novella, Stevenson has taken some care to figure Hyde as a man of lower rank.[3] Although he refers to himself as a "gentleman" (32), Hyde in action is not in the least "gentle." He is given to brutal violence and bestial snarls (e.g. 40), his constitutional "impatience" regularly overrides his politeness (78), his clothes are variously described as plain (39) or ill-fitting (70), and Jekyll's butler Poole revealingly assures Utterson at Jekyll's house, "O dear no, sir. [Hyde] never *dines* here" (41). That Hyde could obviously never appear alongside Jekyll as the doctor's personal dinner guest does nothing to undermine Poole's rough-and-ready socio-economic assessment of the little man as no gentleman, and thus an extremely unlikely devotee of fine vintages. More importantly, since Stevenson's original readers would have had no way of knowing that Hyde's rooms were, in essence, Jekyll's rooms as well, one can assume that this unanticipated discovery of the wine (as of the silver plate, the "napery," and the artwork) is a calculated tipping of the mystery writer's hand that the déclassé villain is not precisely what, or who, he seems. For the narrative "trick" to work, of course, the contrast between Hyde's plebeian nature and his patrician tastes would have to be clear enough to be noticeable, if not exactly unambiguous in its implications. As it happens, readers of *Treasure Island* (1883) would have been especially well primed for the ploy. When the wounded but scheming low-life, Israel Hands, asks Jim Hawkins to go below decks to fetch a bottle of wine as "this here brandy's too strong for [his] head" (thereby angling for a chance to secure a weapon to murder the lad), Jim draws on his experience serving all classes at the Admiral Benbow Inn to intuit that something is amiss: "As for the notion of his preferring wine to brandy, I entirely disbelieved it. The whole story was a pretext" (146). Yet given the social stereotypes we've just examined, even the neophyte reader of Stevenson is likely to have raised a skeptical brow: "Wine in a working-class flat? There must be more to it."

When it came to such matters of "class," in fact, one of Stevenson's original readers did find something substantially wrong with this Soho vignette. Claiming J. A. Symonds as a mutual friend, proto-psychologist, psychical researcher, and cultural gadfly F. W. H. Myers wrote to the author in February of 1886 to say that Jekyll would never have sent a "good picture" to Hyde's rooms (Maixner 215). When Stevenson replied that he "rather meant that Hyde had brought it himself" (Maixner 219), Myers persisted in his sociological scruple, invoking a kind of aristocracy of taste: "Would Hyde have brought a picture? I think — and friends of weight support my view — that such an act would have been altogether unworthy of him" (Maixner 219). Myers' reluctance to see Hyde as refined enough to be an art buff is directly paralleled by his additional complaint that Hyde's rhetoric in the climactic transformation scene with Lanyon is "too elevated.... These are not remarks that fit the husky broken voice of Hyde" (Maixner 216).[4] Stevenson obligingly (if perhaps disingenuously) acknowledged in a reply to Myers "the gross error of Hyde's speech at Lanyon's," blaming the lapse in style on the "white-hot haste" with which the tale was written (Maixner 219).

Given what we know of Victorian drinking patterns, Myers could obviously have found fault with the Soho wine closet as equally "unworthy" of a de facto low-life like Hyde. One influential London wine merchant informed Parliament in 1879 that beer and spirits sales would always predominate "in the East End and *low* neighborhoods where wine was almost unknown to the consumers" (Briggs 85; emphasis added). It may be that Myers' observations on the picture and the speech subsumed the need to offer that additional criticism of the work's social proprieties. We shall return in fact to the matter of Hyde's speech at Lanyon's house in order to argue that Stevenson was actually writing less "erroneously" than he was able (or chose) to acknowledge to Myers (whose fastidious recommendations for revisions to the novella, by the way, Stevenson very significantly never undertook despite Myers' years of fervent urgings [Maixner 213]). Suffice it to say for now that, beyond planting an important clue to Hyde's refined primary identity, the apparent incongruity of a Soho resident's relishing wine dovetails very nicely with a landlady (Hyde's) whose "manners were excellent" despite her "evil face" (49) and also with the central paradox of the brutal Hyde co-existing with the gentleman Jekyll. Utterson has earlier found Hyde's manner "a sort of murderous mixture of timidity and boldness" (40). If, as commentators like Brantlinger and Boyle persuasively argue, *J&H* attends on some level to some revolutionary developments in late–Victorian Britain that threatened the hegemony of traditional institutions and power groups, then the overt, initial image of a diminutive yet murderous boor with a socially ambitious taste for vintages and fine art is surely an eloquently chilling one. Writing in 1855, W. Bosville James addressed the cultural exclusivity fostered by high tariffs on wine. Beneath the oenophile elite, however, he saw lesser classes "rising to equal importance, and far exceeding that class in numbers, intelligence and influence. Those classes will not long be excluded," he portentously claimed, "from the use of wine, because legislation, by high duties, grossly violating free-trade principles, declare it a luxury" (Briggs 23). James clearly lends his voice to bids such as Gladstone's to reduce the excise; nevertheless, the image of an underclass hankering after wine is one that was likely to have appalled as many Tories as it appealed to Liberal free-traders. It is an image, one suspects, that is deployed in *J&H* with a double edge — both as a narrative clue and as a challenge to facile ideological assumptions — especially if one recalls (as is admittedly so hard to do with a text whose basic secret so many readers know even before they ever pick the book up) that Stevenson's original audience could not have known at this point that Hyde is the emanation of the wine-loving gentleman Jekyll. Whatever the naïve reader may subsequently learn, he is obliged to "live" for some time with the image of a boorish killer who boasts a refined taste for vintages. The scene anticipates, in this rather wrenching cultural incongruity, the effect of serial-killer Hannibal Lecter's subscription to the Italian edition of *Vogue* in Thomas Harris's *Silence of the Lambs*. In any case, we shall return shortly to some of the implications of Stevenson's postulated challenge to the socio-economic significations of drink.

Stevenson once very memorably claimed that "wine is bottled poetry" (*Silverado* 189), and the beverage's next appearance in *J&H* supports that romantic contention in a passage of striking evocativeness and deceptive thematic depth. On a bitter and foggy London night, Utterson shares with his head clerk Guest both a glowing fireside and "a bottle of a particular old wine that had long dwelt unsunned in the foundations of his house" (53).

> The procession of the town's life was still rolling in through the great arteries with a sound as of a mighty wind. But the room was gay with firelight. In the bottle the acids were long ago resolved; the imperial dye had softened with time, as the colour grows richer in stained windows; and the glow of hot autumn afternoons on hillside vineyards, was ready to be set free and to disperse the fogs of London. Insensibly the lawyer melted [53–4].

This is assuredly *Wine Spectator* or *Sideways* stuff, the kind of inspired appreciation of bottled goods that could send a suggestible and bibulous reader dashing off to the nearest package store. It patently re-endues wine with the positive aura that the previous passage (indeed the two previous passages) might have qualified. One is told that "there was no man from whom [Utterson] kept fewer secrets than Mr. Guest" (54) and this, together with the reference to the lawyer's "insensibly melting," takes us back to the vision of vinous fellowship and humanity that graces the novella's opening page. Wine's traditional association with "good blood" subtly re-surfaces in the passage as well, informing the image of the "town's life" coursing powerfully through its "great arteries"—a cardiovascular effect that is reinforced by the subsequent reference to the wine's liquid warmth.

There is even more to be found here, however, as the oenological subplot thickens. A careful reading suggests that something very like what is elsewhere "the horror" of a Hydean "release" might be seen, under another aspect, as a great blessing. Hyde is elsewhere described by Jekyll as some kind of pent-up lust, hidden from public view, and the longer he is contained, we are assured, the more violent he becomes: the doctor accordingly confesses, "My devil had been long caged, he came out roaring" (90). Conversely, however, Utterson's rare old bottle, "that had long dwelt unsunned in the foundations of his house," improves with age and concealment. As the passage suggests, the wine's "acids" have been "resolved" by passing years, not intensified by them, as "the imperial dye had softened with time." The dye itself, vaguely analogous to the swarthiness of Hyde's complexion (88), is seen here as positive, "as the color grows richer in stained windows"—presumably windows in the hallowed fabric of a church. More importantly, so also is the release seen as a sweet whisper rather than a roar, as "the glow of hot autumn afternoons on hillside vineyards, was ready to be set free and disperse the fogs of London." Jekyll claims to have felt, under the influence of his chosen poison, horrid "pangs of dissolution" (85), a finally troubling "solution of the bonds of obligation" (83 and 92). Hyde is a creature of "brutish physical insensibility" (90). Here, however, both dissolution and "the insensible" are represented in demonstrably positive ways, as "insensibly the lawyer melted," offering to Guest, as we have seen, "secrets" that bring not anguish and disgrace but warm fellowship instead. Even the "gaiety" that is later more or less demonized by Jekyll when he attributes Hyde's origins to "an impatient gaiety of disposition" (81) is represented here in a positive way, as "the room was gay with firelight"— and as, indeed, drink and "gaiety" are elsewhere associated in an *predominantly* positive way in the account of Jekyll's wine-loving "cronies" for whom a dinner party and its jovial toasting involve "the expense and strain of gaiety" (43). The Utterson-Guest passage is crucially important to a reader like Elaine Showalter, who plumbs the latent homoeroticism of the text. Yet it seems even more striking as evidence that Stevenson's treatment of alcohol is tightly intertwined with his central plot and theme. Here is a microcosm of the whole story of sequestration and release, albeit with values rather puzzlingly reversed. If, despite Hyde's depravities (or perhaps because of them), the work's final warning is against an over-long deferral of gratification — precisely because of the subsequent danger of a violent "release"— this scene seems to extol the singular joys of uncorking a bottled-up "spirit" after a long, long time indeed.

To return from suggestive formal patterns to the letter of the text, wine's next appearance, on "The Last Night," is somewhat less intriguing. The distraught Poole comes to Utterson for help with the domestic turmoil that has followed from his master's disappearance, and he is offered a seat and a glass of wine to help compose himself (62). Several paragraphs later, Poole still sits "with the glass of wine untasted on his knee" (62). And, when Utterson agrees to go along and see for himself what is amiss at Jekyll's house, "he observed with wonder the greatness of the relief that appeared upon the butler's face, and perhaps with no less, that the wine was still untasted when he set it down to follow" (63). The cause of Utterson's "wonder" is unspecified. It was customary in the Victorian era to ply good servants with drink. Thus, a sample temperance resolution appended to John Dunlop's storied 1839 condemnation of British drinking customs accordingly stressed the need for tee-totaling employers to refrain from giving alcohol to their servants (315). Poole's refusal to drink suggests one of several things: (1) the man is too distracted even to notice what he's been offered, which might well surprise Utterson, who himself seems always to have one eye peeled for a glass of something bracing; (2) he's devotedly "on duty" and is unwilling to impair his faculties, which probably shouldn't surprise Utterson, given what we've seen of Poole's general level of competence and commitment; (3) he's not a wine drinker any more than most members of the working classes were, which again shouldn't surprise Utterson; or (4) he's not a drinker at all, which might well leave a confirmed tippler like Utterson "wondering" that any man should have the capacity to turn completely away from drink.[5] We shall consider a bit later the possibility that Poole's portrait is effectively the sketch of a teetotaler, total abstinence having been in fact exponentially more common among the lower ranks of society than among the upper (Longmate 55). For now, however, one should simply observe that Stevenson once again offers alcohol as one available index of class. Poole belongs to the working class and, in one way or another, his rejection of the wine confirms his social position.

Gin, as opposed to wine, is mentioned only twice in *J&H*, but both times in a way that also clearly attends to social status. The second reference is the most conventional and is probably the best to begin with. On his way to Hyde's house with Inspector Newcomen in order to investigate the murder of Sir Danvers Carew, Utterson passes through a "dismal quarter of Soho":

> As the cab drew up before the address indicated, the fog lifted a little and showed him a dingy street, a gin palace, a low French eating house, a shop for the retail of penny numbers and two-penny salads, many ragged children huddled in the doorways, and many women of many different nationalities passing out, key in hand, to have a morning glass [48].

Stevenson's lexicon figures here a hellish, entropic, nether world: "dingy" streets, "low" food shops, "penny" and "two-penny" sales of various sorts, "ragged" children "huddled" in doorways. This is the very lowest that Stevenson takes the reader into the depths of his London, and the reigning spirit is clearly Gin, just as it had earlier been in William Hogarth's famous engraving of social decline. *Gin Lane* (1751) epitomized the dangers of strong drink in the horror of maternal neglect, representing as the famous image did, front-and-center, a suckling child tumbling from its nodding mother's breast right off a high stone staircase onto the pavement. Stevenson follows suit, with his children's "raggedness" all-but-certainly compounded by their mothers' premature taste for a "glass." That the women are most likely prostitutes is in line, as will be seen, with gin's traditional ties to crime and the social "residuum." Gin cost next to nothing to make and to purchase, which meant far more often that its devotees never saved anything at all than that they had any money left after drinking to spare for the real necessities of life. Smollett's *History of England* (1757–8) famously notes that "the retailers of this poisonous compound ... invit[e] people to be drunk for the small expense of one penny, assuring them that they might be dead drunk for twopence" (Longmate 10). Henry Fielding, fulminating against gin as the prime cause of what he took to be London's ruination, claimed that it was "the principle sustenance (if it may be so called) of more than a hundred thousand people in the metropolis.... The intoxicating draught itself disqualifies them from any honest means to acquire it, at the same time that it removes sense of fear and shame and emboldens them to commit every wicked and desperate enterprise" (Hibbert 160). Even after police inquiries of the 1810s and '20s had revealed no direct causal link between gin and crime, the two were persistently and religiously seen as the one-two punch of urban and social decay (Harrison 69). Gin, for example, is the amiable whore Nancy's drink in *Oliver Twist*. John Dunlop cites the neglect of children by their inebriated, prostitute mothers as one of the greatest banes of gin (58). And W. T. Stead, in his inflammatory "Maiden Tribute of Modern Babylon," published the same year *J&H* was written, goes so far as to claim of gin's nefarious impact that "drunken parents often sell their children to brothel keepers," especially "in the East-End" (37). If the stereotypical "Soho crimes" of child neglect and abuse are not identical to Hyde's own when he tramples the little girl in the midnight streets, they are not altogether different, in ways that Stevenson may press home when he imagines Jekyll's laboratory doorway itself as at times every bit as crowded with errant children as the portals of Hyde's chosen neighborhood (30). If we recall that, in Hyde's own case of child abuse, "the child was not much the worse, more frightened" (31), then what happens to children in Soho may actually be worse.[6]

Gin's other overt appearance is fully as intriguing as the Utterson/Guest wine episode. The third sentence of Chapter One reveals that Utterson "was austere with himself; drank gin when he was alone, to mortify his taste for vintages" (29). On one level, there's nothing surprising here. If wine betokens "High" and gin "Low" in the bulk of the text, just as they did in contemporary British social ideology, then it makes some sense that Utterson could drink gin as an exercise in humility, in perfect keeping both with his concerned tolerance for "downgoing men" and his twenty-year avoidance of the theatrical high life he had formerly enjoyed (29). As perhaps an heir to Dickens' sanctimonious Mr. Bumble — the beadle who drinks gin "with a little cold water, and a lump of sugar" (*Oliver Twist* 6) — Utterson sounds almost like a puritanical closet Christian, eschewing, when he can, the proud excesses of the Pharisees. Jekyll, by way of contrast, problematically shuns the "downgoing" side of his own nature and is finally himself brought down by an "imperious desire to carry [his] head *high*" (81; italics added). But, beyond the oddity of seeing any form of tippling as "austere" behavior, could any version of Christianity really consider stealing a slug of gin as an act of humility or penance? Moreover, Utterson claims to "incline to Cain's heresy," to "let [his] brother go to the devil in his own way" (29), which obviously frustrates any provisional attempts to read him as some kind of modest Nonconformist. Stevenson is undoubtedly having a bit of satirical fun here.

Even if one sensibly resists the temptation to follow the language of self-mortification into the realm of conventional religion, then, there is still the odd fact that a passage which begins by extolling drink as a spur to warm fellowship should then turn its attention to a man's tippling "when he was alone." More curious still is the ill fit between gin's positive role in this apparently commendable "mortification" and its overwhelmingly negative contemporary reputation as a catalyst of poverty, depravity, and crime (as in the novella's own Soho scene) — unless, that is, the mortification Utterson seeks for himself is the mortification of a temporary and completely private descent to something like criminal status. One might provisionally argue that Stevenson is toying with the idea that a sort of wallowing in the social depths can sometimes be a good thing, spiritually or intellectually — as for Shakespeare's Prince Hal or, perhaps, for Stevenson himself in his formative days as a carousing Edinburgh undergraduate. But if that's the case, then the overt morality of the rest of the tale appears to be prodigiously out of line: Jekyll hardly seems to be made better by his fall into Hyde, nor do the Soho women look like particularly good mothers. Alternatively, Stevenson may want us to see that Utterson's obsessive humility, because it drives him towards a type of liquid spirit that is just as pernicious as it is humble, could be every bit as dangerous as Jekyll's obsessive pride — which drives him, too, to the secret use of a strong "liquor." In either case, the "simple," traditional association of gin with the lower classes is merely Stevenson's point of departure in a text that is more complicated in its treatment of spirits than conventional attitudes prepare us to see.

So, having surveyed Stevenson's direct, literal references to alcohol in *J&H*, where do we stand? We can conclude, first of all, that Stevenson knew and exploited drink's capacity to signal social rank. Whether he also appreciated drink's capacity to alter that rank in a positive or a negative way remains to be seen. He celebrated, as well, drink's ability to forge social unity, and he seems to have endorsed the commonplace notion that a certain amount of drink fostered good health. Again, we shall see if these conventional stances hold up throughout the novella. In the matter of Utterson's gin, *if* we should take it at all seriously, Stevenson may also begin to reflect on the way one value system can work at dangerous cross purposes to another. The discourse of Humility (be it religious or social) might well be at odds with the discourse of Responsibility (whether physiological or moral) — if gin is salutary in one sphere and murderous in the other. The same theme is of course played out in a major key when Jekyll is caught between the conflicting Victorian discourses of Liberty (or perhaps Self-Help) and Moral Piety (or Respectability). As for Stevenson's literal treatment of wine, one finds equal complexity. The Utterson/Guest scene suggests the great beauty and even sanctity of a cycle of encapsulation, claustration, and an eventual inebriated release and "dissolution"; while the main Jekyll/Hyde plot overtly condemns the same cyclical strategy (while also drawing, as the next chapter will reveal, on the lore and language of wine.) Thus, a close attention to representations of alcohol and its consumption begins to deconstruct not only facile assumptions that the novella *recommends* some form of abstinence from transformative chemical agents — but also more subtle assumptions that Stevenson really *attacks* the bottling up of instincts. Why he should have embraced such fundamentally incongruous attitudes towards drink is a matter to which this study will naturally return. Suffice it to say for now that an attention to the novella's literal treatment of liquid intoxicants takes one with uncanny speed right to the heart of its plot and to the crux of its morality. Even if one were to discover nothing else in the novella that touched on the theme of drink, this might well suggest the signal importance of alcohol to Stevenson's exploration of human duality.

THREE

Alcohol in the Text: The Spirit

As the previous chapter has revealed, Stevenson had effectively drafted a significant portion of his alcoholic sub-text well before he turned his attention to the novella's last segment, "Henry Jekyll's Full Statement of the Case." It is Jekyll's own, confessional language, however, that is most likely to focus a reader's attention on the theme of alcohol — and then perhaps to spark the kind of contextual exegesis this study pursues. It may seem at first that the doctor is simply naming the gothic fantastic in terms of the relatively quotidian, resorting to the language of drink in order to describe the effects of what is at times specifically called either a "drug" (83, 89) or a "potion" (83). Not everyone in his audience, after all, was a drug-fancying Thomas DeQuincey, or even a Samuel Taylor Coleridge — while the vast majority would have had some experience with alcohol, either as a potent intoxicant or simply as a hygienic beverage, as the next chapter will discuss.[1] Norman Kerr had aptly written in 1882, "in intoxication there is usually an exaltation" and "alcohol is the exaltant generally resorted to in this country, because it is in common use" (30). Nevertheless, the more one looks at Jekyll's metaphorical language in the context of other details of plot, setting, and character, the more it emerges that drink is as much the tenor of Stevenson's strange narrative of addiction as it is the vehicle.

Let us begin by revisiting a few crucial passages that have already been touched upon. When Jekyll first samples his perfected potion, he is wracked by what he says were horrid "pangs" (83). Soon, however, the feelings alter:

> There was something strange in my sensations, something indescribably new, and, from its very novelty, incredibly sweet. I felt younger, lighter, happier in body; within I was conscious of a heady recklessness, a current of disordered sensual images running like a mill race in my fancy, a solution of the bonds of obligation, an unknown but not an innocent freedom of the soul. I knew myself, at the first breath of this new life, to be more wicked, tenfold more wicked, sold a slave to my original evil; and the thought, in that moment, *braced and delighted me like wine*. I stretched out my hands exulting in the freshness of these sensations; and in the act, I was suddenly aware that I had lost my *stature* [83; italics added].

This is the last of the text's references to wine and, in spite of its telling use to describe Jekyll's first experience as Mr. Hyde, it may initially seem less interesting and useful than the other, literal treatments. Jekyll doesn't say that he felt as though he'd just had a stiff drink, but rather that his sudden *awareness* of a new and utter wickedness "braced and delighted" him just as a good dose of wine might do. The delight is apparently in his apprehension of this new access to evil, not in any physical feeling. The first thing to say, however, is that the text's more conventional representations of wine are being substantially altered here, just as Jekyll is altered in becoming Hyde. Widely considered the traditional drink of the "reputable," as we've amply seen, wine is now linked to evil, completing a change in moral valence that begins when Utterson discovers the wine in Hyde's rooms in Soho. Wine functions here more as gin was widely held to do, as a prod to baseness and depravity. As though to make this precise sociological point, Stevenson evinces the image of slavery ("sold a slave"), a commonplace Victorian figure for alcoholism that he and his friends were wont to use in that very sense.[2] Even more tellingly, Jekyll's taste of a "wine-like-gin-like-" potion leads to a second shocking realization: that he has lost his "stature." The process of *physical* diminution that marks Jekyll's early transformations into his dark alter-ego will in time reverse itself, as Hyde becomes increasingly powerful (and symbolically "big"); but for now Jekyll drinks something that knocks him a few rungs down the *social* as well as the physical ladder, and perhaps down the Darwinian ladder as well.[3] The drink turns him, in other words, into the kind of man Poole claims would never "dine" with a gentleman like Jekyll (41).

By the middle of the nineteenth century, "problem drinking" had come to be associated almost exclusively with the lower classes (in ways that are perhaps ironically in line with Utterson's determination to "mortify" his taste for wine by drinking that far riskier spirit, gin.) Dickens wrote of drunkenness in 1849, "it is the vice of the poor and wretched, ... not the vice of the upper classes, or of the middle class (whose improvement within the last hundred years is in no respect more remarkable than this" ("Demoralisation" 163). Six years later, J. A. Roebuck affirmed, "It is a mark now that a man is not a gentleman if he gets drunk" (Harrison, *Drink* 316). Yet, in the absence of a dependable science of sampling, judgments like these were largely based on what men were seen to do and to be in public, most consequentially by the local constabulary — and subsequently in whatever information the constables chose to divulge *to* the public (Harrison, *Drink* 389–90).[4] As a result, such intrinsically elitist claims need to be seen against the fact that, by even the early part of the century, the privileged classes had virtually abandoned the public houses and inns of Fielding's day for the more "respectable" and private (read also, intrinsically more "secret") environs of club and home (Harrison, *Drink* 319). Before George Cruikshank took the teetotal Pledge some time after the huge success of his series of admonitory images, *The Bottle* (1847), he had himself been an abandoned and disorderly tippler, a fact which in and of itself might have obliged his friend Dickens to qualify his elitist observations. If in 1885 reformer David Lewis could still maintain that drink was overwhelmingly the problem of "the lower classes" (*Drink Traffic* 226), *J&H* significantly challenges such a comfortable assumption in that very same year. As a portrait of the brutal alcoholic emanation of the overtly respectable Jekyll, the wine-drinking Hyde could well have been modeled on someone like actor Teddy Henley, the brother of Stevenson's long-time friend and collaborator, W. E. Henley, of "Invictus" fame. Despite the man's respectable family origins, Stevenson ultimately (and colorfully) found him to be a "drunken whoreson bugger and bully living himself in the best hotels, and smashing inoffensive strangers in the bar!" (*Letters* 6.93). When Stevenson once answered charges that many of Hyde's transgressions were undoubtedly sexual, he protested that the story's real target was "hypocrisy" (*Letters* 6.56). The century's overt claims that privileged drinkers seldom did society much harm — which incidentally contributed to a massive middle- and upper-class desertion of the temperance movement once teetotal abstinence displaced moderation in drinking as the prime goal — these were claims that Stevenson knew to be patently false. "What is a peer without wine on his table?" *The*

British Critic had asked. "What might a gentleman become *with* wine on his table?" Stevenson asks instead.[5]

There is more in the passage. The "racking pangs" and "grinding in the bones" that Jekyll experiences when he "[drinks] off the potion" soon give way to something "incredibly sweet," suggesting the way the initial bite of alcoholic drinks characteristically softens on the palate into something rounder and sweeter. The draught further inspires in Hyde a "heady recklessness," cousin to gin's deadening of "fear and shame" as described in Henry Fielding's famous jeremiad; and an extravagant disregard for consequences is, of course, a stereotypical effect of alcohol—as distinct, for example, from the contented languor that is bred by opium. Jekyll later significantly testifies to feeling, when he is Hyde, "a greater boldness, a contempt for danger"(92). To return to the immediate passage, however, just as Hyde is "braced" as though by wine when he begins to appreciate his newly evil nature, the drink leaves him feeling "younger, lighter, happier in body." He looks at his hands, "exulting in the freshness of these sensations." Jekyll later claims that as Hyde he is "conscious of a more generous tide of blood" (88–9) and that on reverting to Jekyll he must sadly say farewell to "the comparative youth, the light step" and "leaping pulses" he enjoyed as Hyde (90). And on the "Last Night," when Utterson and Poole wait outside the red baize door, they hear Hyde walking inside, but notice that "the steps fell lightly and oddly, with a certain swing" (69). This scene may complete the rewriting of some of the traditional *societal* and *moral* associations of wine, but we are still clearly in the bailiwick of something very close to alcohol as the promoter of *physical* vitality, as we see in Lanyon's initial description in the story; or in Dickens' assertion that "pure wine makes good blood"; or in Bram Stoker's consummately seductive villain offering Jonathan Harker a jolting shot to warm him on his chilly carriage ride to Castle Dracula (16); or in Sir Henry Baskerville declaring to Holmes after his brush with death by hound, "Give me another mouthful of that brandy and I shall be ready for anything" (Doyle 132).

Despite her own avid temperance stance, Dr. Kate Mitchell conceded in 1880, "The glass of wine ... creates a sensation of warmth through the body, which seems to *brace up* the flagging nerves, to whip the heart into increased motion, to accelerate the motion of the blood through the blood vessels, to bring the brain into livelier action, to assist the stomach in digesting, [and] to restore muscular energy" (158; emphasis added). Similarly, the 22 August 1885 number of *Punch* (published the month before

Stevenson began the novella) featured Lord Randolph Churchill extolling beer as "that great national drink, which sustains the powers, and invigorates, in times of exhaustion, our labouring population" (85). Stevenson himself resorted to liquor for dependable shots of energy, looking to a "stiff drink" to stave off physical exhaustion when he first arrived in Monterey — or sustaining himself and Fanny in the hills at Silverado with rum punch and cinnamon (McLynn 157; 178). He had learned from Burns among others that whisky "strings the nerves o' labour sair" (Dunlop 91), and he distinctly echoes Dr. Mitchell when in *The Ebb-Tide* Davis says to Huish, "You have a glass of champagne.... [I]t's just the pick-me-up for you; it'll put the edge on you at once" (276). Given the popular sentiments of the time, reinforced by august medical authorities such as Louis Pasteur (Sournia 90), the passage supports the claim that alcohol of some sort is Stevenson's prime model for Jekyll's potion, be that modeling a calculated one or no.

The argument strengthens when one turns to the "blood-red liquor" that Lanyon discovers among Jekyll's supplies. "Liquor" could in 1885 mean anything from a distilled or fermented beverage (including "blood-red" wine) to a physician's prescription to an infusion of tea or rendered meat-stock (*OED* 8.1014–15). Nevertheless, the context in which it appears in *J&H* again supports an alcohol-centered reading. Lanyon retrieves from Jekyll's cabinet the phial of liquid and a "wrapper" of "a simple crystalline salt of a white colour" (76), the elements that Hyde then mixes to form his "compound" (79). It's at this point, after he turns to Lanyon with "an air of scrutiny," that Hyde soars to the heights of rhetoric that F. W. H. Myers found so inappropriate for a man of his effective "class."

> "And now," said he, "to settle what remains. Will you be wise? will you be guided? will you suffer me to take this glass in my hand, and go forth from your house without further parley? or has the greed of curiosity too much command of you? Think before you answer, for it shall be done as you decide. As you decide, you shall be left as you were before, and neither richer nor wiser, unless the sense of service rendered to man in mortal distress may be counted as a kind of riches of the soul. Or, if you shall so prefer to choose, a new province of knowledge and new avenues of fame and power shall be laid open to you, here, in this room upon the instant; and your sight shall be blasted by a prodigy to stagger the unbelief of Satan" [79].

If Hyde had already swallowed the glass, one could perhaps explain this "boor's" unwonted eloquence by citing alcohol's contemporary reputation for sharpening the mental and rhetorical faculties as well as the physical. James Boswell felt very strongly that wine improved his conversation (Crouch 25), even as Coleridge believed that educated men were mentally energized by wine (Taylor 112). Dickens similarly writes in *Barnaby Rudge* that drink "brightens eyes, improves voice, enlivens conversation" (Merrett 10). Temperance historian Lillian Shiman in fact reports that many Methodist ministers, notoriously slow to join the temperance ranks, resorted to alcohol before and after preaching (43). A Nottingham drinking song recorded by Thomas Whittaker tellingly celebrates the way ale "moistens our throats [such that]/ We can preach without notes" (*Brighter England* 144). William Gladstone, although he was firmly and abidingly devoted to the Liberal program of alcohol reform, admitted that he'd made it through his ticklish budget speech as Chancellor of the Exchequer in 1860 only with the help of "a great stock of egg and wine" (Harrison, *Drink* 248). And while some temperance campaigners denied the elocutionary benefits of drink — as in 1870 when Bishop Fraser of Manchester was roundly assailed for claiming that bitter beer was an aid to good sermonizing (Harrison, *Drink* 184) — others ceded some significant ground. Dr. Mitchell, for example, cites Joseph Frank's observation that "in the first period of intoxication we observe mental excitement, rapidity of thought, fullness of the heart, brightness of the eyes, [and a] garrulous tongue" (204). Returning to its favored theme of hypocrisy, *Punch* weighs in on a pet peeve with a drawing entitled "An After Thought" in its 11 September 1880 number: the "Professional Temperance Orator" depicted in the image asks, *sotto voce*, for a jolt of brandy to be slipped into his soda water (189). And when Stevenson complained to his Cousin Bob in 1875 that he had "been working like Hell at stories" but that "[his] dialogue [was] as weak as soda water" (McLynn 103), he was reflecting his own latent assumption that alcohol and potent language go hand in hand. Thus, when in *Treasure Island* the sorely injured Israel Hands has "had a swallow or two more of the brandy, he began to pick up visibly, sat straighter up, *spoke louder and clearer*, and looked in every way another man" (144; added italics). But what of the fact that Hyde delivers his eloquent speech *before* he drinks off his potion?

One could always argue that Hyde's mere anticipation of a stiff drink does half the energizing work of the actual drinking, or even that he has begun to be energized by the "small fumes of vapour" that are thrown off by the bubbling brew (79). Stevenson was in fact sensitive to what might be called the atmospheric, "second-hand" effects of alcohol. In his short story "The Suicide Club" (1878), Prince Florizel's "exquisite affability" towards his guests is both prefigured and augmented by "a long glass of some effervescing beverage which diffused an agreeable odour through the room" in which they are brought into his presence (*Complete Stories* 64). An even more satisfying explanation, however, is happily to hand.

One prime association that a Victorian audience would have brought to a scene in which one eloquent man mixes up a potent brew in front of another in private quarters is the concocting of a punch or a cocktail. The convivial ritual was highly ceremonious and arcane. The mixer, commonly and suggestively called the "compounder" (Hewett 55), prepared the drink with paraphernalia that was at least as well suited to the laboratory or chemist's shop as it was to the public house. A Phiz illustration from *The Pickwick Papers*, for example, shows Messrs. Sawyer, Allen, and Winkle gathered around a table that is covered with various bottles, bits of fruit, and a large mortar and pestle (592). Sawyer, the text tells us, is brewing "a reeking rum punch," "stirring up and amalgamating the materials with a pestle in a very creditable and apothecary-like manner." The sole tumbler in the house goes to Winkle to drink from, while Allen gets a corked funnel, and Sawyer "content[s] himself with one of those wide-lipped crystal vessels inscribed with a variety of cabalistic characters, in which chemists are wont to measure out their liquid drugs in compounding prescriptions" (593). The language establishes a rather striking parallel to Hyde's visit to Lanyon's home, down to the real and implied role of chemists or apothecaries, the invocation of cabalistic wisdom, and the resourceful use of laboratory glassware: recall that Hyde requests "a graduated glass" to mix his drink (79). Lanyon significantly calls the brew a "compound," following Jekyll in that appellation: the doctor elsewhere tells us very insistently how he "managed to *compound* a drug" (83) in order to affect the desired transformation; that "one accursed night, [he] *compounded* the elements" (83); that later he "once again *compounded* and swallowed the transforming draught" (90); and that "Hyde had a song upon his lips as he *compounded* the draught, and as he drank it pledged the dead man [Carew]" (91; all emphases added). Chemists were "compounders"—but so, obviously, were convivial hosts.

That this last passage features an obvious toast to "auld lang syne" goes some further way towards clinching the argument that one conscious or unconscious model for Stevenson's Hyde/Lanyon scene is the hallowed rite of the punch bowl. There are, however, a few more useful observations to be made. The "punchmaster" was also known to Victorian aficionados of drink by a term other than "compounder." When George Eliot pens a genteel tippling session in *Janet's Repentance*, one of 1857's *Scenes of Clerical Life*, she describes the way "Mr Dempster as the '*Vice*,' undertook to brew the punch" (223; emphasis added). Social historian Robert Malcolmson accordingly identifies the punch-brewer as a traditional Lord of Misrule, who frequently and appropriately parodied the rhetorical pretentiousness of the upper classes in "a speech full of large promises" (82). Hyde, of course, plays exactly "the Vice" in the morality of the tale, and his speech is appropriately made possible by his temporary overthrow of established personal, social, and moral hierarchies. One wonders, then, whether the quibbling Myers wasn't mistaking a Bakhtinian "parody" of refined language in this scene for the thing itself.

As for the compounder's wonted "promises," Hyde offers Lanyon access to "a new province of knowledge and new avenues to fame and power," albeit at the risk of his succumbing to the "greed of curiosity" at the expense of what is "wise." The awesome solemnity of the fictional moment is, exactly like the level of diction and the fact of the promise, again very much in line with nineteenth-century British drinking customs. Reformer John Dunlop cites one Cyril Thornton on the portentous demeanor of a particular gentleman-compounder who was famous in Glasgow:

> You read in the solemnity of his countenance his sense of the deep responsibility which attaches to the duty he discharges. He feels there is an awful trust confided in him. The fortune of the table is in his hands. One slight miscalculation of quantity, one exuberant pressure of the fingers, and the enjoyment of a whole party is destroyed. With what an air of deliberate sagacity does he perform the functions of his calling [107].

Of course Stevenson is exploring as deeply serious some choices and consequences that for Thornton remain self-evidently in the realm of playful inconsequence. But the Glaswegian could perfectly well be describing Hyde's arguable solicitousness for himself and for Lanyon. Myers was right when he characterized Hyde's speech as "too elevated" for a low-life, but for a gentleman mixing drinks before a friend, the rhetoric is in fact bang-on!

The last aspect of the scene that requires some exploration is the specific promise (or perhaps warning) of knowledge that Hyde makes to Lanyon. Whether or not it was born of ancient cults of Dionysus or Bacchus, the secularized notion that there is a Truth to be found in Wine (as in other forms of alcohol) was readily available to Stevenson through the omnipresent Latin tag line. As a drink-loving Scot, he would also have known Robert Burns' infamous encomium on the life of the tavern:

> Leeze me [Blessings] on Drink! it gies us mair
> Than either School or Colledge:
> It kindles Wit, it waukens Lear [learning],
> It pangs [crams] us fou o' Knowledge [Taylor 35].

One late–Victorian epistemologist, Dr. William Sharpe, gave the notion slightly more scientific foundation in 1882, affirming that "the stimulus of alcohol, when judiciously controlled, always leads to higher mental efforts ... in which the mind ... sweeps intuitively into the veiled and distant regions of universal truth" (Longmate 178). But Stevenson is mining a slightly different vein in the Lanyon scene, one that is fraught with considerably more ambivalence. Hyde is at this point, indeed like the classical Vice figure, a type of the Serpent offering Adam/Lanyon a forbidden and ultimately destructive knowledge. Once again, however, the age's lore of alcohol is a propos. The Victorians, like the Romantics, had been taught by Milton to associate alcohol with Knowledge and the Fall (Taylor 159–90). Milton in fact strikingly anticipates the account of Jekyll's first, damning taste of the potion when he describes the just-fallen Eve as being "height'n'd *as with Wine*" (*PL* 9.793). And accordingly, once Adam has joined her in eating the forbidden fruit, "*As with new Wine* intoxicated both, / They swim in mirth" (*PL* 9.1008–9). Keats notably borrows the trope when his young Apollo prays for a consummate knowledge, "*as if some blithe wine* / Or bright elixir peerless I had drunk, / And so become immortal" (*Hyperion* 3.118–20; all emphases added). Stevenson could easily have taken the wine/wisdom notion from either Milton or Keats, but it is evident that, if he is inventing the Hyde/Lanyon scene against the pseudo-august ritual of the punch bowl, he is doing so in a way that injects an especially dire note into the jocular conviviality that a Dickens brought to the drinking rite. Stevenson himself loved to concoct a good mixed drink. Recall, for example, the cinnamon-rum punch of his Silverado days. Moreover, an acquaintance he made on the return trip from California to England in 1880 suggestively recalls his time with Stevenson as involving "such talk as I had never heard before, and now do not expect ever to hear again. To the accompaniment of ... a perilous cocktail which he had compounded with such zest from a San Francisco recipe, the stream of romantic and genial talk flowed on" (McLynn 179). To the end of his life, he continued his "experiments" in American mixed drinks on the verandah at Vailima (McLynn 404). Yet in the scene with Lanyon, Stevenson endows Hyde's liquorish compound with all the perils of drink seen under the worst aspect.[6] Rather like the children of London blighted by the second-hand effects of gin, Lanyon needn't even imbibe to be consequentially damaged.

The third of the metaphorical passages that most convincingly establish *J&H*'s subtext of alcoholism (as opposed, say, to another kind of drug addiction) is the one that associates Jekyll very specifically with the shallowly reflective moments of a binge drinker: "I do not suppose that, when a drunkard reasons with himself upon his vice...," etc. (90), a piece that has been adequately treated above. Once one recognizes that *J&H* is about a man who is at least *like* an alcoholic, however, the language of the novella comes alive with telling resonances—and, again, does so in ways which confirm that the real-life addiction that hovered closest to the front of Stevenson's mind is alcoholism. The "graduated glass" from which Hyde drinks at Lanyon's (79) may initially seem to be an apt vessel for drinking alcohol only when we recall the curious, moribund custom of punch-brewing. Nevertheless, the beaker then becomes a simple "glass" three times in the next six paragraphs, allowing for its long-standing metonymic association with strong drink—as in *The Ebb-Tide* when the newly-abstaining Captain Davis gives Herrick leave to shoot him "if you see me put a glass to my lips till we're ashore" (224)—or indeed in *J&H*'s own Soho scene when the women trail out for "a morning glass" at the local gin palace. When the "glass" from which Jekyll tells us he *first* drank (83) elsewhere becomes a "cup" (as for example twice on 85), nineteenth-century usage again supports an association with alcohol. Keats had significantly called *Endymion*'s Bacchus the "Great God of breathless cups" (Taylor 163), while James Hogg, in a novel that was much beloved by Stevenson, tells of "the evening cup of joy" tipped in a Scots pub (*Confessions* 36). Accordingly, the infamously inebriated Edgar Allan Poe was mourned in an obituary that warned, "Taste not the cup that poisoned him" (Pollin 130). And William Booth, founder of the Salvation Army, famously decried the lot of the sad multitudes who sought forgetfulness "in the intoxicating cup" (183). The commonplace expression "in his cups" as denoting drunkenness was one that Stevenson knew, and he frequently used it himself, as for example in the short story "When the Devil Was Well" (*Complete Stories* 1.43) and *The Master of Ballantrae* (264). And when the central character Keawe in "The Bottle Imp" is about to leave

The GIN-JUGGARNATH. Or, The Worship of the GREAT SPIRIT of the age
— It's Devotees destroy themselves — It's progress is marked with desolation, misery and Crime —

Figure 1—George Cruikshank, "The Gin Juggarnath" (1835). Courtesy of the British Museum.

his wife to "carouse with [his] jolly companions," he admits that he "will take more pleasure in the cup" if she forgives him for doing so (603).

The potion itself is also five times called a "draught" (86, 90, 91, and twice on 96)—most suggestively, as we've already seen, when "Hyde had a song upon his lips as he compounded the draught, and as he drank it, pledged the dead man" (91). In Stevenson's time, the term "draught" could simply denote "a drink" or "a portion of something drunk," including a "potion or dose of medicine" (*OED* 4.1020). Yet the immediate context, here, of the ironic toast and the convivial "song" strongly suggests that Stevenson has in mind "an extract obtained by distillation" or, even more likely, the results of "drawing liquor from a vessel" (*OED* 4.1021)—as when Fielding decries the dire effects upon London of the "intoxicating draught," gin; or when Dickens refers more appreciatively (and adjectivally) to "a pint of the real draught stout" (*OED* 4.1023). Wordsworth's

"Benjamin the Waggoner" had featured a toast to the hero of the Battle of the Nile:

"A bowl, a bowl of double measure,"
Cries Benjamin, "A *draught* of length,
To Nelson, England's pride and treasure" [Taylor 50; emphasis added].

And Stevenson elsewhere embraces conventional usage when he describes Israel Hands as he "took a great draught of the wine and spoke [as Hyde speaks to Lanyon?] with the most unusual solemnity" (*Treasure Island* 148).[7]

In a notable satirical drawing from 1835, George Cruikshank described the nation's devotion to gin as "The Worship of the Great Spirit of the Age" (see Figure 1). Given that "spirit house" was the British liquor trade's customary term for establishments like Stevenson's Soho gin palace (Spiller 33), Cruikshank's pun was predictably commonplace in popular and literary discourse alike. A Dublin clergyman thus declared in 1839 that "Sunday is especially devoted to the worship of the great spirit, Gin ... [when] the lower orders ... wander forth in maudlin, unwashed multitudes to the temples of the great Gin" (Longmate 10). Back in England, George Eliot echoes Cruikshank's word-play in *Janet's Repentance* (Federico 20). *Punch* rings a slight change on the formula, but keeps the punning alive in its number of 23 April 1881, in which a drawing shows a spectral bottle drifting out of a cupboard towards a frightened young girl, chanting to her, "I am thy mother's *spirit*" (191). The word "spirit" in fact appears a dozen times in *J&H*, sometimes with equal suggestiveness. Perhaps most tellingly, we learn towards the middle of the novella's first paragraph that the lawyer Utterson "had an approved tolerance for others; sometimes wondering, almost with envy, at the *high pressure of spirits* involved in their misdeeds" (29; added emphasis). This in fact represents a significant authorial emendation of the Printer's Copy of the text, which originally read "the pressure of high spirits" (Veeder, *Drafts* 14). The change that Stevenson chose to make not only reinforces the specifically liquorish denotation of the word but also brings the passage more directly in line with the contemporary notion that alcohol afforded an almost mechanical motive force to outrageous behavior. John Dunlop, for example, decries the pitiful carriage of loose women "under the guilty *pressure of liquor*" (58; added emphasis), while an 1870s street ballad describes drunkards "rid[ing] to Hell in their pride, / With nothing but steam from [beer] barrels inside" (Neuberg 194). Given that Utterson is introduced largely in terms of his drinking habits, it's hard to think that the expansive, "spirited" behavior that he comes so close to envying is not the conduct of hard-core drinkers, always ready like Hyde to burst, "roaring," out of their restraining "cages" (90), just as Utterson's wine waits to be "set free" from its dusty bottle (54).

A reader who is sensibly attuned to that early reference to "the high pressure of spirits" will find other suggestive uses of the term scattered throughout the text. When Jekyll first experiences the "racking pangs" that are caused by a sip of the potion, he describes an initial (and somewhat ambiguous) "horror of the spirit" (83) that nonetheless yields to an acquired taste for the drink, as what had been "horrid" becomes "incredibly sweet." "Spirit" in this case most readily denotes the sensing and evaluating faculty—"spirit" as synonymous with "soul" or "conscience"—but it may also suggest the sensed beverage, as Stevenson's word-choice is driven by a brace of concerns, one of them broadly moral and the other narrowly topical. When the doctor ultimately looks at his altered self in the "glass," it is somehow invested with the heightened vitality that was one traditional effect of drink: "it bore a livelier image of the spirit" (84). But, once again, one might ask whether it is his own, intrinsic "spirit" that has become more lively, or whether his face has been imprinted with some sort of image of the intoxicating draught itself, physically marked by the "stamping efficacy" of "the evil side of [his] nature" (84) as energized and informed by the drink. Compare this, for example, to the way Israel Hands "looked in every way *another man*" after his brandy pick-me-up (emphasis added). Hyde's effect on Jekyll is that of a "spirit of hell" that "rages" inside the doctor (90). He infuses even "the unimpressionable Enfield" with "a spirit of enduring hatred" (38). Like the *Punch* drawings to which Stevenson was so given, and in ways to which we shall return, Hyde can almost be seen as an embodiment of the murderous *spirit* of alcohol, the "ugly idol in the glass" (84)—or in the bottle—or in the cask.[8]

A look at the opening of the novella's second chapter takes one even further into a linguistic web spun with either a conscious or an unconscious eye for things alcoholic. "That evening, Mr Utterson came home to his bachelor house in sombre spirits and sat down to dinner without relish. It was his custom of a Sunday, when his meal was over, to sit close by the fire, a volume of some dry divinity on his reading desk, until the clock of the neighboring church rang out the hour of twelve, when he would go soberly and gratefully to bed" (35). Although the word "spirits" assuredly resonates less powerfully here than elsewhere, the mention of "dinner without relish" might well alert one to the presence of other puns in the passage. On a Sunday, when Utterson is obviously weaning himself from even the temptation of the misdeeds that flow from "the high pressure of spirits" of whatever kind, the lawyer structures his day not by visiting the "temples of the great Gin" but, far more appropriately, by harking to the church bells. Moreover, he selects as his reading "some dry divinity." "Dry" here primarily denotes "feeling or showing no emotion," "lacking adornment," or "frigidly precise" (*OED* 4.1088). Yet, once again in the specific context that Stevenson's work provides, "dry" also suggests "not accompanied or associated with drink" or "wanting or desirous of drink" or "thirsty" (*OED* 4.1088), very much in keeping with the lawyer's Sabbath-day abstemiousness. Later, when Jekyll is specifically documenting the wild joys of his "cups," he accordingly and significantly refers to his "aversion to the dryness of a life of study" (85). To be Hyde, then, is to abandon this Apollonian "dryness" for the Dionysian pleasures of drink.

Sunday's "dry" Utterson appropriately goes "*soberly* and gratefully to bed" (italics added).[9] Later in the same chapter he feels "a sober and fearful gratitude" (42) that his own past has been relatively free of the contrasting profligacies that marked Jekyll's "wild youth" and, in even more secretive form, that continue to dog the doctor's later years as well. The concept of sobriety is established even more literally in a nicely whimsical passage in which we learn that, after a long evening of drinking, Utterson's friends enjoyed "his unobstrusive company, practicing for solitude, *sobering* their minds in the man's rich silence after the *expense and strain of gaiety*" (43; added emphases). Once again, the explicit language of alcohol finds its way into the innermost fibers of the text. On the level of character, Utterson is very intriguingly the embodiment of the fatal potion in its restorative, Hyde-back-to-Jekyll mode, offering himself as a "human antidote" for gentlemen who've evidently drunk a little too much wine. And on the level of morality, the passage strongly and revealingly suggests that to make amends for a distinct version of the "straining," "impatient gaiety" that is both *Hyde's* initial constitutive element (81) *and* the essence of "manly vinous recreation"— is appropriately to be "sober." Sobriety and Hyde are thereby, if very subtly, established as polar opposites. This thematic clash of the Official and the Carnivalesque is also tellingly played out in Lanyon's subsequent comment that Hyde looks "laughable" in what turn out to be Jekyll's clothes, "although [the clothes themselves] were of rich and sober fabric" (77).

There is at least one last link in the compelling if sometimes subtle chain of evidence that ties Stevenson's basic language to the business of drink. Jekyll confesses that Hyde's "every act and thought centred on self;

drinking pleasure with bestial avidity from any degree of torture to another" (86; emphasis added). Somewhat later, when Jekyll is describing one of his spontaneous, "flashback" reversions to Hyde, the same notable phrasing recurs: "I was stepping leisurely across the court after breakfast, *drinking the chill air with pleasure*, when I was seized again with those indescribable sensations that heralded the change" (94–5; italics added). When Hyde clubs the defenseless Carew to death, the language varies slightly: "Instantly the spirit of hell awoke in me and raged. With a transport of glee, I mauled the unresisting body, *tasting delight from every blow*" (90; emphasis added). But even in this passage, a "spirit of hell" is present. Thus, each of these variations on what it means to be or to become Hyde involves all three points of the drink-pleasure-pain/discomfort triangle that lies at the thematic heart of the novella — and, as we'll shortly discover, at the ideological core of the case that the temperance movement made against drink as well.[10]

To summarize these opening chapters, then, a careful, focused look at the action and language of *J&H* reveals: (1) that the tale is, first and foremost, a narrative of destructive addiction; (2) that Stevenson studiously characterizes the principals in his most famous text by what and how they drink; (3) that he sees the nature and impact of what drives Jekyll to become Hyde as most broadly comprehensible in terms of alcohol; and (4) that the principals themselves analyze their moral status in language that evinces the use, abuse, and forswearing of intoxicating drink. Thus, the last movement of the novella is introduced in this highly significant fashion: "There comes an end to all things; the most capacious measure is filled at last; and this brief condescension to my evil finally destroyed the balance of my soul" (92). Here, time itself is defined in terms of a "capacious measure" that is inevitably filled to the brim. Be time a cup or a graduated glass, however, the life that is significant here is the taking on of liquid — a lot of it — and that immoderate burdening of the vessel leads to a loss of balance (and the inevitable Fall.) Moreover, this moral disorientation (and implied tumble) is rendered in terms that could just as readily describe the literal loss of equilibrium (and consequent stumbling) of a drunkard. What one finds in *Jekyll and Hyde*, if only one reads it carefully, is something very close to another, more explicit "Drinker's Tragedy" that was in press precisely when Stevenson was drafting his novella — Hardy's *Mayor of Casterbridge*. That this curious alignment may have been something more than coincidental is a possibility that we shall consider two chapters hence.

FOUR

RLS and the Drinking World

Which liquids did Stevenson and his companions "take on," and how might his personal and his more vicarious experiences with alcohol have shaped the conception of *J&H* and its compelling exploration of human duality? These questions are best set against the drinking practice and principles of his age. The most arresting historical fact to consider is that, until a steadily growing public dread of gin gave birth first to the Sale of Beer (a.k.a. "Beerhouses") Act of 1830 and then to the fully-fledged temperance movement, most Britons drank some alcohol with some regularity, cradle to grave. The point is nicely if indirectly made by the *Times* of London on April 20, 1885, less than a year before *J&H* appeared, when a tee-totaling Member of Parliament is said to have bolstered his credentials by claiming that "personally he had been an abstainer from the age of 15" (7). The reasons are many for the kind of broad and early indulgence in drink that might allow someone who reformed himself in his middle teens to think himself as somehow exceptional. They can, however, be surveyed quite economically.

When the medical world proved in the 1850s that cholera was a water-borne disease, it merely brought the scientific imprimatur to a long-standing awareness that Britain's water supply was in a parlous state — especially in the cities, where clean, piped water was essentially a luxury of the well-to-do (Clark 296). *Punch* harped on the concern for decades.

A year before Stevenson was born, the 10 November 1849 issue featured a drawing entitled "Mistaking Cause for Effect": two boys are watching a man open the water mains, and one quips, "I say, Tommy, I'm blowed if there isn't a man turning on the cholera" (185). The enduring hygienic crisis warranted Lord Shaftesbury's alarmist complaint in 1871 that "There was scarcely a pint of water in England which was not distinctly unhealthy, and ... a great deal was positively unsafe" (Harrison, *Drink* 299). Since at least the Middle Ages, one "safe" answer for young and old alike had been to drink ale instead of water, such that the school boys of Winchester College drank beer with meals until 1872, as did their peers at Eton until 1875. Because matters were worse with the working class—and because porter was virtually as cheap as clean water (Harrison, *Drink* 289)—the little girl that Hyde tramples could even have had a half pint with her supper (not that the text ever hints at the likelihood or explores the implications.)

Well before he took on the depredations of "The Bottle" in his vastly popular 1847 series of prints, George Cruikshank decried the pollution of the Thames in his widely-circulated satirical image, "Salus populi suprema lex" (Feaver 22). Temperance strategists routinely followed suit, perfectly aware as they were that alternatives to what was, *de facto*, "hygienic alcohol" had to be made widely available and affordable before the sway of strong drink could be in any significant way reduced. The changes that reformers initiated or endorsed included improvements to the public water supply; the ready distribution of "railway milk" (shipped post haste from the countryside to the cities) and bottled soft drinks (from increasingly successful beverage companies like Schweppes); and the establishment of various "dry" alternatives to the public house, generally serving either coffee or tea (Harrison, *Drink* 298–304).

Working against reformers, however, was the well-established popular conviction (very carefully nurtured by the liquor trade!) that alcoholic drinks were not only safe but also positively salutary—as in the long-enduring claim that "Guinness Is Good for You." On the solely nutritional front, as we've already begun to see, the boost in physical vitality that Jekyll feels when he downs his potion and becomes Hyde reflects the common faith that drink was a potent food. Benjamin Disraeli called ale "liquid bread" (Shiman 34), and British laborers throughout the nineteenth century prepared for their work accordingly. One London coal-backer was widely celebrated for quaffing "sixteen glasses of beer with a measure of gin in each of them regularly before breakfast each morning"

(Hibbert 214). There were, as a result, employers who actually refused to hire non-drinkers, assuming that lily-livered abstainers could never bear up under the demands of hard labor (Longmate 103). Temperance pioneer Joseph Livesey, widely-known for his reformist "Malt Lecture" of the 1830s, tried for decades to explode the myth of alcohol's nutritional value — all in "scientific" ways that would likely have pleased Dr. Lanyon with his inveterate bias against "unscientific balderdash" (36). Nevertheless, claims that agricultural workers needed their strong "harvest beer" were still fueling parliamentary debate as late as the 1880s (Harrison, *Drink* 120–5; 309). Beer, after all, had itself once been hailed a temperance drink, at least in comparison to strong spirits (Harrison, *Drink* 87); thus the Beerhouses Act of 1830, which obviated the need for a license for purveyors of malt brews, who were thereby encouraged to flourish as salutary competition for the increasingly-ubiquitous gin palace. So when the Bishop of London made his own case for moderation in 1886, he nonetheless allowed that "a man who had to toil with his hands until the body was thoroughly weary" would never find it as easy to curtail his drinking habits as a man in a less demanding trade (*Times* 10-25-86.6).

Buttressing nutritional arguments for the benefits of intoxicating drink were medical ones. Alcohol was widely and, in many respects, legitimately regarded both as a pain-killer and as a palliative for psychological as well as physiological stress. Granted, Dickens may be drawing a bead on the misguided pediatric wisdom of old wives when, in *Oliver Twist*, Mrs. Mann slips a shot of gin "into the blessed infants' Daffy, when they ain't well" (6). Yet, as we've seen, Fanny Stevenson documents child Louis' actual, doctor-prescribed dosing with that "antimonial wine." And just as Fanny herself poured brandy onto her husband's silent lips after the fatal stroke, Dickens consistently and confidently "dosed" himself and other adults when illness struck (Howett 80–1). It was a century in which, on the one hand, eminent physicians like Louis Pasteur confidently endorsed the hygienic properties of beer and wine (Sournia 90)— while, on the other, Sir Andrew Clark of the London Hospital portentously claimed that seventy percent of his patients "directly owe[d] their ill-health to alcohol" (Mitchell 114). In this light, it's perhaps no accident that the primary intellectual (as opposed to moral) conflict in *J&H* is between two doctors. Lanyon, although a social drinker, emulates the tone of reformist organs like the *Medical Temperance Journal* (established in 1869), calling the experiments which lead to Jekyll's cataclysmic self-medication "unscientific balderdash" (36). Jekyll/Hyde, in turn, so thoroughly demonstrates the restorative power of a glass of tonic that Lanyon's objections are forever silenced after he watches Jekyll be reconstituted by a singularly potent draught, "like a man restored from death" (80). But the prime point to be made here is that many of Stevenson's contemporaries saw alcohol as a useful "food" or "drug," and the result was that many more people drank than would otherwise have done so. James Greenwood might in 1869 bemoan the fate of one temporarily reformed alcoholic who sadly relapsed after his doctor prescribed regular doses of stout to check an infection (221); but even Joseph Livesey had exempted "medicinal alcohol" from the prohibitions of his historic, 1832 Preston Pledge of "total" abstinence (Longmate 44). And fifty years later, the prohibitionist physician Kate Mitchell was still confidently endorsing the utility of medicinal spirits (93).

Even more central to Victorian drinking patterns than questions of hygiene and health, however, were strongly established social customs. Before he took the teetotal pledge, George Cruikshank had revealingly allowed that "no man was considered a gentleman unless he had made his companions drunk" (Jones 88). This may fly in the face of Dickens' claim that drunkenness was a distinctly lower-class plague, but it's perfectly consistent with Stevenson's portrait in *J&H* of professional "old cronies" whose wonted recreations require a marked and regular need to "sober their minds" after the "straining" rituals of fellowship are over. Even when a gentleman was wooed to the temperance cause, for him to sign the reformers' "long pledge" (which committed him to serve no alcohol whatsoever in his house) as opposed to the "short pledge" (which called merely for the signatory's personal abstinence from strong drink) was essentially to commit social suicide (Shiman 22). Men of refinement not only valued the company and the free-flowing hospitality of other "judges of good wine," they also expected to engage with them in the traditional social rites of drink. When Hyde "compounds the draft" and "pledges the dead man," he is (again) essentially offering a "toast," something that was very much *de rigeur* at any sophisticated gathering and frequently enough ran into dozens and dozens of increasingly-debilitating iterations, as indeed in *Kidnapped*, when David is obliged by his Highland hosts "to sit and hear Jacobite toasts ... till all were tipsy and staggered off to the bed or the barn for their night's rest" (103). John Dunlop accordingly judged that this kind of "health drinking" constituted "one of the highest provocations to drunkenness" (267) in Britain, and it indeed became a prime bugbear for temperance forces. One of the strangest dilemmas surrounding the royal celebrations of 1887, in fact, turned on how the British could responsibly toast the Queen on her fifty-year reign. "Let wine prevail at public banquets during this year of Jubilee," warned one especially anxious voice, "and thousands will never live a decent life again" (Longmate 241). The many and varied solutions that were proposed for this anniversary dilemma — among them toasting with water or with an empty glass — merely testify to the irreducible strength of alcoholic custom.

The classes among whom Hyde dwells and presumably carries on were perhaps even more tangled than their "betters" in the webs of social necessity. John Dunlop's remarkable testament, *The Philosophy of Artificial and Compulsory Drinking Usage in Great Britain and Ireland* (1839), documents not only the extensive and effectively compulsory drinking rituals of "meals, markets, fairs, baptisms and funerals" (3) but also a stunning array of *workplace* rites of passage that brought the provision and consumption of drink into the very center of a workingman's life. Joiners and carpenters, for example, were essentially shut out of the craft if they refused to lubricate with proffered drink the tracks of their advancement: Dunlop attests that, "on obtaining a new bench or station in the work, 4s. for drink must be paid; this is given to benchmen exclusively. Unless an apprentice pays something for drink at making his first window sash, or other difficult operation, he will not be assisted in his work, and no explanation regarding business will be given to him" (185). Since the midday meals of working men were often taken at the very same public houses where these statutory drinks were purchased and consumed, the ethos was one that regularly blurred the line between work and leisure, not only in the symbolic terms of linking the social obligation of "footing" drinks to progress up the ladder of one's profession but also by literally bringing workers back into the shop in an intoxicated state. The increasingly industrialized nineteenth-century workplace ultimately required a clearer separation of work and play in the interests of both productivity and safety (Malcolmson 89), in ways that we shall discover to have been distinctly relevant to *J&H*. A drunken cobbler might smash his thumb with his hammer, but a drunken machinist might either lose his life or kill a coworker. Suffice it to say for now, however, that the practical matters of earning a living joined ranks with, each in turn, (1) social usage, (2) practical hygiene, and (3) the frequent advice of medical men to persuade many Victorians to continue drinking alcohol even while temperance forces upped the pressure either to be moderate or to abstain entirely from strong drink.

Finally, as the last paragraph indeed suggests, the public house itself played a wide range of social roles in the nineteenth century that put far more individuals in the regular way of drink than one might expect. The pub's most egregious ancillary function, according to Dunlop and other reformers like him, was as a *de facto* bank. Many employees were paid jointly on Saturday evenings, as a group, with single large bank notes. In search of individual "change," they necessarily flocked after all other businesses had closed to the only establishments still open that could offer such a financial service: public houses. "Nothing can exceed the tyranny and folly of such masters," Dunlop complained, since the timing and mode of payment guaranteed that a good portion of the men's wages would find its way back to the publican's till (185). An even more problematic variant for disbursement, common for public employees, was the actual payment of wages *at* the pub. "It was no uncommon thing in the past," claimed teetotal activist Thomas Whittaker, "to have secret arrangements between middle men in public works and publicans by which a mutual advantage was secured at the cost of the workmen." Thus, when an 1883 bill finally outlawed this questionable method of pay-rolling, Whittaker righteously claimed "it was not a moment too soon, but fifty years too late" (*Life's Battles* 70).

Other functions of the pub were perhaps less prone to this kind of exploitative manipulation but were no less significant for luring common citizens up to or inside public house doors on a regular basis. Beyond providing food and drink, pubs offered lodging to travelers and meeting places for groups and societies not possessed of their own property. Ironically, William Booth's tee-totaling Salvation Army was itself born in a Whitechapel public house for want of an alternative indoor venue. Pubs served as employment bureaus, auction rooms, campaign headquarters, gambling halls, and centers for various commercial entertainments, including drama, prize fights, and musical performances. Having long served as clearing houses for oral news, pubs evolved in an age of exploding literacy into *de facto* libraries and book-shops (one specifically recalls, in *J&H*, Stevenson's multi-purpose "shop for the retail of penny numbers and two-penny salads" [48]) — or reading rooms for those with an appetite for books and papers but without the requisite means to purchase them. For the very poor, the pub and gin palace offered heat, light, cooking facilities, furniture, and even the lavatories they couldn't afford for themselves. For the lonely, they afforded ready companionship, including the services of prostitutes. Their importance as hubs in London's transportation system is reflected to this day in the names of tube stations like "Royal Oak," "Angel," "Swiss Cottage," and "Elephant and Castle" (Thompson *The Rise of Respectable* Society 322–23; Girouard 10). In sum, when Stevenson says of his days in Edinburgh "I used to have my headquarters in an old public house — where there was a room in which I could go and write" (*Letters* 1.210), he is describing a semi-domestic situation that would not have been at all uncommon for other young British men, from any of a number of rungs on the social ladder. Stevenson may then have had little money for copious drink (Calder 7), let alone to purchase the affections of the friendly prostitutes that haunted the place. But the fact that he was drawn to the pub as the perfect place to conduct "his life" testifies to the broad effect that the culture of drink exerted upon his age. Even those people whose finances or principles led them to be moderate, or even to abstain, inevitably lived for a substantial portion of their lives in the very shadow of Bacchus.

Pub culture marked Stevenson and his novella in ways we shall revisit, but his direct immersion in the publican's world of beer and boisterousness was largely over by the time he left Edinburgh. He did once tell Charles Baxter, "Happiness is a matter of bottled stout" (McNally and Florescu 76), and he later fondly recalled to the same old 'varsity chum those heady years,

> When I was young and drouthy ["thirsty," or "addicted to drinking"]
> I kent a public house
> Whaur a' was cosh ["snug"] and couthy ["comfortable"];
> It's there that I was crouse ["cheerful"]! [*Letters* 4.111].

Just like the "respectable" folk he so despised, he inevitably if ironically transferred the bulk of his drinking to the more private confines of club and home.[1] Yet, if he essentially deserted the tap-rooms and public bars of ale, stout, and gin for the dining- and smoking-rooms of claret and port, his devotion to the gentleman's customary draught was still extraordinary. It's scarcely exaggerating to say that, for Stevenson, wine was essential to life. His metaphors tell the story. If the Utterson/Guest passage likens wine to the warmth of the sun, an especially jubilant passage in his semi-autobiographical short story "The Misadventures of John Nicholson" equates it to the very oxygen in one's lungs, as the hero "looked all about him, drinking the clear air like wine" (180). Similarly, "The Treasure of Franchard"'s Dr. Desprez "inhale[s] the air, tasting it critically as a connoisseur tastes a vintage" (*Complete Stories* 2.23.) For the man who lived to write, another writer's brilliance was tellingly like a perfect vintage: parts of Meredith's "Love in the Valley," Stevenson once confessed to W. B. Yeats, "haunted me and made me drunk like wine" (*Letters* 8.262). Outlining plans for his Samoan estate at Vailima, he writes to Charles Baxter, "The price of the house will be considerable: many expenses have to be faced before we have cattle, feed, and vegetables. On the other hand, once faced there is my livelihood, all but books and wine, ready in a nutshell" (*Letters* 6.397). A loaf of bread, a jug of wine, and a good book: tantamount to life itself. This was the truth that Stevenson's most steadfast literary confidant and fellow oenophile, Henry James, acknowledged when he sent a case of champagne to Louis and wife Fanny's stateroom as they set sail for America in 1887 (*Letters* 6.3). This is the Stevenson to whom J. A. Symonds dedicated *Wine, Women, and Song*, "in memory of past symposia when wit (your wit) flowed freer than our old Forzato" (*Wine* n.p.).

Stevenson's first taste of that early "antinomial wine" can't have been his doing, but from the time he eagerly shared his school-mate's raisin wine, he regularly went to some lengths to ensure his steady supply of fermented drink. A substantial portion of the thousand pounds with which his father set him up "for life" at age 25 went exceedingly quickly to his wine merchant (Bell 90). Writing to Thomas Stevenson from France in 1883, RLS describes an ambitious, family-intensive cellaring project: "I am bottling my wine: i.e. Valentine [the maid] is filling, Fanny corking and every little while, when they have made some progress, I go down and carry in the bottles. There are now two dozen in the cellar, so, as my cask is *supposed* to contain 210 bottles, the work is but beginning" (*Letters* 4.161). While stocking a cellar was easy enough to manage in Europe, the job was distinctly challenging once the Stevensons moved to the Pacific. Sometimes Louis managed reasonably well. In Honolulu in May of 1889, he arranged for a shipment of excellent claret to be brought in by the ship *Equator* (*Letters* 6.21). At other times he barely made do—not that the fact diminished his dependence on the stuff. When Henry Brooks Adams first visited Stevenson's Samoan estate Vailima in 1890, he noted rather mean-spiritedly, "Stevenson himself seems to eat little or nothing, and lives on cheap French vin ordinaire when he can get it" (McLynn 398). The expatriate writer's ultimate solution was to charge his old friend Baxter with shipping him a regular supply of superior European vintages. A letter of 4 November 1892 documents both the need and the arrangement:

If we can afford to make this order just now—I mean if you can afford to pay for it—*it will save money*, as we have to buy bad wine dear in driblets or go without—which is unpleasing and *infra dig*. If we could get the Corton and the Rauenthaler alone, it would be one great want satisfied. And perhaps you could meet these and the bins if not the other. The Rebello Valente, I should scare care to have you order at all, unless you could taste it. I have no use for port unless it is *old and dry*, and spotted this on the list for its age. Perhaps you may know of an *old, dry, light* wine yourself [*Letters* 7.423].

The communiqué is interesting not only as a testament to Stevenson's love of the grape but also for the sense of social status that he attaches to it. Locally available wines are "*infra dig.*," beneath his dignity. We must assuredly allow for the self-deprecating humor that was his custom with Baxter; and there's no evidence that Stevenson's distaste for the available *vin ordinaire* extended to a disdain for his Samoan compatriots themselves. It was only Colvin who decried the slumming new life of his old *émigré* friend, "drinking with dusky majesties ... [in] isolation from anything like equals" (McLynn 340). But the old link between fine wine and elevated class rank, so evident in *J&H*, is very much present in this missive to Baxter.

While it may be fanciful to hear in Stevenson's plea for an "*old*" port and for "an *old, dry, light* wine" echoes of Jekyll's plangent request for more of the Maws' original chemicals—"For God's sake, find me some of the old" (66)—animation very much like the fictional doctor's is interestingly enough a staple of Stevenson's Samoan wine correspondence. In November, 1893, he complains to Baxter, "I am dying of bad claret—literally. As one grows up in years, the wine must be good" (*Letters* 8.181). In early December of the same year, he writes even more suggestively, "For the Lord's sake, order another case of liqueurs: *Eau de vie de Dantzig* and *Oranges Amere*, same as last year" (*Letters* 8.189; see also 8.266). The point to make is that Stevenson wrote about wine (and, here, about spirits as well) with much the same passion that his fictional protagonist brought to the provision of his vital potion. It begins to suggest that the novella could have cut very close to the bone.

Writing again in November of 1894, Stevenson's language evokes even more strongly the imaginative conflation of his own life and the text for which he is probably best known:

O! I have forgotten that I wish another cask of wine from the timorous [wine merchant] Dieppe. Please tell him that the last gave great satisfaction. It is sound and wholesome; perhaps I might prefer a lighter wine, and perhaps some other time *he might make the experiment*, but for just now we shall just have a repetition of the order [*Letters* 8.390; emphasis added].

The language of the laboratory experiment brought to the stocking of the cellar is assuredly suggestive for readers of *J&H*. It is not, however, unique either for Stevenson or for his age. His essay on the Napa Valley observes that "wine in California is still in the experimental stage," as "bit by bit, they grope for their Clos Vougeot and Lafitte" (*Silverado* 189). "But these are but experiments. All things in this new land are moving farther on" (192). And to move beyond Stevenson to the age in which he matured as a writer, when Gladstone's policies made the amateur's sampling of a broad range of vintages a substantially easier exercise, Dr. Robert Druitt expressed in 1866 his personal gratitude as an avid "experimenter" in wines (Briggs 38). A *Times* advertisement of the same year claimed that "a practical distiller, having been experimenting for the last seventeen years, can now produce a fair port and sherry, by fermentation, without a drop of grape juice" (Briggs 76). Of course the greatest oenological "experiment" of the age, as called for in a *Punch* poem of 22 October 1881, was the grafting of European vines onto imported American roots, a vinicultural need occasioned by the catastrophic *phylloxera* blight (183). Not only was wine, then, as constant a concern in Stevenson's life as "the war of the members" was in Jekyll's; he and others regularly talked about it in ways that more or less collapsed the distinction between the drinking place and the laboratory just as thoroughly as the novella does — or as did the rituals of punch and cocktails with which the author also "experimented."

So how did Stevenson feel about his own obsession with wine? In a revealing, Janus-faced letter to his oldest and closest friend, Baxter, he wrote of his early Edinburgh days: "How I feared I should make a shipwreck, and yet timidly hoped not; how I feared I should never have a friend far less a wife, and yet passionately hoped I might; how I hoped (*if I did not take to drink*) I should possibly write one little book" (*Letters* 6.207 [6 Sept. 1888]; italics added). This wrenching sense that drink could always do him in, could cast his ship of life onto deadly rocks, was a constant of his self-reflective moments. He had written to Baxter in 1873, "I'm getting tired of this whole life business.... Let me get into a corner with a brandy bottle; or down on the hearthrug, full of laudanum grog; or as easily as may be, into a nice, wormy grave" (*Letters* 1.271–2). The following year, he confessed with equal morbidity to his idolized confidante Fanny Sitwell, "I have had a bad struggle with myself day by day and night by night. Opium and wine and everything that is death for soul and body, tempt me, one after the other. And in bed at night, ... I often make up my mind that I shall begin to descend to the mouth of the pit" (*Letters* 2.84).

Was Stevenson an alcoholic, then? Or, to use the contemporary medical term introduced by the Swede Magnus Hess and employed by Stevenson in his Menton letter to Colvin, was he a "dipsomaniac"? There is no doubt that alcohol was his crutch as well as his love. When his physician at the tubercular colony in Davos required him to give up smoking and limit himself to two hours of writing per day, his wine consumption jumped to three litres a day (McLynn 187). Stevenson certainly joked about the way his excesses defined his character. 1887's poem "On Himself," a trifle of self-mockery inspired when he and Fanny rather unexpectedly found themselves employing a butler, begins, "He may have been this or that, / A drunkard and a guttler" (*Collected Poems* 354). Writing to an Edinburgh Burns collector in 1891, Stevenson referred to the Scots poet's considerable artistic debt to Robert Fergusson, "the poor, white-faced, drunken, vicious boy that raved himself to death in the Edinburgh madhouse"; "I believe," Stevenson continued fairly revealingly, "Fergusson lives in me" (*Letters* 7.110–8.290). And six weeks before he died, he wrote once again to Colvin expressing the fear that he would in the end die "a drunken pantaloon, a driveller" (*Letters* 8.383). There were times, as with the "antimonial wine" of his early years, that he drank on the best available recommendations: part of the formal "cure" prescribed by his doctors in Davos was, after all, "Valtelline wine" (*Letters* 3.298). There were other times, however, when he knew it might be best for his fragile health if he were to stop. Yet when he tried to do so, he invariably registered the prodigious difficulty of the effort. To his parents he writes of his first documented experiment with abstinence in March of 1884, "I now take NO GROG: eheu! but I am better without it, as I must with groaning reluctancy admit. But what is life without pleasures of the table?" (*Letters* 4.249) He wrote the same day to cousin Bob and his wife Louisa Stevenson: "I am now shorn of my grog forever. My last habit — my last pleasure — gone. I am myself no more. Of that lean, feverish, voluble and whiskyfied young Scot, who once sparked through France and Britain, bent on art and the pleasures of the flesh, there now remains no quality but the strong language" (*Letters* 4.249).[2] That "forever" proved in the event to be ironically short-lived, but the dependence on drink for a sense of mental tranquility and even personal identity re-emerges in June of 1893 in Stevenson's letter to Henry James:

> I have had to stop all strong drink and all tobacco; and am now in a transition state between the two which seems to be near madness.... If I live through this breach of habit I shall be a white-livered puppy indeed. Actually I am so made, or so twisted, that I do not like to think of a life without the red wine on the table and the tobacco with its lovely little coal of fire. It doesn't amuse me from a distance. I may find it the Garden of Eden when I go in, but I don't like the color of the gateposts [*Letters* 8.108].

The closest Stevenson came to a definitive personal judgment on his drinking habits is in a letter to Baxter in 1893, when his old friend's financial crises were spinning him ever more deeply into the ruinous vortex of drink. "You have before you one of the hardest battles possible," Stevenson affirms, begging Baxter to find a supportive but "rugged" friend as a domestic companion and moral monitor to help him reverse his decline. "When I lived alone in San Francisco [while pursuing Fanny in 1879–80], I found I must never have a drop of anything to drink in the house, for in my black isolation and gloom I could not measure what I was taking" (*Letters* 8.109). It is possible Stevenson was exaggerating his own experience to maximize the therapeutic effect on Baxter; but the confessed incapacity to "measure" his consumption suggests he may himself have tasted a version of Jekyll's plight, what Jellinek would call "gamma alcoholism" (37). On the other hand, his focus on the psychological rather than on the physiological trials of his abstinence ("I am myself no more" and "near madness") and the apparent lack of any "progressive process" in his condition markedly differentiates him from Jekyll as being, perhaps at worst, an "alpha alcoholic" (Jellinek 36). Compared to writers like Baudelaire or the fatally dysfunctional Poe, to be sure, Stevenson was not by any means a serious alcoholic by his own contemporary standards. Yet if he ultimately found ways to drink with some moderation, he seems to have had a very full appreciation for the prodigious "battle"—perhaps even the "war of the members"—that managing alcohol could involve.

Well before (and indeed well after) he may have given literary embodiment to that appreciation in *J&H*, Stevenson evinced a sustained fascination with the drinkers and drunkards that he met along life's road. Predictably, he tends to locate them all somewhere on a continuum between the personable, humanized tippler of the Utterson sort and the irascible, threatening drinker of the Hyde mold. One of the first was John Adam, an Edinburgh court clerk whose notorious drunkenness became a great prod to nostalgia in one of Stevenson's 1873 letters to Baxter: "Is there anything new about Johnny Adam? Dear man! How my heart would melt within me and the tears of patriotism spring to my eyes, if I could but see him reel towards me, in his dress clo' like a moon at midday and smiling his vulgar, Scotch grin from ear to ear!"(*Letters* 1.397). When he learned that the man had died "o' Aqua-vitae" (as another "Johnny Adam*s*" suggestively and perhaps derivatively succumbs to poisoned gin in *The Beach at Falesá* [18]), Stevenson wrote a memorial poem which comes a mite closer to evoking the darker themes of *J&H* (*Collected Poems* 106–8). Adam is "aye drunk," fraught with pure "sensuality," always full of "kindled spunk," and fit for a prime role "in ane o' the auld worl's canty [cheerful] hells, / Paris or Sodom." "Whusky an' he were man an may [spouse] / Whate'er betided"—markedly like Jekyll, with Hyde (as "drink"?) bound to him "closer than a wife, closer than an eye" (95). But, for Stevenson and Baxter, Adam was the spirit of life, not the "slime of the pit." Thus Baxter writes in July of 1892 that life goes on in Edinburgh, but with "no Johnny Adams [*sic*], no R.L.S., nor other *joyeux compagnons* to laugh at the dreariness of the whole blooming bag of tricks" (*Letters* 7.348).

Another of Stevenson and Baxter's iconic drinkers, somewhat less "joyeux" perhaps, was an irascible Edinburgh wine merchant named Thomas Brash, who died in 1873 but whose memory was strong enough to inspire the ribald "Brasheanna," a series of comic poems which the two friends exchanged for decades. RLS sends one to Baxter in March of 1882, recalling times when,

> Thoughtless we wandered in the evening hour;
> Aimless and pleased we went our random way:
> In the foot-haunted city, in the night,
> Among the alternate lamps, we went and came
> Till, like a humourous thunderbolt, that name
> The hated name of Brash, assailed our sight.
> We saw, we paused, we entered, seeking gin.
> His wrath, like a huge breaker on the beach,
> Broke instant forth. He on the counter beat
> Danced impotent wrath upon the floor within.
> Still as we fled, we heard his idiot screech [*Letters* 3.303–4].

The poem curiously anticipates both the setting and characterization of *J&H*: first the lamp-lit streets at night and the proto–Enfields wandering through them; then the seemingly unprovoked wrath of a proto–Hyde, whose own "infantile fury" will in the novella involve striking "in no more spirit than that in which a sick child may break a plaything" (90), and whose own impotent feet and ape-like screeches will sound to Utterson and Poole from behind the locked cabinet door. Although Stevenson called Brash "the Caliban of God" (*Letters* 3.319), the mood of the poems is nonetheless distinctly light, and Stevenson kept the playfulness alive through decades of correspondence. Another outburst of verse, for example, restores something like Jekyll's originally innocuous "impatient gaiety" to the wonted vision of drunken, Hydian rage. Stevenson invites Baxter to "share the eternal destiny of Brash": "Let us be fools, my friend, let us be drunken, / Let us be angry and extremely silly" (*Letters* 3.296)

More complex and troubling in his presentation is B. M. Haggard, brother to the novelist, H. Ryder Haggard. One of the Stevenson's constant companions in Samoa, the fellow "drank too much," reports the writer on one night's bingeing, "and kept the ... men in [Stevenson's stepson] Lloyd's house awake till 3 A.M." (*Letters* 8.213) "He eats little or nothing, drinks perpetually; and," wrote Stevenson to his mother Maggie, "well, for his own sake, I hope he will not live to go home. There seems to be no place possible for him" (*Letters* 8.229). Stevenson at times brings this house-wrecker very close to Hyde when Jekyll's alter-ego is described as "the slime of the pit," or "amorphous dust," or "what was dead" (95): "By seven Haggard had joined me, as d___k as they make 'em. As he sat and talked to me, he smelt of the charnel house, methought.... That interview has made me a tea-totaller" (*Letters* 8.383).[3] Yet he is clearly restored to the comic mode by the curious narrative embodied in *An Object of Pity, or The Man Haggard*, a mock-romance in the "Ouida fashion" scribed by Stevenson and five others which lionizes Haggard, his "ten-finger glasses," and his defiance of the conspiracies of "that ass Teetoo-tum" (another possible dig at the temperance movement, characterized as spinning top; 23–4). Similarly, although the family's drunken cook Paul Einfurer often drove the Master of Vailima to a rage, Stevenson kept him on and referred to him with Uttersonian tolerance and humor. Thus he describes him to Sidney Colvin in 1890: "Paul—a German—cook and steward—a glutton of work—a splendid fellow: drawbacks, three: (1) no cook, (2) an inveterate bungler ... continually falling in the dishes...: (3)

a dr___ well, don't say that — but we daren't let him go to town, and he — poor, good soul — is afraid to be let go" (*Letters* 7.24).

Joe Strong, artist-husband to Stevenson's step-daughter Belle, was another drunken presence in the Vailima household, although his predilections were necessarily viewed and documented rather patiently by the writer (McLynn 342). Rather more ominously presented, and far less tolerantly, is another hard-drinking wine merchant of Stevenson's Pacific acquaintance, R. M. Weir, an "insincere and dangerous" man (*Letters* 8.353). Or a drunken acquaintance from Samoa named Carr, "a genuine raving lunatic, I believe, and jolly dangerous" (*Letters* 7.305). Or, once again, W. E. Henley's brother Teddy, "the drunken whoreson bugger living himself in the best hotels, and smashing inoffensive strangers in the bar" (*Letters* 6.93). W. E. was himself a hard-drinking "Falstaffian" (McLynn 90), but Stevenson used him as a model for Long John Silver, a man well aware of the dangers of drink whom some critics have likened to a "teetotal Jacobin" (Swearingen 69–70; Harvie 120). Henley's prodigal brother Teddy, in contrast, is perhaps the closest Stevenson came to finding a real, pure, alcoholic Hyde-without-a-Jekyll living in the real world outside of the novella. It was perhaps type casting that actually gave the man the lead role in *Deacon Brodie*, the Stevenson–W. E. Henley collaboration that brought an earlier Stevensonian vision of criminal duality to the London stage.

Stevenson's humane concern for Pacific islanders was legendary, and he regularly documented the varied effects of alcohol and other drugs on their society and lives. King Kalakaua of Hawaii both amazed and delighted him, as though he were a tropical John Adam. "A bottle of fizz [champagne] is like a glass of sherry to him," the author wrote to Baxter in 1889. "He thinks nothing of five or six in the afternoon as a whet for dinner.... He carries it, too, like a mountain with a sparrow on its shoulders" (McLynn 339). The darker side of drink, however, emerges in an account of a massive native binge at Butaritari in the Gilbert Islands, renewed proof for Stevenson that if "any one can start [a man] drinking, not any twenty can prevail on him to stop" (*South Seas* 248). To celebrate the Fourth of July, the king had lifted a *tapu* against drink, and "for ten days the town had been passing the bottle or lying ... in hoggish sleep; and the king, moved by the Old Men and his own appetites, continued to maintain the liberty, to squander his savings on liquor, and to join in and lead the debauch" (248). Stevenson described a deteriorating scene in ways that recall Jekyll's "dissolution" almost point for point: the once-resolute king "melted and streamed under his cocked hat" (250), the court smoldered in drunken "impatience" (249), the people reveled like "intoxicated children" (252), then succumbed to the "brutal impulse" (252) of armed riot. Stevenson knew where the bulk of the blame lay. The natives weren't drinking native brews but rather "din" (gin) and "perandi" (brandy), imported sprits which the white traders were keen enough to sell: "The whites were the authors of the crisis; it was upon their own proposal that the freedom had been granted at the first; and for a while, in the interests of trade, they were doubtless pleased it should continue" (248). Unlike the *laissez-faire* Utterson, Stevenson was finally moved to confront the key trader, demanding, at some perceived risk to his own neck, that the maddening supply be cut off. Sobriety prevailed, the *tapu* was re-imposed, and Stevenson drafted a petition to the American government to declare the liquor trade in the Gilberts illegal. While he supposed the tract would lie "probably unread and possibly unopened, in a pigeon-hole at Washington" (264), the dire business ultimately and revealingly inspired the inveterate drinker to take a highly restrictive stance on alcohol.

The same solicitousness led him to urge King Malietoa of Samoa to supplement his ban on hard liquor by outlawing opium as well (*Letters* 6.354–55). One might facilely suppose that a commonplace European condescension led Stevenson to see the Pacific islanders as insufficiently civilized to govern their own affairs and appetites, and thus in need of a moralistic paternalism he would never have accepted in his own society and life. Yet he long battled to disencumber his beloved Samoa from the colonializing toils of England and Germany and the United States alike. And his "last word" on the crisis in Butaritari is instructive: "to be just to barbarous islanders we must not forget the slums and dens of our cities; I must not forget that I have passed dinnerwards through Soho, and seen that which cured me of my dinner" (*South Seas* 244). A decade and a half after his famous novella first appeared, Stevenson was still seeing the dipsomaniac drama of *J&H* played out by another people in another hemisphere — and still re-evincing London's Soho as the symbolic epicenter of the problem. But by then, perhaps, the ambiguities of a human tragedy had begun to resolve themselves into the relative certainties that enable both judgment and action.

FIVE

The Literary Contexts of Stevenson's Tale of Alcohol

When at eighteen Stevenson wrote to his favorite cousin Bob about the alluring but dizzying possibility of "becoming great," he confessed to feeling a stabilizing "self-consciousness or common sense ... that would prevent me poisoning myself like Chatterton or drinking like Burns on the failure of my ambitious hopes" (*Letters* 1.143). Here is a curious and suggestive anticipation of Jekyll's own "imperious desire to carry [his] head high," coupled with a sense that failure might lead to inebriated self-destruction, should the "balancing instincts" of common sense not prevail. Nevertheless, the salient point is that Stevenson saw himself as aspiring to greatness. How, one might ask, would the thinly-veiled allegory of inebriation for which he is best known find its place in the literary market of his age? How, in turn, would it place him among the ranks of esteemed writers? The novella was, from its first appearance, phenomenally "popular," garnering a favorable review in *The Times* of London and selling close to 40,000 copies in England in the next six months alone, according to Stevenson's cousin and biographer, Graham Balfour. And by 1901, Balfour reckoned, some quarter of a million authorized and pirated copies had sold in the United States (Linehan 79). Where, however, did *J&H* "fit" in the literary galaxy of its time, chilling tale of addiction that it was?

The temperance movement had by 1885 affected English letters and publishing in ways that influenced Stevenson as well. John Cassell, who would eventually buy and print *Treasure Island*, *The Black Arrow*, and *Kidnapped*, had founded a thriving publishing business squarely on his teetotal convictions, and one of his most successful offerings, *Cassell's Illustrated Family Paper*, was a favorite of the young Louis and his nanny, Alice "Cummy" Cunningham (*Letters* 1.92; 5.291, 296, 307). Cassell significantly sponsored a competition for "moral tales" to be published in the paper, all entries required to be "illustrative of the triumph of religion, temperance, morality, industry, energy, and self-control over idleness, apathy, intemperance, and habitual self-indulgence" (Nowell-Smith 42). Thus, Stevenson would have been steeped from an extremely early age in insistently melodramatic treatments of the very issues *J&H* explores. In a letter to Jane Balfour dictated to Cummy when he was six or seven, he accordingly refers to "a very interesting story" in a "bound up *Cassell's Paper*," and then goes on to say, "Cummy gives me my lessons, and I've good behaviour ones and bad behaviour ones" (*Letters* 1.92). Predictably, however, the literary merit of much of the most avid moral polemic in Cassell's paper and beyond was, at best, questionable. Stage adaptations of Cruikshank's *The Bottle* (1847) and Zola's *L'Assommoir* (Charles Read's *Drink* from 1879), for example, deservedly fell into oblivion (Booth, "Temperance Drama" 207). While they afforded perfect matter for street ballads like the 1870s "Railroad to Hell" (Neuburg 194), the lurid sins of the tavern translated less successfully into the subtleties of high culture. Although Walt Whitman dabbled in the popular trend in *Franklin Evans; or The Inebriate* (1842), he ultimately condemned his own exercise as "damned rot" (Matheson 72). This opportunistic novel is assuredly not among the works for which Stevenson expressed admiration, either in 1878's "Gospel According to Walt Whitman" or 1887's "Books Which Have Influenced Me."

As Stevenson joked about his dependence on drink, he also postured for comic effect as an impecunious hack writer. Recall, for example, the letter to Will Low in which he calls *J&H* his "gothic gnome" (*Letters* 5.163). Comments he made to Sidney Colvin, wife Fanny, and Dr. Thomas Scott—before, while, and after the story took shape—were even more archly self-deprecating: "I'm pouring forth a penny (12 penny) dreadful"; "I drive on with *Jekyll*, bankruptcy at my heels"; "I've got my shilling shocker" (*Letters* 5.128; 5.135; Brantlinger and Boyle 265). On only the second day of 1886 he cannot yet have known how exceptionally well the newly-published novella would do on both sides of the Atlantic, but he nonetheless wrote to Edmund Gosse, "There must be something wrong in me or I would not be popular" (McLynn 263).[1] Despite Stevenson's self-mockery, however, and his driving desire to make a living with his writing, there's no reason to think that he was truly and completely "slumming" when he penned what was in substantial measure a tale of alcoholic addiction, thereby playing either the literary demagogue to the growing temperance market or the lurid panderer to those with a taste for muck. A look at "the grand tradition" of nineteenth-century literature reveals almost as consistent an interest in drink as anything in either the Cassell's or the "penny number" range. And among these "higher" treatments of alcoholism, Stevenson's tale is the equal of any in both nuance and humanistic insight. James Ashcroft Noble testified early on to the gap between the novella's unprepossessing appearance and its substantial literary clout. In an *Academy* review of 23 January, 1886, he wrote, "in spite of the paper cover and the popular price, Mr. Stevenson's story distances so unmistakably its three-volume and one-volume competitors, that its only fitting place is a place of honour. It is, indeed, many years since English fiction has been enriched by any work at once so weirdly imaginative in conception and so faultlessly ingenious in construction as this little tale" (Maixner 203).

We might well begin our canonical mise-en-scène with Dickens.[2] As any number of citations earlier in this argument have suggested, Dickens' work is as full of drink and drinkers as was the London life in which he traded. Daniel Quilp, the villainous, rum-guzzling dwarf of *The Old Curiosity Shop* (1840–41), anticipates the "dwarfish" Hyde (40) in his symbolically degenerate stature as well as his addiction. *Hard Times* (1854) documents alcohol's dire impact on a highly sympathetic central character, as Stephen Blackpool's life is blighted by his drunken spouse (who is literally as "brutish" [87] and "impatient" [67] as Hyde). The same theme is played out in minor keys and lesser characters by Mrs. Sparsit's husband, whom she claims plunged her into poverty when he died at twenty-four of a surfeit of brandy, and by Bounderby's drunken grandmother, very likely a figment of his self-serving imagination but for him an apt example of why he's stuck on the lower rungs of the social ladder. Dickens' most extravagant alcoholic must surely be *Bleak House*'s rag-and-bone man, Krook (1852–53), whose spirit-doused ways lead to his rather spectacular death by spontaneous combustion. Yet Dickens' most significant and triumphant drinker would be Sydney Carton from *The Tale of Two Cities* (1859), who, like a prototypical Cassell's hero, finds it in himself to make the ultimate, redemptive sacrifice of his own life to save his look-alike, his own "upright twin," Charles Darnay. If the doubling of characters in this novel doesn't anticipate Stevenson's plot in exact ways, the text nonetheless establishes alcoholism as a theme of some importance for the mid–Victorian novel.

The Brontë sisters were profoundly affected by the notorious drunkenness of their brother Branwell. As Charlotte suggested, the man's incorrigible alcoholism found its way to the very heart of *The Tenant of Wildfell Hall* (1848), providing sister Anne her model for the drunken and debauched Arthur Huntingdon. Hindley Earnshaw, too, undoubtedly owes something to Branwell as well as to Hogarth's gin drinkers when, deeply into his cups early in *Wuthering Heights* (1847), he accidentally drops young Hareton over an upstairs banister. *Jane Eyre*'s John Reed (1847) is a problem drinker too, and even Bertha Mason can wreak her pyrotechnic vengeance only after her custodian Grace Poole has drunk herself insensible—further testament to Branwell's impact on his sisters and, thus, to his lasting effect on English letters.

Charles Kingsley's fittingly-named *Yeast* (1848) features a young man who, driven to drink by rural poverty, drowns while in an alcoholic stupor. Moreover, Kingsley's *Alton Lock* (1849) could perfectly well have been ghost-written by John Dunlop, given its evocation of the customary alcoholism fostered by, in this case, the tailoring trade. Elizabeth Gaskell explores the traditional tie between drink and prostitution in *Mary Barton* (1848), when Mary's aunt Esther confesses to the wracking need for alcohol that she experiences in the flesh trade: "Such as live like me could not bear life if they did not drink. It's the only thing to keep us from suicide.... Oh! You don't know the awful nights I have had in prison for want of it" (McCormick 976). The power of drink returns with overwhelming irony in Gaskell's *North and South* (1855), when Betsy Higgins spends her last consumptive breath warning her father to forswear drink, but grief at her loss drives him instead to "a sup o' drink just to steady [him] again sorrow" (McCormick 976). And of course George Eliot's *Janet's Repentance*, the final segment of *Scenes of Clerical Life* (1857), anticipates *J&H* not only in its central, chilling representation of the violent alcoholic male, Dempster, but also in its correlative portrait of a prime victim — the downtrodden (and herself addicted) woman of the title.

Any one of these works might have given Stevenson reason to believe that addiction in general, and alcoholism in particular, were legitimate themes for an ambitious writer of English. It is two other classic texts of alcoholism, however, that are likely to have had the most significant impact on *J&H*. The first has for some time been loosely connected with the novella. When Andrew Lang, a reader for Longman's publishing firm, first saw Stevenson's story in manuscript in the Fall of 1885, he wrote to ask if Louis knew two other pieces that shared its theme of the mysterious double (Maixner 199). One, Theophile Gautier's *Le Chevalier Double*, Stevenson claimed never to have read. As to the other, he replied affirmatively: "Dear Lang, Yes, I know William Wilson" (*Letters* 5.158). Stevenson was in fact well acquainted with Poe, having written a review of John Ingram's edition of *The Works* for *The Academy* in January, 1875 (Swearingen 18; *Letters* 2.83). The parallels between "William Wilson" and *J&H* are fundamental, numerous, and (to this point) largely if curiously unexplored in Stevenson criticism.

Poe's story reads like what one might flippantly entitle "Edward Hyde's Foul Statement of the Case," as it gives prime narrative authority to "the dark half" rather than, as in Stevenson, to the "upright twin." The narrator begins, like Jekyll, with an account of his family and youth, but confesses to being "self-willed, addicted to the wildest caprices, and prey to the most ungovernable passions" (Geduld 55). He first meets his moral alter-ego late at night when he steals to the "other" William Wilson's school bedside, just as Utterson twice imagines Hyde approaching Jekyll's own bed — and stares at his alter-ego with "an iciness of feeling" (60) that is close kin to the "thin and icy" sensation in Jekyll's blood when he sees himself as Hyde (*J&H* 88). The "Bad" Wilson leaves the "Good" behind and goes off to Eton, where at a social gathering and "wildly excited with wine," he is unexpectedly visited by his better half, who is wearing clothes identical to his own, approaches him with "a gesture of petulant *impatience*," and delivers a "singular, low, *hissing* utterance" of warning (60; italics added), close kin to Jekyll or Utterson in his moral solicitousness, to be sure, but also very much like the impatient and hissing Hyde (*J&H* 39) so frequently dressed in Jekyll's clothes. Some years later, at Oxford, Bad Wilson is in the process of gulling a fellow whom he's disarmed by inducing him to "drink deeply" (61) when Good Wilson re-appears to foil his scheme, leaving behind a cloak identical to Bad Wilson's own.

Bridling at his better half's continual "imperious domination" and appalled by his own "utter weakness and helplessness" to continue doing Bad things in the presence of utter Good (and here the complete inversion of Jekyll's dilemma is most striking!), Bad Wilson now flees to Rome, where he confesses, "I had given myself up entirely to wine; its maddening influence upon my hereditary temper rendered me more and more impatient of control. I began to murmur, to hesitate, to resist. And was it only fancy which induced me to believe that, with the increase of my own firmness, that of my tormentor underwent a proportional diminution?" (60) The alcohol, the impatience, the "mutter" and "struggle" (cp. *J&H* 95), and perhaps especially the reciprocal changes in "stature" (cp. *J&H* 88) — are all there in close anticipation of Stevenson's tale. And just as the repentant Jekyll resolves to end his "slavery" (*J&H* 85), Bad Wilson says, "I now began to feel the inspiration of a burning hope, and at length nurtured in my secret thoughts a stern and desperate resolution that I would no longer be enslaved" (64). But his life is inextricably bound up with the other Wilson's such that, after he has mistaken his antagonist for his own image in a mirror but then sorted things out sufficiently to kill his more upright twin, he admits with some Stevensonian pronominal complexity, "I fancied I was speaking when he said: *In me did you exist — and in my death, see by this image which is your own, how utterly you have murdered yourself*" (65). In the same way of course (although at two very separate moments in time and perhaps according to two different definitions of "life") Hyde becomes a "self-destroyer" (70) and his better self equivalently brings "the life of that unhappy Henry Jekyll to an end" (97).

The parallels throughout the two tales are marked, down to the crisis of subjectivity at the very end of each, mirrored in the interplay of pronouns. Again, it's surprising that commentary on *J&H* has been so slow to document the specifics of Stevenson's apparent debt to the American writer, be they conscious or (more likely) unwitting. As that debt is acknowledged, however, it is important to note that the perverse and personally revealing fascination with alcoholism that Poe displays in "The Black Cat," "The Cask of Amontillado," or even *The Narrative of A. Gordon Pym* informs "William Wilson" as well.[3] Thus, when Stevenson happened upon the idea of the problematic double in Poe's tale, it too came trailing its own clouds of dipsomania — all to be filed away, perhaps, for future reference.

Poe's notoriety in Stevenson's day was as much for his own losing battle with alcohol as for the literary or humanistic merit of his work.[4] Stevenson himself judged that "he who could write 'King Pest' had ceased to be a human being" (*Letters* 2.89). One other author and alcohol-centered work seem likely to have had an impact on the composition of *J&H*, however, with both scribe and script being well-established in the "high" world of literary ambitiousness. Stevenson wrote to Thomas Hardy in August of 1885, citing Edmund Gosse as a mutual acquaintance and asking if he and Fanny might pay the Dorset writer and his wife a visit on an impending trip that would take them near Dorchester (*Letters* 5.125). Hardy readily agreed, and the pair indeed met later in the month. Exactly what they discussed was most unfortunately not recorded for posterity, although Fanny later claimed that she and her husband "felt an instinctive sympathy" for the great novelist and liked him "exceedingly" (McLynn 250). Given Stevenson's unfailing bent for literary conversation, however, and given that *The Mayor of Casterbridge* had been completed only that April and was due to begin its serial appearance in both the *Graphic* and (across the Atlantic) *Harper's Weekly* in January (*Casterbridge* 295), it seems unlikely that the two men could have failed to touch upon Michael Henchard's own forthcoming "tale of two natures." It is, in any case, a certainty that Hardy's own tragedy of addiction greatly affected Stevenson. In early June of 1886, he wrote to his new Dorset acquaintance: "My Dear Hardy, I have read *The Mayor of Casterbridge* with sincere admiration: Henchard is a great fellow, and Dorchester is touched in with the hand of a master. Do you think you could let me try to dramatise it?" (*Letters* 5.259) Hardy was flattered and gave Stevenson his permission to rewrite the story for the stage; but, even though the two men met again that month at Colvin's rooms at the British Museum (*Letters* 5.262), nothing further came of the project. Or at least of that *particular* "dramatisation" of Hardy's subject.

Heading home from the Dorchester visit, Stevenson suffered a pulmonary hemorrhage and was unable to return to Bournemouth until September 12 (McLynn 250). His recovery was slow, and he experienced still more severe bleeding at the end of the month. When he finally returned to energetic work, however, it was very significantly to "pour forth [his] penny dreadful"[5]; "I drive on with *Jekyll*," he told Fanny on October 20th, "bankruptcy at my heels" (*Letters* 5.135). Stevenson's account of the story's imaginative origins is well known. On November 1, he told publisher Charles Longman that the "main incident occurred [to him] in a nightmare: indigestion has its uses. I woke up, and before I went to sleep again, the story was complete" (*Letters* 5.150). "I had long been trying to write a story on this subject, to find a body, a vehicle, for that strong sense of man's double being," he later confessed, adding that the nightmare gave him two central scenes that grew into the novella: ostensibly 1) the vision of the ailing Jekyll sitting at the window above the Sunday strollers Utterson and Enfield, and 2) the dramatic transformation from Hyde back to

Jekyll in front of Dr. Lanyon ("A Chapter on Dreams" 208). If his preconscious creative geniuses—his "Brownies"—gave him detailed dramatic inspiration, it is at least tempting to think that a conversation with Hardy about his own soon-to-appear addictive hero had some impact on Stevenson's more general topical invention. The timing is too suggestive to overlook.

The Mayor of Casterbridge shares at least as many of Stevenson's themes and images as "William Wilson" does. At the heart of Henchard's character — as at Jekyll's and (as Jellinek tells us) the archetypal alcoholic's as well — lies a "restless impatience" (156) that drives him in turn to sell his wife, to hire Farfrae, to confess his dark story to Elizabeth-Jane, to fire and then assault Farfrae, and even to persecute the ne'er-do-well minor character Abel Whittle. The fatal catalyst is the old lady's rum-spiked furmity, which precipitates the tragedy by unbalancing Henchard's character and leading him to treat Susan and Elizabeth-Jane as cruelly as Hyde treats the women he encounters— the match-girl and the trampled child. Like Jekyll and so many other addicts, Henchard swears a solemn oath to abstain from his ruinous drug, but he finds himself unable to keep the vow, "busting out drinking" (176) much as Hyde bursts roaring from his repressive "cage." Like Jellinek's gamma alcoholic, both principals blame their lot on powers beyond their control, either Fate/"the curse of mankind" (*J&H* 82) or another, alien self: "I cannot even allow that I'm the man you met then," Henchard says to Newson about selling Susan; "I was not in my senses, and a man's senses are himself" (223).

Moreover, displacements and doublings abound in Hardy's tale, suggesting that the older writer could have spoken engagingly to Stevenson's quest for an appropriate fictional vehicle to advance his driving interest in human duality. Farfrae replaces Henchard as the town's alpha corn-merchant, as mayor, and, for a spell, as that prime object of Elizabeth-Jane's affection. A new Elizabeth-Jane takes the name and place of a dead original. Come to meet with her old amour, Lucetta appears to Henchard like a new Susan, "appearing here as the double of the first" (192). The townsfolk's censorious "Skimmington" parades the effigies of the former lovers through the streets of Casterbridge, and Henchard later has a most Jekyllian specular moment as he stares down into the mirroring pool he means to make his grave and sees a body: "he perceived with a sense of horror that it was *himself*. Not a man somewhat resembling him, but one in all respects his counterpart, his actual double, was floating as if dead in Ten Hatches Hole" (227). And just as Stevenson's psychological drama is played out on either side of Regent Street—in a struggle between the "reputable" professionals of Mayfair squares and the murderous denizens of Soho—Hardy's involves the symbolic movement of characters to either side of a central bridge, "the merging point of respectability and indigence" (170). Some low townsfolk, very much like Hyde, "did not mind the glare of the public eye." Others, "the inefficient of the professional class—shabby genteel men," rather seek to hide their shame, as Jekyll does, from the public view (171).

If we knew that Stevenson read *The Mayor* before he began *J&H*, some of these parallels might perhaps rise to the level of establishing direct literary influence, as would appear to be the case with William Wilson's comments, say, on his stature gradually surpassing that of his alter ego (cp. "WW" 60 and *J&H* 88). We must certainly assume, however, that Stevenson read the story only after it was formally published—and accordingly acknowledge that Henchard's constitutional "impatience" is far more likely to have shown up as a central trait of Hyde because *both* authors knew a little something about addictive personalities than because Stevenson could have read about (or even *talked* in any detail about) the man's fateful inclinations. Nevertheless, given the timing of his visit to the real "Casterbridge," it is difficult to believe that Stevenson's conversation with Hardy gave no added shape whatsoever to the tale of man's double-ness he had long been wanting to write. *If* they discussed the character that Stevenson so evidently admired, their conversation would at the very least have given him the sense that the "12 penny dreadful" on which he next began to work turned on an "enslaving" habit that could be the stuff of serious English literature—and could treat them in ways that were estimably artful. *J&H*'s veiled condemnation of alcoholic excess may not have earned the endorsement of the Church of England's temperance journal, something which was actually afforded to *The Mayor of Casterbridge* for its perceived support of the reforming cause (Lilienfeld 235). But a careful reading reveals much the same topicality, albeit couched in a narrative that continues to be better known and better appreciated than Hardy's—if not until now as an implicit temperance tract.

The scent of literal alcohol wafts through much of the rest of Stevenson's creative work as freely as it does through his letters or the literature of his age—enhancing, one trusts, the relative likelihood of an "alcoholic" reading of *J&H* seeming "right for this particular author." Writing to Baxter in December of 1873, he refers to a story he composed "a long while ago" called "The Curate of Anstruther's Bottle" (*Letters* 1.417–18). The piece has unfortunately been lost, but its subject is undoubtedly the old Scots legend that Stevenson tells again in "The Coast of Fife" (1888): one black night, an old, drunken cleric is stumbling home with the help of a little girl parishioner when suddenly "a huge bulk of blackness seemed to sweep down" upon them (266). Badly unstrung by what the girl is certain is a spirit of hell, they make it safely to his dwellings, but the next morning the townsfolk find that the curate has disappeared; "the devil had indeed come for Mr. Thomson" (267). John Falconer in "An Old Song" (1877) forfeits his avuncular inheritance in a scene of drunken abandon, leaving his uncle's house with the Jekyll-like confession that he has made a "beast" of himself and will do what he can to make up for it: "I understand your feeling in this matter," he allows to his gravely disappointed uncle. "You cannot have a drunkard in the house; of course not. I am not going to promise amendment; I do not aspire so high. But you shall be rid of me today" (*Complete Stories* 1.94). And in "The Merry Men" (1882), Gordon Darnaway gives himself over to the bottle and revels in the sea's destruction of passing ships—diabolically endangered by the wreck plunderer's studied refusal ever to warn those in dire risk of the devouring rocks which give the story its name. Stevenson's description of the fearsome breakers themselves recalls Hyde's (and indeed the Edinburgh spirit-merchant Brash's) lethal blend of gaiety, drink, and wanton violence, "As when savage men have drunk away their reason, and, discarding speech, bawl together in their madness by the hour; so ... these deadly breakers shouted by Aros in the night" (*Complete Stories* 1.464). Drink is violent death, and its allure is all the more dangerous for its beginning in, and sometimes reverting to, merriment.

Treasure Island (1883) boasts the memorable piratical refrain that could serve as the Curate of Anstruther's epitaph: "Drink and the devil had done for the rest." Heavy drinkers litter the British shore, the ship, and the desert isle, all of them much the worse for the drinking habit in ways that even their ringleader Silver belabors. The pirates may aspire to prosperity ("You would ride in carriages, you would," Silver sneers), but their addiction to drink keeps them down (instead of a fancy ride, "You'll have your mouthful of rum tomorrow, and go hang," the sea cook grimly predicts [65]). The daft but shrewd castaway Ben Gunn remarks of the dreaded Captain Flint, "Barring rum, his match were never seen" (106)— but drink was Flint's unshakable nemesis, "and he died of rum at Savannah" (65). The virtuous Dr. Livesey could himself easily have been based on the famous temperance man of the same surname, Joseph Livesey.

Five. The Literary Contexts of Stevenson's Tale of Alcohol 73

"One glass of rum won't kill you," he allows to the failing Billy Bones, "but if you take one you'll take another and another, and I stake my wig if you don't break off short, you'll die.... I clear my conscience — the name of rum for you is death" (14). For the ship's doctor, in fact, right conduct with regard to alcohol is so central to morality that, in his mind, it displaces Scripture's "sowing" and "reaping" as a measure of a life's outcome: "As you have brewed," he sententiously pronounces to young Jim Hawkins towards the end of the story, "so shall you drink, my boy" (178). Of course, the novel also effectively revisits the nautical symbolism of "The Merry Men," as drink not only turns Israel Hands into a murderer but also leaves him totally oblivious when Jim intentionally runs the *Hispaniola* aground. It's perhaps no surprise that temperance-man-turned-publisher John Cassell chose to purchase the story, or moreover (given the heatedness of the contemporary alcohol debate) that it was Stevenson's first commercial and critical success — something that the writer incidentally very much wanted to "match" in the Fall of 1885.

Even while he worked on *J&H*, Stevenson also labored at "The Misadventures of John Nicholson" (1887; *Letters* 5.152), a partly-autobiographical tale as full of literal drunkards as *Treasure Island*. The young hero, a haunter like Stevenson had been of Edinburgh pubs, flees from his stern, sabbatarian, temperance-minded father and runs off to California to make his fortune. He initially succeeds beyond his wildest dreams, but then is completely ruined when a clerk "with what is called a weakness for drink" violates his great fiscal trust at a particularly crucial pass (*Complete Stories* 2.182). Nicholson returns home completely penniless, counting on the solicitousness of an old friend, only to find this man, too, "utterly lost," a complete "slave" to alcohol, and evidently, like Hyde, a murderer into the bargain: "what a dreadful thing was drink," observes the newly circumspect John (194).

The perpetually drunken pirates of *Treasure Island* re-appear, as it were, in a cameo role in *The Master of Ballantrae* (1889), Stevenson's darkest fiction. Liquor is a blight on more than the minor characters, however — on men such as the pirates, or Macconochie the "old, swearing, ranting, drunken dog" (19), or John Paul for whom "drink was the root of his malady" (22). Strong drink irrevocably alters the character and fate of the principals as well. The Master himself, James Durrisdeer, is an inveterate lush, thoroughly exploiting "the run of the cellar" (202) at his patriarchal manse or wherever else he happens to find himself. On the fateful night when a quarrel with his brother Henry erupts into the duel in which Henry believes he has killed the family Cain, James "had been drinking freely" (123). Consequently, in the midst of an ostensibly tempered conversation, rather like Hyde's initial exchanges with Sir Danvers Carew, something snaps in the man. His language "shift[s] from ordinary civil talk into a stream of insult" (123) which precipitates the apparently fratricidal combat and all but shatters Henry's life as a result. Ultimately fleeing Scotland to begin a new life in New York, Henry is unable to escape the ghosts of his past and, as his loyal servant Mackellar sadly observes, becomes "altogether too convivial in his habits. I was often in bed, but never asleep," his man goes on, "when he returned; and there was scarce a night when he did not betray the influence of liquor" (261–2). Just like Poole, Mackellar seeks to intervene in his employer's down-going life. "I wonder," Henry asks him, "why I am never happy now." "My lord," Mackellar bravely replies, "if you would drink with more moderation you would have the better chance. It is an old by-word that the bottle is a false consoler" (264). But the happy reversal proves impossible to effect, given that James' vice has effectively transferred itself to his brother, from Cain to Abel, from Esau to Jacob (96). Mackellar accordingly laments the constitutional decline that heralds Henry's eventual death—"To behold the man thus fallen; to know him accepted among his companions for a poor, muddled toper, welcome (if he were welcome at all) for the bare consideration of his title; and to recall the virtues he had once displayed against such odds of fortune; was not this a thing at once to rage and be humbled at?" (264) The novel isn't narrowly a tragedy of drink, but it nods strongly in that direction. McKellar's dirge for his master recalls, in that, Utterson's poignant concern for another fallen "Henry," and indeed Jekyll's own elegy for his dashed fortunes: "A moment before I had been safe of all men's respect, wealthy, beloved—the cloth laying before me in the dining room at home; and now I was the common quarry of mankind, hunted, houseless, a known murderer, thrall to the gallows" (93).

Not surprisingly, the humane activist of the Vailima years continued to write of drink and drinkers, arguably with added moral certainty and fervor. *The Beach of Falesá* (1892) features a scathing portrait of a former sea-captain who is all but destroyed by drink. The man Randall may tipsily recommend to the unlikely hero Wiltshire the traditional salutary virtues of alcohol—"Take gin for my health's sake, Mr Wha's-ever-your-name—'s a precautionary measure" (8)—but when Wiltshire looks at the old wretch "squatting on the floor native fashion, fat and pale, naked to the waist, grey as a badger, and his eyes set with drink," the protagonist concludes that "any clean-minded man would have had the creature out at once and buried him; and to see him ... and remember he had once commanded a ship, and come ashore in his smart togs, and talked big in bars and consulates, and sat in club verandahs, turned me sick and sober" (8). If Randall somehow recalls Hyde as fallen "slime of the pit," he also shares the man's destructive disposition. His room, too, is in ruins: "there was no standing furniture; Randall, when he was violent, tearing it to laths" (9). As indigent as he seems, Randall is nonetheless the business partner of the arch-villainous trader Case, and thus he's a crucial part of the diabolical cartel that Wiltshire must defeat if he and his native wife Uma are to survive. Case, incidentally, is said to have done away with an earlier competitor named Johnny Adams by poisoning him with a "white powder" mixed into his gin. In this business rivalry elevated to moral combat, Wiltshire triumphs against long odds, with Uma's help. But importantly, even though he originally took to trading specifically to lay up enough cash to buy a pub back in his native England, he decides to stay on the island with his wife and children: "My public-house? Not a bit of it, nor ever likely. I don't like to leave the kids, you see" (71). *Falesá* is primarily the tale of a European who, almost unwillingly, learns to embrace indigenous culture in a remarkably free-thinking way, very much in the line of a Mary Kingsley rather than a Cecil Rhodes. But it is also, in a marked if slightly subordinate way, an antipodean temperance tale and casts a useful retrospective light back upon the characters and themes of *Jekyll and Hyde*.

Published in the year of Stevenson's death, *The Ebb-Tide* (1894) returns with a vengeance to a motif that was central to the author's ruminations on alcohol. It may have been inevitable for the scion of a family of lighthouse engineers to think more than the average man about dire maritime perils, but Stevenson's many voyages to Europe, America, and the Pacific islands will have made him especially aware of the mortal dangers that drink posed for seafarers. *The Ebb-Tide* goes "The Merry Men," *Treasure Island* and *The Beach of Falesá* one better by inventing a schooner laden with a full cargo of champagne but left entirely without officers after the men in command die of smallpox—a disease that they've significantly contracted during a drunken spree ashore. A trio of fatalistic ne'er-do-wells who are stranded on the beach in Tahiti take the ship over, but two of them have an overwhelming taste for "the fizz" and, despite the sympathetic character Herrick's "sicken[ing] at the thought of his two comrades drinking away their reason" (213) and despite his timely and vociferous warnings, the vessel is almost lost when the drunken new master refuses to take in sail during a violent squall. Thereafter, the undeservedly fortunate Captain Davis resolves to stay dry, and imagines himself reformed and wealthy, settled back in his native (and celebratedly prohibitionist) Maine, "smoking a cigar, a blue ribbon [traditional symbol of the teetotaler] in his buttonhole, victor over himself and circumstances" (289). Although he does succumb once more to avarice and wrath, he indeed ends up turning his life around, like his abstemious shipmate Herrick. Huish, the inveterate Cockney drunkard, tellingly ends up dead. Begun in concert with his step-son Lloyd, *The Ebb-Tide* was completely overhauled by Stevenson and, despite his confession to Henry James that the characters were "such a troop of swine" that "I wonder I have been able to endure them myself until the yarn was finished" (*Letters* 8.107), it embodies some of the writer's most mature insights into the human condition. The novel has long been neglected, and it surely wants and deserves sustained study. At base a darkly honest meditation on human autonomy, theology, and the functions of narrative, *The Ebb-Tide* also takes a hard look at what alcohol does to and for the men who use it, all in ways that reflect back most artfully on its central triad of serious themes. It's yet another example from Stevenson's prose fiction that exercises his obsession with the far-reaching realm of Bacchus.

Finally, alcohol works its way with fair consistency into Stevenson's verse as well. Often enough the references are incidental, and fall into the stereotypical tropes of the age: drink proffers joy, escape, and companionship. Poems to Baxter, cousin Bob and other Stevensonian pals frequently nod in their nostalgia towards the "gay" bacchanal, extolling days and nights long past in "the inn of the shining wine" when old chums would "drown care in jovial bouts" or bring each other "brave wines to strengthen hope" (*Selected Poems* 19, 11, 16). "Brave lads in olden musical centuries," begin the "Alcaics to H. F. Brown," "Sang, night by night, adorable choruses, / Sat late by ale-house doors in April / Chaunting in joy as the moon was rising" (*Selected Poems* 35). If this is fairly predictable chaff, "The Cruel Mistress" is slightly more pithy, turning as it does on the narrator's unrequited spiritual longings in the face of Nature — but it still resolves itself in facile consolation: "Better be drunk and merry / Than dreaming awake! / Better be Falstaff than Obermann!" (*Selected Poems* 22). "I am a hunchback, yellow-faced" affects a convincing reformist zeal. It's a poem to which we shall return, featuring, amidst the "residuum" of society very much in need of a tolerant and supportive embrace, "a drunkard's lass" in whose bowed and whitened head "gin dances" (*Selected Poems* 27). The poem could almost be a warm-up for the opening page of *J&H*, and we should note the way one of its principals owes her decline to the noxious spirit of Soho.

In a few of his poems, alcohol becomes Stevenson's central subject. In one of the "Brasheanna" mentioned above, for example, the fancifully villainous Edinburgh spirit merchant "doles / Damned liquors out to Hellward-faring souls" who, like Utterson's acquaintances and perhaps like Jekyll, "all journey downward by one common way" (*Selected Poems* 38). While he was living in California in 1880, Stevenson "published" the first two verses of "Not I" in stepson Lloyd Osborne's juvenile paper, *The Surprise* (*Collected Poems* 558).

> Some like drink
> In a pint pot,
> Some like to think;
>   Some not.
> Strong Dutch cheese,
> Old Kentucky rye,
> Some like these;
>   Not I [*Collected Poems* 412].

At the risk of overburdening a child's poem, one might suggest that these lines anticipate the contrite moment when Jekyll denies his kinship with his evil twin through a kind of pronominal surgery: "He, I say — I cannot say, I" (52). In both cases, the "self" refuses to define itself by its relationship to things or persons addictive (as Stevenson himself in fact so often did do in playful letters to fellow-drinkers Baxter and James) but rather does so by separation and denial. Hyde, conversely, seems to make a poetic appearance in "Heather Ale," a work that echoes *J&H*'s dedicatory poem in its focus on wild upland moors and "the bonny bells of heather" which become the wine (*Collected Poems* 236–39). When a domineering "king of Scotland" defeats the Picts, he finds it no joy to "rule in a land of heather / And lack the Heather Ale" that his defeated foes once brewed and drank so exuberantly that they "lay in a blessed swound / For days and days together / In their dwellings underground." The king searches for the brewers, and finally turns out from under a rock a "dwarfish and swarthy couple," father and son, from whom he seeks the recipe. (Recall that the "*dwarfish*" Hyde has hands "of a dusky pallor and thickly shaded with a *swart* growth of hair" [40, 88; added italics].) The two will brook no lowlander's mastery, however, and despite all his efforts, the king is outsmarted by the paternal — and, it turns out, infanticidal — dwarf, and the secret of Heather Ale is lost to the world. And still more lives, finds Stevenson, are lost to strong drink. It was a theme to which both he and his Age were wed, and it was very much canonical stuff.

SIX

"Self" and "The Other Fellow"

Having established the general place of alcohol in Stevenson's life, in his works, and in the literary world he sought to inhabit, we may now wish to refine our sense of the specific models Stevenson had to hand for his portrait of Henry Jekyll's "double being," be they prototypes he consciously drew upon or troubled faces from the past that were offered up to him, restored but altered, by his Brownies. We have already seen disparate bits and pieces of the doctor and his dark alter-ego peeking out from the life and from the fiction — from the Brashes and the Teddy Henleys to the Randalls and the Huishes — but it will repay the effort to look a little more concertedly for the individuals who may have offered Stevenson the most compelling, most integrated paradigms for both sides of Jekyll's character (provided "integrated" isn't the wrong term to use in relation to the archetypal split personality.)

There's assuredly no need to look for a *single* fictive or real-life "original." As Jekyll says of his psyche, it may be that Stevenson's principal character was essentially compounded of a varied "polity of multifarious, incongruous and independent denizens" of his world (82), a kind of amalgamated quintessence of the "divided" characters he knew the best. From the realm of literature, William Wilson and Michael Henchard are both likely candidates to have been in the mix — Poe offering the radical, dramatic vision of an "other half" as a physically separate being some years before *J&H* was begun, and Hardy offering the immediate contemporary incentive to write about a man whose constitutional impatience was tragically sensitive to pernicious liquors. Another (and this time) well-acknowledged inspiration was James Hogg's quintessentially ambiguous *Private Memoirs and Confessions of a Justified Sinner* (McLynn 258; Letley x–xi). In this strange, almost pre–post-modern thriller, Robert Colwan, "cloaked" not by a separate physical identity but rather by the belief that he is among the spiritually Elect, succumbs to the influence of the malign and increasingly-dominant Gil-Martin and murders his own brother, together with a minister. Subsequently, Colwan's mother and "a young lady of great beauty" are also killed, either by Gil-Martin in the likeness of Colwan or by Colwan himself, his body "possessed by a spirit over which it had no control" (125) — and perhaps also, it is suggested to him, under the influence of alcohol![1] Hogg's refusal to clarify whether the dark "other" is an aspect of the self or actually the Devil in person is a trick that Stevenson may imitate more overtly in "Markheim" (1885) than in *J&H*. Nevertheless, the general form of Hogg's narrative, including an "editor's" contextualizing account which both precedes and follows the sinner's actual confession, could have suggested the ultimate shape that Jekyll's story takes. Stevenson in any case said of Hogg's *Confessions* in 1891, "the book since I read it, in black, pouring weather on Tweedside, has always haunted and puzzled me" (*Letters* 7.125). There is no reason to assume that it wasn't very much in his mind in the Fall of 1885.

If Hogg twice inspired Stevenson — in both "Markheim" and *J&H* — another Scot matched his record. Stevenson's fascination with the historical William "Deacon" Brodie, cabinet-maker by day but thief by night, is once again well-documented, most recently in a highly readable popular-market study by Raymond McNally and Radu Florescu. Stevenson in fact counted one of Brodie's wooden chests amongst the furnishings of his childhood room in Edinburgh (Letley ix) and the curiosity seems to have inspired some of Alice Cunningham's most vivid moralizing for the growing lad. He wrote his first draft of a play on the infamous character as early as 1864, when he was only fourteen, and later collaborated with W. E. Henley on *Deacon Brodie, or, The Double Life*, produced in 1882, 1883, 1884, and 1887, before being revised in 1888 (Swearingen 36–7). A devotee of both the plentiful drink and the violent sport that characterized the Edinburgh tavern scene, the historical Brodie retains his tippling habit in Stevenson and Henley's play, previewing in one of his soliloquies the night-world of disguise, appetite, alcohol, violence, and self-liberation that is *Jekyll and Hyde*: "The city has its vizard on, and we — at night we are our naked selves. Trysts are keeping, bottles cracking, knives are stripping; and here is Deacon Brodie flaming forth the man of men he is" (1.9, p. 21). Unlike the actual criminal though, hanged for his crimes after more than three months in the hands of the law, Stevenson and Henley's 's Brodie precipitates his own death by virtually running onto the sword of his Bow Street pursuer, appropriately named Hunt. Like Hyde in his end, then, he also succumbs to the close cousin of Utterson's ad hoc persona, "Mr. Seek" (38).

The historical Brodie obsessed Stevenson too consistently not to have played a major role in the conception of Jekyll and Hyde, a conclusion that is well supported by Fanny's later claim that "a paper he read in a French scientific journal on sub-consciousness ... combined with memories of Deacon Brodie, gave the germ of the idea that afterwards developed into the play, was used again in the story *Markheim*, and finally ... culminated in the dream of Jekyll and Hyde" (Swearingen 101).[2] Yet Stevenson often looked even closer to home for his fictional prototypes. For example, an 1890 letter to Lloyd Osborne reveals that *Treasure Island*'s Long John Silver was based by the author on his dramatic collaborator Henley, that both *The Prince*'s Otto and *The Dynamiter*'s Somerset were set on his cousin Bob Stevenson, and that *Kidnapped* and *Catriona*'s David Balfour was founded on yet another cousin, Willie Traquair (*Letters* 7.35). One of Stevenson's acquaintances claimed in 1902 to have been with him "the moment that he conceived the germ of the idea of 'Dr. Jekyll and Mr. Hyde.'" The author, or so alleged C. H. E. Brookfield, was horribly miffed at a tradesman named Samuel Creggan who (much like the hypocritical Jekyll) promised a helpfulness on which he wouldn't deliver. "Creggan's the *real* man," Brookfield claims that Stevenson muttered: "Samuel's only superficial." Another acquaintance, however, thought the incident had actually involved one of Stevenson's publishers, C. Kegan Paul, with the actual comment being "Kegan is an excellent fellow, but Paul is a publisher" (Swearingen 101). Given that neither of these alternative scenarios involves any form of a "transforming draught," however, we might tentatively take them less as direct clues to the novella's most profound "origins" than as confirmation that Stevenson's sense of "man's double being" could just as well involve the ill fit between pose and character, or person and profession, as the essential "war of the members" that lies at the heart of *J&H*. Actually, the rage that Brookfield witnessed in the bona fide tippler *Stevenson himself* may take us closer to Jekyll's prototype than either Creggan or Kegan do. If "The Misadventures of John Nicholson" repays an autobiographical reading, so might *J&H*.

Along with the consuming interest in alcohol that we have documented above, Stevenson had a very telling and life-long habit of inventing alter-egos for himself, being as apt when he was writing to friends to sign himself "T. Brash" or "John Bunyan" as to use his own name (e.g. *Letters* 4.148; 4.248). Biographer Frank McLynn observes that, when he was ill (as he so often was), Louis almost invariably distanced himself from infirmity by pretending to be someone else, a trait that McLynn shrewdly relates to Jekyll's rejection of the deathly "thing" that always lay within him. Down with flu in Samoa, for example, Stevenson transformed himself rhetorically into a "Mr. Dumbey" (453). Yet he was partial to literal disguises as well. While staying in London in 1879, crushed by some particularly depressing news from Fanny a world away in California, he wandered through the city streets dressed as a ragged tramp, hoping to be arrested (McLynn 143). In the same era, driven now by proto-sociological curiosity rather than by lovelorn misery, he walked around a London suburb on two successive days, dressed first as a member of the upper classes and then as a member of the lower — noting the way the "gentleman" was warmly greeted by shopkeepers and passers-by while the "artisan" was treated "with extreme distaste" (McLynn 159). These could well have been model experiences for the universal esteem accorded Jekyll and for the consistently chilly public reception of Hyde. The novella's references to Jekyll "plod[ding] in the public eye with a load of genial respectability" but then, in turn, "strip[ping] off these lendings" in order to assume his Hyde self as a "thick cloak" or an "impenetrable mantle" (86) surely strengthen the case.

Stevenson's most enduring (and specifically drug-enhanced) charade actually began years before his London sojourn in Deacon Brodie's Edinburgh, when he and Charles Baxter began to live their own hypocritical "double lives"— spending their days as affectedly staid university students, but squandering their nights as the self-proclaimed, hard-drinking "Holy Wullies," "Johnston" and "Thomson" (Bell 57; McLynn 45).[3] Along with a few others, the pair founded a Society that anticipated the broadly patricidal values of Hyde, the motto of their organization being "Disregard everything our parents taught us" (Bell 68). Throughout a life-long correspondence, the two friends reverted to the broad, affected Scots dialect of these hedonistic wastrels who, as far as one can tell, once cut something of a swathe through the pubs and lower haunts of the city's Old

Town (Bell 55–9). As the poetastic "Brasheanna" verses bear witness, they fancied themselves at least Enfields and perhaps even Hydes—"a couple of heartless drunken young dogs" (*Letters* 1.42). In a letter written in March of 1884, Stevenson says to his old crony, "Ye've been, since ever I kent ye, a drunkard, a whoremonger, a blasphemer, and mair that I wouldnae like to name" (*Letters* 4.254). In November of the same year, he styles *himself* somewhere between an Utterson and a Jekyll — "jist aboot as honest as he can weel afford, an' but for drink an' weemen an a wheen [few] auld scandals, near forgotten noo, ... a pairfeckly respectable and thoroughly *decent* man" (*Letters* 5.30). A year earlier, he had described just as suggestively the conditions of his on-going "Wullie's life" while living with Fanny in Argyll: "For society, there isnae sae muckle [much]; but there's myself—the auld Jonstone, ye ken ... and there's the wife, puir wean [child] — an' there's Powell the druggist, a fine canty body; and man, there's a grog shop whaur, every afternoon, twa auld men sit crackin [talking], that taydious that the diel [devil] wad die of't, an it's grand sport for once in the week" (*Letters* 4.178–9). It was powerfully little to live with, but with the right woman, a good chemist, and strong drink, it was enough for any "Hyde" to survive. It's clearly no accident that Baxter became Stevenson's *de facto* European wine-agent once he'd moved his entourage to Samoa. Throughout their lives, the pair kept the "Soho world" of Old Town Edinburgh forever alive in their restless imaginations.

Yet Stevenson didn't need Baxter to see himself as a Jekyll cum Hyde. Looking at himself in the mirror would evidently serve the purpose well enough. In a letter to J. M. Barrie from April of 1893, he describes himself in a way that brings first Utterson and then, in fact, both the gracious "elderly doctor" and the swarthy "child of hell" (94) variously into view:

> Exceedingly lean, dark, rather ruddy — black eyes ... crow's-footed, beginning to be grizzled, general appearance of a blasted boy — or blighted youth — or to borrow Carlyle on DeQuincey "Child that has been in hell." ... Drinks plenty. Curses some. Temper unstable.... (When he's well he looks like a brown boy with an uncertain temper, but when he is ill he's a rose-garden invalid with a sainted smile.) [*Letters* 8.44]

Even before the novella was conceived, the imaginative ground-work for an authorial appearance in its pages was perhaps being laid. In a letter to Henley from September of 1881, four years before *J&H* was begun, Stevenson complains (in verse!) about a respirator he's been obliged to wear by his doctor, George Balfour (the same man who decried the effects of that early antimonial wine). He claims the thing leaves him looking like a pig, or perhaps like a proto–Hyde, "a gnome of olden time / Or boguey in a pantomime" (*Letters* 3.232). Stevenson was of course later to tell the American Will Low that *J&H* was a "gothic *gnome*" who answered to the name "Stevenson"; and Fanny claimed that, when she'd wakened her husband from the dream in which he was essentially given the story, he reproached her very much as Coleridge may have berated the meddling man from Porlock, saying "I was dreaming a fine *bogey* tale" (Swearingen 100; all italics added). This could all be linguistic coincidence. It could, on the other hand, be all the more reason to look at *J&H* as a window into its author's sense of self.

As a glance in the mirror put Stevenson in touch with his innate duality, so apparently did a look at his handwriting. Richard Dury has recently and very usefully noted that a few of the writer's letters suggest an autobiographical cast to the scene in *J&H* in which Utterson and Guest inspect the differently-sloped "hands" of Jeykll and Hyde (55). "I have two hand-writings," claimed Stevenson a few months before he began the novella. In March of the previous year, in fact, he had written to P. G. Hamerton about the impact of a recent illness: "I have been obliged to lean my hand the other way, which makes it unrecognizable; the hand is the hand of Esau" (*Letters* 5.122; 8.417). As Dury concludes, "This sounds very much like Jekyll 'sloping my own hand backwards' to give Hyde a signature, and the uncouth hand of the instinctive Esau sounds much like the hand of Hyde" (112).

Those who knew Stevenson best, in youth or maturity, frequently spoke of him as a creature of duality, or even of multiple "polities." Sidney Colvin (the man to whom Stevenson confessed his persistent "dipsomania") seemed to preview the clash of Jekyll and Hyde in the young writer when he was still immersed in the "ferment of youth":

> There met in him many various strains and elements, which were in these days pulling one against the other in his half-formed being at great expense of spirit and body. Add the storms, which from time to time attacked him, of shivering repulsion from the climate and conditions of life in the city which he yet deeply and imaginatively loved; the moods of spiritual revolt against the harsh doctrines of the creed in which he had been brought up...; the seasons of temptation, most strongly besetting the ardent and poetic temperament, to seek solace among the crude allurements of the city streets [*Selected Letters* 7–8].

Colvin was Stevenson's literary executor and as solicitous of the author's reputation as anyone short of his parents and wife, yet here he clearly identifies in his talented protégé a version of Jekyll's "warring members"— as significantly complemented by a low yearning for the "undignified pleasures" of a "Soho."

Stevenson's school friend H. B. Baildon may have succumbed even more explicitly than Colvin to the temptation to read the lineaments of the novella back into pliable memories of the old boy. Stevenson, as recalled in 1901 by his chum at Robert Thomson's school in Edinburgh, was "long, lean, and spidery"— very like the "lean, long, dusty" Utterson. But then Baildon all but reproduces the revealing physiognomic complexity of Jekyll, the "smooth faced man of fifty, with something of a slyish cast perhaps, but every mark of capacity and kindness" (*J&H* 43): "About the mouth," Baildon recalls of schoolboy Louis, "and in the mirthful mocking light of the eyes there lingered ever a ready Autolycus mockery that rather suggested sly Hermes masquerading as a mortal. The eyes were always genial, however gaily the lights danced in them, but about the mouth there was something a little tricksy and mocking, as if of a spirit that already peeped behind the scenes of life's pageant and more than guessed its realities" (McLynn 27). The "slyish cast" that betrays the lurking Hyde is, of course, the ineffaceable mark of the "impatient gaiety of disposition" that is Jekyll's birthright.

Fanny spied that Puckish mirth in her husband as well, claiming that the "genius and wide humanity" he had inherited from his father was counter-balanced by "the natural *gaiety* of Margaret Stevenson" (McLynn 182; emphasis added). Unfortunately, Stevenson found that his wife ultimately tolerated his self-acknowledged "tricksy spirit" no better than Jekyll did his own "impatient gaiety," complaining about her to Henley that "I am what *she has made me*, the embers of the once gay RLS" (McLynn 253). Fanny wrote to Colvin in December of 1885 — the month *J&H* was to have been published — that her husband appeared in two photographs taken by Sir Henry and Lady Taylor as, on the one hand, an "angel" and, on the other, as a "devil" (McLynn 259). That she was far more interested in promoting the moral rectitude that she felt Louis inherited from his father than the impish gaiety he got from Margaret is nowhere more forcefully confirmed than in her virtual insistence that the original draft of *J&H* be re-written to capture the implicit "allegory."

Aside from his utter dependence on his potion, Hyde's most salient characteristic is ultimately his "inordinate anger, strung to the pitch of murder, lusting to inflict pain" (93). And if Stevenson was finally as dependent on wine as his fictional creation was on his "transforming draught," he also showed throughout his life the little man's impatient rage, as noted in the "blasted boy" portion of the self-portrait cited above. One of his aliases in his correspondence is "The Old Man Virulent" (e.g. *Letters* 6.2040): "The signature," explained Colvin, "alludes to the fits of uncontrollable anger to which he was often in youth ... subject: fits occasioned sometimes by instances of official stolidity or impertinence or what he took as such" (Wolf 63). Looking back on his Edinburgh escapades with his cousin Bob, Stevenson confessed to a version of the "impatient gaiety" that erupts into Hyde's wrath: "Laughter was our principal activity ... laughter and a deep anger against the life we discovered all around us" (McNally and Florescu 79). When asked what he would do if he were cast away on a desert island, he once claimed "I wouldn't die of thirst; I'd die of rage!" (McLynn 482). Fanny noted what a tyrant he could be with his servants (*Letters* 7.100). Harry Moors, who worked as a kind of factotum for the Stevensons in Samoa, puts it most pointedly:

> When in a rage he was a study. Once excite him, and you had another Stevenson. I have seen him in all moods. I have seen him sitting on my table, dangling his bony legs on the air, chatting away in the calmest manner possible; and I have seen him become suddenly agitated, jump from that table and stalk to and fro across the floor like some wild forest animal [McLynn 388].

Moors and Sir Danvers Carew, who is immolated in Hyde's "great flame of anger" (47), could well have exchanged notes and commiserations with each other.

Although that rage was evidently always smoldering in Stevenson, it was alcohol that seems to have brought it out especially. One of "Johnston's" poems recalls the nights in an Edinburgh pub when the author and Baxter would drink "like Samson" and then quarrel till they cried (*Letters* 4.112). Stepson Lloyd Osborne in turn described the wrath of the stepfather "whose very mien as he once raised a row about a corked bottle of wine had emptied half a restaurant" (Bell 175). Osborne suggests that, when the waiter first served the poorly-opened bottle, Stevenson was merely irritated. But when the man simply poured the wine into another bottle and brought it back to the table for a second try, the pique gave way to rage and the infuriated writer/connoisseur dashed the container to smithereens against the restaurant wall (McLynn 115–16). Years later at a club he had joined in Hawaii, Stevenson is said to have repeatedly prepared for dinner by ordering "a light-red California burgundy ... and then launch[ing] into a tirade against [William T.] Stead," whose repeatedly anti-royalist editorials the writer found maddening. "When he had worked himself up into a rare fury," goes the account, "he would finish his peroration and then glare around the room, waiting for anyone to answer him. Nobody ever did, and RLS was reduced to gulping down his burgundy and storming out of the room" (McLynn 469). It's hardly surprising that one of Stevenson's alias signatures was "T. Brash" (*Letters* 4.148), for he shared the fabled Edinburgh spirit merchant's liquorish rages—and perhaps Mr. Hyde's into the bargain.

It's safe to say, then, that one of Stevenson's principle inspirations for Jekyll was himself—as a notoriously gay, impatient, irascible "crony" and a thoroughly dedicated "judge of good wine." Thus the comment to Low about his "gothic gnome," or the assurance to Katherine de Mattos that the novella was dedicated to her by the part of him that was "Jekyll, and not Hyde." In some very real way, he wrote the story from his inside out. He confessed to Symonds two months after publication, "*Jekyll* is a dreadful thing, I own; but the only thing I feel dreadful about is that damned old business of the war in the members. This time *it came out*; I hope it will stay in, in future" (*Letters* 5.220–21; emphasis added). Two months before he died, he was still evidently suffering the internal throes, the old psychomachia of elderly doctor and impetuous child of hell, and still trying to bite it all back: "I was born a young man," he told Colvin; "I have continued so; and before I end, a drunken pantaloon, a driveller— Enough again. But I do not enjoy getting elderly" (*Letters* 8.383). Curiously, if Stevenson's last completed task was to fetch and uncork a bottle of burgundy from his Vailima cellar, his last recorded word was the first in the full title of the novella—*Strange Case of Dr Jekyll and Mr Hyde*. Helping Fanny mix some salad dressing for the evening meal, he suddenly clamped his hands to his head and cried out, "What's that? Oh, what a pain! Do I look strange?" (McLynn 504). There is indeed, as Vladimir Nabokov observed in passing, "a curious thematical link between this last episode in Stevenson's life and the fateful transformations in his most wonderful book" (204). And, as Nabokov also noted, there is a present in both instances a very distinctive "winey smell."

The "strange" was always there inside the man's head, be it in the form of the Brownies who gave him the dream images from which his narratives grew, of an impatient gaiety inflamed by alcohol, or of the final, irreversible dissolution of his mind itself. Stevenson told Myers in 1892 that, from the time he was a child, he had suffered from "night fears," "wanderings" of the mind, feverish states that "impaired sanity" (*Letters* 7.331). They regularly separated his mind, he said, into two antagonistic "parts": that "which I ventured to think was *myself* ... engaged with *my other self* in a perpetual conflict." That second, "impaired" self he revealingly termed "*the other fellow*" and ultimately linked him to "the dreamer described in my 'Chapter on Dreams'" (*Letters* 7.333). That particular text, written for *Scribner's Magazine* in 1887, accounts for the imaginative sources of *J&H* and, in the process, documents with remarkable richness Stevenson's distinction between "what I call I, my conscious ego ... the man with the conscience and the variable bank account" (207) and "the Little People" (206), the "Brownies" "whom I keep locked up in a back garret" (207), who inspire creativity but "have not a rudiment of what we call a conscience" (208). Jekyll's pronominal psychomachia, his moral compunction, and his crucial bank account are all there in autobiographical embryo, along with Hyde and his dwarfish stature, his swarthiness, his repressive "caging," and his "complete moral insensibility" (90). Sleep regularly freed the writer's "other fellow," even as, towards the end, Jekyll regularly wakes as Hyde (95). Fever and that final embolism evidently did the same. The other precipitating agent, for Stevenson as for so many others of his time, was alcohol.

"People mayn't be like their books," Stevenson wrote to Barrie in April of 1893; "they *are* their books" (*Letters* 8.48). The insight is stunning, and all the more compelling when one considers the volatile responses of both Jekyll and his creator to the power of alcohol, "the transforming draught." While autobiographical resonances have been detected in *J&H* at least since G. K. Chesterton's perceptive commentary of 1928, the present study is the first to tie the novella consistently to the drinking of the author and of his age. It's also, as far as can be determined, the first to make in anything more than a cursory way the complementary case that closes this section of our argument. If Stevenson somewhat unaccountably felt "dreadful" about *J&H* unleashing "that damned old business of the war in the members"—and I say "unaccountably" because he'd in fact long wanted to write just such a story "of man's double being"—he will have felt more understandably dreadful about an actual death by alcohol in which he was made to feel personally complicit.

By far the most troubling and poignant of Stevenson's real-life drunkards was James Walter Ferrier. An intimate friend of the author's univer-

strangely concerned about it" (*Letters* 4.155). "Poor Ferrier," Stevenson confided to his cousin Bob, "it bust me horrid" (*Letters* 4.170). "He was, after you, the oldest of my friends," Louis added, squarely anticipating Utterson and Lanyon when they identify themselves as "the two oldest friends that Henry Jekyll has" (36). Even Fanny appended in postscript to the letter to Bob, "I was surprised that Louis was so broken down by Ferrier's death. I had somehow believed in his philosophical talk, and that he would regard the death of a friend simply as a longer absence. He has not been well since he first heard ... I fear he has a touch of fever" (*Letters* 4.171). All this surely smacks of a watershed moment.

Stevenson likely saw the handwriting upon the wall. "This has been a strange awakening," he wrote to Henley, in language that subtly prefigures Jekyll's own when he recounts his own "strange" case; "Last night, when I was alone in the house ... I could swear he was in the room with me" (*Letters* 4.157). Very tellingly, Stevenson's wonted metaphors of danger at sea creep into the language of his grief. "Dear, dear, what a wreck," he writes to Henley of his dead friend. "Alas to sink so low." "Few have made such a *plunge*." "If anything looked liker irony than this fitting a man out with these rich qualities and faculties to be wrecked and aborted from the very stocks, I do not know the name of it" (*Letters* 4.157; 156; 159–60; 159). Significantly, Jekyll will later "la[y] aside restraint and plung[e] in shame ... into the sea of liberty" (81; 86), only then to bemoan his own "dreadful shipwreck" (82) and appeal to Lanyon to keep his conscience clear of either "[Jekyll's] death or the shipwreck of [his] reason" (75).[5] His initial problem, of course, is that he also was "fitted out" with "excellent parts" that he claims were tragically countered by those ruinous "polar twins" of human nature.

Stevenson's anguish was compounded immeasurably by the fact that Ferrier's mother had savaged him in a letter that all but held the writer personally accountable for the lethal habit that was ravaging her son's life: "He now exists among the number of those degraded ones," she ranted, "whose society on earth is shunned by the moral and virtuous among mankind" (McLynn 213). Sorely stung once her words proved to be prophetic, Stevenson wrote to Ferrier's sister Elizabeth, informing her of his careful attendance at her brother's deathbed — this despite Mrs. Ferrier's playing the Harpy who "lay in wait for me and flashed out upon me..., looking splendid with contempt and anger, and 'gave it to me' in the most withering style. Finally, she went to my father and mother and told them I was ruining their son" (*Letters* 4.165–6). Subsequently, very

sity days and another charter member of the anti-patriarchal "L. J. R." club (the initials standing for "Liberty, Justice, and Reverence" [McLynn 60]), Ferrier fell seriously under the sway of alcohol. Stevenson observed of Ferrier, while they were both still in Edinburgh, "the curse was on him. Even his friends did not know him but by fits" (*Letters* 4.158). The writer was able to joke with the doomed man in the Johnston-Thomson mode, as in a letter of 23 November, 1872: "By common repute, there is scarcely a crime that you have not committed.... If you go on at this rate, you will become a very famous man — a 'bug to frighten babes withal'" (*Letters* 1.257–8). But Stevenson writes on, hinting at his growing concern for the fellow carouser who was to become for him a "poor, besotted gentleman," or "a Nathaniel though a sordid drunkard" (*Letters* 4.154; 183): "Seriously, however, you have left a very motley reputation behind you; and godly people, when your name is mentioned, draw closer round the fire and look fearfully over their shoulders" (*Letters* 1.258). In a fragmentary autobiography written early in 1880, Stevenson's concern reaches a premonitory intensity. He calls Ferrier the "most complete and gentle gentleman... I have known";

> But he was consumed and wrecked by a miserable craving for drink. Will he ... outlive the tendency, and become a conscientious, and kind gentleman as we knew him in his sober hours? Or will he go downward to the sot, the spunge [sic] and the buffoon? When last I parted from him, five months ago, he and I, for the first time in our intimacy, shed tears together over this alternative; he promised me, for my sake as well as his own, to continue the good fight; and yet ever since I have feared to write him [*Letters* 3.64].

If the last sentence hints that Stevenson may already have felt implicated in Ferrier's peril (albeit no more compelled than Utterson to intervene any more forcefully in the life of a down-going friend) the ones that precede it suggest that the alcoholic was well on his way to being an additional and arguably more crucial model for Jekyll and Hyde.[4] Compare Jekyll's "feverish" vows to Utterson to have done with Hyde (52) — or his final, haunting question, "Will Hyde die upon the scaffold, or will he find the courage to release himself at the last moment?"(97)

When Ferrier died in September of 1883 — from a chronic kidney a ment exacerbated by years of alcoholism — Stevenson was upset beyond his expectations. He wrote to Sidney Colvin that his frie untimely demise "has much upset me. I did not fancy how much.

much like Jekyll (who knows what he's been as Hyde and who, when Utterson remarks on his "escape," replies "I have had what is far more to the purpose ... I have had a *lesson*" [53; emphasis added]), Stevenson closes his letter to Elizabeth by confessing, "This has been a sharp lesson" (*Letters* 4.167). His selfless and persistent attentions to the dying man, along with his obvious contrition, earned him first the forgiveness and ultimately the favor of Ferrier's surviving sibling. Stevenson and "Coggie" Ferrier indeed became fast friends. But if the fact that he signed many of his letters to her as "Thomson" might ultimately betoken an easy familiarity between the two that rivaled his intimacy with Baxter, it also suggests that he realized perfectly well that the Edinburgh bacchanals in which he'd played a key part would always define his relationship with the whole Ferrier family. A casual poem in a letter to Henley from May of 1884 looks back at those crucial university days with a curious blend of nostalgia and moral sobriety:

> I had companions, I had friends,
> I had of whisky various blends.
> The whisky was all drunk; and lo!
> The friends were gone for evermo! [*Letters* 4.287].

The lines are, in the context of Ferrier's death, more ambiguous than they might initially appear. Was Stevenson loved only for his liquor? Or, except for him, have all the rest been "done for," just like Billy Bones, by "drink and the devil"?

Stevenson's father Thomas had earlier — and often — warned his only son about the responsibility that true gentlemen owe to their friends: "I would ten times sooner have seen you lying in your grave," he once claimed with a truly chilling paternal candor, "than that you should be shaking the faith of other young men and bringing such ruin on other houses, as you have brought already upon this" (*Letters* 1.312). Accordingly, Stevenson wrote contritely to the aging patriarch in October:

> This curious affair of Ferrier's death has sent me back on our relation and my past with much unavailing wonder and regret. Truly, we are led by strange paths. A feeling of that which lacked with Ferrier and me, when we were lads together has put me upon a task which I hope will not be disliked by you: a sketch of some of the more obvious provinces and truths of life for the use of young men, and particularly of those who may be, in their youth entire unbelievers. The difficulty and delicacy of the task cannot be exaggerated. Here is a fine opportunity to pray for me; that

> I may lead none into evil. I am shy of it; yet remembering how easy it would have been to help my dear Walter and me, had anyone gone the right way about it, spurs me to attempt it [*Letters* 4.172].

That admonitory "sketch"—addressed to the budding Jekylls of the world ("to any young man, conscious of his youth, conscious of vague powers and qualities, and fretting at the bars of life")—was embodied in part in "Lay Morals." That it took yet another form altogether in "Old Mortality" attests both to the depth of Stevenson's contrition and to his instinct to help others learn from his own and from Ferrier's mistakes.

"Old Mortality," written in the Fall of 1883, is essentially Ferrier's emblematic Life. The narrative was in some ways so personal, in fact, that Stevenson delayed publication until (as Fanny later claimed) "he sent the proof sheets to his friend's sister, leaving it to her to say whether it should see the light or not. She responded with an urgent request for its publication" (Swearingen 85). The narrative recalls a man who, like the original Jekyll with his mix of traits, "in his youth ... was most beautiful in person, most serene and genial by disposition; full of racy words and quaint thoughts. Laughter attended on his coming. He had the air of a great gentleman, jovial and royal with his equals, and to the poorest student gentle and attentive" (*Memories* 50). Thereafter, the narrator moves him into the dangerous realms of Enfield and Hyde (or perhaps of Johnston and Thomson):

> I can still see and hear him, as he went his way along the lamplit streets, *La ci darem la mano* on his lips, a noble figure of a youth, but following vanity and incredulous of good; and sure enough, somewhere on the high seas of life, with his health, his hopes, his patrimony and his self-respect, miserably went down [*Memories* 51].

Stevenson's favored maritime metaphors return with a vengeance: add to the ones above the narrator's further "marvelling that so rich an argosy had sunk" (55), "his whole armada lost" (53). Yet while the language may hint at the drink that was Ferrier's actual nemesis, it is crucial to note that drink is present in the story neither literally nor in the form of the clearly-coded language and explicit metaphor we find throughout *J&H*. Stevenson warned Henley in March of 1884, "Ferrier's grave gapes for us all" (*Letters* 4.262). Yet if the grim memento mori that was his friend's life was to be fully taken to heart, how useful was it to withhold or so deeply submerge the central fact of his ruinous *addiction*? One wonders whether an overriding solicitousness for Ferrier's reputation didn't lead Stevenson to soften the contours of his exemplum, perhaps enhancing the essay's role as an encomium to a fallen friend but seriously diminishing its effectiveness either as a sharply pointed warning or as an honest and direct grappling with a regrettable truth. One further wonders whether a more honest and consequential admonitory engagement with the dangers of addictive draughts didn't emerge from Stevenson's conscience late in 1885, in the blunter but essentially anonymous form of *Strange Case of Dr. Jekyll and Mr. Hyde*.[6]

In a letter to Henley from September, 1883, Stevenson has in fact already invented an "evil double" for Ferrier. After copiously lauding the man as "the only gentleman of all my friends," "the only modest man among the lot," "the only man I ever loved, who did not habitually interrupt" (one wonders, incidentally, how Henley himself would have taken all of this), Stevenson allows,

> When I come to think of it, I do not know what I said to his sister [in a recent letter], and I fear to try again. Could you send her this? There is too much both about yourself and me in it; but that, if you do not mind, is but a mark of sincerity. It would let her know how entirely, in the mind of (I suppose) this oldest friend, the good true Ferrier, obliterates the memory of *the other*, who was only his *"lunatic brother"* [*Letters* 4.158; italics added].

What he actually did say to Coggie Ferrier in a letter which survives was almost as significant: "My dear Walter, set apart that terrible disease, was, in his right mind, the best and gentlest gentleman. God knows he would never intentionally hurt a soul. Well, he is done with his troubles and out of his long sickness, and I dare say is glad to be at peace and out of the body, which in him seemed the enemy of the fine and kind spirit" (*Letters* 4.155). The "good fight" that Stevenson had earlier hoped Ferrier would keep up, the "brave battle" and "energy to fight" that he so admired after it was all over (*Letters* 4.159; *Memories* 54), would seem to be precisely Jekyll's ongoing "war of the members" as exacerbated by the use of alcohol.[7] The good Ferrier, "the most complete and gentle gentleman," was possessed of a dark, "lunatic brother"—"the other Walter," as Stevenson terms him a few sentences earlier, in contradistinction to "the ... gentle one"; and although he "kept back his secret," it ultimately put him in his grave (*Letters* 4.157). Stevenson could speak quite honestly and frankly with Ferrier's sister, as his assuming with her the role of Thomson ironically confirms. Yet to write a "lunatic brother" into the finally encomiastic "Old Mortality," giving all the sordid particulars of a man who pickled his organs with an uncontrollable appetite for drink, was something Stevenson evidently wasn't prepared to do. A more comprehensive and frank memorial to Ferrier seems likely to have taken shape in *J&H*, where the street-side depredations of Hyde could more discreetly evince the grim, child-frightening depravities of Ferrier when Walter himself "was walking very wild and blind, and had no true idea whether of himself or life" (*Letters* 4.166). One wonders whether the man's sister might ever have seen it for what it was.

Stevenson wrote to Henley in September, 1883, "My dear friend, Walter Ferrier. O if I had only written to him more!" And again to Coggie, "Well, I had the courage to go every day [to visit Walter despite his mother's ire] ... and I am glad now. Had there been one or two others who did the like, or had I been older and wiser, he might—would, I think, have been saved" (*Letters* 4.159; 166). But if Stevenson had lost the chance to write more *to* or do more *for* Ferrier before he died, he could still seize the opportunity to write more *about* and do more *with* Ferrier and his salutary example after the fact. If the theory of inspiration that has just been tendered is indeed a "full statement of the case," then Stevenson produced two—and two very different—portraits of the most poignant drunkard he knew. One, the *Jekyll* version, is seen through the harsh lens of tragedy. The other, "Old Mortality," is instead seen through the ultimately gracious eyes of redemptive comedy in the Dantean sense. For Jekyll, there is wisdom in the end, but no possible recovery. Once "Ferrier" has hit bottom, however, his fortunes are effectively reversed.

> From this disaster, like a spent swimmer, he came desperately ashore, bankrupt of money and consideration; creeping to the family he deserted; with broken wing, never more to rise. But in his face there was a light of knowledge that was new to it. Of the wounds of his body he was never healed; died of them gradually, with clear-eyed resignation ... still joying in his friend's successes; his laugh still ready but with kindlier music; and over all his thoughts the shadow of that unalterable law which he had disavowed and which had brought him low. Lastly, when his bodily evils had quite disabled him, he lay a great while dying, still without complaint, still finding interests; to his last step gentle, urbane and with the will to smile [*Memories* 52].

"Old Mortality" finds Stevenson moving his explorations of alcohol past the tenacious and troublesome pendulum swings between carnivalesque indulgence and official restraint—the reactive opposition which tears Jekyll apart—to a wise and balanced emergence into a new, and newly gracious and accepting, sobriety. The hero is the prodigal son, welcomed back because he has reformed, but especially welcome because he has retained the humanity and joviality of his heady days even while he has embraced the seriousness of his own mortality. He is Hyde forgiven by Jekyll and Jekyll humanized by Hyde, it may be, and thus restored to equanimity. His excesses have destroyed him, but they have also allowed for his redemption. "The tale of this great failure," as Stevenson said, "is, to those who remained true to him, the tale of a success" (*Memories* 53). Given his affection for Ferrier and his family, it's clear why "Old Mortality" tells the tale it does. Whether or not he saw its outcome as either plausible or sufficiently cautionary, however, remains an open question. As we'll see, even the reformers of his age were of mixed minds about whether the fallen drunkard could, or should, be reclaimed. And if *J&H* trumped "Old Mortality" in its implicit frankness and admonitory potential, it also will have reached a far wider audience. We needn't postulate a hypocritical Stevenson in order to assume that he and Fanny warmly welcomed the added revenue that came along with that kind of broadened moral currency. Whether the blatantly oenophilic scenes of the novella fit comfortably with its central moral burden, however, is another matter.

So, "models" for Jekyll and Hyde? They would seem to have been many and varied, some of them fictional, some of them live human beings. The most compelling, however, appears to have been a kind of "Edinburgh polity" of dualistic men, compounded of elements of Deacon Brodie (the criminality), Baxter (the drunken levity), Stevenson himself (the drunken anger), and poor Walter Ferrier (the tragic mortality). Under the withering tandem criticism of Ferrier's mother and his own father, Stevenson was clearly devastated by his friend's death. As much as he will have questioned his own responsibility for Ferrier's untimely end, he also realized that his old companion's fate could perfectly well have been his own: "Ferrier's grave gapes for us all." The most telling mirror any individual can hold up to society is undoubtedly the mirror in which he can see his own face — past, present, or potential. If *Jekyll and Hyde* is Ferrier's story, it is Stevenson's as well. It was also, as we shall continue to see, the story of the drinking Victorian Everyman.

SEVEN

The Temperance Agenda

For reasons that go well beyond Stevenson's sustained anguish over Ferrier's death or his timely visit with Thomas Hardy, 1885 was arguably a perfect year for a "temperance thriller *cum* moral mirror" to have emerged from the writer's fecund imagination. William Gladstone had returned to prime-ministerial power a half decade earlier, determined to move past what he called "the stage of experiment" in the matter of alcohol reform (Harrison, *Drink* 20). As a result, observes social historian Lilian Shiman, "For almost five years, England was gripped by a temperance fever that rose and fell continuously like the temperature of a sick man" (112). Reforming voices were strident and strong, none more so than that of Sir Wilfred Lawson, Liberal M.P. for Carlisle and President of the prohibitionist United Kingdom Alliance, whose resolution for "Local Option" in the licensing of public houses was carried by the Commons in June of 1880 (Longmate 223). "Never before in the history of the [temperance] movement," wrote reformer David Lewis in 1885 about the years immediately preceding, "have the forces at work, and the energy displayed ... been so earnest and powerful" (*Drink Traffic* 25). "And yet," Lewis must regretfully allow as he goes on to consider how unsuccessfully this reforming energy was translated into economic reality, "the [nation's] drink expenditure has somewhat increased." Progressively well-organized collaboration between the liquor industry and the Conservative party, nicely evidenced when a number of rich brewers were somehow raised to the peerage, made common cause with enduring social custom to effectively stem the rising tide of reform (Girouard 75; Gutzke 243). If Gladstone had hailed the 1880 General Election as a triumph *over* the liquor interests (Lewis, *Drink Problem* 250), his party's failure to win a definitive majority in the penultimate weeks of 1885 — which in turn paved the way for Lord Salisbury's ascendancy as Conservative Prime Minister in '86 — could have moved him to recycle the grimmer judgment he had uttered after a previous electoral loss: "We have been borne down in a torrent of gin and beer," he had colorfully lamented in 1874 (Gutzke 1). Leading temperance spokesman Wilfrid Lawson in fact lost his seat in '85 without ever seeing Local Option reach the stage of a signed and implemented Act. The activist *Brewer's Guardian* understatedly deemed "the results of the late election ... satisfactory" (Gutzke 97).

This portion of our argument makes the case that Stevenson's psychomachia of "warring members" is profitably seen against the struggle between reformist and traditionalist social forces on the matter of alcohol, as that conflict came to a climactic head in the early 1880s. Because many of the lines of moral and legislative battle were drawn out earlier in the century, however, and because Stevenson's own exposure to the ideology and imagery of temperance began as early as his nursery-room immersion in *Cassell's Illustrated Family Paper*, we'll do well to begin with a brief survey of the general campaign against drink in nineteenth-century Britain.

Prior to 1830's Sale of Beer (or "Beerhouses") Act, gin had looked poised to eclipse beer as England's national drink (Clark 295). As a result, the century's first real temperance initiative was, paradoxically enough, Wellington's bill to legalize the sale of beer without a traditional license. The hope was that cheap beer would become universally available, cutting strongly into the gin market and yielding much more "moderate" drinking as a result (Girouard 25). The strategy was not, however, resoundingly successful. The Canon of St. Paul's wrote in the very month that the law was introduced, "The new Beer Bill has begun its operations. Everybody is drunk. Those who are not singing are sprawling. The sovereign people are in a beastly state" (Longmate 25). Although wry observations like this one may have overstated the case,[1] what had begun as a focused anti-*spirits* campaign soon enough evolved into an initiative that spoke to the drawbacks of alcohol of every sort. Joseph Livesey, the man whose celebrated "Malt Lecture" sought to demonstrate that the purportedly "nourishing" alcohol in beer was identical to the "maddening" alcohol in strong spirits, effectively launched the full-fledged temperance movement when he and six other reformers signed a pledge in the northern town of Preston in August of 1832, promising "to abstain from all liquors of an intoxicating quality ... except as medicine" (Harrison 120–25; Longmate 43–44).

Although the campaign against gin had fired reforming zeal in *all* ranks of society, the more strongly Livesey's Preston initiative took hold, the more deeply a wedge was driven between "moderationists" from the middle and upper classes and "teetotalers" from the lower (Longmate 55; Shiman 18). And as teetotalism more and more evinced the zeal of a religion, the Church of England significantly absented itself from the temperance vanguard for some thirty years, especially the wealthier and more powerful members of the clergy (Olsen 45–6). On the secular side, a developing cult of bourgeois "respectability" had already begun to persuade prosperous tradesmen and professionals alike to cut down on their drinking (Clark 308–09), such that growing calls for total abstinence increasingly struck "reputable men" not only as unnecessary for them and their kind but also, for that very reason, as a *de facto* rhetorical earmark of the "unrespectable classes" (Longmate 55). The fact that so many of them were, like *J&H*'s professionals, "judges of good wine" rather than avid drinkers of spirits only reinforced the smug reaction. Dickens' remarks on drunkenness being the bane of the lower classes alone are, in this context, akin to his disdain for the "low" teetotal cause, as memorably expressed in his acerbic essays "Whole Hogs" and "A Plea for Total Abstinence." The great novelist's "Sunday under Three Heads" might in large part support the temperance zealots' call for effective recreational and comestible alternatives (or "counter-attractions") to alcoholic drink, but he clearly thought that his old friend George Cruikshank's decision to sign the teetotal pledge was a version of social suicide.

While men such as Dickens kept their distance from the movement, temperance reformers themselves soon enough fell into two warring camps. Proponents of what was called "moral suasion," men like itinerant American orator James B. Gough, held that to drink or not to drink was a matter of individual will, and that experiments in total prohibition like 1851's Maine Law were therefore essentially immoral and unethical. Reinforcing traditional Christian emphases on the importance of free will in matters of moral judgment was the pragmatic philosophy of the Self-Help movement, together with the powerful, buttressing libertarian thought of John Stuart Mill (Shiman 10, 81–2; Harrison, *Drink* 150). Gough's arch-rival Frederic Lees, however, heralded the Maine Law as a milestone in human history and joined other veteran teetotalers like Livesey, John Cassell, Thomas Whittaker, James Silk Buckingham, and Ireland's Father Mathew in supporting the United Kingdom Alliance for the Suppression of the Traffic in All Intoxicating Liquors, founded in 1853 on a strictly prohibitionist platform (Longmate 136).[2]

In the face of an overwhelming popular hostility to the idea of universal prohibition, the Alliance's strategy was to work with Gladstone to build gradual support of the "Permissive Bill," whereby a majority of ratepayers would be empowered to ban the sale of drink in their own localities. The hope was that any local restrictions that could be enacted would prove to be so overwhelmingly successful that a truly universal measure could finally be adopted (Harrison, *Drink* 260, 198). As it evolved into Lawson's "Local Option" on licensing (based now not on a direct plebiscite but rather on the will of extant representative governmental bodies already charged with administering local affairs), this was the strategy that was pushed the hardest and failed the most consequentially in the years during which *J&H* was slowly taking shape in Stevenson's mind. In essence, and a little like Dr. Jekyll, the U.K. Alliance empowered the very opposition that ultimately foiled it. Long known for its Liberal sympathies, the British brewing trade was for all intents and purposes driven by the specter of prohibition into the Conservative camp, with more than one brewer finding himself a newly-made Lord as a direct result (Gutzke 60–64; Girouard 75). A *Punch* drawing of 24 June 1882 makes this point as well about the on-going drink question. Sir Arthur Bass is shown mounted on a very equine beer-bottle with a cork-screw for a tail and a beer-cask for a saddle-bag. "A new Beeronet," reads the caption, "whose Father refused a Beerage. *Motto*—'Bass is the Trade that pays'" (298). Thus energized in the Election of 1885 by a distinct version of Stevenson's "high pressure of spirits," the Conservatives were able to bring down Lawson and a number of other reformist Liberals.

Earlier and more modest attempts at restriction had met significant opposition as well. The enacted Wilson Patten Bill of 1854 had successfully curtailed Sunday opening hours in London (Harrison, *Drink* 280). But when Lord Grosvenor's Sunday Trading Bill of the following year was widely if erroneously perceived to seek a ban on all Sunday liquor sales, the city erupted in dismay, with outraged citizens filling Hyde Park for three successive Sundays of violent protest. Karl Marx, witness to one of the riots, sententiously proclaimed that "the English Revolution began yesterday in Hyde Park." Such was the impact of the uprising that a full quarter of a century later, in 1880, Home Secretary R. A. Cross warned that if Sunday closing were carried on his watch, he "would not be responsible for the peace of London" (Harrison, "Sunday Trading Riots" 220–24; 232; 238). Thus, if Britain's own "war of the members" (of *parliament*) over the matter of drink didn't finally bring down the monarchy itself, it could consequentially threaten the peace of the capital and contribute mightily to the shaking and the ultimate fall of a government. These kinds of threats and facts are unlikely to have been lost on any thinking man of Stevenson's generation.

Stevenson not surprisingly refers to temperance matters with some regularity, often with a kind of dismissive, jocular superficiality. In the 1881 letter to Henley complaining about the "pig's snout" respirator that his doctor George Balfour had obliged him to wear, he allows that the dreadful experience at the very least insulates him from any further disaster:

> Let *Lawson* triumph, cakes and ale,
> Whisky and hock, and claret, fail;–
> Tobacco, love and letters perish,
> With all that any man could cherish:
> You it may touch, not me. I dwell
> Too deep already — deep in hell [*Letters* 3.232; added emphasis].

In his 1883 poem for Baxter ("When I was young and drouthy"— "drouthy" meaning either "thirsty" or "addicted to drink"), he says wistfully of old cronies, "some hae been convertit / An' weirs the ribbon blue" (*Letters* 4.112) of the "Blue Ribbon Army," a Gospel Temperance movement brought from America by reformed drunkard Richard Booth in 1880 (Shiman 109–121). In the same year he writes to Sidney Colvin, "Yesterday morning, after a day of absolute temperance, I awoke to the worst headache I had had yet. Accordingly temperance was said farewell to" (*Letters* 8.119). And Stevenson's letter to Baxter about the strictures of life in Argyll is signed in a playful Jekyllian hypocrisy, "Yours te-totally, Drucken An'ra" (*Letters* 4.179).

Sir Wilfred Lawson reappears in a letter to Walter Simpson, written in November of 1884, and the reformer is accorded some respect. "I have nearly finished Lawson's most lively pamphlet [possibly 'The Drink Difficulty' from 1879, in which the M.P. lays out his plans for Local Option]. It is very clear and interesting." But these words are significantly prefaced by Stevenson's forceful commitment to the very kind of educating indulgence that Hyde would endorse: "I am persuaded we gain nothing in the least comparable to what we lose, by holding back the hand from any provinces of life; the intrigue, the imbroglio, such as it is, was made for the *plunger* and not for the *teetotaler*" (*Letters* 5.21) This resolution not lightly to abstain is reiterated in response to Baxter's writing to him as "Johnston" in December of 1885, "an noo a'm on the tee tottle." "Damn Tetottle say I!" Stevenson replies, in the very month *J&H* was intended to be published (*Letters* 5.62). As for the Samoa years, Stevenson's wonted devotion to wine is confirmed in the very language of "the movement" when he writes to Henry James that to be kept from "drink[ing] to comfort all the days of [his] life" is to be forced to wear an unwelcome "teatotal [*sic*] badge" (*Letters* 8.109). And while Ferrier's fatal "plunge" apparently gave Stevenson considerable pause about that commitment to being a "plunger" that he expressed in the letter to Simpson, it's dangerous to read too much seriousness into his report of a conversation with the drunken B. M. Haggard: "That interview has made me a tea-totaller [*sic*]" (*Letters* 8.383). The bare facts of his drinking at Vailima argue very much the opposite.

The fiction, too, reveals Stevenson's ear for the reforming rhetoric of his age, albeit sometimes with something of the wry amusement that we see in the letters. Frank Cassilis in "The Pavilion on the Links" (1880) allows of a time of particular stress in the story's action, "I have always been a temperance man on principle; but it is useless to push principle to extreme, and on this occasion, I believe that I finished three-quarters of the bottle ['of good burgundy']" (51). More soberly, *Treasure Island*'s Dr. Livesey shares, as we've seen, both a surname and a particularly dire attitude towards drink with temperance pioneer Joseph Livesey. "If you keep on drinking rum," this doctor warns Billy Bones, "the world will soon be quit of a very dirty scoundrel.... One glass of rum won't kill you, but if you take one you'll take another, and I stake my wig if you don't break off short, you'll die" (8; 14). *The Ebb-Tide*'s drunken cockney Huish, half-way through a good bottle of Brâne-Mouton, alludes sarcastically to the Band of Hope (264), a hugely popular wing of the temperance movement that focused on the protection of children, even as he ribs Captain Davis for refusing to crack a bottle with him after their schooner is nearly lost in the squall: "Turned teetotal, 'ave you?" (226). Davis, conversely and as we've seen, imagines himself as a kind of latter-day reformed Ferrier, safely ashore back in Maine (forever the quintessential temperance state after its adoption of prohibition in 1851), "smoking a cigar, a blue ribbon in his buttonhole, a *victor over himself* and circumstances" (289; italics added). Back on the other side of the issue, the mock-heroic "Man Haggard" of *An Object of Pity* defies the conspiracies of "that ass Tee-tootum" (23–4). And finally, the staunch but spiritually benighted missionary of the short-short story "Something In It," when he is offered the "kava of the dead" that will reveal to him the real truths of the spirit world that his narrow religion has kept him from seeing, replies, "I thank you. It smells excellent. But I am a blue-ribbon man myself; and though I am aware there is a difference of opinion even in our own confession, I have always held kava to be excluded [prohibited]" (256). He's left at story's end as a kind of Horatio or Ishmael, clearly deprived of an ennobling wisdom.

So, Stevenson's attitudes towards the temperance movement are somewhat difficult to pin down. He accords Lawson respect for a "clear and interesting" argument, he celebrates the historical Ferrier and the fictional Davis alike for their triumph over their addictions, and, at that crucial moment in his later life, he goes so far as to advocate prohibition in the Gilberts and Samoa. On the other hand, his character Frank Cassilis concedes that any moral stricture can be taken too far, Stevenson himself chafes at wearing the "teatotal badge," and "Something in It" evinces in a demonstrably approving way all the old associations between alcohol and a very positive idea of Knowledge that informed the traditional rituals of the punch bowl or the cocktail carafe. The more one considers it, the more Stevenson's writing on alcohol looks like a palimpsest of Dionysian endorsement and Apollonian restraint, a kind of "double text" very like Jekyll's own "pious work ... annotated, in his own hand, with startling blasphemies" (71). The majority of his remarks about abstinence are humorous and even dismissive. But a strong counter-current is often enough in evidence as well.

If Stevenson's feelings about temperance ebbed and flowed with circumstances and the moment, the rhetoric and imagery of the social movement nonetheless left an indelible imprint on the writer and his most famous work. As we've seen, Louis cut his moral teeth on *Cassell's Illustrated Family Paper*, and he in fact claims to have learned to read precisely in order to understand what the pictures were about in the two bound volumes of that publication as he found them in his father's library (*Letters* 1.85).[3] Among his earliest literary models will therefore have been Cassell's prescribed, proto–Jekyllian "moral tales"—all of them "illustrative of the triumph of religion, temperance, morality, industry, energy, and self-control over idleness, apathy, intemperance, and habitual self-indulgence." Cassell's sponsored writers' competition for a cash prize and for publication in the paper actually required that entries juxtapose the stories of *two* men: one of "humble birth" who rises to "eminence and opulence," another "possessed of great natural advantages both of mind and person," who nonetheless falls "into infamy and ruin" (Nowell-Smith 42–3). The fit isn't quite right, but the ultimately upward trajectory of "Old Mortality" and the resolutely downward path of *J&H* look especially interesting in this regard. In any case, in an essay entitled "Popular Authors," which he published in *Scribner's Magazine* in July of 1888, Stevenson ironically attributes to Cassell's moralistic *Family Paper* his ultimate interest in the low "penny press," one product of which was in fact *J&H* itself, the "penny (twelve penny) dreadful" which he confessed to Colvin he was "pouring forth" in the early autumn of 1885. He recalls Alice Cunningham taking the paper "on confidence" that "the tales it contained were Family Tales, not novels. But every now and then, something would occur to alarm her finer sense," he continues; "she would express a well-grounded fear that the current fiction was 'going to turn out a Regular Novel'; and the family paper, with my pious [and proto–Jekyllian] approval, would be dropped" (Linehan 122). Stevenson goes on to allow, however, that neither he nor his nurse could ever quite free themselves from their prurient interests; "we would study the windows of the stationer and try to fish out of subsequent woodcuts and their legends the further adventures of our favorites." He doesn't mention whether his censorious companion ever indulged those interests again. But it is certainly tempting to see *J&H* as one of the paper's temperate "Family Tales" transmogrified, over the course of experientially-laden decades, into a "Regular Novel."

Perhaps even more suggestive of an early inspiration for *J&H* than the publisher's moralistic fiction contest is an illustration from another of Cassell's papers, *The Popular Educator*, entitled "The Influence of Morality or Immorality on the Countenance" (see Figure 2). First published in Britain in 1852 (the image itself having originated in France), the drawing asks about a *single* young boy, "What will he become?" and then shows two life courses that are open to him. The "high road" at the top of the page leads successively to "School," "Literary Institution," "Profession and Marriage," and "Head of a Family"; the latter to "Faubourg," "Beer-shop," "Vice and Misery," and "Beggary." Each stage offers its fulfilled "Jekyll" and its fallen "Hyde." Especially in the first two iterations, the high and low characters look hauntingly like each other, as though (but for hair-do and clothing) the latter could be the former, but

Figure 2 — "The Influence of Morality or Immorality on the Countenance." From Cassell's *Popular Educator* (1852). Reproduced with the permission of the British Library.

(to cite the novella) with "something wrong" (34), giving "the impression of deformity without any nameable malformation" (40), projecting "the haunting sense of unexpressed deformity" (50). Take away the discipline of "school," and you have the disarray of a "Faubourg" like Soho. Add alcohol, and "Literary Institution" dissolves into the "Beer-shop." Utterson tells Poole late in the novella that Jekyll is "plainly seized with one of those maladies that ... deform the sufferer" (66). If his hypothesis is more apt than he realizes and the root malady really is somehow alcohol — what Stevenson duly termed the "disease" that turned Ferrier into the "bug to frighten babes withal" (*Letters* 4.159; 1.258) — then Cassell's image could have afforded the pictorial case study.

Read "vertically" in this way, then, the drawing could itself easily have offered early inspiration for the long-sought fable of "double being" that became *J&H* — a "visual aid," if you will, for thinking about both a "good and gentle" Ferrier and his dark "lunatic brother." Read "horizontally" instead, the two alternative possibilities are precisely and eerily those that Stevenson mentions in his letter to Baxter of 1888, when he recalls himself as a young man hoping for a wife and a lifetime of moderate literary success—"if [he] did not take to drink," thereby frittering his own "Literary Institution" away into the depredations of "Beer-shop" (*Letters* 6.207). The drawing could also stand as an illustration of either of two portions of Stevenson's novella that contemplate in similar ways the idea of a whole life's course as affected by good and bad choices: first, the point where he claims "I saw my life as a whole: I followed it from the days of my childhood, when I had walked with my father's hand, and through the self-denying toils of my professional life, to arrive again and again, with the same sense of unreality, at the damned horrors of the evening" (91); or, second, of his dire discovery that he has uncontrollably become Hyde, when "a moment before I had been safe of all men's respect, wealthy, beloved—the cloth laying for me in the dining room at home; and now I was houseless, a known murderer, thrall to the gallows" (93). From "Head of family" to hunted pariah in the blink of an eye.

It is more than plausible that Stevenson knew the illustration. After appearing in the pages of *The Popular Educator*, the image was extensively used in "poster" form in street advertising campaigns throughout Britain, with the title "The Child: What Will He Become?" (Nowell-Smith 47). Its impact in that setting was sufficiently strong that it inspired a *Punch* parody a full thirty years later. The 12 August 1882 number of the magazine asks about "The New Member" of Parliament, "What will he become?" (64; see Figure 3). This proves at the very least that Cassell's famous temperance imagery was sufficiently "in the late–Victorian air" to be adapted with full confidence by a popular illustrator in the very decade *J&H* appeared, as confidently as someone like David Letterman might allude today to Nancy Reagan's "Just say No!" campaign with full faith that the audience will "get it." We know from his letters that Stevenson was reading *Punch* in August-September of 1882 (3.531). As a life-long devotee of satirical prints, he was very much the kind of person who would have appreciated this effective homage to Cassell; and he would very likely have been reminded of—or at least found out about—the specific temperance application which inspired it.

Even if we were to dismiss the likelihood that Stevenson knew either of the drawings, the truth is that Cassell's wonted dichotomies were everywhere in temperance rhetoric and imagery, exaggerated by the moral absolutism of the teetotalers. Kate Mitchell kept Cassell's head-to-head contrasts alive for the 1880s with her long-term comparative analysis of the lives of two workmen: "The one is a total abstainer, the other believes

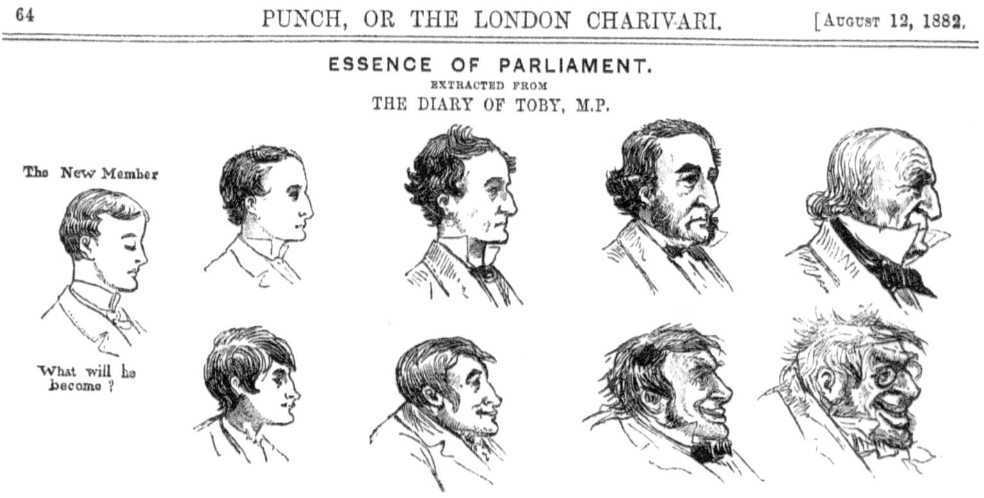

106   THE TRANSFORMING DRAUGHT

64   PUNCH, OR THE LONDON CHARIVARI.   [AUGUST 12, 1882.

ESSENCE OF PARLIAMENT.
EXTRACTED FROM
THE DIARY OF TOBY, M.P.

The New Member

What will he become ?

Figure 3 — "Essence of Parliament." From *Punch*, August 12, 1882. Courtesy of the University of Canterbury Library.

in his beer." "No longer a workman," she says of the first, "he is a capitalist at the end of ten short years, and, through his foresight and industry, can carry his head amongst the highest. But where is the beer-drinker?" (230–31). Charles Lamb had asked in 1812, "is there no middle ground betwixt total abstinence and the excess which kills you?" ("Confessions of a Drunkard" 174). "No," answered Thomas Whittaker most emphatically seventy-two years later, "there can be no middle course" (*Life's Battles* 203). And as with decisions on individual conduct, so too with judgments on institutions like the liquor trade. "The Alliance believes that when the people suffer a great wrong the best policy is to proclaim that wrong entire, and not part of it," reasons David Lewis (*The Drink Problem* 178). Whittaker goes on to decry a version of Jekyll's self-division by noting the way "the drinking system makes it easy to do wrong and difficult to do right, so we are distinct races.... All who drink belong to one lot; all who do not belong to another. These are two distinct and separate classes" (*Brighter England* 161–61). And discussing the nefarious impact of music halls as close kin to pubs, the *Times* of 15 October 1883 similarly expresses concern for the way these recreational institutions

Opposite: Figure 4 — "Which Way Shall I Turn Me?" From *British and Foreign Temperance Intelligencer*, November 2, 1839. Courtesy of the Livesey Collection, University of Central Lancashire.

THE BRITISH AND FOREIGN
Temperance Intelligencer.

[*In consequence of an accident which happened to the wood-cut intended for this number, just as we were going to press, we have been compelled to substitute the cut now given. The fifth of the "STEPS OF INTEMPERANCE," will appear in our next.*]

Vol. III.   No. 156.   SATURDAY, NOVEMBER 2, 1839.   PUBLISHED WEEKLY. PRICE ONE PENNY.

"WHICH WAY SHALL I TURN ME?" *or, Ruin and Salvation.*

OLD FUDDLER.—Come along, Charley my boy; come along! *Only just one glass!* A short life and a merry one! that's my ticket.

CHARLES.—Well, your'e a good natured fellow, tho' you've ruined yourself by drinking. I was thinking about abstaining; but surely *one glass* won't hurt me!

TEE-TOTALLER.—Don't listen to him, my dear Charles. You see what drinking has done for him. If you take *one glass* you won't know when to stop. You promised to go to our meeting. Come, and learn the blessings of Total Abstinence.

PRINTED AND PUBLISHED BY J. P. &CO, 90, BARTHOLOMEW CLOSE, LONDON.

"intensify the tendency of the nation to become two" (Bailey 166).[4] As we shall see, this tendency of reformers to see social schisms as the macrocosmic equivalent of psychological and moral duplicity is something that *J&H* reflects as well.

From the days of Hogarth's "Gin Lane" and "Beer Street," temperance dichotomies had also informed the imagery of popular publications other than Cassell's. The "perennial war in [Jekyll's] members" is suggestively modeled in an image from the *British and Foreign Temperance Intelligencer* of November 1839, entitled "Which Way Shall I Turn Me?" (see Figure 4). A modestly dressed man is accosted, on his right side, by a well-dressed and -groomed gentleman (the "Tee-totaller"), on his left by a slovenly lout in ill-fitting clothes (from his expression, clearly the spirit of drunkenness). Behind them lie two blocks of buildings, one cut away to reveal a scene of domestic comfort, with some children secure in their parents' laps, the other a doorway crowded with miserable characters and, nearest the drunkard's boots, a small body lying in the street. The image is interesting not only for the way it links drunkenness to the domestic decay we see so vividly portrayed in Stevenson's Soho but also for the language of its title. Although the picture and the dialogue printed below it represent the meeting of three distinct people, the title reduces sociology to interior psychology, with one aspect of a multiple self contemplating how best to control the other. It essentially embodies, then, an early version of Jekyll's pronominal psychomachia.

The general potency of the "Upright vs. Evil Twin" motif that we find in *J&H* is further evidenced in a series of cover drawings and poems that ran in six issues of *The Temperance Intelligencer* from February to April, 1840. "Temperance and Intemperance" follows, as Kate Mitchell was later to do, the career of two young men from their apprenticeship in the same print shop to radically different ends—Tommy's fortune made by total abstinence and hard work, Harry's hopes crushed by the "love of drink" instilled by the very workplace customs that John Dunlop detailed a year before (29 February 1840 [1]). J. W. Kirton's *Four Pillars of Temperance* (1865) revisits the metaphor fifteen years into Stevenson's life and anticipates Hyde's dependency on Jekyll's cheque book (see Figure 5). The frontispiece pictures the confrontation of two men, one dressed for labor and pointing the way to the "Post Office Savings Bank," the other another ill-kempt wastrel slouching in front of a sign touting "Fine Cordials and Gin."

Given the specialized publications in which these particular images

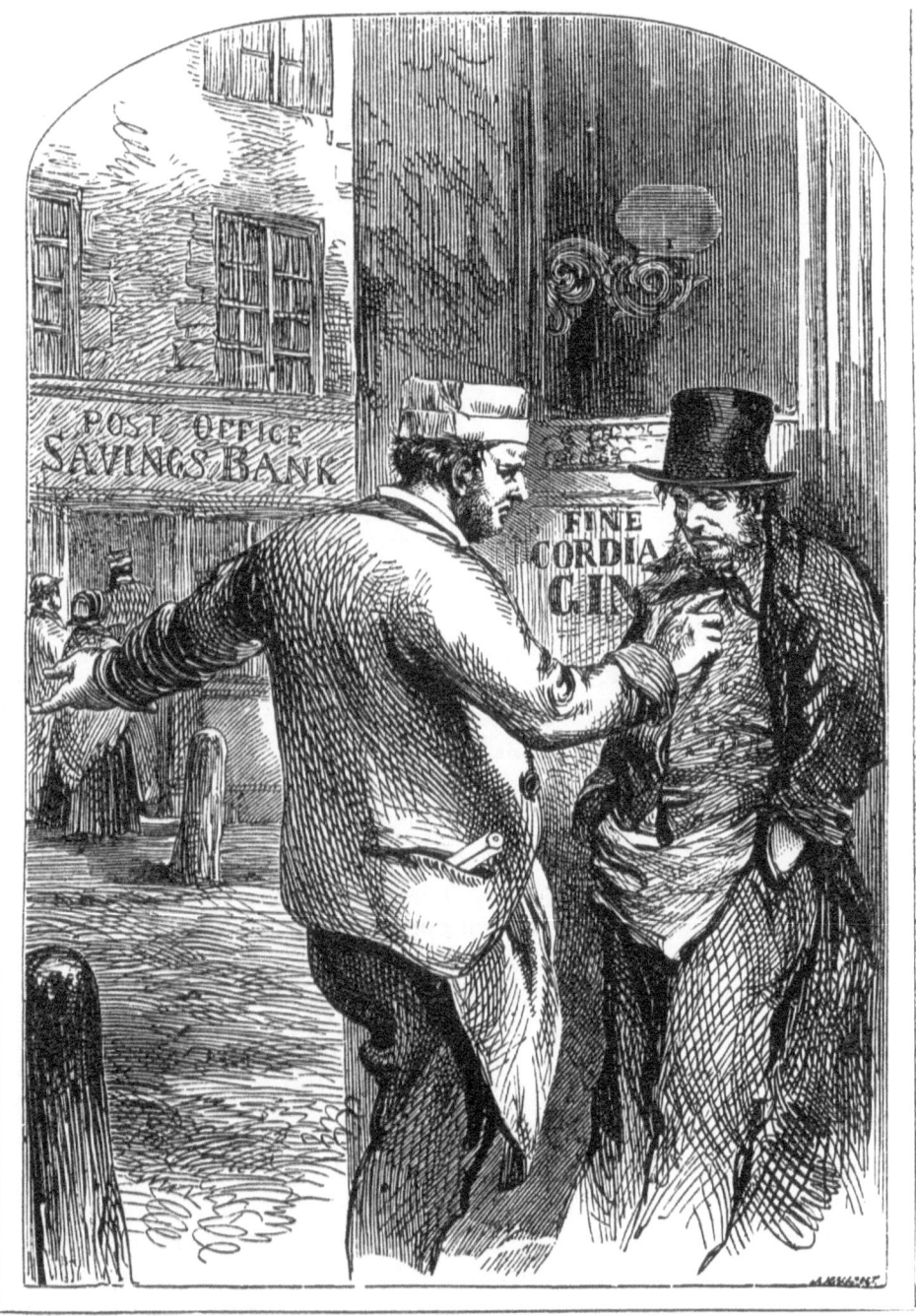

Figure 5 — "The Savings' Bank and the Losings' Bank." From John W. Kirton, *The Four Pillars of Temperance* (1865). Reproduced with the permission of the British Library.

appeared, it's unlikely Stevenson would have seen any of them. Far more probable is that, among drawings that predate his enthusiastic nursery browsing, he could have known such Phiz illustrations as "Effects of Tea" or "John Bull Recovering from his Watery Humour" (1846), both of which contrasted the traditional, robust vitality of drinkers with the physical debility of teetotalers (Longmate 103); or, among images from his maturity, something like the flyers that brewer-turned-reformer Frederick Charrington distributed in the streets of London in 1883, showing angels and devils fighting for the souls of drinkers (Shiman 126). We can again be virtually certain, however, that he knew a range of topical drawings from *Punch*, given that he was reading the magazine at the time when a story about man's "double being" was very much on his creative shortlist.

The magazine that had (as we've seen) featured a top-hatted bottle greeting a stout tankard in "Sunday Equality: A Re-union of Champagne and Porter" (11 Aug 1855; 57) kept the satirical ball rolling in the "temperance-fevered" 1880s. The 20 March 1880 number featured "Beer and Water: An Election Eclogue" (122–23). The 14 August issue of the same year tweaked the "Extreme Sabbatarian Party" with a pair of drawings entitled "Dark Monday" vs. "Bright Monday" (61). "Dark Monday" shows the men of London hung over but "not quite discontented," because, although museums had been closed the previous day, pubs had been open; "Bright Monday" conversely shows men hard at work, but "not quite contented," because museums had been open and the pubs closed. 15 November 1884 brought the image of an upright gentleman, with tall top hat, gloves, spats, and a rolled umbrella, contrasted with a staggering member of the lower classes: "Neat and Tidy!" reads the one caption, versus "Tight and Needy" (230).

The explicitly combative nature of Jekyll and Hyde's relationship is more closely anticipated in two other *Punch* images from the '80s, both of them inspired by the heated debate over Local Option. 20 October 1883 offers "Pot and Kettle" (182; see Figure 6). A foaming pewter tankard, representing "the intemperate bunkum" Dean of Bangor and the liquor interests, squares off against a tea-kettle, an embodiment of "Teetotal extravagance" who stands menacingly on an inverted saucer, steam jetting out of his spout as he threatens to "finish the bout." Stevenson was in France when the issue appeared, but was evidently still keeping up with his favorite old magazine (*Letters* 4.218). Even more suggestive than "Pot and Kettle" is another water vs. beer image that had appeared the previ-

PUNCH, OR THE LONDON CHARIVARI. [October 20, 1883.

POT AND KETTLE.
(*A New Version.*)

[The Dean of Bangor says, that if he had his own way there would be much less tea-drinking among people of all classes. Excessive tea-drinking created a generation of nervous, discontented people, who were for ever complaining of the existing order of the Universe, scolding their neighbours, and sighing after the impossible. In fact, he suspected that over-much tea-drinking, by destroying the calmness of the nerves, was acting as a dangerous revolutionary force among us. The tea-kettle went before the gin-bottle, and the physical and nervous weakness that had its origin in the bad cookery of an ignorant wife, ended in ruin, intemperance, and disease.]

"Kettle began it."—Dickens's *Cricket on the Hearth.*

Kettle (*turning up its Spout contemptuously*). You horrible, mischievous creature! You pewter-built Borgia, get out with you!
Before very long, Saints be praised! our Sir Wilfrid will finish his bout with you;
And then——
Pot (*frothing over with wrath*). Oh! now come, this *is* cool! Who are *you* calling Borgia? Blow you!
You, who beat the Brinvilliers to fits! Ah! it's time honest people should know you,
You false mollycoddling old *Mawworm.*
Kettle (*sputtering*). Ah! *always* abusive in anger. What have you to say against me?

Pot. I? Oh, nothing, of course. Go to—Bangor, And just ask the Dean what *he* thinks about tea-drinking. Talk of *my* doings?
What are they compared with the woes that are wrought by your worse than witch-brewings?
Kettle. Mine?
Pot. Yes; you and the teapot between you are simply upsetting creation.
Kettle. What, I and the cup that——
Pot. Oh! come now, enough of that stale old quotation
From maudlin emasculate Cowper, it's blown on, played out. Bless you, Pekoe
More mischief has wrought in this world than all strong drinks from Four-half to Clicquot,
And Gunpowder Tea's worse than Dynamite, looked at as one of the forces
That aid Revolution and Murder—the Dean my opinion endorses.
Kettle. The Dean be——
Pot. Exactly. That's just it; profanity coarse, anti-clerical! Regular Communist, *you* are; result of the weakness hysterical
Caused by all dealings with Tea, which is simply distilled condemnation,

Figure 6 — "Pot and Kettle." From *Punch*, 20 October, 1883. Courtesy of the University of Canterbury Library.

Figure 7 — "Publican-Barrel and Pharisee-Pump." From *Punch*, 28 October, 1882. Courtesy of the University of Canterbury Library.

ous year: "Publican-Barrel and Pharisee-Pump," from 28 October 1882 (see Figure 7). A portly and blustery beer barrel plays Sir Toby Belch to a willowy and sanctimonious water-pump-Malvolio. "What," reads the caption, "Though you be virtuous, shall there be no more (cakes and) ale?" (194). We shall return to the image very shortly, but again we know that Stevenson was following *Punch* in the Fall of 1882 (*Letters* 3.351), and the image mirrors to perfection the pieties of Jekyll and the reactive violence of Hyde — once again in the suggestive context of Local Option on Sunday closings. It's therefore very tempting to think that the image took its place in the Brownies' pre-conscious scrapbook right alongside Cassell's "What will he become?"— ready for the momentous dream that loosed the floodgates of creativity.

In sum, from his earliest days poring over the latest number of *Cassell's Illustrated Family Paper* under the morally dichotomizing eye of Alice Cunningham to his habitual browsing through *Punch* in the years during which *J&H* was taking shape, Stevenson would have found in the rhetoric and imagery of the temperance debate among the most consistent and compelling articulations of social and personal duality going at the time. Given the importance of Gladstone and Lawson's temperance reforms to the General Election that was gearing up precisely while the story came into being, it would thus be somewhat surprising if some substantial allusion to the issue of alcohol reform hadn't found its way into *J&H*'s excursus on "man's double being." Add, among other things, Stevenson's lingering angst over Walter Ferrier's death, and one of the novella's most significant themes might seem to have been guaranteed.

EIGHT

Dream Scenes: Neighborhoods of Nightmare

Stevenson's ultimate indebtedness to the rhetoric and imagery of the temperance movement is readily apparent in the seminal "scenes" that Stevenson claims were given him by the Brownies, and perhaps even more obviously in the "major offenses" that the novella shows him committing (to be treated in the next chapter). The dream scenes—the first seeds of the entire narrative and thus arguably the most likely to contain its thematic DNA in the purest (if also perhaps the least rationalized) form — are admittedly hard to identify with absolute certainty, owing to a bothersome inconsistency in the various accounts that Stevenson gave of them. In an initial reckoning in the *New York Herald* (8 September 1887), he claimed, "All I dreamed about Dr. Jekyll was that one man was being pressed into a cabinet, when he swallowed a drug and changed into another being. I awoke and said at once that I had found the missing link for which I had been looking so long" (Swearingen 99). In his subsequent "Chapter on Dreams" (1888), however, he asserts that, "I dreamed the scene at the window, and a scene afterwards split in two, in which Hyde, pursued for some crime, took the powder and underwent the change in the presence of his pursuers. All the rest was made awake, and consciously.... All that was given me was the matter of three scenes, and the central idea of a voluntary change becoming involuntary" (208). Thus 1887's single scene becomes 1888's two, one of which then splits to yield "three" total scenes, together with the "central idea" of the alteration in physical states. The scene most explicitly identified, albeit in only one account, seems to be embodied in the chapter called "Incident at the Window," in which the Sunday strollers Utterson and Enfield witness what is apparently the initial stages of Jekyll's spontaneous reversion to Hyde.[1] The other scene about which we might feel reasonably certain is contained in "Dr. Lanyon's Narrative," in which Hyde indeed "took the powder" and "underwent the change" in the presence of a witness. Lanyon, however, is not at all a "pursuer" in the way that Utterson and Inspector Welcomen are; he expresses no curiosity at all about Jekyll, but rather an increasing resolve to have nothing to do with him (36, 57). As for the nature of any second or "other half" of the bifurcated "*non*-window" scene that was mentioned in 1888, we're left at a complete loss; unless the "pursuit for the crime" somehow constitutes a "scene" separate from "taking the powder"— or, somewhat more plausibly, unless "taking the powder" *in general* and "taking it and changing in front of somebody" *in particular* constitute two separate scenes. If the reader is befuddled by all this, it is no surprise. No interpretive option seems totally satisfactory. The best course of action, then, may simply be to reduce the confusing accounts to what seem the lowest common denominators, taking the *Herald* vision of Jekyll "swallow[ing] a drug and chang[ing] into another being" as one core image that the text indeed embodies (and embodies over and over again!), and the "Incident at the Window" as the other. What, we might ask, lies at the imagistic hearts of these two "visions" as they have been expressed and preserved in the novella?

We've in fact made a reasonably good start with the first. As Norman Kerr observed in 1882, the most common "drug" for any Briton of Stevenson's day to swallow if he wanted to change into another "being" was alcohol. From Dr. Johnson to Charles Booth, analysts of the world of drink documented the escape that alcohol afforded a man from any number of the trials and pressures of life—from anything and "all that was unbearable," in Jekyll's terms (82); "drown[ing] care in jovial bouts," in Stevenson's own ("Epistle to Charles Baxter," *Selected Poems* 11). Long identified by people like Henry Fielding as a prime precipitant of crime, drink was also sometimes seen to absolve criminals of a measure of responsibility for their actions, given that alcohol so impairs one's rational judgment (Harrison, *Drink* 327).[2] Kerr, for example, noted with a measure of approval that "judges have allowed a plea in defense when the crime has been committed during frenzy arising from habitual intemperance" (359).

And if Jekyll's denial of moral responsibility for his actions as Hyde smacks of this traditional legal defense — "It was Hyde, after all, and Hyde alone, that was guilty" (87) — the salient detail of Jekyll's "voluntary change becoming involuntary" is also perfectly in line with the realities of dipsomania as understood by Stevenson and his age.

It's when we look at the precise kind of "other man" that Jekyll becomes, however, that the ideological and imagistic underpinnings of Stevenson's dream become most evident. If Jekyll's "blood-red liquor" thrills and delights him "like wine" in all of the suggestive ways that have been treated above, it also reduces his "stature" (84), turning him into a violent and largely uncivilized "little man" (31) who is "dwarfish" (40) and "troglodytic" (40), a manner of cave-dweller (89), "hardly human" (40), with hands "of a dusky pallor and thickly shaded with a swart growth of hair" (88), who "snarl[s]" in a "savage laugh" (40), has "haunches" (78) instead of a proper derrière, jumps "like a monkey" (68), and manifests the "tricks," "spite," and "fury" of an "ape" (96, 97, 47). It makes good sense that Jekyll should imagine the constellations looking down on Hyde as "the first creature of that sort that their unsleeping vigilance has yet disclosed to them" (84) — or that Lanyon should be so curious not only about Hyde's "life, his fortune and status in the world" but also about his "*origin*" (78; italics added): Jekyll's alter-ego is clearly being seen through the lens of contemporary thought on degeneration and criminal recidivism as it followed from Darwin's *Origin of Species*, *Descent of Man*, and *Expression of the Emotions in Man and Animals* (Arata 33–43). It may even be significant that Stevenson told the *Herald* newspaper that, in hitting on the dramatic image of Jekyll's change into another man, he had found "the missing link" for which he had so long been searching.[3] Small, dark, hairy, and snarling, Hyde stands, as often as not, half-way between ape and civilized man.

Not at all surprisingly, proponents of temperance followed B. A. Morel and Max Nordau in citing alcohol as a key precipitator of disastrous tumbles back down the evolutionary ladder. Charting the increased consumption of alcohol in Great Britain between 1830 and 1888, Nordau names the "poisons" that, over time, yield the "dwarfish" likes of Hyde:

> A race which is regularly addicted, even without excess, to narcotics and stimulants in any form (such as fermented alcoholic drinks, tobacco, opium, hashish, arsenic) ... begets degenerate descendants who, if they remain exposed to the same influences, rapidly descend to the lowest degrees of degeneracy, to idiocy, to dwarfishness [*Degeneration* 34)].[4]

If Thomas Whittaker accordingly asserted that drink separated the English into "two races," David Lewis went him one better when he claimed that alcohol was "one of the most powerful factors in the deterioration and debasement of the race" (*The Drink Problem* 4). William Booth's *In Darkest England*, as its title suggests, likened the drink-ridden slums of London to the darkest jungles of Africa, filled as a place like Soho was with "sinking classes" of "dwarfish, dehumanized inhabitants," "sodden with drink" (Preface n.p., 12, 24). The human condition might even be worse in England than in Africa, Booth added, because "Darkest England has many more public-houses than the Forest of the Aruwimi has rivers" (24). Lending authority to this notion that men "devolved" under the influence of drink — in ways that we would call genetic and not simply behavioral — was weighty medical opinion (Sournia 49). Thus Lewis continues, "The drink appetite ... has become chronic, and according to a hereditary law is being transmitted from generation to generation. We here discover one of those hidden and hostile forces which even those carrying on the temperance work are apt to overlook" (*The Drink Traffic* 26). One thinks of the "impatient gaiety" with which Jekyll is born, but which devolves under the influence of his drug into the driving motive of "the *brute* that slept within me" (94; emphasis added).

In *The South Seas*, as we've seen, Stevenson himself later likened the degrading alcoholic dissolution of the Gilbert Islanders to the "Darkest English" depravities of Soho. *J&H* starts that ball rolling with an onslaught of coded language. Beyond the examples that have already been mentioned, Jekylls harbors an "animal within" who "lick[s] the chops of memory" (92). Hyde appropriately "hisses" like a snake (39), bridles at being "caged" and "c[o]me[s] out roaring" (90) in resentment, torturing others with "bestial avidity" (86) and "brutish physical insensibility" (90). Especially in context, this is the lexicon of temperance as borrowed from Darwin, Nordau or Cesare Lombroso. Jekyll's initially "undignified" pleasures become, "in the hands of Edward Hyde, ... monstrous" (86). Prohibitionist doctor Kate Mitchell talks about habitual drinkers "sinking lower and lower to the level of brutes," echoing Fielding in her allegation that "most of the horrible and brutal crimes which are a blot upon our civilization are committed in this country by persons under the influence of drink" (250, 12). Thomas DeQuincey had earlier distinguished the drunk from the drug addict by observing that alcoholic inebriation is "a condition which calls up into supremacy the merely human, too often the brutal, part of his nature" (Taylor 107). Dickens accordingly reveals Mrs.

Blackpool's "brutish instinct" (*Hard Times* 87), invents another version of Bill Sykes in "Bill Brute" ("Demoralisation" 161), and complains of the way the gin drinker, "reduced to a worse level than the lowest brute in the scale of creation, lies wallowing in his kennel" ("Sunday under Three Heads" 646). Similarly, Mary Woolstonecraft's Maria in the novel of the same name labors "to reform her embruted mate" (Taylor 213), while George Eliot deemed Branwell Brontë a "drunken brutal son" and copiously documents the vile behavior of the drunken lawyer Dempster in his "ill-tempered and brutal phase" (McCormack 19; *Janet's Repentance* 270). Elsewhere, Stevenson describes the "brutal impulse" of the drunken natives in Butaritari (*South Seas* 252) and terms the drunken ex-skipper of the *Farallone* a "brutish man" (*The Ebb-Tide* 170).

As for "animals within," we've heard Dr. Johnson speaking of the way humans escape from the pain of being men by becoming "beasts." Coleridge observed that wine, although it inspired civility in the refined drinker, turned the uneducated man into "a frantic wild beast" (Taylor 113). Woolstonecraft claimed in her *Vindication of the Rights of Women* that "drunken husbands are irrational beasts" (Taylor 211), and George Eliot in turn vindicated her feminist predecessor when Janet likens the drink-maddened Dempster to a "wild beast within his den" (273). Never personally one to abstain from drink, Dickens nonetheless claims that a drunkard imitates a hyena ("The Great Baby" 316), even as he berates those who "make wild beasts of themselves under the influence of strong liquor" ("Demoralisation" 161). Among James Greenwood's "Seven Curses of London" is the "bestial intoxication" that turns even women to "she-creatures" swarming like a "horde of human tigresses" (185, xvii). And Kate Mitchell concludes very memorably of the inveterate drinker that "base instincts are yielded to, the passions ride triumphant over the reason; no four-footed animal is capable of showing such degraded tendencies, and such an utter want of decency, or committing such unnamable offences as a man in a state of intoxication. He is lower than a beast; he can be compared with nothing in the animated world but a loathsome object, deserving only the censure, and sometimes the pity, of his sober fellow creatures" (200). Noting the way Mitchell's disdain modulates into the budding sympathy that could power a salutary intervention, one might recall Jekyll's condemnation of Hyde as "the slime of the pit" and an "insurgent horror"—but also, almost unaccountably, as a great lover of life whom, Jekyll says, "I find it in my heart to pity" (96). Perhaps unfortunately, that seed of pity is never given a chance to take effective root.

Beyond the pages of *J&H*, Stevenson describes the drunken John Falconer making "a beast" of himself (*Complete Stories* 1.94) and decries the "fizz"-pickled Captain Davis's "hoggish slumber" (*The Ebb-Tide* 165). He was furthermore appalled in the Gilberts by the bingeing and violent islanders, shocked by "the vision of man's beastliness, of his ferality ... the image of our race upon its lowest terms, as the partner of beasts, beastly itself, dwelling pell-mell and hugger-mugger, hairy man with hairy woman, in the caves of old" (*South Seas* 254). But then he remembers Soho. And if Jekyll explains about the "troglodytic," cavern-dwelling Hyde (89) that, "as the first edge of my penitence wore off, the lower side of me, so long indulged, so recently chained down, began to growl for license" (92), so does Thomas Whittaker warn that "when we take [liquor from] the drinking adult, it is butter out of the dog's throat. It is difficult, and the dog barks, growls, bites" (*Life's Battles* 314). In sum, when the Brownies gave Stevenson the idea of the drug that changed Jekyll "into another being," they could well have been drawing on memories of Cassell's "What will he become?" with the higher line of man ("higher" both morally and on the page) always alarmingly prone to devolve into the lower. And as the story took fuller shape, the notion of the change took on more and more of the specific ideology and language of temperance.

While the evidence is more subtle, the same can be said of the other scene that the Brownies "gave" Stevenson and that he subsequently expanded in "Incident at the Window." The salient details for analysis are these. It's Sunday, and once again "Mr Utterson was on his usual walk with Mr Enfield" (60). As on their first Sabbath-day stroll that opens the novella, they happen by the dilapidated door that Hyde uses to enter Jekyll's laboratory. Utterson proposes that a visit with Jekyll might "do him good," so they enter the dark court that is overlooked by the doctor's three back windows, finding it "very cool and a little damp, and full of premature twilight, although the sky, high up overhead, was still bright with sunset." Jekyll sits at a half-open window "with an infinite sadness of mien, like some disconsolate prisoner." Asked about his health, he admits to being "very low," to which Utterson replies, "You stay too much indoors.... You should be out, whipping up the circulation like Mr. Enfield and me." Jekyll turns down the invitation to join their excursion, but agrees that a chat would be very welcome, provided they stay where they are: "I would ask you and Mr. Enfield up, but the place is really not fit" (61). It is at this point that "the smile was struck out of [Jekyll's] face and succeeded by an expression of ... abject horror." The doctor slams the window down, and the cousins leave the court, traverse the by-street, and refuse to speak "until they had come into a neighboring thoroughfare, where *even upon a Sunday* there were still some stirrings of life" (emphasis added).

The episode nicely complements the other, "powder-taking" scene that Stevenson claims to have dreamed as well, for it apparently represents the imminent onset of "the change" in Jekyll's nature once it has progressed from being "voluntary" to being "involuntary." If there is any scene in the novella that explores Jekyll's dread of his true nature being laid bare to the very public whose respect he has always craved, this is it. It is also a scene that is significantly, if subtly, laden with the ideological and imagistic freight of the temperance movement. Let us begin by recalling that Utterson and Enfield walk *every* Sunday: "the two men put the greatest store by these excursions, counted them the chief jewel of each week, and not only set aside occasions of pleasure, but even resisted the calls of business, that they might enjoy them uninterrupted" (30). That passage, prominently set at the very beginning of the tale, stresses the way the cousins' set aside not only "business" but also "pleasure" for the sake of vigorous exercise on the Lord's Day. For Enfield, this involves a significant break from his undisclosed but perhaps questionable routine as a "well-known man about town" (29), as he instead keeps Sunday company with the very cousin whose fellowship other men actively seek when they want to "sober their minds" (43). For Utterson, the walks are also part of an altered Sabbath-day program that culminates in that self-denying evening at home, conspicuously attending to the church bells and reading "some dry divinity" before going "soberly to bed"—and therefore evidently having skipped his customary dose of "mortifying" gin (35). The aggregate picture, then, involves at the very least an enforced and regular Sunday abstinence from work-a-day labors *and* recreations—and arguably (given the implications of Enfield's reputation as a late-night bon vivant and the suggestive language associated with Utterson) from the specific "pleasures" of the bottle. In any case, the two men choose instead to "whip up the circulation" with a good walk prior to an evening of staid pieties. Jekyll, on the other hand, proves disinclined—and ultimately unable—to join them. What might these facts reveal about the social realities on which Stevenson and his Brownies may have been drawing? And how might the novella's original readers have taken this creatively central scene?

The first thing to treat is the insistently rendered (and repeated) Sunday setting. The Sabbath had obviously long been a day for altered routines, but it was perhaps especially so in Victorian Britain. The venerable British Lord's Day Observance Society (L.D.O.S.) was founded in 1831, significantly the same decade that Joseph Livesey and his Preston colleagues gave new focus and drive to the campaign against drink (Wigley 34). The organization's titular charge, as articulated by spokesmen like Sir Andrew Agnew, M.P. from Wigtonshire, was essentially to encourage Britons to spend their Sundays like Utterson and Enfield, both "resisting the calls of business" and "setting aside occasions of pleasure" (at least pleasures of the "undignified" sort to which Jekyll confesses he is so partial). Stevenson's London itself subtly reflects Sabbath-day traditions and perhaps the impact of the movement. "On Sunday," we are told early on, Jekyll's distinctly commercial neighborhood "veiled its more florid charms and lay comparatively empty of passage" (30); and when the cousins leave Jekyll behind the hastily slammed window, they find only "*some* stirrings of life" in the neighboring thoroughfare (61; emphasis added).

L.D.O.S. "Sabbatarians" like Agnew and temperance campaigners such as Livesey weren't always in perfect lock-step, since some of the dry "counter-attractions" to alcohol that drink reformers wished to offer on what had long been the biggest drinking day of the week were deemed inappropriate by the pious Sir Andrew and company. As late as 1884, controversy over whether or not to open a reading room on Sundays was sufficiently divisive to split the ranks of a mechanics' institute (Wigley 1). And whether or not to allow the British Museum to open on Sundays— the exhaustingly persistent issue that inspired that 1880 *Punch* cartoon on "Dark vs. Bright Monday"— divided the House of Lords right down the middle five years later (Wigley 142). The Lord Chancellor voted with the closers, and as a result Sunday museum openings were effectively delayed until 1896 (Bailey 93). Sabbatarian and temperance forces were nevertheless firmly united on two related issues: limiting liquor sales on Sunday, and providing for adequate recreational space and activity in locations other than pubs.

Predictably, legislators felt safer ordaining Sunday closing in the hinterlands than in the Home Counties. The Forbes-Mackenzie Act of 1845 prohibited Sunday sales of liquor in Scotland, effectively reducing instances of Sabbath-day drunkenness in Edinburgh by thirty- to forty-per-cent over a two-year period and thereby cutting sharply into the "drunken brawls" that David Lewis found to be such a profound grievance on the Hibernian Lord's day (Longmate 159; Lewis, *The Drink Problem* 187; Lewis, *The Drink Traffic* 81–2). Wales eventually got a Sunday Closing Act as well, in 1881 (Harrison, *Drink* 254). As for London, the Metropolitan Police Act of 1839 had closed all licensed premises within fifteen miles of Charing Cross from midnight Saturday until Sunday afternoon at 1, with further curtailments and modifications being imposed in 1854, 1864, 1872, and 1874 (Longmate 159; Harrison, *Drink* 280; Girouard 14). But, as we've already seen, when Lord Grosvenor's Sunday Trading Bill of the following year was widely if erroneously construed to propose Sunday closing, all hell broke loose. Evidently not everyone in the city was content to be an Utterson.

Ironically, the Sunday Trading Riots of 1855 took place in one of the very same public venues that sabbatarians and temperance advocates alike thought were absolutely necessary to encourage Sunday sobriety — Hyde Park. As early as 1834, James Silk Buckingham had advocated a massive public works program, "to draw off by innocent and pleasurable recreation and instruction, all who can be weaned from habits of drinking." That year's Select Committee on Drunkenness accordingly mandated "the establishment by the joint aid of government and the local authorities and residents on the spot, of public walks, and gardens, or open spaces for healthy and athletic exercises in the open air, in the immediate vicinity of every town" (Bailey 58, 50.) Continental visitors like Montesquieu and Hippolyte Taine had long attributed the Britons' stereotypical affection for cozy pubs to their beastly insular climate, but the twin effects of land enclosure and the rapid, un-orchestrated development of the industrial city were seen as additional culprits, depriving people of the open space that they needed for wholesome, outdoor recreation. "When the village maypole fell, and the commons were inclosed [*sic*]," lamented one British radical, "the fiend, intemperance, was ushered into birth" (Harrison, *Drink* 48). No less a moral authority than John Ruskin notably concurred, admitting *this* to members of a working class that had for half a century effectively been trampled by "The March of Bricks and Mortar" lampooned in Cruikshank's "London Going out of Town" (1829): "if I were in your place, I should drink myself to death in six months, because I had nothing to amuse me" (Harrison, *Drink* 322). Reformers like Buckingham, Joseph Livesey, Joseph Strutt, and Octavia Hill pushed hard to make amends. In London, Regent's Park was opened to the public in 1841, with the *Times* avidly commending this move towards "the redemption of the working class through recreation" (Bailey 63). Towards the same ends, Primrose Hill, Victoria Park, Battersea Park, and the Embankment were all successfully established in the mid-century, augmented by the preservation initiatives of the Metropolitan Commons Act of 1866 (Harrison, *Drink* 322–3). The same thinking that led Lord Hill to mandate in 1841 the establishment of cricket grounds near every military barracks in the kingdom led Octavia Hill's Open Space Movement of the 1870s to provide for "the common man's need for healthy outdoor sports" (Bailey 202, 145). And in addition to luring potential drinkers from the pub and fostering the hallowed Victorian *mens sana in corpore sano,* taking a Sunday walk in a public park or garden became a symbol of the civilizing process itself. "A man walking out with his family among his neighbors of different ranks," argued Robert Slaney, M.P., "will naturally be desirous to be properly clothed; ... [and] this desire duly directed and controlled, is found by experience to be of the most powerful effect in promoting Civilisation and exciting industry" (Bailey 53). One potent means of enlightenment for "Darkest England," then, was a good stroll along The Serpentine. That a good portion of new East End park furniture calculatedly bore images and messages of temperance and godliness closed the ideological circle with unmistakable emphasis (Malchow 122–3).

So, when Utterson and Enfield are engaged in their Sunday walkabout, they are duly enacting the sabbatarian blend of sobriety and vigorous outdoor activity that was a particular wont of the Victorian middle-class (Wigley 183).[5] Very significantly, when Jekyll responds to the murder of Carew by re-doubling his charitable activities, turning at last to "religion," and totally abstaining from his potion for two month's time, we are told that "he was much in the open air" (56). "Now that the evil influence had been withdrawn," the narrator avers a few sentences earlier, "a new life began for Dr. Jekyll"— almost as though Hyde were himself the "influencing" draught salubriously "with*drawn*" and Jekyll were born again into a temperate new self-discipline.[6] Conversely, when Jekyll later refuses to join Utterson and Enfield on a subsequent salutary outing, he shuts himself back inside the unhealthy world of his intemperance (regardless of how one defines it) as definitively as if the window he closes were the frosted glass "snob screen" that afforded wealthier drinkers their desired privacy — and thus a hypocritical "respectability"— in the pubs of 1880s London (Girouard 60–4). It may be no accident that the way to the laboratory from Jekyll's house passes through "a yard which had *once* been a garden" (18; emphasis added). The doctor is finally no more interested in the health of his civilized soul than he is in a healthy diet of greens.

"You sit too much indoors," complains Utterson. Jekyll's cloistered existence — his "disconsolate imprisonment" — is nicely accentuated by the tight and clammy confines in which the interview takes place. "The court was very cool and a little damp, and full of premature twilight." The sky, bright with sunlight, is admittedly visible, but it is "high up overhead," as out of reach to Jekyll at the moment as the "sweet spring odours" he later enjoys in Regent's Park (92). Again, the text is fraught with ideological potential, however consciously or unconsciously Stevenson may have implanted it. When the Metropolitan Public Gardens Association was founded in 1882, it drew upon an argument for open space that took as a given the inadequacy of London housing. Parks, the founders urged, "cleanse cities by opening them to purifying sunlight and air, dissipating the airborne contagion" associated with cholera. In addition to affording an escape from pub culture and an exposure to the example of the respectable classes, parks and gardens were "more easily policed than the warren-like back courts and dark alleys of the impacted slum" (Malchow 98). But if parks afforded a kind of remedy for the blight of alcohol and the blight of poor housing alike, was there perhaps a causal link between the two things being remedied?

There was generally felt to be, indeed, although cause and effect were hotly contested. With between £125 and £140 million a year reckoned to have been spent on drink in Britain in 1880, by contemporary estimates (Mitchell 28; Lawson 405), most people assumed that drink effectively destroyed housing as a direct result of this massive diversion of resources. "Let the missionaries go where hard drinkers reside," asserted Joseph Livesey in the 1830s; "Dirty doorsteps, broken windows and other indications of the effects of drink will not be long to seek" (Longmate 44). Drink "leads to the bad home rather than the bad home ... to the drink," a Church of England temperance man continued to argue in the 1880s (Gutzke 37). "Wherever a home is found in wretched condition, and unwholesome owing to squalor and filth, in 99 out of 100 the cause is the use of alcoholic liquors," David Lewis resoundingly agreed in the very year that *J&H* was written (*The Drink Traffic* 90). The most influential evocation of the position was undoubtedly George Cruikshank's famous print sequence from 1847, *The Bottle*. Of the eight images in the series, six show the sitting room of the respectable middle-class man who succumbs to drink. Plate One's well-furnished abode of a happy and healthy family visibly decays throughout the sequence, in pace with the man's physical and moral degradation, as its furnishings are pawned, its utensils are broken, and its plaster cracks and then falls off the laths. When Charles Dickens reviewed his friend's artistic sequel, *The Drunkard's Children*, however, the great author took the other side of the causal debate: "Drunkenness, as a natural horror, is the effect of many causes. Foul smells, disgusting habitations, bad workshops and workshop customs, want of light, air, and water, the absence of all easy means of decency and health, are commonest among its common, everyday, physical causes" ("The Drunkard's Children" 104). Dickens' thinking was broadly enough shared that extensive mid-century efforts to improve housing throughout Britain were widely heralded as crucial temperance initiatives (Harrison, *Drink* 320). Close to the year in which *J&H* was composed, Andrew Mearns of the London Congregational Union concurred, asking of the myriad dwellers in the "rotten and reeking tenement houses" in "Outcast London," "Who can wonder that the public house is 'the Elysian field of the tired toiler?'" (*Bitter Cry* [1883] 50–61).

Regardless of one's feelings about cause and effect, however, drink and decayed housing were seen to be irrevocably bound together, invariable concomitants to each other. As we've noted, the reformist image "Which Way Shall I Turn Me?" associates domestic comfort with the teetotaler and domestic chaos with the drunkard. Thomas and Harry in Plate Four of the *Temperance Intelligencer*'s "Temperance and Intemperance" are shown living respectively in "Domestic Happiness" and "Domestic Misery," with the rooms and furniture to match (21 March 1840 [1]). James Greenwood describes among the "curses of London" a relapsed drinker "laid in a bed of straw" in "such a home as none but the drunkard could inhabit" (221), while the imperiled home became, quite predictably, an absolute cliché of temperance drama (M. Booth 206–7). In sum, when the Royal Commission on the Housing of the Working Classes pursued its reforming ends in the two years preceding *J&H*'s publication, one of the group's prime operating assumptions was that alcohol and urban decay invariably went hand in hand (Ledger and Luckhurst 50). Accordingly, as we have seen and as we shall soon expand upon, Hyde's Soho digs are square in the middle of an entropic "city in a nightmare" filled with "embattled vapours," "muddy ways," "dingy streets," and what one must assume are negligent mothers off to the "gin palace" for "a morning glass" (48).

Fictive or real, the century's stereotypical sots almost invariably looked back with fumy nostalgia on the comfortable digs they had actually *lost* through drink. Dickens' archetypal drunkard "thought of the time when he had a home—a happy, cheerful home" ("The Drunkard's Death" 492). Reformer David Lewis recalls "the many cases where the occupants of commodious and comfortable dwellings have in consequence of their drinking habits been compelled to herd with the denizens of the slums, as the penalty of their improvidence and dissipation" (*The Drink Problem* 131.) Conversely, the reformed drinker's dream was to own a comfortable home: Thomas Whittaker delighted in telling the tale of a certain "man in the west" who saved enough money from four and a half years of abstinence to build himself a cottage (*Brighter England* 55). For a century that had increasingly come to see drink as a problem of the lower classes, to possess a respectable house was not only a tangible reward for overcoming a debilitating habit but also a symbolic mark of social recovery or advancement. Once safely on the wagon, Whittaker confessed, "the home that had satisfied my wants as a drinker was not in harmony with my self-respect as a teetotaler, and I soon put myself in possession of a house rented at twelve pounds a year" (*Life's Battles* 66). In fact, more than one temperance reformer sought to redirect into this kind of domestic materialism the male competitiveness that otherwise all too often fuelled the drinking contests and violence of the pub (Harrison, *Drink* 321). Albeit with tongue in cheek, Stevenson's own poem "On Himself" registers something of this concern for domestic status, set against the implicit assumption that drink and residential luxury are mutually incompatible: "He may have been ... a drunkard," reads the poem, but (just like Jekyll) "at least he kept a butler" (*Collected Poems* 354).

We might thus consider reading the damp, dark, sun-deprived nature of Jekyll's court with a reasonable eye to this ideological association of drink, poor hygiene, and domestic decay. In the very year *J&H* was written, David Lewis complained, "our great scheme of city improvement, while undoubtedly conferring very great benefits ... by the demolition of unhealthy tenements, thus letting in light and air, has been rendered almost nugatory ... by the prevalence of intemperance" (*The Drink Traffic* 91). It is literally Jekyll's intemperate addiction to his drug that accounts for his unwillingness to let his friends come into his house; and when he excuses himself from asking them in by claiming "the place is really not fit," he not only explicitly keeps at bay some potentially problematic witnesses to his condition but he also at least hints at his being one of those stereotypical addicts who can't keep their domestic space in any better order than they keep their moral houses.

Of course, parts of Jekyll's accommodations are admittedly top-drawer. His door on the square—*the* way in for the moderate wine-drinking gentlemen of his professional acquaintance—wears a "great air of wealth and comfort"; and Utterson, when he first calls, is shown into a "large, low-roofed, comfortable hall, paved with flags, warmed (after the fashion of a country house) by a bright open fire, and furnished with costly cabinets of oak"—"the pleasantest room in London," according to Utterson (41). But the other half of this very property, in addition to the fetid, ill-ventilated court, is "a sinister block of building" that,

> showed no window, nothing but a door on the lower storey and a blind forehead of discoloured wall on the upper; and bore in every feature the marks of prolonged and sordid negligence. The door, which was equipped with neither bell nor knocker, was blistered and distained [30].

That this—distinctively *Hyde's* entrance (32)—could for contemporary readers be one the "dirty doorsteps" that for Livesey almost infallibly signal "the effects of drink" is confirmed when we recall that the tramps and malingering children who huddle in its recess are effectively mirrored in the novella's explicitly gin-soaked Soho scene.

When it comes to Jekyll's various residences, in fact, everywhere we look there's a half-refined but half-degraded quality that reflects not only his personal "double being" but also (now that we've heard from Dickens and Lewis) the relative sobriety and relative inebriation of his two "halves." We've seen it in his house—in the two "wings" and entrances. He also lives in a symbolic "neighborhood in transition": "Round the corner from the by-street," we are told, "there was a square of ancient, handsome houses, now for the most part decayed from their high estate, and let in flats and chambers, to all sorts and conditions of men: map-engravers, architects, shady lawyers, and the agents of obscure enterprises. One house, however, second from the corner, was still occupied entire ... [and] wore a great air of wealth and comfort" (40). As Jekyll's court-yard window is "half-way open" when his friends come to call—only to close all the way when he reverts to Hyde—so his neighborhood is poised halfway between "high estate" and debased "obscure enterprises," and it is clearly headed in the very same direction as Utterson's "down-going men." A number of things might admittedly bring on this kind of urban blight. As Cruikshank teamed with Dickens to attest, however, the stereotypical cause of this kind of urban decay for the late–Victorians was drink. Thus David Lewis again reports the shameful way that "good houses have been subdivided" (like most of the other buildings on Jekyll's square), "and thus become over-crowded, and the worst evils of former years have been reproduced in dilapidation, squalor, and filth, due, I have no hesitation in saying, to the improvidence of the tenants and the curse of intemperance" (*The Drink Traffic* 91). Jekyll's neighborhood is going down just the way he is—with houses and men alike giving shelter now to multiple and debased characters—both of them arguably destroyed by the predations of "the glass." The tenuous hold that his own house still maintains on elegance and propriety is simply a measure of how far he has yet to fall.

A variation on the same duality obtains in what is more properly Hyde's neighborhood, Soho. The area is clearly represented in the novella as the same low enclave of drunken savagery that Stevenson recalled it as being when he wrote *The South Seas*. Precinct of "gin palaces" and sluttish tipplers, it shares the same "hues of twilight" as Jekyll's court—vapour-filled, fog-bound, criss-crossed by "muddy ways" and "slatternly passengers"—once again "like a district in some city in a nightmare" (48). If ever there was an area that Livesey or Lewis or Whittaker would say was blighted by drink, this is it. Yet when we enter Hyde's rooms, we rather anomalously discover they are "furnished with luxury and good taste" (49). Stevenson virtually reproduces the effect he created in Jekyll's square: a neighborhood blighted by "obscure enterprises" and entropic forces, among them drink (explicitly present in Soho if only implicit on the other side of Regent Street); but within that neighborhood, we find a little sanctuary of refinement and good taste. In both cases there seems to be a "Hyde space" surrounding a "Jekyll space." Although this neatly and somewhat curiously reverses the notion that Hyde is the "animal within" and Jekyll the surrounding "cavern" (89) or "mantle" (86) within which Hyde "hides," it perfectly captures the all-encompassing threat that the "insurgent horror" (95) represents for the doctor. It's as though that tidy little store of wine and its neat surroundings represent the potential for drink to be handled in a moderate and orderly way, as by Utterson and Guest—and even perhaps by Hyde.

But then the roof caves in. Given what Hyde has been up to, given what his blood-red liquor has inspired him to do, the place in Soho starts looking like a plate from *The Bottle*: "At this moment, however," we are told about Utterson's entry, "the rooms bore every mark of having been recently and hurriedly ransacked; clothes lay about the floor, with their pockets inside out; lockfast drawers stood open; and on the hearth there lay a pile of gray ashes, as though many papers had been burned. From these embers the inspector disinterred the butt end of a green cheque book, which had resisted the action of the fire; the other half of the stick was found behind the door" (49). Like so many other things in the novella, the scene is over-determined. In the simple terms of the plot, Hyde is evidently trying to cover his tracks, however ineffectually. But, if we attend to deeper themes, he is also treating his digs as destructively as Cruikshank would hold that an alcoholic inevitably does—and as the lethally besotted pirates intriguingly do to the *Hispaniola's* cabin and the stockade alike in Stevenson's own *Treasure Island*.[7] The burnt cheque book and broken walking stick may be seen to represent, in turn, the financial ruin and loss of "balance" that alcoholism also entails. It's no accident that the cane had been Utterson's gift to Jekyll (48). It effectively represents the temperate civility that he and Enfield manifest every Sunday in their vigorous walks. Jekyll refuses to join them because the quintessentially intemperate Hyde has literally and figuratively broken the walking stick

Lanyon notes "the odd subjective disturbance caused by [Hyde's] *neighborhood*" (77; emphasis added). In a curious way that many temperance men would surely have recognized, his story is in part not just the story of Hyde's troubling "proximity" or "nearness" but also the tale of "neighborhoods" themselves "disturbed" by the ruinous forces he epitomizes (as we'll shortly further explore). But then neighborhoods, of course, are made up of individual homes. And when, in a climactic spontaneous reversion to Hyde, the changing Jekyll looks down and sees that "the hand that lay on my knee was corded and hairy" (92), his first thought is this: "I was once more Edward Hyde. A moment before I had been safe of all men's respect, wealthy, beloved—the cloth laying before me in the dining-room at home; and now I was the common quarry of mankind, hunted, *houseless*, a known murderer, thrall to the gallows" (92–3; emphasis added). The passage is full of reasons to feel anguish and remorse, but the most insistent emphasis may well be on the loss of social status and the attendant comforts of the home. Hyde has destroyed Jekyll's domestic security, and he significantly finds himself, like the stereotypical Victorian drunkard, "homeless."

In sum, if Stevenson's "powder scene" strongly recalls the atavistic "brutalization" which many late–Victorians deemed the most common bane of excessive drinking, the complementary "window" scene offers its own more fleeting glimpse of the novella's concern with strong drink and its sociological (as well as psychological) effects. If the central image of men in the street confronting the dual-natured protagonist was what the Brownies gave to Stevenson, many of his "finishing touches"—the dank court, the invitation to stroll, the "unfitness" of the rooms within the surrounding decay of his neighborhood — may be seen as bound together most logically by the abiding concern with alcohol that we've seen throughout the text. Utterson, neatly and consistently characterized as a moderate drinker, appropriately balances his week-day indulgences with a Sunday program of outdoor exertion — to be followed by those pious evening readings we have earlier discussed. Jekyll, in contrast, remains ensconced in his unwholesome and partially-decaying digs, the victim of an addiction he is unable to subdue even on the Sabbath. Despite the lawyer's solicitousness as so generously displayed in Jekyll's dark court, he proves once again and with his oldest friend that he is finally little more to the doctor than "the last good influence in the lives of down-going men" (29). Directly before this chapter, we read of Utterson's understandable but rather disillusioning relief when, showing up to visit with Jekyll, he is turned away at the door: "Perhaps in his heart, he preferred to speak with Poole upon the doorstep, and surrounded by the air and sounds of the open city, rather than be admitted to that house of voluntary bondage" (59). Utterson *is*, for all his love of drink, most regularly a temperate man of the open air and city. But if, like the vigorous reformers of his age, he extends what he hopes will be a salutary hand of invitation to his failing compatriot, Jekyll is unable to grasp it. "Like some disconsolate prisoner," indeed, he remains helplessly trussed up in his house and in his habits — in ways that will have reminded some of Stevenson's original readers of a struggling but inveterate dipsomaniac.[8]

NINE

"Street Crime"

If the two scenes which made up the original, "dream-scripted" imaginative core of *J&H* are laden with the ideas and concerns of the temperance movement, so also are the two major "crimes" that we see Hyde commit. The first is, to be sure, less overtly criminal than the second: it involves what is apparently an inadvertent collision between two late-night pedestrians, "one a little man who was stumping along eastward at a good walk, and the other a girl of maybe eight or ten who was running as hard as she was able down a cross-street." "Well, sir," says Enfield in reporting the incident, "the two ran into one another naturally enough at the corner" (31). This is nothing like the brutal and intentional clubbing of Sir Danvers Carew which occurs later in the text. Enfield in fact allows that "It sounds nothing to hear," even though "it was hellish to see" (31). Then, to substantiate just how hellish it actually was, he adds this: "It wasn't like a man; it was like some damned Juggernaut."

This orientalist embellishment achieves its desired rhetorical effect: the image of the "Juggernaut" that is Mr. Hyde becomes an obsession for Utterson. He's unable to sleep that night because "Mr. Enfield's tale went by before his mind in a scroll of lighted pictures. He would be aware of the great field of lamps of a nocturnal city; then the figure of a man walking swiftly; then of a child running from the doctor's; and then these met, and that human Juggernaut trod the child down and passed on regardless of her screams" (37). Then, almost immediately, we're told again that, "if at any time [Utterson] dozed over, it was but to see [the figure of Hyde] glide more stealthily through sleeping houses, or move the more swiftly, and still the more swiftly, even to dizziness, through wider labyrinths of lamp-lighted city, and at every corner crush a child and leave her screaming" (37). If the image of the child-crushing "Juggernaut" obsesses Utterson, it clearly drove Stevenson as well, sufficiently for him to add the image to Enfield's original, "little man" account when he undertook his revisions in the Printer's Copy. In what had been the penultimate draft, the word "Juggernaut" was used only *once*—and appears to leap directly from Utterson's own imagination, rather than taking potent root there after having been planted by his cousin's appalled, initial description (Veeder, *Manuscript* 15). What might account for the enhanced prominence that is thereby given to the image?

Part of the answer lies in the initial passage itself. Mentioning the "Juggernaut" is in fact the second thing Utterson does to explain the horror of what he's seen. After describing the two pedestrians colliding "naturally enough at the corner," he says, "then came the horrible part of the thing; for the man trampled calmly over the child's body and left her screaming on the ground." It's not the fact of the violent collision that is "horrible"; it's that the unintentional collision becomes a "calm trampling" over the child's body, with Hyde impervious to the child's distress. He simply "left her screaming on the ground." The other people who are on the scene—or who come to be there—all react with appropriate human emotions: Enfield pursues and collars Hyde; the doctor, although he's said to be "about as emotional as a bagpipe," "turn[s] sick and white with the desire to kill him"; and, although the men are "pitching in red hot," the women manage to outdo them, "for they were as wild as harpies." Hyde, on the other hand, "was perfectly cool." "It wasn't like a man; it was like some Juggernaut," says Utterson, anticipating Jekyll's pronominal trickery and, in the process, de-humanizing Hyde to the state of an "it." Human beings feel the appropriate human emotions, among the most powerful and important of them being protectiveness for children. Yet Hyde has no more fellow-feeling, Enfield concludes, than the inanimate, processional death-chariot of an un–Christian Eastern religion, crushing the bodies of hapless devotees beneath its mindless wheels.

One might be tempted to read the scene as an example of a drunkard "walking under the influence," un-reactive to the child's screams because of the "brutish physical insensibility" that the novella attributes to Jekyll's intoxicated other half (90). The image would literalize a term Stevenson used in *Treasure Island*, when Jim Hawkins describes the drunken Billy Bones—terror to all the denizens of the Admiral Benbow Inn—as "the most *overriding* companion ever known" (5; added italics). Valerie Martin's brilliant redaction of *J&H* in her novel *Mary Reilly* in fact begins with just such a scene of brutish, drunken child abuse, offered in clear, formal parallel to the novella's own opening pages. After Martin's young Mary has committed the unpardonable sin of breaking a tea-cup, her inebriated father locks her under the dark stairs, tossing a loosely-bagged rat in there with her for good measure. As for Stevenson's century, although Britain's young were admittedly the literal poster-children for any number of liberal social causes—from labor reform to initiatives against prostitution to the expansion of the ragged schools—they were throughout the nineteenth century among the most frequently cited and poignantly bemoaned victims of drink. "Little children, guiltless of sin, are crying for bread," observes Dr. Kate Mitchell, "and yet every year we spend nearly double upon intoxicating liquors that we do upon the staff of life" (233). Or an Essex magistrate documents the sad case of a man who took his four-year-old to the beer-shop and turned him into a capital resource: "The wife went to look for him and found the man drunk and the child stripped of his clothes" (Longmate 30). The moral implicit of either account could just as well be drawn from Stevenson's own portrait of the neglected children of Soho, loitering in rags in the murky streets while their mothers trudge off "for a morning glass."

Children were themselves believed to be terribly prone to getting caught up in the crushing toils of drink. "Neglected by their parents, educated only in the streets and falling into the hands of wretches who live upon the vices of others," reads the first plate of Cruikshank's *The Drunkard's Children*, "they are led to the gin shop to drink at that fountain which nourishes every species of crime" (Feaver 56). Moreover, parental "neglect" could be active as well as passive: Andrew Mearns observes in 1883 of London's imperiled children, "Many of them are taken by the hand or carried in the arms to the gin-palace, and not seldom may you see mothers urging and compelling their tender infants to drink the fiery liquid" ("The Bitter Cry" 62). John Dunlop had lamented years earlier that, owing to the pernicious and widespread social rites of drink, "many ... children are now gone in firm and hardened habits of adult drunkenness" (317). And, returning to the decade of *J&H*, Kate Mitchell cites fellow doctor Moore Madden, who tells the shocking tale of "a little girl five and a half years old, brought in suffering from acute meningitis, the result of a savage blow in the head inflicted some time previously by her drunken mother. During her ravings in the course of the disease, and even during her convalescence, this poor child babbled repeatedly, and craved earnestly, in her own words, 'for a drink of porter from the gallon'" (134). While Stevenson's Jim Hawkins and David Balfour drink moderately, *The Covenant*'s rascal cabin boy in *Kidnapped*, young Ransome, is in fact a notorious tippler, and accordingly suffers a fate more dire than Dr. Madden's poor little girl—beaten to death by the drunken navigator, Mr. Shuan (40, 49, 53).

To return to the particulars of the passage at hand, children were repeatedly seen, in fiction and the popular press alike, as the victims of accidents caused in one way or another by drink. Drunken Hindley Earnshaw drops baby Hareton over the balustrade in *Wuthering Heights*. And *The Birmingham Mail* reported that "In the course of a year, hundreds of accidents occur to young children ... engaged in fetching beer for ... their parents. Sometimes they are knocked down in crossing the horse-roads, but generally the accident is caused by the youngsters falling with jugs and bottles in their hands" (Longmate 238). In any case, Stevenson evidently wanted the child to figure throughout the novella as much as he wanted the Juggernaut. He actually emended the Notebook Draft in order to get her into Jekyll's "Full Statement," re-writing his earlier, cursory account of some unspecified, impersonal, late-night altercation—"detected in an act of infamy," Jekyll confesses rather generically, "I had to bribe a party of young fools to set me free"—in order to give us the fuller, and more fully "casted," melodramatic vignette we now have (Veeder, "Texts" 7).[1] *Whatever* the girl is there to be the victim of, Stevenson very much wanted her as part of the tale.

Aside from the fact that Hyde is knocking about town at 3 A.M., there's nothing in the scene to suggest that he is literally intoxicated. His manner is "cool" and controlled, and when Enfield and the doctor threaten him with scandal unless he pays up to the girl's family, he answers with the kind of measured eloquence Myers found so unlikely in a "lowered" character: "'If you choose to make capital of this accident ... I am naturally helpless. No gentleman but wishes to avoid a scene'" (32). One might, to be sure, cite Norman Kerr and his nearly contemporary observation on the difficulty of telling when some men are inebriated. He cites the case of a barrister who, "when actually drunk ... seemed to be more sober than when he had not been drinking. In his cups, when so drunk that he could with difficulty stand upright, his tongue moved more slowly, his speech became more deliberate, his argument more lucid and well weighed" (148). Recall in support of this kind of linguistic oddity Jim Hawkins's observation that Israel Hands became unexpectedly eloquent in the throes of drink (*Treasure Island* 144). Yet if Stevenson had consciously intended to represent Hyde's inebriation here, it's doubtful he would have done so by endowing the man with the felicity of expression that Kerr and Jim are *surprised* to find in a drunkard. A better alternative — and one that reflects the contemporary iconography of the "Juggernaut" that we shall soon explore — is to see him not narrowly as a virtual drunkard but rather more broadly as a man *of* drink. Beyond all of the suggestive language, and action, and associations that we've examined in previous chapters, Hyde may in fact be characterized in this scene with a consequential — if not necessarily a calculated — eye towards the thoughtless, impersonal, and crushing impact that the general liquor trade was seen by the temperance movement to have had on the people of Britain, adults and children alike. If the scene basically constitutes an odd sort of traffic accident, the "traffic" most consequentially in Stevenson's or his Brownies' sights may have been the "drink traffic" that found its way into the long title of the United Kingdom Alliance ("for the Suppression of the Traffic in all Intoxicating Liquors") and that also gave David Lewis the title of the book he published in London the year *J&H* was written — *The Drink Traffic*. Dickens captured with memorable vividness the *literal* scene of the capital's late-night streets flowing with their diurnal supply of liquor: "The gaslit public-houses are the first shops to open in the darkness before dawn.... From Southwark the great brewers' drays begin to rumble over the bridges; the quayside wharves and warehouses are awake, where the kegs and barrels and hogsheads wait, of gin and rum and wine. The essential London, that feeds and gives drink to the whole, wakes and works long before the rest, getting ready for another day" (Hewett 4). Thomas Whittaker, recalling dark years between Gladstone's reforming Liberal governments, significantly translates Dickens' literal image into a morally-charged metaphor of *physical* peril: "Those were the days when the whole nation was dragged at the tail end of the brewer's dray" (*Brighter England* 144). "The liquor traffic never sleeps," Lewis goes on to say, "but is ever uniform and persistent in its operations" (*Drink Traffic* 25). Just like Hyde, it's up all night and it slows its pace for no one.[2]

Some fifty years before Hyde, however, "drink traffic" had been likened to something else, equivalently wheeled and dangerous but even more suggestive for a deep understanding of Stevenson's first street crime. When in 1833 Sir Andrew Agnew introduced a bill in parliament to restrict

Sunday labor, George Cruikshank was outraged that the servants of the rich were to be exempted from the relief offered by the proposed bans. He persuaded John Wight to write up his arguments in a pamphlet that he himself would then illustrate, the result being *Sunday in London* (Patten 374–5). When he came to the relevant subject of gin, Wight called it a "giant demi-god." "Jaggernaut [*sic*] is but a fool to him!—for the devotees of Jaggernaut do but put themselves in the way of being crushed to death beneath his chariot wheel, and are put out of their misery at once; but devotees of the Great Spirit Gin devote themselves to lingering misery" (Patten 380–81).

Wight's image was translated by Cruikshank into a striking etching published in 1835 in *My Sketch Book* (Figure 1). No less prominent a cultural commentator than William Makepeace Thackeray subsequently described the piece in his essay "On the Genius of George Cruikshank," published in J. S. Mill's widely-read *Westminster Review* in August of 1840:

> Gin has furnished many subjects to Mr. Cruikshank, who labours in his own sound and hearty way to teach his countrymen the dangers of that drink. In the *Sketch Book* is a plate upon the subject; it is called the 'Gin Juggernaut,' and represents a hideous moving palace, with a reeking still at the roof and vast gin-barrels for wheels, under which unhappy villains are crushed to death. An immense black cloud of desolation covers over the country through which the gin monster has passed, clearly looming through the darkness whereof you see an agreeable prospect of gibbets with men dangling, burnt houses, &c. The vast cloud comes sweeping on in the wake of this *horrible body-crusher*; and you see, by way of contrast, a distant, smiling, sunshiny tract of old English country, where gin as yet is not known. The allegory is as good, as earnest, and as fanciful as one of John Bunyan's, and we have often fancied there was a similarity between the men [Wardropper 55–6; italics added].

The picture and description are certainly striking, and could perfectly well have given Stevenson not only the image of the "Juggernaut" (so in Thackeray; Wight has "Jaggernaut" and Cruikshank "Juggarnath") but also a prototype for the sooty fogs of Soho, the decayed housing in Jekyll's neighborhood, the "gallows" that Hyde so dreads, and even some of his wonted puns on "spirit": Gin is, after all, the image's "Great Spirit of the Age." And while the assault on Sir Danvers Carew is a rather different matter from the collision with the little girl, it's interesting to note that what begins as a clubbing ends up with Hyde, again, "trampling his victim

The Struggle.

THE ENGLISH JUGGERNAUT.

TEMPERANCE AND NATIONAL ECONOMY.

The prime cause of our distress I believe to be the *Corn Laws*. Among the foremost of the *secondary* causes, I place the mighty evil INTEMPERANCE. Drinking intoxicating liquors is not only the bane of thousands of families, but it is a great *national loss*; and *abstinence* from the same would be found, beyond all belief, a great *national benefit*. He that quietly abstains and persuades others to do so, is a much greater patriot than he who vociferates about liberty, and yet spends his time and money at the public house.

No. 22.

Figure 8 — "The English Juggernaut." From *The Struggle*, No. 22 (1842). Courtesy of the Beinecke Rare Book and Manuscript Library.

under foot" while "the body jumped upon the roadway" (47). Like the Gin Juggernath's, Hyde's terror is indiscriminate, all-over-running, "crushing" the "bodies" of young and old alike.

The trio of Wight, Cruikshank, and Thackeray evidently gave the Juggernaut metaphor sufficient currency that it spread into the popular temperance press as well. The reformist journal *The Struggle* (1842) works an interesting variation on the earlier "Gin" formula (see Figure 8). No longer a "hideous moving [gin] palace," "The English Juggernaut" has come to look more like a man, with a huge beer barrel for a body, a still for a [death's] head, bottles and punch bowls for arms and hands and feet, and port-, brandy-, rum-, and sherry-casks for legs. While he does sit on a gin barrel, this grim avatar of death has moved from being "the demigod *Gin*" to something closer to "The Drink Traffic" in *general*. We may recall Dickens' account of the way the "great brewers' drays begin to rumble over the bridges" and "the kegs and barrels and hogsheads wait, of gin and rum and wine." *The Struggle*'s villain has also taken in his humanoid form a significant step closer to looking like the "damned Juggernaut" that is Hyde — the somehow indeterminate "little man" who is nonetheless an "it" that actually "wasn't like a man."

Which if any of these possible inspirations for his own Juggernaut Stevenson might have known it is impossible to say. The general notoriety enjoyed by Cruikshank and Thackeray alike makes them more probable sources than Wight or *The Struggle*. If the argument isn't too arcane, it might conceivably be that the attention Stevenson pays to street lamps in all of his relevant "Juggernaut" passages gives a nod to Cruikshank, whose moving liquor palace sports two lanterns more than six feet high, by scale: "there was literally nothing to be seen but lamps," says Enfield (31), paving the way for Utterson's "great field of lamps of a nocturnal city" and the "wider labyrinths of lamp-lighted city" (37). Dickens' "Boz" sketch of "Gin Shops" documents the notorious "light and brilliancy" that characterized the stereotypical spirit shop: "its profusion of gaslights in richly gilt burners, is perfectly dazzling," he says (*Sketches*, Slater 1.183). Given that the lighting technology of drinking houses tended to keep well ahead of regular street lighting precisely in order to have the kind of "moth-attracting" economic impact that Dickens describes (Girouard 128), Stevenson's emphasis could in part signal his theme in a way that Cruikshank inspired. His own "Plea for Gas Lamps" (1878) mentions the "blinding glare" of a Paris bistro where "love and laughter and deifying wine abound" (423). Yet the argument seems a trifle precious. The anthropomorphic form of *The Struggle*'s Juggernaut is much more insistently present in the fictional scene's core image.

Stevenson may actually have known none of these texts or images, although it wouldn't be at all surprising to learn that he was familiar with the Cruikshank as a signal work by one of the century's most prominent popular artists. From the days when he and Alice Cunningham scanned *Punch* for amusing images to those when he showcased two purported Hogarths in the house at Vailima or wrote Baxter in 1893 of his "need" for some Thomas Rowlandson prints (*Letters* 8.289, 8.20), he had a lifelong passion for satirical drawings. This abiding taste was both consistently stimulated and professionally sharpened by Sidney Colvin, who was Slade Professor of Fine Art at Cambridge when Stevenson first met him and later became Curator of Prints and Drawings at the British Museum, where he made his rooms available for a meeting between his writer protégé and Thomas Hardy. But even if Stevenson didn't know "The Gin Juggernaut," his contemporaries regularly talked about drink in ways that could readily have inspired Stevenson to "re-invent the imagistic wheel" in this very way. As we've seen, before John Wight contrasts gin with "Jaggernaut," he calls strong drink a "great demi-god." The fact that Enfield's streets are "all lighted up as if for a procession" certainly paves the way for the specific procession of the idol of Krishna, but their also being "all as empty as a church" suggests the same broader sense of a "surrogate divinity" that we find in Wight.[3]

The image of Hyde as Juggernaut explicitly associates his thoughtless mayhem with the careless might of a god. What of the might of the drink traffic that is the tenor of Cruikshank's metaphor? The perception that brewers, especially, had become virtually all-powerful was commonplace by the decade in which *J&H* was written, and the impression was founded on some firm realities. The phenomenal growth of railways and the equally phenomenal growth of new, "national" breweries went hand in hand, affording men like Sir Arthur Bass the kind of power that *Punch* targets in that 1882 cartoon with its jokes about "The Beerage." One of the more nefarious developments, according to many social critics, was the "brewer barons'" calculated strategy of buying up retail premises and re-opening them in a variety of ways that ensured their beers would be the only ones sold (Girouard 18). After a modest start in the 1860s, the phenomenon gained pace through the '70s, and by the 1880s reached what were, for some, alarming proportions (Spiller 88; Gutzke 5). For all of the temperance movement's fervor and dedication, alcohol was a quintessential growth industry in late–Victorian Britain. As a representative example, William Hughes' Victoria Wine Company, founded in 1865, had by 1886 expanded to include 98 shops throughout England (Briggs 9). Public awareness of liquor's huge economic potential was such that, when Guinness first offered its stock as a limited company in 1887, its issue of £6 million in shares was twenty-eight times oversubscribed (Levy 211). If we couple this with a longstanding public conviction that brewers had always been thick with magistrates (Clark 264, 266), then Brian Harrison's evocation of the "nightmare opponent" that Gladstone and Lawson feared in the liquor trade becomes fairly compelling: "the great landowners, the legal system, the Anglican church, the London clubs, the armed services, the magistrates and the great London [and, we should add, Burton] brewers were constituents of a great Leviathan which obstructed social and political progress" (*Drink* 29). Speaking for himself, Lawson decries "an enormous government system for tempting the weak and the poor to courses which ruin them for the benefit of the rich and the strong" ("The Drink Difficulty" 416). David Lewis agreed: "The position of the drink traffic is established and defended by all the authority and force of Parliament; its strength consists on well nigh one million of the population being directly interested in its prosecution, while upwards of thirty million sterling are annually drawn from it in the shape of revenue; and its power of endurance is exhibited in its being able to bear up against all moral and religious agencies, however varied, formidable, and expansive" (*The Drink Traffic* 2–3). Imagine the impact "in the streets" of this sort of socio-economic construction, and it's actually hard to avoid Stevenson's image of a Juggernaut. As for its most poignant victims, because of the "satanic superstructure" of the drink trade," laments John Dunlop, "many more children are now gone in firm and hardened habits of adult drunkenness" (317)—crushed, one way or another, beneath the wheels or the anthropomorphized feet of the industry.

One of the more interesting voices in the temperance camp was, in fact, that of Frederick Charrington, scion of the famous brewing company and patron of a London ragged school. Leaving his family's Mile End brewery one night in 1873, he witnessed a drunken man knocking his wife into the gutter after she had asked him for money. When Charrington looked up at the sign board of the pub that the man had just left and he saw his own surname blazoned there in huge, gilt letters, he "realized in a moment the hypocrisy involved in his family's good works," gave up all his brewing income, and dedicated his life to alleviating East End poverty (Harrison, *Drink* 341). At a subsequent rally for school board candidates, when an active brewer rose to lament the fate of London's uneducated street-children, Charrington turned on him and his fellows and belabored *their* hypocrisy: "Why, it is you, Mr. Hoare, with your beer, and you, Mr. Buxton, and you, Sir Edmund Hay-Currie, with your gin, who are causing these wretched, ragged children to be roaming about our streets" (Harrison, *Drink* 341). The same man who had in 1882 distributed leaflets that showed angels and devils fighting for the souls of drinkers, Charrington was very much in the news in the year Stevenson wrote *J&H*, having been convicted of libel and slander in a much-publicized case involving his harassment of a music hall owner (Shiman 126). If Stevenson followed the story, he could have found (or confirmed) a number of the novella's themes in the principal's life history, not the least of them the spotlight on the hypocrisy involved when men (like Hoard and Buxton) who make a show of doing good nonetheless refuse to, as it were, "give up the house in Soho" (90). Of course, once Charrington witnessed the literal effect on the street of his wonted pursuits, he succeeded in turning his life around. Conversely, for all of his parallel determination to "redeem the past" (92), Jekyll ultimately fails.

"Leviathan," "satanic superstructure," "enormous government system," even that *Punch* cartoon of Sir Arthur Bass and "the Beerage" on bottle-back — any one of these could have gotten Stevenson or his Brownies to the image of Hyde as a "Juggernaut," had he never seen or heard of the specific images of Wight, Cruikshank, Thackeray, or *The Struggle*. In any case, that Hyde may stand as much as an allegorical type for an abstract socio-economic problem as a disguised version of Ferrier or Baxter or Stevenson is something that the text itself may suggest. Utterson repeatedly imagines the "Juggernaut" charging through the streets of London. Over and over he sees the child crushed. "And still the figure had no face by which he might know it; even in his dreams, it had no face, or one that baffled him and melted before his eyes; and thus it was that there sprang up and grew apace in the lawyer's mind a singularly strong, almost an inordinate, curiosity to behold the features of the real Mr Hyde" (37–8). The passage is curiously reminiscent of Stevenson's confession that he had long waited for a "vehicle" to convey the idea of "man's double being." But it also strongly suggests the way Hyde may go beyond simply representing the archetypal nasty drunkard to, in essence, give the "face" of allegorical embodiment to something as abstract as "the drink traffic," something that David Lewis rather suggestively referred to as "this enemy of God and men [that] rides rough-shod over the bodies and souls of [our] countrymen" (*The Drink Traffic* 109). Hyde, in other words, may in some ways give Alcohol (with that capital "A") "a local habitation and a name."

One final note before we leave this first "street crime" behind. After hearing from Enfield the grim "Story of the Door," Utterson lies restlessly in bed, reliving his cousin's account in a nightmarishly amplified way. After recounting the lawyer's imaginings of the way "that human Juggernaut trod the child down and passed on regardless of her screams," the narrative moves on to state that, "if at any time he dozed over, it was but to see it glide more stealthily through sleeping houses, or move the more swiftly, even to dizziness, through wider labyrinths of lamp-lighted city, *and at every street corner crush a child and leave her screaming*" (37; emphasis added). *If* one is prepared to see "Hyde the Juggernaut" as in part a figure for the drink trade (and one hopes that the case has been made to seem plausible), then the lurid reference to *multiple* crushings at multiple *corners* looms rather larger than it might otherwise seem to. Utterson hears about one accident at "*a* corner" and then he imagines it repeated, with compounded horror, "at *every* corner" in the city. In Stevenson's as in earlier times, of course, "corners" were largely infamous for one thing: they literally had "a corner" on drink. When liquor was to be encountered in the streets of Victorian Britain, it was with overwhelming frequency to be encountered at crossroads and corners. Two of the temperance images we've treated above, "Which Way Shall I Turn Me?" (Figure 4) and the illustration from Kirton's *Four Pillars of Temperance* (Figure 5), depict gin palaces that are clearly located at urban intersections. Following up on Charles Booth's contemporary observation that corners were favored locations for drinking houses (*Life and Labour* 224), Brian Harrison has determined of Booth's era that "of the 160 pubs in the area bounded by Bethnal Green Road / Commercial Street / Whitechapel Road / Cambridge Road, 131 [and that's a full 86% of them] were situated on corners or opposite road junctions" (*Pubs* 169). Thomas Whittaker accordingly speaks of "decent working men ... swept away into the corner dram-shop and nearest public house by passing influences" (*Life's Battles* 58). Kate Mitchell bewails "the dazzling gin-palace, rearing its mighty head at every corner" (28). And William Booth denounces the "flaming gin palace at each corner" (*Darkest England* (50). "The public house is ubiquitous," complains J. London as well in *The People of the Abyss*; "It flourishes at every corner" (Smith 373). But if the spokesmen of temperance decried the inevitability of the corner location for licensed houses, many with money and an eye to development counted on it. As London evolved in the second half of the century with more sense of advanced planning and control, builders almost invariably *put* a pub on a corner site if their plots included one (Girouard 39). As a result, reported the trade journal *Building News* in May of 1857, "All parts of the metropolis discover, *at every turn*, large buildings of splendid elevation fitted up in a style of grandeur, not to say elegance.... The *corner public* is radiant of gas, redolent of mahogany, and glittering in mirrors" (Girouard 36; emphasis added). Stevenson obviously knew the tradition and the value of the corner location. Thus, in "The Pavilion on the Links," the tiny town of Graden Wester boasts two main streets, "and, at the corner of these two, a very dark and cheerless tavern" (ML 157). Long John Silver's Spy-glass Tavern in *Treasure Island* is similarly situated with "a street on each side and an open door on both" (46). And when the man Wiltshire longs for the life of a tavern-keeper in *The Beach of Falesá*, he dreams about "the looks of [his] public, by a cant of a broad high-road like an avenue" (17)— "cant" meaning either "corner" or "angle." It would thus seem to be suggestive that Hyde's hit-and-run takes place at "cross streets"— or perhaps even that, on the most momentous night of his life when he first drinks the fateful potion, Jekyll should say that he "had come to the fatal cross roads" (45). The "patricidal" drift of some of the narrative surely suggests that Oedipus is on Stevenson's mind here (Veeder, "Children of the Night" 126). An even stronger sub-textual current, however, confirms that he will have seen an urban intersection as a perfect location for a collision between one of England's innocents and his own Gin Juggernaut. He certainly goes out of his way to put it "at the corner" in particular ways that he wouldn't have found in Sophocles. In his revision of the Printer's Copy, Stevenson in fact added the phrase "at the corner" following his original version of Enfield's statement, which simply read thus: "Well, sir, the two ran into one another naturally enough"— period (Veeder, *Drafts* 15). Coming as this minor addition does directly after "down a cross street," the sentence may seem in no grave need of clarification. Yet clarification Stevenson gave it, and in ways that may offer us the ghostly image of a gin palace — or at least of a gin palace's neighbor and client — haunting this "labyrinth of lamp-lighted city."

Turning now from Hyde's "misdemeanor" with the little girl to his capital crime against Sir Danvers Carew, the simple fact of Hyde's violent and largely unprovoked rage may be a telling clue that he stands for the effects of drink. Men as influential as George Cruikshank seem to have believed not only that alcohol made an inordinate number of men violent but also that there was scarcely any kind of crime, let alone violence, that *didn't* owe something to drink. "Fearful Quarrels, and Brutal Violence, Are Natural Consequences of the Frequent Use of the Bottle," reads Plate Six of *The Bottle*. "I challenge anyone," the artist later said, "to point out any teetotaler who has been committed for a brutal assault upon his wife, or for garotting, or picking pockets, or house robbery, or murder" (Patten 244). While Cruikshank's second position may have been relatively extreme, a remarkable number of Victorians agreed with the first. David Lewis claimed that the effect of 1830's Beer Act, "passed as it was in the interest of sobriety, was to open the flood-gates of intemperance and to deluge many cities and larger towns throughout England with violence and crimes of the most horrible and disgusting character." Nine out of every ten cases of violence in the kingdom, Lewis reported, were owing to drink (*The Drink Problem* 151; 113). Kate Mitchell thus called for the immediate establishment of counter-attractions "to the innumerable places where drink is sold and night brawls are a common occurrence" (253); John Dunlop documented the ease with which drink can turn "playful fellowship" to "deeds of blood" (320); and even John Stuart Mill conceded the way a substance that he believed men must be left free to consume could nonetheless excite them to do physical harm to others ("On Liberty" 90). During the half-decade in which *J&H* was conceived, Norman Kerr's *Inebriety*, which offers so many fleeting glimpses of Jekyll amongst its case studies of gentleman sots, accordingly describes a "type of inebriate" that is represented by "a highly educated gentleman of mature years" who "when under the excitement of alcohol, though of a peaceful disposition he exhibits marked pugnacity. He tries to fight 'tooth and nail' with everyone near him" (21–22). Within the Stevenson canon and ken, Hyde's lethal rage could just as well be the homicidal drunkenness of Israel Hands in *Treasure Island*, or of *Kidnapped*'s Mr. Shuan, or of the Gilbert Islanders in *The South Seas*, or of the trader Randall in *The Beach of Falesá*, or of Teddy Henley in Samoa.

If Stevenson's textual revisions specially signal the topicality of the "Juggernaut" scene, they do the same for Hyde's second "crime" as well. Hyde's victim in the early Notebook Draft had been a "Mr. Lemsome," someone whom Utterson had met in advance when he came to the lawyer "bleating for help under the most ignoble and deserved misfortunes," "a man of about twenty-eight, with a fine forehead and good features; anoemically pale; shading a pair of suffering eyes under blue spectacles; and dressed with that sort of outward decency that implies both the lack of means and a defect of taste. By his own confession, Mr. Utterson knew him to be a bad fellow ... an incurable cad" (Veeder, "Texts" 8). The first thing Stevenson gained by replacing Lemsome with Sir Danvers Carew was to make Hyde's crime all the more dark. Instead of killing an "incurable cad" who labors under "the most ignoble and deserved misfortunes"— and thereby perhaps doing society a favor — Hyde snuffs out the life of "an aged and beautiful gentleman" with "a pretty manner of politeness" and "an innocent and old-world kindness of disposition" (14). William Veeder makes a compelling case that the change served Stevenson's need to put another "father" into the text, affording a parallel to Jekyll as a patriarchal "opposite" of the "bad son" Hyde and a useful object of the author's own vicarious animosity towards his moralistic father, Thomas. Carew's "professional initials," "M.P." (53), Veeder argues, are paralleled to the long list that follows Jekyll's own name (35) to make the two older men a kind of composite, professional father at whom Hyde (and behind him Stevenson) can then strike out, at each in his own way ("Children of the Night" 113). As plausible as this reading may be for the psychodynamics of the text, however, what could we say about its "politics," as intimated not only by Carew's being made specifically a Member of Parliament but also by Jekyll elsewhere suggesting that the archetypal human psycho-drama of "duality" may some day be seen as involving a "polity" of conflicting principals (82)? If the current study has begun to make a convincing case that Hyde stands for both the drinking man and for the drink trade, both the little individual and the mammoth institution, what then comes of the author's deleting a victim with whom Hyde might have rubbed shoulders and then traded insults and finally exchanged blows in a tap room — and replacing him with a kind, civil, well-intentioned Member of Parliament?

Assuming that images like *Punch*'s "Pot and Kettle" (Figure 6) and "Publican-Barrel and Pharisee-Pump" (Figure 7) really were in the Brownies' mental portfolio as Stevenson worked on *J&H*, Stevenson's revision significantly brings what could reasonably be claimed to be the caricature of a reformist politician into the text as the pointed target of Hyde's rage. The beer tankard's opponent in *Punch* is a tea-pot dressed as a Chinaman, for obvious geo-commercial reasons; but the flyer that is being shaken angrily in the tankard's left hand is labeled "Wilfred Lawson." The drawing thus reflects British brewers' and publicans' passionate opposition to the drive for Local Option which so exercised political debate until the Tory victory in the General Election of 1886 muted the cries of temperance. The tea-kettle, however, voices the hopeful aspirations of the movement in 1883 when it boasts, "Before very long, Saints be praised! our Sir Wilfred will finish his bout with you" (182).

Punch's image of "Publican-Barrel and Pharisee-Pump" is even more suggestive for our purposes. The drawing is prefaced by a quotation from Lawson's speech at the Annual Meeting of the United Kingdom Alliance's General Council. "The publicans are getting into hysterics at the ruin impending over their trade; ruin to them, but bringing countless blessings to the people. When we get as far as Local Option for the Sunday, we shall be within measurable distance of the time when Parliament will give the counties the power of preventing the drink traffic during the rest of the week" (194). If the image itself, as noted earlier, anticipates the opposed sanctimonious and indulgent alter-egos that constitute Jekyll's "double being," it also offers a prototype of Carew's encounter with Hyde. The pump, who clearly stands for Sir Wilfred Lawson, M.P., could just as well stand for Sir Danvers Carew, M.P. He opens the moralistic dialogue, as *Punch*'s text tells us, with "a superior swagger," a more pointed version of Carew's "something high too, as of a well-founded self-content" (46) — and then he echoes the quotation on the "publicans' hysterics" (curiously anticipating Lanyon's comment on Hyde's approaching "hysteria" [78]) by claiming that his opponent is "becoming hysterical" (194). Barrel replies "indignantly," suggestively declaring "unqualified war" on Pump and berating his opponent for "tracing all Evil that happens to *me*," rather as Hyde might do when Jekyll claims "It was Hyde ... and Hyde alone, that was guilty" (87). Rather than delving too deeply into a speculative point-for-point comparison of drawing and fiction, however, it's best simply to conclude that *Punch* offered a potent image of "the liquor traffic" or "Juggernaut" squaring off in the street against a frail but self-satisfied teetotaling Member of Parliament. It might have been too good a "scene" for Stevenson to pass up, as he refined the material given to him by his subconscious muses.

Given Lawson's prominence on the political landscape of the 1870s and '80s, amply demonstrated by his frequent appearance in *Punch*[4] and, indeed, in Stevenson's letters to Baxter, he could have made an ideal model for the "kindly disposed" Carew. James Greenwood spoke in 1869 of the recent appearance "on the temperance stage of a set of well-meaning

Nine. "Street Crime" 147

"OUR ONCE FACETIOUS CONTEMPORARY IS BY NO MEANS FUNNY THIS WEEK."
[*Vide* BRIGHT, *in his Great Political Organ, the* "*Morning Star.*"

Figure 9 — "Our Once Facetious Contemporary Is By No Means Funny This Week." From *Punch*, 5 February, 1859. Courtesy of the University of Canterbury Library.

gentlemen" who are "good-natured enough" to work in good faith with the liquor trade: "Sir Wilfred Lawson is the acknowledged head and champion of the party" (224). Suggestively decrying acts of incivility towards temperance advocates in 1884, Thomas Whittaker assured supporters that "flour bags hurled at the head of a bishop will not settle the question, and the refusal to hear a man of such honest intentions and genial motives as Sir Wilfred Lawson, will not harmonize with the sense of fair-play which has ever characterized our people" (*Life's Battles* 271). But Lawson needn't have been Stevenson's only model, if indeed he had one, and more than

Ferrier was Jekyll's. The temperance call had been sounding for years, and any number of M.P.'s had joined the chorus. Another *Punch* cartoon from 5 February 1859 shows outspoken parliamentary reformer John Bright, with the magazine's eponymous character standing over his crumpled and unconscious body, holding a raised club: "Our once facetious contemporary is by no means funny this week," reads the caption, demonstrating that Mr. Punch's own "impatient gaiety" could be turned to violence as readily as Jekyll's, given the right provocation (51; see Figure 9). A political cartoon from 1870 actually shows Bright, coat off and shirtsleeves rolled up, standing behind the figure of Bacchus mounted on a gin barrel, ready to club the drunken god with a sledge hammer (Ausubel 192). Despite his cooperation with the United Kingdom Alliance in the years following 1876, however, Bright's contention that temperance was a matter not for Westminster but rather for local Town Councils made him a less likely figure than Lawson to stand for explicitly "parliamentary opposition" to drink (Harrison, *Drink* 243, 263).

If Carew were indeed like Long John Silver in boasting a real-life "original," tireless sabbatarian Sir Andrew Agnew is another intriguing possibility to consider — and not simply because "Danvers Carew" is tantalizingly close to one possible anagram for Agnew's own name — *Danwer Ganew*. Considered by Dickens to have been a consummate hypocrite ("Sunday under Three Heads" 646), Agnew was nonetheless almost universally considered to be "genial and kindly" (*DNB* 1.178). "He exuded an air of good nature, had an even temper and possessed a reserve of moral courage," claims John Wigley, "but he had a weak voice" (36), a vocal trait that John Bailey confirms when he describes it as "peevish and almost inaudible" (31). Interestingly enough, the maid who witnesses the fatal encounter in *J&H* is unable to hear what Carew says to Hyde. She describes the old man's appearance and manner, but as to what he's saying, we only learn that "it did not *seem* as if the subject of his address were of great importance; indeed, *from his pointing, it sometimes appeared* as if he were only inquiring his way" (46; emphasis added). Stevenson might have known that one of the most famous reformers of the century had a weak voice and might conceivably have built the trait into this scene, be it fully consciously or no. What in fact seems *far* more compelling and convincing, however, is that Hyde's very name suggests the violent response to Agnew's brand of sabbatarian reform that Stevenson may have meant to reflect in this climactic scene.

The commonplace search for a meaning in Hyde's surname is actually (and, for a careful interpreter, rather encouragingly) initiated by Utterson himself when the excruciatingly dry (if not exactly abstinent) lawyer manages what is for him an uncharacteristic pun: "If he be Mr. Hyde, I shall be Mr. Seek" (38). Commentators regularly treat the dark Other as a manifestation of Jekyll's "hidden" desires and qualities, some of them likening his "dusky" skin, "thickly shaded with a swart growth of hair," to an animal's "hide." Among the more intriguing exegeses to date, however, is Wayne Koestenbaum's claim that the villain's name reflects Stevenson's awareness of and thematic interest in a popular demonstration against the immoral behavior of high officials that took place in Hyde Park on 22 August, 1885, in the wake of the Labouchère Amendment: "At this rally," Koestenbaum observes, "an orator said, 'Our public men should remain pure.' Hyde Park was known as a site for homosexual assignations. The surfacing of once-secret impurities — dirt finding its voice — prompted a demonstration in Hyde Park and a novel about a man named Hyde who embodies impurity, and who exists by drinking a draught tainted by some 'unknown impurity'" (48). Koestenbaum's argument is often compelling, especially in tandem with readings like Veeder's and Showalter's which also explore the novella's homo-social and homosexual sub-texts. Looking to Hyde Park for Hyde's name makes good sense; throughout the nineteenth century, the place was (as it remains today) the prime London venue for vocal eruptions of popular sentiment (Richter 62–71, 90). Yet, given the inordinate violence that Hyde displays in Stevenson's novella, something far more cataclysmic than a "demonstration" at which an orator "spoke" about the need for purity in public officials may well have been in Stevenson's mind — something rather more in line with the novella's most prevalent language and imagery. In fact, Hyde Park was arguably as notorious for the Sunday Trading Riots of 1855 as for *any* public demonstration prior to the appearance of *J&H*. When, after Gladstone's return to power in 1880, Home Secretary R. A. Cross declared that if Sunday Closing were carried he "would not be responsible for the peace of London," it was back to the frightening events of a quarter-century earlier that he looked with admonitory dread.

As we've seen, Lord Grosvenor's Sunday Trading Bill did not in fact propose the Sunday closing of drinking places; but the general public, stung by the reduced hours that had been mandated by the Wilson-Patten Act of the previous year, certainly assumed that it did. That was enough to set off thousands of Londoners who, like Dickens, believed that restrictive legislation favored the privileged over the common ("The Great Baby"

318). Scores of posters, almost certainly financed by the drink trade, duly advertised a meeting to be held in Hyde Park on the afternoon of Sunday, June 24th, "to see how religiously the aristocracy is observing the sabbath" (Harrison, "Sunday Trading Riots" 227; 223). No less keen a social observer than Karl Marx reported that more than 200,000 people appeared, chanting to the wealthy on horseback and in their carriages, "Go to church." As we've seen, their numbers and vehemence in fact inspired the father of socialism to proclaim that "the English Revolution began yesterday in Hyde Park." Writing three days later to Mrs. Burdett Coutts, Charles Dickens explains the public outcry in a way that curiously anticipates Stevenson's account of Hyde's impatient fury after he has stood speechless in Carew's company: "Some don't understand how things can be so, many more don't care, and the dangerous result is brought about that the people get no hearing until they break out into tumult — and then the business is done in a moment" (*Letters* 7.659). As yet, however, no blows were recorded in the park's confines.

More posters appeared the following week, prompting the Metropolitan Police Commissioner to issue a notice forbidding the renewed assembly that was planned for July 1. When huge crowds gathered in the park nonetheless, violence finally erupted. Police were attacked with a number of makeshift weapons, including (most resourcefully and memorably) a live eel that had been fished out of The Serpentine. The constabulary struck back at assailants with their truncheons, ultimately making 72 arrests (Harrison, "Sunday Trading" 223). With the new work week, Lord Grosvenor prudently withdrew his proposed Bill from parliamentary consideration, but his conciliatory move nevertheless failed to quash the rioting, which continued a week later on July 8th. Chartist and Radical journalist Thomas Frost then reported seeing many of the rioters armed with sticks and staves (if no canes), some of them brought in from outside the park and others distributed by organizers within; he also claims to have heard "many remarks as to the use that was to be made of them" (Harrison, "Sunday Trading" 226; Wigley 69). Come July 8th, the police stayed in the background, forestalling serious mayhem, but the riot spilled out into considerable hooliganism in Belgravia, such that *The Manchester Guardian* reported on July 11th that the protest had escaped from the control of "its original and well-meaning authors into the hands of a set of ne'er-do-wells for whom there is no expostulation so suitable as a thick stick" (Harrison, "Sunday Trading" 224). In sum, *Reynold's Newspaper* saw the protracted incident as reflecting the same kind of class struggle that we see mirrored between each of the novella's old gentlemen—Jekyll, Lanyon, and Carew—and the brash and youthful spirit of indulgent "liberty" (86) that is Hyde: "the struggle has been one betwixt the Aristocracy and Democracy; and the Aristocracy has been most soundly beaten" (Harrison, "Sunday Riots" 230).

This was the actual, historical, anti-temperance "Hydian reaction" or "violence in Hyde" that Home Secretary Cross specifically recalled in 1880 when he warned the government about the political explosiveness of the Sunday Closing issue. Even more significant for our purposes, however, was Lord Salisbury's campaign speech in Newport in the autumn of 1885 itself, in which he too looked back to the way Londoners, once they'd learned of the odious Sunday Trade Bill, "took effective measures [and] marched into Hyde Park and broke the windows of every member of parliament they could find; ... the remonstrance had its effect and the Bill was immediately withdrawn," he observed. "I do not know that the population of London has since changed very much." In fact, "the trouble in Hyde" was still being discussed before the Royal Commission on Liquor Licensing in 1896, so indelibly associated was it with the public's violent protectiveness of its right to drink (Harrison, "Sunday Trading" 238). More significantly, Salisbury's speech was printed in the *Times* on 8 October, 1885, during the second or third week that Stevenson was working on *J&H*. The author first names his infamous characters in a playful letter to Colvin, describing his fevered process of composition: "I am pouring forth a penny (12 penny) dreadful; it is dam [*sic*] dreadful; ... they call it Doctor Jekyll, but they also call it Mr Hyde, Mr Hyde, but they also, also call it Mr Hyde" (*Letters* 5.128). It is unfortunate for our purposes that the communiqué is undated; but the editor of the Yale *Letters*, Ernest Mehew, suggests "Late September/early October" as the likeliest time frame. It may have been on the 8th of the month, then, that Stevenson's daily reading of the newspapers gave him the actual, historically-resonant name for Jekyll's violent, stick-wielding, liquor-quaffing alter-ego.

It is as a result extremely tempting to see the novella's villain as in part an embodiment of the anti-temperance anger that so infamously united drinkers and the drink trade alike in Hyde Park in the mid-century—and his Member of Parliament victim as, in turn, an imaginative conflation of the sabbatarian Agnew and Stevenson's favorite teetotaler and champion of Local Option, Wilfred Lawson—acknowledged star of "Publican-Barrel and Pharisee-Pump." That Lawson lost his seat in the General Election that was held the very month Stevenson was putting the finishing touches on *J&H*—including his replacing the low-life Lemsome with M. P. Carew—may suggest that it was he who was the prime "model," if indeed there was one. Temperance activists, however, so often suffered indignities or violence at the hands of drinkers and drink purveyors that the scene would have been thematically apt even if Carew were a physician and Hyde were named Magoo. Lawson himself described the parameters of what was a virtual war between opposing factions: "When the preachers of [teetotalism] set to work to proclaim it, the liquor dealers— Demetrius like — at first stirred up tumultuous opposition. One speaker had to creep through a window and fly for his life from a meeting in the Dudley Town Hall. The Bishop of Exeter [Frederick Temple] was pelted with flour-bags for the space of half an hour in his own city, drunken ruffians scaling the platform, and breaking up the meeting and the ribs of one of the Alliance zealots at the same time" ("The Drink Difficulty" 413).

At the moderate end of the scale of harassment, temperance speakers could expect to be pelted with rotten eggs, drenched with paint, or even struck with "a dusty stuffed imitation fish"—shades of battery by Serpentine eel (Longmate 70; Whittaker, *Life's Battles* 87). Irate Londoners who came to heckle the Irish reformer Father Mathew dressed head to foot in hop leaves and shook weighty staves, while the Briton Henry Gale had his glasses trampled at a rally in Birmingham (Longmate 116; Harrison, *Drink* 341). As Lawson's comments suggest, however, many reformers had reason to fear worse. Off to a meeting on the Permissive Bill in 1871, H. J. Wilson wrote to his sister, "very doubtful if I shall get home with my skin complete" (Harrison, *Drink* 244). As witness to a "Teetotal procession" some years earlier, Dickens had "perceived in some [spectators] so moody an implacability towards the magistrates of the scaffold, and so plain a desire to tear them limb from limb" that he feared for their lives ("A Plea for Total Abstinence" 360). Stevenson's own publisher, John Cassell, was once assaulted physically after he convened a temperance meeting outside a pub, sharing that fate with hosts of others like James Teare (Nowell-Smith 6; Longmate 51). It is Thomas Whittaker, however, who in 1884 leaves perhaps the most chilling account of life's literal "battles in temperance armor." Whittaker was on separate occasions flogged, burned, and drowned in effigy; stoned in a Baptist chapel and nearly overturned in his carriage by hecklers as he made his escape; attacked by a score of drunken maltsters and brewers' men who screamed "Burke him!" and "Set fire to him!" and hurled the broken legs and arms of chairs at his head; and attacked once again by sixty men "armed with sticks and other weapons" who surrounded his house, smashed the windows, and broke down the door, rushing in to "demand [his] body" (*Life's Battles* 200, 296, 192, 257). Given that at least one teetotaler was actually killed by thugs hired by publicans—like the very Hydian "bravos" that Jekyll mentions "men have before hired ... to transact their crimes" (86)—it was hardly an exaggeration for Kate Mitchell to claim that temperance activists suffered a "martyrdom not unlike that suffered by the early Christians" (Shiman 24; Mitchell 8).

Once again, the immediate years leading up to the composition of *J&H* were particularly charged, as popular and drink-trade opposition to William Booth's increasingly powerful Salvation Army coalesced into a dark, antagonistic double — the so-called "Skeleton Army." Nefariously supported by brewers and publicans alike, those who marched and gathered under the black flag with its lurid skull and crossbones (partial inspiration for *Treasure* Island's drunken villains?) were initially content to heckle their teetotaler foes. But "in the early 1880s physical attacks increased alarmingly. The Skeleton Army pelted the Salvation marchers with mud, stones, dead cats, paint, even live coals." By 1881, the claims of Army harassment were being presented to the Home Office. In 1882, a female Salvationist nearly died from injuries sustained in a clash in Chester and one male comrade was totally blinded, only one of the more serious casualties among six hundred Salvation soldiers injured by mobs that year (Richter 75, 77, 80, 81). In August of 1885, the month Stevenson visited Hardy in Dorchester and may have discussed the dire consequences of Michael Henchard's alcoholism, a number of Salvation Army contingents met in Derby. They were attacked by between six and seven thousand people, who "soundly trounced them in a vicious hand-to-hand melee in the market place, then shattered every window in the Salvation Army barracks and smashed the band instruments." The next day, the Skeletons celebrated by hurling rotten pears all around the commercial battle-ground (Richter 82). So marked were the excesses of this reactionary "slime of the pit," to use Stevenson's morbid metaphor for Hyde, that even the pro-trade *Licensed Victualler's Guardian* felt obliged to take a disapproving stance: "We cannot ... see the advantage of the use of violence, in lieu of argument, against our Teetotal opponents" (Gutzke 219).

Violence, then, was the way of drink in the second half of the nineteenth century, whether we consider the stereotypical irascibility of the common drunkard, or the spontaneous public protest of aggrieved populace, or the calculated strategy of an anti-temperance organization. Hyde's second and most odious narrated crime looks distinctly as though it may have been shaped by Stevenson's awareness of all three manifestations. It's a notoriously hard scene to get a handle on, not least because it treats information that originates with a romantically naive woman who wasn't really able to hear what was going on and doesn't even get to speak directly to the reader. But Carew's good intentions, and his self-content, and his frequent "pointing" are consistent with the portrait of some kind of *reformist* M.P., as indeed is "the air of one very much surprised and a trifle hurt" when his comments aren't well received by his auditor. Dickens wrote plaintively to Mrs. Coutts about the kind of naiveté that regularly set the parliamentary foes of drink up for a rude awakening: "I am sorry for what occurred in Hyde Park, but it is an illustration of what I endeavoured to put before you ... — I mean the extraordinary ignorance on the part of those who make the laws, of what is behind us, and what is ever ready to break in if it be too long despised" (*Letters* 7.659). Hyde could just be a psychopath, but the novella consistently likens him to a heavy drinker. Here, he seems frighteningly like a stick-bearing rioter in his namesake park, or a raging witness to the William Booths of the world: a one-man Skeleton Army who can be driven to murderous violence by nothing more than another man's words. Carew just happens to have been carrying a sealed and stamped envelope addressed to Utterson. The plot essentially requires the thing, as it quickly puts Utterson in touch with these highly relevant developments in the matter of Mr. Hyde. But it may serve the novella's dominant topical theme as well, suggesting that this Member of Parliament had written something for the consideration of the Law — but which Hyde's savage reaction kept from its routine delivery as effectively as the Hyde Park rioters put paid to Grosvenor's Sunday Trading Bill. In any case, that Hyde should evidently have been enraged by nothing more than a kindly M. P.'s gesticulating speech goes some way towards confirming that that scene is, indeed, somehow innately political.

As a coda to this section, it is worth noting that Hyde's major offenses against child and man are supplemented by a passing act of cruelty to a woman. As Hyde is on his way to Lanyon's to fetch his chemicals, Jekyll recalls, "a woman spoke to him, offering, I think, a box of lights. He smote her in the face, and she fled" (94). William Veeder reads the swiftly narrated detail as evidence of a deep-seated misogyny in Hyde, the woman being quite possibly (Veeder claims) a street-walker who offers her "inflaming," venereal "box" in ways Jekyll cannot in his repressed account overtly acknowledge ("Children of the Night" 141). It's an intriguing suggestion, especially given that Stevenson's youthful, "Johnston-and-Thomson" interest in prostitutes may have informed the implied profession of the novella's Soho gin-drinkers, together with the carefully-constructed metaphor of the shops in Jekyll's neighborhood as resembling "rows of smiling saleswomen," variously displaying and veiling their "lurid charms" "with an air of invitation" and "coquetry" (30). Yet the first thing to note is that Stevenson's age saw women as virtually co-equal with children as the most poignant and frequent victims of drunken violence (Booth, M. 211). Again, as with children, one must sensibly acknowledge that the great suffering of women was commonly and convincingly attributed by late–Victorian reformers to *many* causes other than drink. A battered match-girl does not, necessarily, another victim of gin make. But it would be senseless to pursue the current argument without considering the frequency with which the female of the species was represented as particularly vulnerable to the curses of drink — or, correspondingly, the fact that the three people whom we know are struck by Hyde consist of two females and (in curious keeping with them) "an aged and *beautiful* gentleman" with "a very *pretty* manner of politeness."(46; emphasis added) What, to put it most simply, do Hyde's interactions and associations suggest here *if* we read the man as a figure for the effects of strong drink?

Cruikshank's *The Bottle* established the Victorian popular stereotype of alcoholic decline as consequentially as Hogarth's *Gin Lane* had done for the Georgians. The series' unquestioned climax is the plate (No. 6) in which the husband attacks and ultimately kills his wife. Dempster's alcoholic wife-abuse, of course, drives Eliot's *Janet's Repentance*. In *The Mayor of Casterbridge*, Henchard not only sells his family while under the influence but also hints to Elizabeth that his abuses involved more than criminal abandonment: "I was a drinking man once, and used your mother roughly" (90). Frances Power Cobbe's "Wife-Torture in England" (1878) blamed "seas of brandy and gin" for this heinous and all-too-frequent crime, while we've seen Frederick Charrington's life-conversion to have followed directly from his witnessing a drunk brutally striking his imploring wife in the city street. Further, Charles Booth's *Life and Labour of the People in London* describes the stereotypical drinking husband who, "when sober, was most hard-working and kind, but when drunk would beat the poor woman unmercifully" (62). And when reformed drunkard Nat Bailey talked about turning his own life around, his account made the point about women and drinking men in both negative and positive ways. After "getting mad with drinking," he confessed, "Well, my friends, I got my razor and went to look for my wife. The old woman ... thought I was up to no good, and so she ran. I ... ran after her; but I couldn't catch her ... and it was a good thing I couldn't, for if I had caught her, I should have been hung for her, instead of being here to tell you teetotalers about it.... Look at my wife and children before you. Instead of being ragged and deserted, they looks tidy and comfortable" (Longmate 70).

Stevenson was keenly aware of the link between drink and domestic abuse. Appalled by Randall's degradation at the hands of gin, Wiltshire in *The Beach of Falesá* makes Uma pour an entire case of gin into the sand. "Man he drink, he no good," he tells her ever so temperately; "Suppose I drink gin, my little wifie be 'fraid" (111). It makes good sense, then, that his proto-allegory of alcoholism should involve an assault on a woman as well as a child, as fleeting as it may be. It would also make sense that the woman should be described in an arguably compromising fashion, since one of the ways in which women were held to become the gravest victims of drink was by being lured into prostitution. The last plate of *The Bottle* reads in its original, un-bowdlerized version, "The bottle has done its work — It has destroyed the infant and the mother, it has brought the son and daughter to vice and to the streets, and has left the father a hopeless maniac" (Feaver 56); the girl is shown visiting her father's lunatic cell in the shameless garb of a courtesan. Accordingly, *The Drunkard's Children* (1848) begins with a plate which recounts the way the son and daughter alike were "led to the gin-shop to drink at that fountain which nourishes every species of crime." The third plate reads, "From the gin-shop to the dancing rooms, from the dancing rooms to the gin-shop, the poor girl is driven on in that course which ends in misery," finally committing suicide by hurling herself off a bridge (Feaver 56). Thirteen years later, Kate Mitchell agreed that prostitution was "a direct result of intemperance," hers being one of many teetotal tracts that saw "the first glass as the respectable woman's first step towards the lowest brothel in London" (*The Drink Question* 249; Harrison, *Drink* 175). And in the year *J&H* was written, W. T. Stead published the "Confessions of a Brothel Keeper" who testified to the efficacy of alcohol in staffing his premises:

The getting of fresh girls takes time, but it is simple and easy enough when once you are in it. I have gone and courted girls in the country under all kinds of disguises ... and made them believe that I intended to marry them, and so got them in my power to please a good customer.... I propose to bring her to London to see the sights. I bring her up, take her here and there, giving her plenty to eat and drink — especially drink. I take her to the theatre, and usually contrive that she misses the last train. By this time she is very tired, a little dazed with the drink and the excitement, and very frightened at being left in town with no friends. I offer her lodgings for the night: she goes to bed in my house, and then the affair in managed. My client gets his maid, I get my £10 or £20 commission, and in the morning the girl, who has lost her character, and dare not go home, in all probability will do as the others do, and become one of my "marks"— that is, she will make her living in the streets, to the advantage of my house ["Maiden Tribute" 36].

Alternatively, if time is at a premium, the procurer assures us, "Drunken parents often sell their children to brothel keepers" (36).

Those who acknowledged there were other routes *to* the oldest profession nonetheless agreed that drink and prostitution were irrevocably associated in practice. Echoing both John Edgar's *Female Virtue — Its Enemies and Friends* (1841) and J. Miller's *Prostitution, Considered in Relation to Its Causes and Cures* (1859), the Canterbury Committee on Intemperance of 1867 held beer-houses to be notoriously responsible for "prostitution and other lusts" (Harrison, *Drink* 175; Shiman 101). Streetwalkers could obviously count on finding willing clients among a pub's drinking clientele: B. Seebohm Rowntree therefore decries the number of young women in York who "spend their evenings in public-houses with a view to meeting men for immoral purposes" (313). Some women drank to "prime the pump" of lucrative conviviality. Often enough, however, alcohol was the anesthetic that dulled the pain and anxiety of a demeaning and dangerous life (as for *Mary Barton*'s Aunt Esther), and thus became a key part of a vicious downward spiral (Harrison, *Drink* 175). For a while, Stevenson himself thrived in the heady atmosphere of liquor and love for sale in his Edinburgh public-house "headquarters" (*Letters* 1.210–11). He may well reminisce in a not-altogether nostalgic way in *J&H*, especially with his sketch of those wretched Soho women who are apparently unwilling or unable to start their day without a stiff shot of gin — and perhaps even in the vision of a woman of the streets struck by an enraged potential John. At the very least, one would expect a fiction that explored the dire effects of addiction on an urban man would somehow reflect the impact of his drug on the citizenry at large. These side-long glimpses of "women of the street" would seem to fill the imaginative bill.

Of course the women of the novel can also rage with the best of them. When Hyde tramples the little girl, he's quickly surrounded by a group of vengeful women, "wild as harpies. I never saw a circle of such hateful faces," says Enfield (32). We've noted how frankly the age acknowledged that women in their cups could be as violent and vindictive as men: witness Stephen Blackpool's wife in *Hard Times*, or James Greenwood's drunken "she-creatures" swarming like a "horde of human tigresses" (185, xvii). But Hyde at least in part stands for the Drink Juggernaut here, so, if one *were* moved to read the "harpies" figuratively, the women would somehow have to be arrayed exegetically among the forces of temperance. The campaign against drink was in fact staunchly supported by women and became a *cause célèbre* of early feminists (Harrison, *Drink* 224; Mattingly 39). Different organizations accorded women different roles and degrees of power. While the United Kingdom Alliance profited from their fund-raising and organizational prowess, women rarely filled important positions or spoke in their forums. In contrast, Anne Carlile was a driving force behind the 1847 foundation of the Band of Hope, a temperance organization for working-class children which was subsequently managed by a board of a dozen women and became increasingly powerful as the century progressed. Similarly, the National Temperance league chose three women to oversee its ambitious efforts to expand membership in the 1860s and '70s (Harrison, *Drink* 224–5, 192). When the first issue of the *Church of England Temperance Magazine* appeared in 1862, it featured pieces by Clara Balfour, Mary Howitt, and Julia Wightman (Olsen 39). Meanwhile, across the Atlantic, contemporary American feminists deemed temperance the most important reform issue for women in the nineteenth century, among other things advocating divorce as a necessary escape from marriage to an alcoholic (Mattingly 6, 27). And as the Maine Bill of 1851 gave both heart and a hugely solid talking point to the U.K. Alliance, so did the Women's Christian Temperance Union lend consistent ideological and practical support to their British sisters in the years after its founding in 1874. When Frances Willard crossed the Atlantic to speak at London's Wesley Chapel, Lady Henry Somerset presented her with gifts to express the gratitude of English proponents of women's rights and reform (Mattingly 3–4).

Balfour, Howitt, and Wightman were content simply to lend their voices to a journal that issued a "declaration of war on the pub" (Olsen

39), joining other female teetotalers like Kate Mitchell in a forceful and sober rhetorical onslaught. Elsewhere, however, we catch glimpses of the emotional frenzy and physical vindictiveness that Stevenson's "harpies" display. Carol Mattingly records cases of violence among American temperance women, as in one instance where a spirit seller was physically attacked and his property destroyed by a gang of angry ladies. "Abuse makes me wild," confesses a witness to the violence of drunken men in the 1873 temperance novel, *The Subtle Spell*; "I've got to keep out of it, or I'll be as bad as any of them" (98). David Lewis's *The Drink Traffic* notes in 1885 what was for him the inspiring way in which Swedish women "protect themselves and children from that drink evil which they seemed to hate with a perfect hatred" (76). Closer to home, Dickens documents the inflammatory rhetoric of the Secretary of the National Temperance Association, who "calls upon the women of England ... to 'dash down the cup'" in ways that, taken literally, could certainly lead to blows ("Demoralisation" 162). Even more suggestively, during Father Mathew's crusading visit to Deptford in 1843, the man was guarded by a bevy of formidable Irishwomen with shillelaghs hidden inside their umbrellas (Harrison, *Drink* 168). There's no evidence that they ever used the stout weapons, but they might well have kept any insurgent Hydes at bay.

There's no question that the women of England could be ferocious in protecting their sister victims of alcohol — and perhaps especially their children. The female-led Band of Hope rode such a wave of solicitous maternalism that within four years of its founding, it could organize that massive Edinburgh rally of 30,000 children (Longmate 123). Yet in order to take the impression that might have inspired *J&H*'s "harpy" scene, Stevenson needn't in the least have attended the Edinburgh rally as a precocious one-year-old; nor have come across any wild colonial feminists during his initial trip across America; nor have heard the outraged complaints of one publican who claimed to have been mobbed by women who rushed to scratch his face when he attempted to raise a dissenting voice at a temperance meeting (Harrison, *Drink* 228). The complaints made to his parents by Walter Ferrier's mother would surely have sufficed. Frequent companion to Ferrier in the late-night streets of Edinburgh, he worried that he had indeed been a key component of a youthful "drink Juggernaut" that crushed his old friend, as his letters to his father, Thomas, suggest. In "Old Mortality," Stevenson remembers Ferrier this way: "I can still see and hear him, as he went his way along the lamplit streets, *La ci darem la mano* on his lips, a noble figure of a youth...; and sure enough, somewhere on the high seas of life ... [he] miserably went down" (*Memories* 51). In *J&H*, on the very same lamplit streets, he envisions another "youth" or child going down in a slightly different fashion — and instead of Ferrier's lilting Mozart, he may well be remembering the furious invective of another protective mother. As with so many details of this text, the women Hyde repeatedly encounters in the city's by-ways are susceptible to a range of contextual interpretations. Yet given the insistent impact of "the Ferrier saga" on Stevenson's conscience, this highly personal echo seems the most likely to have driven the invention of Hyde's lurid "traffic accident."[5]

TEN

Jekyll and Hyde: Beginnings and Endings

We come now to the third of three chapters exploring the "major moments" of Stevenson's novella — its germinal scenes, its most vivid representations of villainy, (and now) its opening and closing acts. If we set aside the actual narrative sequence of *J&H* and focus instead on what are in terms of fictional chronology its first and last glimpses of Jekyll's "life" — the important, "bookend" passages that document his initial declaration of purpose and, in turn, his final hours and fate — then Stevenson's temperance subtext again reveals itself. The innate "impatient gaiety of disposition" which is the seed of Hyde, as Jekyll claims when he opens his "Full Statement of the Case," is a trait that the young man "found it hard to reconcile with [his] imperious desire to carry [his] head high, and wear a more than commonly grave countenance before the public." As a consequence, Jekyll tells us, he hid throughout his early life what he considered to be his "irregularities ... with an almost morbid sense of shame" (81). Continually plagued, however, by the "war among [his] members" — by "the two natures that contended in the field of [his] consciousness" (82) — he ultimately formulates a plan to still the dissonance:

> I ... learned to dwell with pleasure ... on the thought of the separation of these elements. If each, I told myself, *could but be housed in separate identities*, life would be relieved of all that was unbearable; the unjust might go his way, delivered from the aspirations and remorse of his more upright twin;

and the just *could walk steadfastly and securely on his upward path*, doing the good things in which he found his pleasure, and no longer exposed to disgrace and penitence by the hands of this extraneous evil [82; added emphasis].

Jekyll's language here is highly resonant. He contemplates sorting out his incongruous "identities" in terms of separate "housing," a bit of internalized urban planning that should incidentally allow his "upright twin" to do the very kind of enlightened and enlightening "walking"— "steadfastly" and on an "upright path"— that any well-situated sabbatarian from Sir Andrew Agnew to Mr. Utterson would so zestfully endorse. Interestingly, the implicit argument on housing and population distribution reasserts itself a bit further on, when Jekyll imagines that his current vision of human "duality" might one day be refined and augmented such that "man will be ultimately known for a mere *polity* of multifarious, incongruous and independent *denizens*" (82; emphases added.) Jekyll keeps thinking in the same metaphorical vein when he subsequently notes that his respectable identity as a doctor affords a "city of refuge" into which Hyde can safely retreat when he must. Most simply, of course, the opening paragraphs of the "Full Statement" reflect Jekyll's quest for a kind of "hyper-respectability," for some shrewd adjustments to his nature, habits, and appearance that will allow him to carry his head preternaturally "high." Yet the words that he hits upon suggest that his personal attempt to re-order his psychological house for the sake of "image" might profitably be seen against some of the more general sociological negotiations of the era. Jekyll surveys his character as though it were an urban space, he identifies two essential "classes" contending for territory there, and he seeks to "house" them in separate quarters or neighborhoods— so that the pristine social reputation of the "high" can be protected, while the "low" is freed, at whatever risk, to do just as he pleases. What might this kind of resonant discourse on residential separation and psychic amendment mean for the argument that we have been pursuing?[1]

The first thing to say is that Jekyll's progressive quest for respectability, for the chance to hold his head "high," mirrors an evolution in social thinking that changed the demographics of Victorian drink — not simply in terms of what and how much was drunk by whom but also in terms of where various sorts of people did their drinking. We've already seen the way the symbolically-opposed choices of gin or wine became, for Britain and Stevenson alike, radical markers of class. The deep inebriation that gin rendered so likely became a stereotypical attribute of the lower classes: "While [drunkenness] is the vice of the poor and the wretched," Dickens wrote in 1849, "it is not the vice of the upper classes, or of the middle class (whose improvement within the last hundred years is in no respect more remarkable than in this); and it is not, generally speaking, the vice of the great body of *respectable* mechanics, or of servants, or of small tradesmen" (*Demoralisation* 163; emphasis added). Westminster grocer George Wilson anticipated Dickens by a decade and a half, testifying in 1834 that excessive drinking was most definitely on the wane, even "among the *respectable* mechanics, those persons who are prudent and *independent* in spirit and endeavour to *keep up the appearance of respectability*" (Clark 308; added emphases). So, if we've justly associated Jeykll and his cronies with moderate drinking (they are all tellingly dubbed "intelligent *reputable* men, and all judges of good wine" [43; my emphasis]) and Hyde with the dire effects of alcoholic abandon, then their customary drinking habits perfectly reflect their differing commitment to Respectability, the Victorian shibboleth to which Jekyll so clearly nods at the beginning of his self-reckoning.[2]

As with the choice of drink (and reasonable expectations for the depth of inebriation that go with it), so with drinking venue. Brian Harrison reveals that, although some segregation of the classes in their drinking activity pre-dated the nineteenth-century, territorial exclusivity was a marked and evolving hallmark of the 1800s, radically altering the social role and architecture of the public house in the process. In London, as early as the 1830s, most members of the higher classes and even tradesmen were drinking at home, and "private as opposed to public drinking was becoming a mark of respectability." "By the 1850s," Harrison continues, "no respectable urban Englishman entered an ordinary public house" (*Drink* 45) — a scrupulousness reflected in *Treasure Island* when Captain Smollett faults Mr. Arrow, the first mate, for being so "free" in his conduct as to "drink with the men before the mast" (52). Statistician G. R. Porter accordingly commented in 1852 that "no person above the rank of a labouring man or artisan, would venture to go into a public house to purchase anything to drink"; and in 1888, closer to the days of *J&H*, *The Licensed Victualler's Gazette* observed that "In these days when taverns are voted vulgar, it would be almost the ruin of a barrister's reputation to be seen entering a public house unless it were called a restaurant" (Girouard 45;12.)[3] Publicans adapted as well as they could to the evolving social mores, constructing separate entrances to separate internal "bars" that catered discretely to the different ranks — or installing "snob screens" and what were essentially private "boxes" to shield more well-to-do customers from the eyes of servers and fellow customers alike (Girouard 63;57). These were all ways, essentially, for drinkers to be more "private," even when they were undeniably in public. But the general retreat of the higher classes towards a more genuinely private respectability was unstoppable and, for a time, irreversible. As the *Victualler's Gazette* suggested, one alternative and more acceptable public venue for imbibing was the "restaurant," a burgeoning institution whose French inspiration was reflected both in the borrowed gallic term itself and in the focus on imported wines that loaned these establishments their elevated social tone. Gentlemen, of course, could increasingly resort to London's expanding web of private clubs such as the Savile, joined in fact by Stevenson on the endorsement of Sidney Colvin (Girouard 36; McLynn 82). But as a general rule, as Harrison again suggests, "whereas at the beginning of the century different classes patronized the same pubs, by the 1860s the respectable classes were drinking at home, or not drinking at all" (*Pubs* 166). One motive for this change in venue was clearly the privacy that the move afforded, allowing for one's drinking to be done safely behind one's own walls, or solely with invited cronies whose tolerance and discretion were largely guaranteed, regardless of how "respectably" a man was really behaving. Recall, if you will, Dickens' sanguine public pronouncements about the higher classes and drink — this despite his chumminess with the erstwhile profligate George Cruikshank. But an additional motive was assuredly to place potentially disgracing drink within the tempering context of the domestic "sphere," sometimes even under the direct aegis of the "Angel of the House" herself. B. W. Whitmore, in an informative pamphlet written in 1854, touts not only the beneficial effects of wine but also the salutary effect of the familial setting in which it was more and more regularly drunk: "I believe nothing, after religious instruction and secular education, would have a greater impact in improving the character of the people, than placing within their reach a light and wholesome beverage — and one that would enliven and not intoxicate — one that could be enjoyed more in the family than in a gin-palace or the ale-house. Give, then, that which is wholesome to the body and safe to the moral condition of mankind" (Briggs 20). Among the practical levers of temperance, slum clearance and universal counter-attractions to intoxicating drink were essential; but they were staunchly reinforced by the largely middle-class concept of "home life." The safest recreations were increasingly believed to be domestic ones (Greenwood xix; Malcolmson 104).

One London manifestation of this social trend was the Duke of Bedford's successful exclusion of public houses from his Bloomsbury precincts (Harrison, *Pubs* 166). The equivalent in Stevenson's novella is Jekyll's literal and initially successful domestic relocation of Hyde to Soho—essentially "Gin City"—while he and his cronies continue to drink moderately from their private cellars in Mayfair. Brian Harrison suggests that, after the flight of "respectable" drinkers from public to private settings, "secrecy shrouded the shared recreation of different social classes" (*Drink* 46). *J&H* essentially reflects that state of affairs, with its "elevated" voices (whichever of its three "narrating professionals" we listen to: Utterson, Lanyon, or Jekyll himself) shrouding Hyde's doings in *almost* complete mystery, while also making it clear (via Poole) that the brutal little fellow is not the kind of man who would "dine" with Jekyll or value the "high" conviviality of professional men (41). That mutual secrecy duly acknowledged, however, the elitism that drove the affluent to drink in private alcohol that they could afford to cellar against future need—but that, conversely, left the poor prey to the vagaries of public house licensing and opening—was *precisely* the elitism that blew up in the Hyde Park Sunday Trading Riots into a very public manifestation of class resentment. As we've seen, Beer- and gin-drinkers wanted to see for themselves how abstemiously the wine-drinkers, snug in their squares or houses or carriages, were "keeping the Sabbath." So, *just* as in Stevenson's novella, the attempt to "house" different types of tipplers in different venues, although it certainly allowed some drinkers to feel more "respectable," ultimately pushed London close enough to civil chaos for Karl Marx to claim that June 1855 marked the onset of the English Revolution!

One could argue with some justice that, although Jekyll, Utterson, and their professional cronies are clearly and appropriately represented as drinkers of wine in private domestic settings, Hyde is less explicitly identified with the public world of the pub. Although film versions of his story invariably, and perhaps intuitively, show him reveling in that realm — whether we consider Spencer Tracy's seduction of barmaid Ingrid Bergman (1941) or Michael Caine's repeated terrorizing of an East End dive (1990)—we admittedly never see Stevenson's villain in an actual place of drink. We do, however, know that his rooms are in Soho, and that there are gin palaces virtually at his doorstep (48). Whatever he does with his nights, he's regularly away from home and out in the streets, divorced from "respectable domesticity" even more markedly than Enfield, who is himself very much more a "man about town" (29) than a creature of home and hearth. In "class" and behavior and geographic range, then, Hyde is at least implicitly a pub-crawler, in ways that much of the language and imagery we have treated here tend to confirm. But what is finally most problematic for a clear-cut social taxonomy of alcoholism in the text is, as we've seen above, that impressive stash of wine in his Soho digs. Although he's overtly a public carouser, Hyde is covertly a private connoisseur. On the other hand, Utterson, a man who relishes wine in the *semi*-privacy of polite company, drinks gin in the *complete* privacy of his own home. It might be that, consciously or no, Stevenson finally confounds the emerging Victorian moral topography of drink that we've just been exploring.[4] Yet suffice it to say for now that Jekyll's "reputable" attempt to distance himself from the "undignified" and ultimately "monstrous" excesses of Hyde (86) is perfectly and revealingly consistent with the evolution of drinking patterns in the historical London where the action takes place. If Stevenson's search for a vehicle to explore man's dual nature took him quite naturally in the direction of a parable on alcohol, then the schism that Jekyll engineers between the "high" and "low" aspects of his character takes on the appropriate lineaments of Victorian social self-definition in the specific terms of drink.

To return our focus for a moment from behavior to urban planning, Lord Bedford's successful exclusion of licensed premises from Bloomsbury needs to be seen against one key demographic impact of the Industrial Revolution — the tendency of both the outright wealthy and the relatively affluent to separate themselves residentially from labor and the poor (Cunningham 80). Their motives were both sociological and hygienic: the prodigious wealth that was generated by industry left significant numbers of the "haves" in a strong position to enhance the visible signs their ascendancy; while both the appalling pollution and the increasingly dense labor populations that were created by the factories made relocation a very attractive option for those with the means and jobs that allowed for it. Although the explosive development of Victorian suburbia is probably the clearest manifestation of the trend (Greenwood ix), with London's great railway-abetted expansion the classic case in point, significant adjustments were made within traditional city limits as well.[5] Perhaps the most striking example is John Nash's Regent's Park/Regent Street project, which not only afforded the wealthy a host of elegant new villas and houses in the terraces and crescents that bordered the park itself but also threw up, in the form of the majestic, curving thoroughfare of Regent Street, an effectively un-breachable dam between the teeming, low, immigration-swollen neighborhoods of Soho to the east and the refined squares of Mayfair to the west (Hibbert 128–30; Porter 130, 217). Nash, in other words, not only established a new neighborhood for the affluent but also insulated and protected their more traditional haunts from any low "insurgency." There was thereafter little danger, for example, that Dr. Lanyon's Cavendish Square would ever turn into another Covent Garden, itself once the exclusive preserve of the well-to-do but ultimately and infamously co-opted not only by the raucous and reeking market it hosted but also by an attending plethora of "taverns, coffee-houses, gambling dens and brothels" (Porter 6).

The same strategy of isolation and exclusion was resorted to by many in the temperance camp. In some instances, reformers established teetotal zones within city suburbs or established city precincts, "drink-free utopias" like the 1870's Bedford Park or the 1880's Queen's Park, Shaftesbury Park, and Noel Park in London — or Toxteth Park in Liverpool (Harrison, *Pubs* 183). As in Bedford's Bloomsbury, no public houses at all were permitted in the new developments. In other parts of the kingdom, avid reformers founded what were essentially purpose-built temperance towns, such as Saltaire or Birstall in Yorkshire, or Bessbrook in Ireland. "Two separate worlds existed for the Birstall teetotalers by the end of the century," observes Lillian Shiman; "the teetotal world centred around the Temperance Hall, and a non-temperance world that was little known to the young teetotalers" (169). In other words, Thomas Whittaker's observation in 1884 that "the country is divided into three towns—the *Moderation* Town ... the *Drunken* Town ... [and] the *Teetotal* Town" (210) charted a topography that could be literal as much as allegorical. And when Jekyll sees himself as "severed" by a "trench" into "provinces of good and ill" (81)—or when he describes his doctor-self as a "city of refuge" to which Hyde can retreat (92)—his language resonates in highly charged ideological and topographical ways.

Jekyll is admittedly not a literal teetotaler in the way that, say, Poole may be. Yet the doctor does effectively banish Hyde to the gin-soaked climes of Soho, and thereby creates for "himself" a more abstemious life in some undesignated western part of the city—presumably not far from Lanyon's Cavendish Square and a neighborhood through which Hyde is, therefore and accordingly, "stumping along *eastward*" when Enfield first sees him (31; emphasis added). And, in ways no previous study has yet noted, it is precisely along the socio-economically and morally significant Regent's Park/Regent Street axis that something which Jekyll describes as the climactic "end of all things" comes to pass. The relevant passage is worth quoting at length, filled as it is with the coded allusions to themes alcoholic we have noted above and with other suggestive turns of phrase to boot (all of them italicized below).

> There comes an end to all things; the *most capacious measure is filled* at last; and [a] brief condescension to my evil finally destroyed *the balance of my soul*.... It was a fine, clear January day, wet under foot where the frost had melted, but cloudless overhead; and the Regent's Park was full of winter chirrupings and sweet with Spring odours. I sat in the sun on a bench; the *animal within me* licking the chops of memory; the spiritual side a little drowsed, promising subsequent penitence, but not yet moved to begin.... And at the very moment ... a qualm came over me, *a horrid nausea* and *the most deadly shuddering*. These passed away, and *left me faint*; and then as in its turn the faintness subsided, I began to be aware of a change in the *temper* of my thoughts, a *greater boldness, a contempt of danger, a solution of the bonds of obligation*. I looked down; ... the hand that lay on my knee was *corded and hairy*. I was once more Edward Hyde. A moment before I had been *safe of all men's respect*, wealthy, beloved — the cloth laying for me in the dining-room at home; and now I was the common quarry of mankind, hunted, *houseless*, a known murderer, *thrall* to the gallows [92–3].

We needn't rehearse anew the language that's already been treated, but should merely add that what could pass for the "nausea" that follows from a night of over-indulgence, along with the "deadly shuddering" of *delirium tremens*, both give way here to a kind of spontaneous re-inebriation which is "Hyde"— bold, contemptuous, dissolute, and of a debased "temper." What is interesting is that the first spontaneous reversion to Hyde for which Jekyll is fully conscious—the first reversion that doesn't occur while he is asleep—takes place in a park that had been opened to the general public in 1841 in large part as a salutary *retreat* from the social pressures and conditions that fostered the altered "temper" that is "intemperance" (Bailey 63). Jekyll is right to see this as the beginning of "the end." For him to revert to a bestial, disreputable self even while he's sitting at the very heart of a calculated refuge from drink suggests that it is not just he who has lost control of his baser elements. It is London itself as well, as the city had been carefully re-engineered by various urban planners and park apologists from James Nash to Octavia Hill. "Soho drunkenness" has overwhelmed "Mayfair respectability" in the very heart of a sabbatarian refuge, as though the 1855 Hyde Park Riots had moved north into royalty's own pastoral fastness.

Ten. Jekyll and Hyde: Beginnings and Endings

Appropriately, Hyde flees straight to a "hotel in Portland Street" in order to strategize. Given that there *is* no actual "Portland Street" in central London, Stevenson must have in mind either Portland *Place*, which extends the grand line of Broad Walk (the park's central avenue), Park Square, and Park Crescent straight down to the top of Regent Street; or *Great* Portland Street, running parallel just to the east; or *Little* Portland Street, which connects the two just below Mortimer Street. In whichever case, Hyde's attempt to re-establish his "city of refuge" is undertaken precisely on the topographical axis that separates Mayfair from Soho, respectable and moderate wine-drinkers from low swillers of gin. Thus, if it is telling that Jekyll *loses* control in the most salubrious spot along this symbolic line, Hyde's attempt to *re-establish* control on that same line is equally so. Significantly, Hyde recalls, "I could write in my own hand," and so he is effectively able to send a message from "Jekyll" off to his old friend Lanyon, who lives just to the west in Cavendish Square, seeking the doctor's assistance. Although Jekyll's and Hyde's literal hands differ markedly (87–8), they share a uniform cursive script. In exactly the same way, Jekyll's Mayfair proprieties and Hyde's Soho depravities could hardly be more different, yet their "territories" unmistakably merge at the Regent Street "border"—at the southern end of which Piccadilly Circus has long provided for the quintessential if notorious intermingling of privilege and the demimonde (Hampson 107). Unfortunately for Jekyll, the exiled Hyde proves to be the quintessential "insurgent horror" (95), and the doctor is finally no longer able to keep him at bay "across town" in his own hedonistic Soho digs. Critics have indeed seen the implicit urban drama of *J&H* as informed by Stevenson's youthful negotiation of the marked social and moral boundaries between Edinburgh's Old and New Towns, frequently suggesting in the process that the novella is scarcely about London at all (Bell 177–8; Calder 5). Yet the story is most definitely about London in a very particular way — and a way that makes special sense when one examines the tale in light of the Alcohol Question and the urban planning that it inspired.

The last topical "separation of elements" worth looking into involves the novel ideological split between work-world and leisure that was precipitated by British industrialization — a conceptual phenomenon that had its own dire ramifications for the temperance movement. Consciously or no, Stevenson invites this line of analysis as well, quite early in Jekyll's "Statement." "Both sides of me were in dead earnest," the doctor affirms; "I was no more myself when I laid aside restraint and plunged in shame, than when I laboured in the eye of day, at the furtherance of knowledge or the relief of sorrow or suffering" (81). Jekyll "labours" as a scientist and a doctor, establishing no greater identity outside his professional life than his chums do. Hyde, however, is defined by his "laying aside of restraint" and "plunging in shame" (with all the coded significance that Stevenson attached to "plungers").[6] His own little "man about town," Jekyll tells us, is not simply the embodiment of "impatient gaiety" (81); he also affords the carnivalesque "disguise" in which Jekyll can discreetly enjoy "the *pleasures* which [he] made haste to seek" (86; italics added). Jekyll is the principle of "work," then, to Hyde's "play." The problem is that the play turns very dark, and the player eventually overthrows all the referees.

Throughout the eighteenth century into the early nineteenth, as Peter Bailey has shown us, Britain was like other pre-industrial societies in that it manifested "no clear-cut division between labour and leisure and the daily round was seasoned with a good deal of complementary sociability.... Work and leisure intermingled in the life of the workshop where traditional craft practices laid down the ritual patterns of celebration and good fellowship" (2, 3). Those "ritual patterns" frequently enough involved alcohol, as John Dunlop documents so copiously. As a result, drinking on the job (or coming to the work place in one's cups) was a common occurrence up through the early years of the Industrial Revolution (Cunningham 68). Predictably, however, the ever-increasing mechanization of production led not only to those unprecedented levels of industrial output and profit that rendered the "wasted time" of ritual hugely "inconvenient" to employers (Harrison, *Drink* 40) but also to a workplace in which inebriation posed a significant threat to life, limb, and expensive machinery alike. It obviously behooved nobody to have bits of drunken workers caught up in the equipment — or, indeed, vice versa.

The obvious response of people in financial and governmental power was to hearken to reformers like Dunlop and devise regulations and policies that purged the workplace of congenial ritual and ceremonial alcohol alike, separating *homo economicus* from *homo ludens* in the same way that Jekyll attempts to do with Hyde.[7] The results, however, were highly consequential for our argument in two main ways. First of all, many in the working class bitterly resented any attempts to impinge on their traditional customs, consequently directing towards employers, magistrates, and collaborating teetotalers alike the kind of popular animus so exuberantly demonstrated in Hyde Park in 1855 (Harrison, *Drink* 309; Bailey 5). Second, and even more significantly for Victorian England and for our study, the more that working-class recreation was dissociated from the work place and, in turn, from the many rituals that had long given it acceptable shape in that setting, the more it was frighteningly "on the loose." "There is no doubt," writes Brian Harrison, "that the nineteenth-century temperance debate was really an argument about how leisure should be spent" (*Drink* 32). After all, leisure — in the sense of time *completely* separate from work and workplace; or of recreation "relocated in the life-space, forming a separate and self-contained section in the increasingly compartmentalized way of life" (Bailey 4) — was something altogether novel and, given the enhanced efficiency of mechanized production, available in ever-expanding quantities. In terms of individuals, "once a man walked out of the factory gates in the big city," Bailey tells us, "he was in a sense freer than in any previous age" (4). Even if he weren't a recent immigrant to the city, with new money in his pocket but bored by impersonal labor and markedly cut off from his wonted communal bonds and restraints, he was no longer bound by what had evolved to be the holistic ethos of a craft, a tried-and-true system for balancing productivity and conviviality in an ultimately symbiotic and sustainable way. In the alternate terms of behavioral institutions, leisure in the abstract now constituted a "fluid and open territory" that Bailey tells us "threatened to outstrip the reach of existing systems of social control" (4–5). The worry, of course, was that both man and institution would be drawn to the control-resistant world of the *pub*, a compensatory but unregulated realm "in which communality and gregariousness were in part a response to the mobility and moral anonymity of urbanism, the tendency for the segmentation of work place, family and leisure" (Smith 330).[8] The expansion of leisure and improved wages were in fact widely seen as a recipe for inebriation — even clinical insanity (Mitchell 27–8; Lewis, *Traffic* 11–12; McCandless 52). As the substantial profits of industry trickled down to the worker, wrote Goodwin Smith in the *Contemporary Review* in 1873, "the period of transition from low to high wages, and from incessant toil to comparative leisure, must be one of peril to the masses." "Our streets are reeking with the abuse of pleasure," a prominent churchman had warned a year earlier; "our society is rotten with it; our best institutions are being shaken and paralysed by it" (Bailey 106; 79). In sum, the "Jekyll" world of productive labor had invented an autonomous monster called Leisure, albeit for ostensibly high-minded ends. And in the hands of Leisure, as in the hands of Hyde, "pleasure" was feared to be devolving ever more alarmingly into "abuse."

If the sometime-liberated masses were to prove unable to exercise an appropriate restraint over themselves, then upper- and middle-class shapers of ideology needed to step into the breach. "Viewed from above," asserts Peter Bailey, "leisure constituted a problem whose solution required the building of a new social conformity — a play discipline to complement the work discipline that was the principal means of social control in an industrial capitalist society. In contrast to the harsh offensive of the earlier period of industrialization, however, the policy was now to be pursued through the reform of popular recreations rather than their repression" (5). From the second quarter of the nineteenth century on, middle- and upper-class employers and reformers came increasingly to believe that their own drying out of the workplace, their own support for Enclosure and for ostensible temperance measures like the Beerhouses Act, together with their own increasing tendency towards the residential and customary exclusivity we have discussed above, "were driving the poor to the ... world of drink and drink-based entertainment" (Cunningham 86). We needn't expand here on all of the varied particulars of the ensuing patrician response, since many have already been touched on above: sabbatarianism, the systematic re-establishment of open spaces, the Self-Help movement, the development of recreational counter-attractions and alternative, non-alcoholic beverages, and so forth — not to mention other forms of "rational recreation" and educational reform. Just as Stevenson's novella reflects many of the problems associated with "separations" or schisms of a behavioral or residential or (in this last instance) ideological sort, it also reflects many strategies of amendment, as we've seen. A few more things need to be said, however, about the increasing awareness of England's "haves" that they themselves were largely responsible for the parlous and threatening state of the "have-nots." Again, attention to the contemporary condition of Britain takes us straight to the heart of Stevenson's thematic interests.

As we've seen and as was so often the case, Dickens had his finger squarely on England's pulse when it came to the socio-dynamics of drink. "Drunkenness is rife among the very poor and wretched, as every other low and sensual vice is rife among them, because, for years, they have been *left behind* in the march of civilization, and have been sinking deeper and deeper down into the mire, left in the track of advancing forces" (*Demoralisation* 168; emphasis added). Whether he is discussing people who were still denied the benefits of an expanded educational system (including the famous ragged schools) or those who were literally left in old neighborhoods by more affluent fugitives to the suburbs, Dickens sees the neglect of the Good as a significant cause of Evil. A generation later, Thomas Whitaker could be speaking to either of Dickens' possible concerns or, alternatively, to the dire threat of "free" leisure: "When the subjects of [base passions and uncontrollable desires] happen to get withdrawn from the influence and surroundings which were enough to keep their forefathers tolerably circumspect, it is then the enemy comes in like a flood, and the house is wrecked" (*Brighter England* 17). The answer is re-engagement, Dickens claimed, "a full determination on the part of all classes of society to co-operate for ... an end." He accordingly railed against the rabid teetotalers who effectively prevented the kind of broad-based coalition of prohibitionists and moderationists alike that might collectively have redeemed poor folks who had been outdistanced by Civil Progress (Dickens once again seeing urban decay as a cause of drunkenness, rather than the other way around): "Are we to be told ... that the removal of ignorance, and the removal of dirt, would not remove the drunkenness because the middle and the upper classes chose to set the example of moderation instead of abstinence? If the lowest classes were bought with the influence of any wholesome example at all, which they are not now, is there no example in that quality of moderation which Tee-Total Societies so sorely need?" (*Demoralisation* 169; 166) William Booth, once again a generation later, agreed with Dickens wholeheartedly in terms of moral duty if not moderationist role models, urging the importance of a re-integrated, collective social initiative against poverty and vice: "Co-operation implies the voluntary combination of individuals to the attaining an object by mutual help, mutual counsel, and mutual effort" (229). Denied any consistent contact with the higher classes by all of the various developments that have been treated above, what the lower classes were seen desperately to need was the moral guidance of Dickens' "wholesome examples," and any number of them into the bargain.

While no one seems to have proposed that moderate, educated drinkers of wine be re-introduced to the rollicking confines of the alehouse — or alternatively that the odd gin-swiller be invited to an occasional, staid Mayfair fête — the mid-century nonetheless gave voice to increasing hopes and convictions that other forms of recreation could and should bring the classes back together to everyone's mutual advantage (Cunningham 110). William Thomson, the Archbishop of York, warned in an 1874 sermon on sport and pastimes that the Church was failing in part of its charge to provide the literal ground on which all God's people might meet, and that it needed to take immediate and imaginative steps towards complementing places and times of prayer with places and times of play. The institution was "losing contact with culture at every level," he lamented, lending his voice to the swelling choruses of the 70s and 80s that called on churches themselves to assume a strong role in affording alternative recreations to drink. While some religious traditionalists argued that initiatives of this sort weren't the legitimate business of people who tended to the soul rather than to the body, one layman attending a Congregational symposium took what was a more widely-shared position on the need both to lure lost sheep back into the fold and to tame the wastes and woods as well — in any way that was necessary: "It would be better to reclaim certain amusements," he observed, "than to abandon them to those who abuse them" (Bailey 82). One naturally thinks of Jekyll's dangerous abandonment of his constitutional "gaiety" to the likes of Hyde.

Not surprisingly, parks and open places were pegged as playing vital roles in the "wholesome re-integration" of society, as we've already begun to see. After discussing the foundation of the Metropolitan Public Gardens Association in 1882, H. L. Malchow adds to his account of the hygienic benefits of parks that, "morally, they reformed by providing an alternative to public house amusements and bringing the poor into visual contact with the respectable bourgeoisie on the park promenade." ("In addition," he adds rather cynically, "open spaces were more easily policed than the warren-like back courts and dark alleys of the impacted slum"; 98.) The necessary incentive for the down-trodden to become more "respectable" could be provided with either a carrot or a stick. Robert Slaney, a Member of Parliament, urged again that "A man walking out with his family among his neighbors of different ranks, will naturally be desirous to be properly clothed; ... [and] this desire duly directed and controlled, is found by experience to be of the most powerful effect in promoting Civilisation and exciting industry." Alternatively, conformist sartorial "civility" could essentially be required: a *Times* piece written after Regent's Park was opened to the general public rather condescendingly endorsed the "redemption of the working class through recreation" by affording them "the liberty of taking a walk in the more plebeian portion of the park, provided they have a decent coat on" (Bailey 63).

Even bolder proposals were floated for a salutary rapprochement of the classes. Planners of Victoria Park, for example, cherished hopes that prosperous city folk might be lured back into the East End by the luster of impressive new housing on the park's periphery (Malchow 123). Unfortunately, the scheme met with little success. Economist Stanley Jevons nonetheless spoke for a substantial number of Englishmen when he identified "a positive *duty* on the part of the middle and upper classes to frequent the well-conducted places of popular recreation" in order to set a refining example (Bailey 106; italics added). Increasingly cognizant of having severed too many ties with "the people," those who were "dutifully" solicitous of the Common Good sought throughout the second half of the century to redress the balance.

"Balance," of course, is Stevenson's prime term in *J&H* for the proper conduct and carriage of the individual, in ways that nicely elide the distinctions between moral deportment and literal equilibrium and thus, arguably and as well, between the errant thinker and the stumbling drinker. At first, the part of him which becomes Hyde seems to Jekyll to be a psychic and moral burden that impedes "his more upright twin" in his desire to "walk steadfastly and securely on his upright path" (82)— and thus to reclaim the guiltlessness of those callow, pre-potion days, when he tells us he "had walked with [his] father's hand" (91), balanced by a parent's moral and literal strength. Yet once Jekyll severs the original ties between the two sides of his nature—the "high" and the "low," the "labourer" and the "pleasure seeker"—Hyde careens out of control, sadly justifying Jekyll's early fear that "the *balance* of [his] nature might be permanently overthrown" (88–9; added emphasis). While at times Jekyll blames the dire results entirely on his swarthy alter-ego ("It was Hyde, after all, and Hyde alone, that was guilty"; 87), at other times he shows the same awareness of his own instrumental complicity that characterized upper- and middle-class reformers of England: "I had voluntarily stripped myself of all those *balancing instincts* by which even the worst of us continues to walk with some degree of steadiness among temptations; and in my case, to be tempted, however slightly, was to fall" (90; italics added). For Jekyll at the start, the "upright path" must have seemed very much the way of Dickens' "march of civilization." But the lower self he leaves behind, abandoned in his "progressive" track, perverts his newfound leisure and freedom into a ruinous pursuit of brutish pleasures— and the "muddy ways" of Soho or the "slime of the pit" into which he figuratively and perhaps literally falls are the direct equivalents of Dickens' "mire." Jekyll attempts to re-impose control, even resorting in that climactic scene in Regent's Park to a classic location for temperate diversion and social rapprochement. But it is too late. Hyde has full access to a doctor's wealth and, ironically, to his "respectable" clothes as well—without ever having to amend his life in any way to enjoy their use.

If we now turn our attention to the other end of Jekyll's personal account, we again discover the framework of the Drink Problem undergirding the plot. "The Last Night" finds Jekyll's butler, Poole, coming distractedly to Utterson's rooms to seek the lawyer's aid in dealing with his master. Jekyll has been acting very erratically, sending off to his chemists for supplies that, once they're delivered, he all but hurls back at Poole for their inadequacy. He finally seems to have disappeared altogether. This is the scene we explored earlier in which the oenophilic Utterson offers Poole a glass of wine which, we're told twice, remains conspicuously "untasted" (62,63). The careful and repeated attention to drink at this climactic point in the story seems important, and readers will recall that Poole's refusing to drink the wine *might* suggest that he is a teetotaler, something that would be perfectly consistent with his working-class origins, as his humble roots are confirmed not only by his professional position but also by his occasionally ungrammatical turn of phrase. ("Yes, sir, he do indeed," he says to Utterson at one point; 41). Poole, in any case, is initiating what a modern counseling center would call an active "intervention," complete with a forced entry into the sufferer's room. And while the terminology is obviously anachronistic, the concept is most assuredly not, for the butler's urgency in responding to the needs of a ruined man is very much in line with the program of the teetotalers, a large part of whose charge was first to embrace those who had plunged to the lower levels of society from which many of their own activist numbers had sprung, and then to "redeem" them and restore them to something of their former estate. Conversely, more "moderationist" factions of the temperance movement tended to limit their efforts to *preventing* such tumbles into perdition, and were wont to wash their hands of any new pariahs who slipped through their fingers—regardless of their social origins. Brian Harrison outlines the rift between classes which characterized the early years of the reform movement, as the moderate, largely middle-class, moral suasionists ceded (or lost) control of the cause to working-class prohibitionists:

> When an anti-spirits society adopted the teetotal pledge, gentility [as in "gentlefolk"] usually departed in a hurry. The rise of teetotalism within the anti-spirits movement constitutes a *coup* by an elite of working men allied with radicals and nonconformists.... For as soon as emphasis

switched from preserving the sober to reclaiming the intemperate, the temperance movement outgrew its original respectable basis of support [*Drink* 137–38].

The issue, as noted earlier, was largely one of will. Moderate, middle-class reformers like Dickens, surrounded by peers who as a class had significantly amended their drinking habits in the ways he forcefully celebrates, naturally saw drunkenness not as a problem of continued availability but rather as a failure of self-restraint: "the drunkard had failed to exert his willpower and deserved denunciation" (Harrison, *Drink* 115). Conversely, working-class reformers, surrounded by the undeniable alcoholic excesses of their peers (ironically compounded in the 1830s by the very Beerhouses Act that had been intended to bring the situation under control), saw the problem less in the drunkard than in the powerful, omnipresent Drink Traffic: "for the teetotaler, the drunkard's will had been paralysed by alcohol, and he deserved sympathy" (Harrison, *Drink* 115). Total personal abstinence was the only abiding solution, ultimately to be buttressed by public prohibition. Again, as a result, working-class reformers were more than willing to get their hands dirty, while moderationists, despite their eagerness to help prevent drunkenness, tended to turn away from anyone who fell to the depths (Shiman 10, 246). Accordingly, reports Harrison, "Teetotalers like [Joseph] Livesey and [Thomas] Whittaker could be seen walking the streets arm-in-arm with drunkards whom moderationists spurned as an embarrassment to their cause" (*Drink*, 115).

Once again, then, it makes perfect sense in a novella that treats Jekyll/Hyde as all but an alcoholic that it should be a working-class man who refuses to drink who provides the impetus for an attempt at salvage. Poole's motives, of course, may well be over-determined by aspects of both plot and sub-plot. He may be both a total abstainer *and* a loyal servant whose livelihood depends on the welfare of his master. But the butler is willing, like the archetypal good teetotaler, to get involved. Lanyon, in distinct contrast, takes the more censorious upper-crust line. Again, once he has seen first-hand the extent of Jekyll's fall, he swears to Utterson with trembling hand, "I wish to see or hear no more of Doctor Jekyll.... I am quite done with that person; and I beg that you will spare me any allusion to one whom I regard as dead" (57).[9] Jekyll, who also shows no marked and purposeful interest in redeeming (as opposed to terminally suppressing) what he considers to be a fallen side of himself, refers to Hyde as "the slime of the pit" or "what was dead" (95), resorting just as

Lanyon does to the lurid rhetoric of drink's great critics.[10] It is in fact Utterson who is, in these terms, the most interesting character in the novella. His characterization as "the last good influence in the lives of down-going men" (29) positions him as a kind of potential Catcher in the Rye for alcoholics, perhaps even a 19th-century "Bill W." He is moved to look into the troubling business of Hyde and Jekyll's will, and he effectively extracts from his friend the timeless promise of the classic alcoholic: "I will tell you one thing: the moment I choose, I can be rid of Mr Hyde" (44; also 52). He tries, as we've seen, to interest his old friend in a program of salutary Sunday exercise. And he agrees, furthermore, to assist Poole in his "intervention." But, when push comes to shove, Utterson is also given to looking the other way. Thus, after Enfield has in the opening chapter told "the Story of the Door" and afterwards proposes, "Let us make a bargain never to refer to this again,' Utterson responds, "With all my heart.... I shake hands on that Richard" (34). As for "The Incident as the Window," what the two men see only leads them to "walk on once more in silence" (61). Early on, we are told that Utterson "used to say quaintly: 'I let my brother go to the devil in his own way'" (29). His actual, demonstrated solicitousness for Jekyll is assuredly such that one cannot seriously charge him with the cavalier indifference that his words affect. On the other hand, it is precisely to the devil that his friend ends up going, and Utterson is able or willing to do nothing to change that. While he promises Poole at the end of "The Last Night" that he will return "before midnight" to take the next step in resolving his friend's misfortune, we never hear that he does. Whether or not he finally turns from his fallen friend as Victorian moderationists turned from those who had ignored their warnings must perhaps remain an unanswered question — if also perhaps one that somehow speaks to Stevenson's central concerns.

Moving to other relevant themes in the "intervention scene," we note that Poole's report on Jekyll's terminal distraction focuses on the doctor's efforts to secure more of the chemicals he requires for his "experiment."

> All this last week ... him, or it, or whatever it is that lives in that cabinet, has been crying night and day for some sort of medicine and cannot get it to his mind.... Every day ... there have been orders and complaints, and I have been sent flying to all the wholesale chemists in town. Every time I brought the stuff back, there would be another paper telling me to return it, because it was not pure, and another order to a different firm. This drug is wanted bitter bad, sir, whatever for [65].

Subsequently, of course, we learn from Jekyll himself that his "transforming draught" is no longer effective not because his new supply of "salt" (83, 96) was *not* pure but rather because it *was*: "I am now persuaded that my first supply was impure, and that it was that unknown impurity which lent efficacy to the draught" (96).[11] It may be fanciful to read Utterson's comment that Jekyll wants his drug "*bitter* bad" as punning evidence of the tale's topical focus on alcohol, "bitter" of course being a noted style of British ale. Nevertheless, Jekyll's problems with the purity of his chemicals is very much in line with one of the era's gravest consumer concerns: the widespread and uncontrolled adulteration of a wide range of products — everything from foodstuffs to drugs to alcohol.

Richard Altick has provided a very useful overview of the consumer crisis in *The Presence of the Present: Topics of the Day in the Victorian Novel* (562–68), despite the fact that he completely overlooks *J&H* and its impure salts. The problem broke into widespread public awareness with Friedrich Christian Accum's *Treatise on Adulterations of Food* (1820), in which this Librarian of the Royal Institution formally exposed the alarming extent of the practice, especially among druggists and the wholesale grocers who supplied breweries (562): Accum offered "a horrendous list of chemicals and other materials introduced by brewers into their liquor" (Clark 294). John Mitchell followed in 1848 with his noteworthy *Treatise on the Falsification of Food*, but the practice persisted and, indeed, became ever more extensive — with breweries and pubs taking a pernicious lead in the abuse (563). William Howitt, for example, had lamented shortly before Mitchell published his exposé that "a new class of ale houses has sprung up under the new Beer Act which, being generally kept by people without capital, often without character, their liquor supplied by public brewers, and *adulterated by themselves*, have done more to demoralize the population of both town and country than any other legislative measure within the last century" (McCormack 59; added emphasis). Parliament responded in 1860 with its Act for Preventing the Adulteration of Articles of Food and Drink, but the measure was fraught with loopholes and it did little to stem the tide of deceptive practices (Greenwood xv). Some of that Act's flaws were addressed and amended in subsequent parliamentary initiatives of 1872 and 1875, but the issue remained insistently topical well into the 1890s and found its way into the work of the most eminent Victorian writers. Altick cites a butler in Dickens' *Our Mutual Friend* whose demeanor as he offers a glass of Chablis to a diner "seemed to say 'You wouldn't if you knew what it's made of'"; and Grimes the publican from Trollope's *Can You Forgive Her?* claims, "It's my belief the more you poison their liquor, the more the people likes it" (567).[12]

The adulterator's prime motive would seem to have been to "stretch" the product and thereby enhance profit. This was commonly the case for food (where "fillers" in sausage continued to be the fodder of popular skepticism and humor well into the twentieth century) and frequently the case for alcohol as well; prior to Gladstone's reduction of high duties on imports in 1860, wine had been a prime case in point, as Dickens' butler suggests. More frequently with drink, however, the way to increased profit involved nefarious strategies to *increase* a beverage's potency and addictiveness (Longmate 14). The real concern was not with self-evidently fortified drinks like Port, although Cyrus Redding's *History and Description of Modern Wines* (1851) decried that popular import as "adulterated with brandy" (Merrett 122) and Kate Mitchell, some thirty years later, ranted against the "doctoring" of imported wines for the sake of preservation and strength (42–3). After all, when Michael Henchard asked that his furmity be spiked with rum, or when chilled boaters on the Thames took their beer in the form of "purl"—"heated nearly to the boiling point and flavoured with gin, sugar, and ginger" (Mayhew 259)—they knew exactly what they were letting themselves in for. It was the "secret" and sometimes addictive fortifiers that were the most frightening to the general public, and that ultimately stirred a strong parliamentary response. Accum's *Treatise* revealed that among the brewers' most frequent and effective additives was opium (Clark 294). James Greenwood's *Seven Curses of London* supplements Accum's "horrendous list" of brewery additives with a daunting panoply of his own, all of them designed to "increase the intoxicating properties of the liquor": cocculus indicus, fox-glove, green copperas, hartshorn shavings, henbane, jalop, multum, nut-galls, nux vomica, opium, oil of vitriol, potash, wormwood, and yew tops (216). In the end, it is exactly this sort of unannounced "impurity" in Jekyll's "blood-red liquor" that renders the doctor's potion so lethally "efficacious," something perhaps by way of the "phosphorous and ... volatile ether" that Lanyon believes he can whiff in the effective version of the brew (76). Thinking that he was simply freeing his alter ego to pursue "undignified pleasures," Jekyll discovers to his dismay that Hyde's wonted recreations "turn towards the monstrous" (86). Shortly before Stevenson penned his story, Frances Power Cobbe had in her "Wife-torture in England" (1878) cried out against the way adulteration was steadily and consistently transforming "seas of brandy and gin" into "infuriating poisons" (McCormack 7–8). *J&H* could have provided her with an almost perfect exemplum.

Stevenson was certainly attuned to the problem, in ways that any sentient Victorian could hardly have avoided. Dr. Desprez, in 1882's short story "The Treasure of Franchard," assures his protégé that, "Pure air..., *unadulterated wine*, and the reflections of an unsophisticated spirit in the presence of the works of nature — these, my boy, are the best medical appliances and the best religious comforts" (33–4; emphasis added). The efficient — and ultimately lethal — agent in Jekyll's potion is a "simple crystalline salt of a white color" which Lanyon watches Hyde add to a phial of blood-red liquor (76). That it might stand in Stevenson's mind not merely for an ingredient in a kind of curious punch but also, in some calculated or uncalculated way, for the kind of adulterating agents that lent both potency and poisonousness to alcohol is rendered more plausible when we consider that Johnny Adams' murder in *The Beach of Falesá* is effected when his rival tradesman Randall slips what a native calls "white sand — bad sand" into his gin bottle: "He got the bottle still," the man warns Wiltshire. "Suppose he give you gin, you no take him" (18). "Now I had heard much the same story in other islands," reflects Wiltshire, "and the same white powder always to the front." There are certainly shades here of *Treasure Island*'s liquor as an "artificially compounded death." And speaking of the liquorish abandon of pirates, the sometime narrator Chevalier de Burke remarks of a frightful shipboard binge in *The Master of Ballantrae*, "I have heard many a drunken bout in my time, many on board that very *Sarah*, but never anything the least like this, *which made me early suppose the liquor had been tampered with*" (54; emphasis added.)

Punch, as with virtually every other mid- to late-century topic that related to alcohol and its abuse, was consistently interested in adulteration. In "A Seasonable Song," which appeared in the Christmas number of 1880, the magazine itself is toasted at "Carnival Time" by a very Cruikshankian death's head sporting evening apparel — the figure being drawn next to the verses — who is compounding a punch in a large bowl. He allows that the "sherry shows traces of sulphate" and that the water "is charged with some deleterious gas," but claims that fact should dampen no one's spirits:

> Let's fill up the tumbler to lighten our toil,
> Though whiskey too often contains fusel oil;
> Though rum, which our sailors imbibe, has been said
> To be charged with red pepper and sugar of lead;

> Though Cocculus Indicus lurks in the beer —
> We'll try them, for Christmas comes once in a year [297].

In the same vein, the May 17 issue of 1884 features a drawing that treats the adulteration of sherry. It is especially interesting, however, that when *Punch* published its parody of Stevenson's novella in February 1886, only a month after *J&H* first appeared, the key psychic transformation is attributed to "powdered acidulated drops." The hero, Trekyl, explains the final crisis thus:

> Well, that acidulated fool Hidanseek got into serious trouble, and I wanted to cut him. But I couldn't; when I had divided myself into him one day, I found it impossible to get the right sort of sugar to bring me back again. For the right sort of sugar was adulterated, and adulterated sugar cannot be obtained in London [64].

This must afford reasonably strong evidence that the magazine's parodists thought Stevenson's original story was somehow about the pernicious effects of adulteration — though certainly not of sugar, perhaps of drugs, and perhaps even of alcohol. Their sense of the novella's topicality on this particular issue was significantly anticipated by an unsigned January review in the *Birmingham Daily Post*, which observed of Jekyll's drug that "his first supply had been adulterated, and it was the unknown adulteration which gave it its strange power" (Linehan 94). We shall return to the *Punch* item shortly to refine our argument about adulterations of strong drink.

The last scene we must consider is essentially the last in the novella, in terms of actual chronology. Certain of their need to intervene in Jekyll's disappearance or indisposition, Utterson and Poole have just burst through the door of the Doctor's "cabinet." In contrast to the violence and clamor of their assault, what follows is something a shock, even to them:

> The besiegers, appalled by their own riot and the stillness that succeeded, stood back a little and peered in. There lay the cabinet before their eyes in the quiet lamplight, a good fire glowing and chattering on the hearth, the kettle singing its thin strain, a drawer or two open, papers neatly set forth on the business table, and nearer the fire, the things laid out for tea; the quietest room, you would have said, and, but for the glazed presses full of chemicals, the most commonplace that night in London [69–70].

For sheer coziness, the setting is unmatched by anything in the novel save the "*Wine Spectator*" scene in which Utterson "melts" by the fireside with

Mr. Guest. It is significant for our argument, however, that while the element that combines with fire to create the warmth of the earlier, implicitly juxtaposed scene is *wine*, in which "the glow of hot autumn afternoons on hillside vineyards was ready to be set free and to disperse the fogs of London" (54), now the presiding liquid genius is insistently *tea*. Given that Jekyll has earlier finished his written statement "under the influence of the last of the old powders" (96) and at that point fully expects to revert to Hyde within the half hour (97), it is only sensible to assume that Hyde has now been Hyde long enough for him to have been the one to put the kettle on the hob — this despite the distinct difficulty of imagining a murderous degenerate, even a very British degenerate, brewing up a "hot cuppa" in a perfectly tidy and cozy room. Valerie Martin seems to come closer to getting it right in a visceral sense when in her thoughtful redaction, *Mary Reilly*, her Hyde *crushes* a tea-cup in his bare hands, smearing the blood over Mary's face. Nonetheless, this is what Stevenson gives us, and in a fundamentally unlooked-for way that is accentuated in a subsequent passage. The kettle suddenly boils over — which again suggests that it was put on quite recently (read, by Hyde) rather than sitting a long time at a low simmer (say since Jekyll was writing his final account) — and thus re-attracts the men's attention: "This brought them to the fireside, where the easy chair was drawn cosily up, and the tea things stood ready to the sitter's elbow, the very sugar in the cup" (71).[13]

In this tale of consequentially transforming draughts, then, the last drink that we are literally and insistently (if somewhat incongruously) shown is tea — hands-down the quintessential (and thus the *stereotypical*) temperance drink. The iconographic status of the beverage was so strongly established by Stevenson's time that, in drawing after drawing in *Punch* — as we've indeed seen — teapots invariably signaled "teetotalism," whether or not any accompanying captions or dialogue reinforced their specific identification with, say, Sir Andrew Agnew or Sir Wilfred Lawson. One assumes, then, that if the specific context of "social satire" that was *Punch*'s focus was sufficient to yield this particular, un-annotated "meaning" for tea, the same might be said for the related context of "late-Victorian drink" provided by the whole of *J&H*. The novella's striking "tea scene," in other words, is very likely to have been read by Stevenson's original audience as a politically significant variant on the earlier Utterson-Guest encounter.

On a practical front, none of the many alternative beverages on which counter-attractionists depended was more central than tea. In the crucial years between 1852 and 1890, when "temperance fever" raged to its height, tea consumption in England rose by a striking *300%*, owing in no small part to Gladstone's very calculated campaign to increase the duty on spirits while reducing that on tea (Longmate 211–12; Harrison, *Drink* 301–2). As early as the crucial Preston temperance initiatives of the 1830s, free teas were among reformers' most successful tools in attracting drunkards to their rallies. In 1876, The British Women's Association successfully diverted substantial numbers of manufacturing workers from public houses by organizing tea and coffee stalls at the entrances of their factories (Sournia 125). So closely was tea tied to public conceptions of abstinence, in fact, that some Britons rather amusingly assumed that, once a teetotaler had taken the pledge, he could drink nothing *but* tea (Shiman 25; 42). In any case, Hardy's Michael Henchard pointedly and representatively confirms his recovery before Farfrae by swearing that, since his fateful furmity binge, he's "drunk nothing stronger than tea" (38); and Elizabeth later takes the fallen former mayor tea "to prevent his taking other liquor" (182). Finally, the paradigmatic counter-attractionist *Coffee Public House: How to Establish and Manage It* images in 1877 a proleptic version of Jekyll's study, albeit one with more company than the doctor and his alter-ego are able to enjoy: "Give the working man a public house where he may meet his friends and talk and smoke ... and where good coffee and tea ... take the place of beer and gin ... a warm and cheerful room and a comfortable seat ... a boon they rarely enjoy" (Longmate 210). The obvious goal was to re-create all of the convivial glow we see in the Utterson-Guest scene, but with a whistling pot instead of a popping cork.

That the inventor of the novella's rather surprising last scene behind the shattered door himself thought of tea as a prime temperance drink is confirmed by the persistence of one of Stevenson's favorite puns, as in his report that a conversation with the drunken Haggard "made [him] a *tea*totaller" (*Letters* 8.383; emphasis added), or his writing to Henry James that to be kept from "drink[ing] to comfort all the days of [his] life" is to wear an unwelcome "*tea*total badge" (*Letters* 8.109; my emphasis). We know from his signing a letter to Baxter "tee-totally yours" that he could manage the proper spelling. So, on balance and in the rich context of the current argument, it would seem significant that he chose to end his story of damaging beverages with his main character, in one or the other of his guises, sitting right in the middle of what amounts to a private and rather surprisingly "respectable" little temperance scene. When Jekyll/Hyde is, perforce, "out of spirits"—when he can no longer partake of his "red liquor" and "transforming draught"—it is tea he evidently drinks as an alternative, either as a tonic to settle his troubled spirits (if we want to read the scene in the simplest possible way) or as the thing that the reformers almost invariably recommended as the antidote of choice for drunken excess (if we wish to follow our sustained argument to another logical imagistic conclusion). The maddening "cups" of his rage have resolved into a humble tea-cup, expectantly laid out by a quiet fireside, pre-filled with its ballast of sugar. It could, in fact, have been this last detail that inspired Stevenson's *Punch* parodist to invent his "sugar" as the antidote to Trekyl's "acidulated drops"; as "sugar" tempers "acid" in the magazine, sugared tea may be called upon to compensate for a mordant "liquor" in the novella.

There are those who might argue that Hyde would be very unlikely to drink tea by choice; that, if he is indeed the one who put the kettle on the hob and the sugar in the cup, this is merely the last, desperate consolation of blackguard who, villainous as he may be, is still British. A more reflective case might be made that Hyde is in fact possessed of a few redeeming qualities and that, in the manner of Michael Henchard, he could be using tea to re-impose on his character a measure of the same kind of order that, one gathers, he has re-imposed (or at least not destroyed) in the room itself, with those "papers neatly set forth on the business table, and nearer the fire, the things laid out for tea."[14] In essence, however, it doesn't really matter for our argument whether it is Jekyll or Hyde who is brewing (and tidying) up here. Unless, that is, we as readers are being asked to decide, like either a teetotaler or a moderationist, whether or not Hyde has it in him to reform; whether he deserves our readerly sympathies (as Poole is almost prepared to accord him; 69) or whether we should completely turn our backs on him. For a tale that has in so many ways suggested a tragic personal and cultural struggle with alcohol, it's a subtle but perfectly apt ending. The man who has assured Utterson that, whenever he chooses, he can be rid of his demon in fact dies in a setting that comes as close as it possibly could to being therapeutic. Push come to shove, he has in at least one of his two incarnations become a tea-drinker. But it is simply too late.

ELEVEN

Stevenson's "Allegory" and Its Reception

In his early biography of Stevenson, nephew Graham Balfour reports that Fanny advised her husband to re-work the hastily-written first draft of *J&H* because "it was really an allegory, and he had treated it as if it were a story" (Swearingen 100). Balfour goes on to say, "In the first draft Jekyll's nature was bad all through, and the Hyde change was worked only for the sake of a disguise," which leads one to conclude that any "allegory" Stevenson was eventually moved to pursue was in the line of Prudentius, a timeless, general psychomachia of virtue and vice, of the "upright" and "unjust" sides of human nature that Jekyll ultimately describes.[1] Since one of the consistent arguments of this study, however, has been that Stevenson and his Brownies between them injected what at times approaches a more specific and topical allegory of alcoholism and temperance into a "story" of fantastic shape-shifting — the kind of typological narrative Thackeray had in mind when he said about Cruikshank's Gin Juggernaut, "The allegory is as good, as earnest, and as fanciful as one of John Bunyan's" — it is worth taking a moment to consider two things: first, the extent to which "The Drinking Question" was presented to him by his Age in a pre-determinedly allegorical way; and, second, the existence of any evidence inside or outside the novella that a writer best known for an eclectic blend of romance and realism was nonetheless sufficiently drawn to the allegorical mode to produce the sporadically polysemous text we claim to have read.

The first task is easy enough to accomplish. *Punch*'s drawings alone deluged Stevenson with allegorical personifications of virtually every issue on the political horizon, from the time he was a six-year-old charmed by the picture of "a man beating a great many drums on an engine" (*Letters* 1.91)) to the time when, at thirty-two, he likely saw "Publican-Barrel and Pharisee-Pump." But the temperance fever of the 1880s also brought red-letter events like the publication of Thomas Whittaker's allegorically titled *Life's Battles in Temperance Armour* (1884), which chronicled in very Bunyanesque fashion "the *Moderation* Town, its dangers and difficulties; the *Drunken* Town, its madness and miseries; the *Teetotal* Town, its triumphs and blessings" (210). John Barleycorn, the traditional personification of British drink, was also alive and well in Stevenson's day, starring in 1879's *Trial of John Barleycorn alias Strong Drink*. 1882 in fact boasted a witty variation on this old chestnut in *The Trial of John and Jane Temperance*, in which characters like "Mr. Muchprofit" complain about things like losing seats in Parliament to teetotallers who spend too little money on their campaigns (Longmate 197). The next year, Frederick Charrington was filling the streets of London with pamphlets that showed angels and demons struggling for men's souls, duly reinforcing the point that the rhetoric of temperance was as regularly allegorical as it was anecdotal. Thus, when one moment Hyde is called "a little man" and the next we are told that, "it wasn't like a man; it was like some damned Juggernaut" (31), Stevenson's villain may be seen as walking the fine line between realistic fiction and the kind of personification allegory the age very well knew.[2]

Admittedly, not many of Stevenson's fictions press especially hard towards the realm of intellectual abstraction. In fact, Fanny's contention that his inordinately speedy first draft had entirely "missed" the potential allegory suggests that his natural, spontaneous mode was far more verisimilar than *J&H* eventually became. "Will o' the Mill" is perhaps something of an exception, with an embodiment of Death playing a key role in the plot. But *Cornhill* editor Leslie Stephen, who well knew what he liked and disliked about Stevenson, faulted the story for its indeterminate oscillation between realism and allegory, and Stevenson himself later deemed it "cat's meat" (McLynn 139). And despite a title that might recall the subject of an old morality play, "Crabbed Age and Youth" (1878) is essentially a veiled, personal rumination on Louis's stormy relationship with his father.

Nevertheless, Stevenson had at least a playful taste for allegory and symbolic representation. He wrote to Fanny Sitwell in 1874, "My father regards this life 'as a shambling sort of omnibus which is taking him to his hotel.' Is that not well said?" (*Letters* 2.47). In 1882, he proposed to Baxter that he devise an "emblematic woodcut" to grace the tomb of the irascible wine-merchant, Brash, and he had earlier humorously allowed that the second man Fanny Stevenson ended up marrying (i.e., himself) was "much fitter for an emblem of mortality than a bridegroom" (*Letters* 4.9, 3.203). When Stevenson decided that he no longer believed in "the strange tea-party dream that Thackeray invented and called life," it was only to substitute a darker figurative vision of humanity, "egg-dancing among crimes and volcanoes" (*Letters* 2.269–70). In fact, when he offered his catalogue of "Books Which Have Influenced Me" (1887), Stevenson allowed that he "must name the 'Pilgrim's Progress,' a book that breathes of every beautiful and valuable emotion" (273).

Bunyan's work curiously obsessed the author of *J&H*. In an 1876 letter to Fanny Sitwell, he vowed to dip into *Pilgrim's Progress* "now and again" for the rest of his life (*Letters* 2.176). His nanny Alison Cunningham had read the work to him in the Edinburgh nursery (*Letters* 1.85), and as late as 1894 he contemplated putting together an edition of the work for Methuen's "English Classics" (*Letters* 8.328, 330). In dedicating *Travels with a Donkey* to Sidney Colvin, he wrote that "we are all travellers in what John Bunyan calls the wilderness of this world—all, too, travellers with a donkey" (9). Yet the extent to which Stevenson somehow identified with the seventeenth-century allegorist is best, if most playfully, suggested by the fact that he essentially signed two of his letters to Henley (in 1882 and 1884) with the earlier writer's name: one "William Pegfurth Bannatyne, witnessed by John Bunyan" and the other simply "John Bunyan" (*Letters* 3.338, 4.248).

Most revealing of all is the end of "A Chapter on Dreams," where Stevenson is talking about the moral cast of *J&H* and the vampire story "Olalla." While he has earlier said that the Brownies who orchestrate his dream-life "have not a rudiment of what we call a conscience" and that he himself does "most of the morality" (208), he subsequently allows that "sometimes a parabolic sense is ... undeniably present in a dream; sometimes I cannot but suppose that my Brownies have been aping Bunyan" (209). So Stevenson himself suspected his imagination could work in ways that partook of allegorical method and content, albeit perhaps in unconscious or pre-conscious ways. He goes on to say that the Brownies "ape" moral allegory, "in no case with what would possibly be called a moral in a tract; never with the ethical narrowness; conveying hints of life's larger limitations and that sort of sense which we seem to perceive in the arabesque of time and space" (209). It may well be that, when Fanny prevailed upon him to treat the "story" of Jekyll and Hyde as an "allegory," he consciously moved the tale *towards* the sort of "ethical narrowness" that drives JeyklI's radical distinction between the "upright" and the "unjust." Whether, however, the *final* morality of the story is narrowly ethical — in the sense, say, of issuing an unambiguous warning against intemperance — that is something we shall shortly consider. For now, it's best simply to propose that Stevenson's imagination sometimes "aped" the wonted topicality and personifying characterization of moral allegory, and that some of the eruptions of temperance language and imagery in *J&H* might best be explained in terms of his creative, and not always fully rationalized, exploration of one of the century's more consistently allegorized issues. If one of Hyde's "apelike tricks" was to write "blasphemies" in the margins of Jekyll's moral books, then perhaps one of the Brownies' converse tricks was to write "temperance vignettes" into the action and imagery and language of a shilling shocker.[3]

A host of minor details betray the novella's allegorical tendencies, whether we consider them in terms of the overt, consistent, psychomachic allegory which Fanny demanded or the more covert, piecemeal, and perhaps less insistently purposeful alcoholic allegory this study has explored. Utterson starts the ball rolling most explicitly when he resolves, "If he be Mr. Hyde ... I shall be Mr. Seek" (38). But Enfield has earlier called the building into which Hyde ducks to fetch Jekyll's cheque "Black Mail House" (33); and then gone on to explain his reluctance to look more deeply into what the blackmail might entail by saying, "the more it looks like Queer Street, the less I ask" (33). Meanwhile, the "lean, long, dusty, dreary" Utterson (29) lives appropriately on "Gaunt Street" (39). It's this kind of authorial wordplay that strengthens one's inclination, later on, to read Stevenson's Soho as akin to Whittaker's "Drunken Town," and perhaps Lanyon's Cavendish Square as "Moderation Town."[4]

Even before Enfield's "blackmail" reference, the ontological line between animate and inanimate objects that is typically erased by personification allegory has been substantially blurred in Stevenson's description of the building with "a blind forehead of discoloured wall" bearing marks of neglect "in every feature" (30). That blurring is in fact anticipated in the previous paragraph, when the shops in Jekyll's neighborhood are likened to "rows of smiling saleswomen," "laying out the surplus of their gains in coquetry," while standing "along the thoroughfare with an air of invitation" (30). Earlier still, Utterson's human affections for Enfield are said to be "like ivy," the mindless, unintentional "growth of time" (29). This is already a world in which things take human form, and the qualities of a "him" can (as Enfield claims is the case with Hyde) accordingly become the qualities of an "it."

The Bunyanesque realm of ideas rubs shoulders with the realism of the "shilling shocker" well beyond these opening pages as well. If Hyde's half of Jekyll's inanimate house has a "blind forehead" and "features," Hyde is himself sufficiently inanimate for his face to become a "hide" or parchment able to bear "Satan's signature" (40). The increasingly uncertain physiological separation between Jekyll and Hyde is reflected in the "buildings so packed together about [Jekyll's] court, that it's hard to say where one ends and the other begins" (33). The city of London emits, at one moment, the "low growl" of a beast (38), while the next moment the "vast hum and clatter of the city" is more appropriate to a machine (38). When Hyde leaves Utterson after their first meeting, the lawyer is "the picture of disquietude" (40). When Utterson and Poole prepare on "The Last Night" to break into Jekyll's study, the lawyer declares, "let our name be vengeance" (68). In a scene representing the epitome of the vinous warmth of gentlemanly hospitality, the lawyer appropriately entertains "Mr. Guest" (53). William Veeder has, along with others, treated the allegorical suggestiveness of some of the novella's other names, like "Hastie Lanyon," and "Dr. Denman," and even the chemists "Maw" ("Children of the Night" 115, 121, 128–9).[5] But this much should suggest the degree to which *J&H* pushes towards the allegorical even in what appear to be the incidental details of the story. Reading Hyde as, in part, "The Drink Traffic" and Jekyll's musty court as a miniature "Mayfair Soho" becomes all the more compelling as a result.[6]

What is the evidence that any of Stevenson's contemporaries felt that interpretive compulsion? Writing to Stevenson in March of 1886, J. A. Symonds said, "The fact is, viewed as an allegory, it touches one too closely. Most of us at some epoch in our lives have been upon the verge of developing a Mr Hyde" (Maixner 210–11). One assumes Symonds is talking about the same "allegory" that Fanny must have been, the "damned old business of the war in the members" that Stevenson mentions in his response — "upright" vs. "unjust," Good vs. Bad, in general. It's also plausible that the intrinsic "Hyde" by which Symonds himself felt most threatened was a life of homosexual abandon, given that Symonds struggled for much of his life to accommodate his sexual desires to the dictates of Victorian convention and respectability. But he was Stevenson's constant drinking companion during the harsh winter months in Davos when Louis's wine consumption rose to three liters a day, and both wit and the "old Forzato" flowed in equal volume, as Symonds recalled in dedicating *Wine, Women, and Song* to his old tippling crony. There's a chance, then, Symonds read past the over-arching "allegory" of Good and Evil to the specific allegorical sub-text of alcoholism. Perhaps, in turn, the Hyde he felt on the verge of developing was a troublesome sexual abandon enabled by alcoholic excess, for he elsewhere decries, eerily like Jekyll, the "painful situation" when a man "should sit down *soberly* to contemplate his own besetting vice" and "tallies *last night's deeds* with today's knowledge ... of a perpetual discord between *spontaneous appetite* and acquired respect for social law" (Linehan 139; emphases added). In any case, Symonds adds that "the art is burning and intense. The 'Peau de Chagrin' disappears; Poe is as water" (210) — implying that the work of Poe is (most ironically, given the American writer's notorious alcoholism) a poor teetotal substitute for the "spirited" intensity of *J&H*— in terms both of the novella's impact and of its subject matter alike. Unfortunately, Symonds gives us nothing more than this.

Other early readers, to be sure, took the text in an insistently literal (if broadly applicable) way. "It is a marvelous exploration into the recesses of human nature," wrote James Ashcroft Noble in his review in the *Academy* of 23 January 1886, as revealed by the effects of "certain chemical agents" (Maixner 204). An unsigned review in the United Church of England and Ireland's *Rock* referred on 2 April to "a medicine which is capable of separating [Jekyll's] two natures into two distinct identities" (Maixner 225). One of the more amusing accounts of the work's reception comes from Stevenson himself, writing to his parents on 25 May 1886. "In Bright's today," he informs them, "the man told me Jekyll had been preached about in St Peter's, and next day a lady came into the shop and asked for 'That book about a *medical man who lives here in Bournemouth*, who took something, and came to a bad end'" (*Letters* 5.259). In all these instances, alcohol seems to be far from readers' minds.

F. W. H. Myers was, as we've seen, one of *J&H*'s most careful and consistent commentators, yet he too read with a determined literalism. One of his more intriguing suggestions for revision mentioned that, after the exhausting rigors of his first transformation into Hyde, Jekyll "might revive himself by wine placed nearby" (Maixner 216). "[H]is new body would be specially sensitive to stimulants," the self-appointed editor observed, adhering to the wonted notion that alcohol boosts vitality, but clearly overlooking the fact that Hyde's "thrill and delight" at finding himself the man he has become is in fact described precisely in terms of the effects of wine! The only glimmer of evidence that Myers responded to the sub-text of drink comes when he asserts that Hyde's handwriting wouldn't look like Jekyll's with a different slant but rather something quite different, "like Jekyll's done *with the left hand* [his italics], or, *done when partly drunk* [mine] or ill: that is the kind of resemblance there might be" (Maixner 215). Yet this is a long way from proof that Stevenson's contemporary audience read the novella as we have—as far away as Julia Wedgwood's judgment in the April number of the *Contemporary Review* that *J&H*, "is one of those rare fictions which make one understand the value of temperance in art" (Maixner 223). Wedgwood is praising not the novella's content but rather its "condensed and close-knit workmanship." While her language, along with Myers,' might be consistent with a subliminal recognition of the work's concern with drink, her perceptions are no more conscious or purposeful than Stevenson's Brownies when they are "aping Bunyan."

With a wonderful kind of propriety, it was *Punch* that in fact offered one of the commentaries that came closest to acknowledging the text's concern with alcohol. The magazine lost little time mounting a parody of Stevenson's surprisingly successful tale, publishing "The Strange Case of Dr. T. and Mr. H." in its number of 6 February 1886. "Chapter III" reads in its entirety,

> And so it turned out that TREKYL made a will, which contained a strange provision that, if he disappeared, Hidanseek was to have all his property. Then Dr. ONION went mad with terror, because, after some whiskey-and-water, he fancied that his old friend TREKYL had turned into the tracked and hunted murderer, HIDANSEEK.
> "Was it the whiskey?" asked STUTTERSON.
> "Wait until the end!" cried the poor medical man, and, with a loud shriek, he slipped out of his coat, leaving the button-hole in the bore's hand, and died! [64].

"Chapter the Last" subsequently explains, as we have already seen, that Trekyl customarily changed to Hidanseek by ingesting "powdered acidulated drops," and restored himself by simply "substituting sugar." Moreover, the passage cited leaves it somewhat ambiguous whether it is Trekyl or Onion who drinks the whiskey. But surely anyone knowing anything about the original story would, at least on a first reading of the parody, assume not only that it was Trekyl who drank "the whiskey" to effect his notorious transformation, but also that Stutterson would be far more interested in Trekyl's behavior than in Onion's qualities of perception. What *Punch* offers, then, is a comic but very commonsensical theory on what might, in everyday *reality*, turn a benign Trekyl into a malignant Hidanseek, a fair indication that someone at the magazine was as attentive to what Stevenson was subtly up to as Stevenson was devoted to the magazine's highly topical words and images. When the "acidulated drops" and "sugar" come into the narrative, it's basically to explain how Hidanseek could turn back into Trekyl, a reverse transformation that's admittedly rather hard to account for in a drink-based reading.[7] But, as we've seen, even the sugar is discussed in terms that reflect substantial topical insight. Trekyl's restorative method ultimately fails because, "the right sort of sugar was adulterated, and adulterated sugar cannot be obtained in London."

Stevenson knew the *Punch* parody. In a letter to J. R. Vernon dated 25 February, he mentions having read the comic piece and contends, "these parodies do good to the book parodied; great good, sometimes; they are kindly meant, and the parodist has usually keenly enjoyed the book of which he sits down to make a fool" (*Letters* 5.211). Unfortunately for us, he says nothing about either the whiskey or the drops and sugar, although he does elsewhere graciously concede that texts may embody meanings of which the author is not necessarily aware. In response to what must have been Vernon's criticism of the clarity or nature of his "allegory," Stevenson replies "others must look for what was meant; the allegorist is one, the commentator is another; I conceive they are two parts." Speaking to his wonted representational modes, he then allows that "I have written some other slighter things in a more or less allegorical vein; but they have not yet been collected."

When *Rock*'s sermonizing reviewer seeks to apply Stevenson's allegory to real-life cases, the very first "commentary" he offers once again revealingly involves drink. At first, he observes, men may, "trifle with their lower nature, always conscious that they can, at any time, reassume their better self. By degrees, however, the unfortunate victim finds that he is losing his better self, and that the lower nature acquires more and more power. *The jovial man does not mean to become a drunkard, though he yields now and then in secret*" (Maixner 227; added emphasis). The anonymous writer goes on to treat "the man whose passions are strong [who] has no intentions of becoming a sensualist" and "the fashionable lady of the world [who] does not mean to become insincere," and then he concludes, "But enough: *ex une omne discit*" (Maixner 227). The case of the "jovial man" turned drunkard, in other words, might just be one of any number of possible examples of loss of control. On the other hand, it may actually be the perfect "bridge" from the veiled particulars of the novella to the more general examples offered in the review's other two vignettes—one appropriately meant for a man, the other for a woman. The first "application" could easily have been inspired by a right reading of Utterson and his "secret" taste for gin, or even more easily by Jekyll, whose all-but-alcoholic downfall is bred of an original "impatient gaiety of disposition" that might just as well be called "jovial."

More evidence of an insightful thematic reading of *J&H* comes through a parody which was published in London in 1886 or 1887. Revealingly titled *The Stranger Case of Dr. Hide and Mr. Crushall: A Rum-antic Story*, this version of "Robert Bathos Staving Son's" story involves a number of hard-drinking central characters. "Mr. Utterduffer," for example, has a consistent yearning for "his drop of Scotch" (Geduld 139). Having heard the grim story of a black man who has kicked a baby through the streets—as repeatedly and callously as a soccer ball—Utterduffer goes to bed and dreams that he is himself the baby. "Even in my most childish moments I have a yearning for the bottle," he chuckles in his sleep (141), suggesting that the parodist read Stevenson's Juggernaut scene as indeed about the crisis of children and drink. "Dr. Layiton" is as given to drink as his lawyer friend: "the nervous exhaustion attendant on an extensive practice had necessitated his habituating himself to rum and milk for breakfast" (143). The tale then dissolves into an absurd narrative in which we learn that a Shelleyan Dr. Hide had resolved to "create a race of mankind" (148), deciding that the best thing to begin with was a pair of electric trousers to provide locomotion. Unfortunately, the trousers then fell into the wrong hands (or onto the wrong legs?), leading to the notorious child-kicking. After what is for our purposes a highly propitious start, alcohol all but disappears from the story, except when the black man in the stolen electric pants is subdued by a brewer's drayman, who "backed his waggon [sic] forcibly and suddenly sideways upon the man" (146), rather like a Brewers' Juggernaut for the Common Good. But the story once again evinces the specifically dipsomaniacal themes that *some* of Stevenson's original readers took from the text.

At least two other contemporary responses suggest the extent to which *J&H* was read as somehow about alcohol. Both are American, and may reflect the fact that the temperance fever of the 1880s raged as powerfully on the western shores of the Atlantic as on the eastern, a fact that Stevenson would have been well aware of through his extensive American travels. Thomas Russell Sullivan's stage adaptation of the novella premiered in Boston in May of 1887, and moved to Madison Square Garden in September, shortly after Stevenson himself arrived in New York (McLynn 280). A highly successful vehicle for its lead actor, Richard Mansfield, the play featured a second act in which Hyde is literally drunk when he is confronted by the ghost of Sir Danvers Carew (McNally and Florescu 169). In a curious twist of fate, the production was temporarily closed down after moving to London's *Lyceum* in 1888, blamed in public forums as eminent as the *Times* of London and New York for its possible instigation of the serial Whitechapel murders—Mansfield himself being for a time one of the suspects (McNally and Florescu 170; Danahay 184–86). London evidently knew perfectly well that no extraordinary "chemical agents" were required to inspire brutality in the streets. In any case, Sullivan's inclination to see Hyde as a drunkard was mirrored later in 1887 by *Punch*'s transatlantic satirical soulmate, Joseph Keppler and Henry Bunner's *Puck*. In its 16 November number, a stand-alone comic drawing entitled "An Explanatory Failure" shows a well-dressed gentleman flopped on a carpet at the base of an elegant staircase, his body hopelessly entangled with a fallen hat rack. A brief dialogue follows:

> VOICE (from the upper landing).—Is that you, Livingston?
>
> MR. VAN ARSDALE (who hasn't come in very successfully).—No, m'dearsh, it'sh Doct' Hyde. Mist' Jekyll did n't (lem me up, I shay!) g-g' out t'-night! [22.188].

Asked by (one assumes) his wife if he, the presumably respectable Livingston Van Arsdale, has returned safely home, the man's drunken alter-ego replies as Hyde, denying that his Jekyll-self ever went out in the first place. The tipsy inversion of the two characters' titles only accentuates the artist's linkage between the effects of alcohol and Stevenson's infamous duo.

The contemporary reception of *J&H*, then, affords modest but significant evidence that Stevenson's "allegorist" and "commentator" could in fact come together on the matter of drink. As the Victorian era passed, however, and multiple suggestive contexts like Cruikshank's images, admonitory evocations of the Sunday Trading Riots, and Sir Wilfred Lawson's Local Option receded into virtual oblivion, what thereby became the semantically denuded language of the text did only an indifferent job calling critical attention to the novella's major sub-text. Thus, from Stephen Gwynn's passing observation in 1939 that "there is no other of all his books where his kindly feeling for vintages makes itself so often felt" (130) through Nabokov, Fraustino, Wright, and Dollar — all of the essays treated in Chapter One above — no one seems to have been sufficiently attuned to the issues and language of the times to ferret out the reading that has been uncovered here.

Amongst extant considerations of alcohol in Victorian fiction in general, Mairi McCormick's "First Representations of the Gamma Alcoholic in the English Novel" (1969) is particularly wide-ranging and useful; but in her careful literalism, McCormick omits *J&H* entirely. (Perhaps more surprising is her overlooking *The Master of Ballantrae* or, especially, *Ebb Tide*.) Annette Federico's "'I must have drink': Addiction, Angst, and Victorian Realism" (1990) treats the works of Dickens, Charlotte Brontë, Mrs. Gaskell, and George Eliot, but, despite her pointed and promising observation that *Mary Barton*'s Huntingdon "changes from a Jekyll to a Hyde," Federico overlooks Stevenson as well (19). The whole issue of alcohol in Victorian fiction has in fact been relatively, if curiously, neglected. Anya Taylor (1999) has written illuminatingly on drink in the work and lives of the age's Romantic predecessors; Edward Hewett and W. F. Axton treat the "Convivial Dickens" (1983); and Kathleen McCormack investigates George Eliot's extensive concern with intoxication of various sorts (2000). But it is revealing that, despite its copious treatment of other "Topics of the Day in the Victorian Novel," Richard Altick's lengthy *Presence of the Present* (1991) lacks any index entries at all on either "alcohol," "drink," or "temperance." The "adulteration" of food and drink, something that we've seen to be a related but considerably less consequential and divisive social issue, is however noted twice, one reference being to a substantial, seven-page treatment in Altick's study.

For all of the curious obtuseness of a gadfly critic like Myers, then, the original readers of *J&H* were obviously in a far better position than their modern counterparts to register the many ways in which the novella alludes to the world of drink. They lived, as we've noted, in the world that *Punch* parodied, they voted for Liberals or Tories on the partial basis of their stances on the drink trade, and they saw or heard of the clashes between the Salvation and "Skeleton" Armies. Themselves new to Stevenson's tale in ways that we can never be, they will even more importantly have read its opening chapters with an eye to determining why a "real" man might "really" act in the way that Hyde does—roaming the midnight streets, randomly abusing child and woman alike, erupting into a murderous rage at the slightest provocation. They will have considered the novella's language and imagery for any ways in which they might bear on such a realistic explanation, while we now read with a dedicated eye to what is essentially a foregone conclusion — and, inevitably, devote considerably more of our attention to the skill with which Stevenson withholds and conveys crucial narrative information than to simply trying to figure out "what's going on." Upon reaching "Dr. Jekyll's Full Statement of the Case," many of those first readers will have heard the temperance resonance in a phrase like Jekyll's "shipwreck of my reason,"[8] while post–Woodstock readers faced with the doctor's spontaneous reversions to Hyde are more likely to think of LSD than gin as a real-world analogue to Jekyll's potion. That said, one of the most powerful readings of *J&H* as in some central way about alcohol is actually Valerie Martin's *Mary Reilly*, published in 1990, in which Jekyll and a housemaid discuss her father's intoxicated abuse of her as a child — and whether alcohol didn't effectively "bring out" or "let out" a version of Hyde in the man. The clues, then, have always been there, if readers have only considered them with sensitivity and care. One hopes that a focused study such as this of Stevenson's broad concerns with alcohol will not only pave the way for more insightful critical readings of *J&H*, but also highlight the need for a more wide-ranging exploration of the momentous role that the "drink question" played in the artistic culture of the late–Victorian era.

TWELVE

Conclusion: Finding the Balance

This study is brief enough to be wrapped up without a lengthy, formal reiteration of every revelation and assertion made in its course. One hopes that it demonstrates the extent to which *J&H* engages with one of the most pressing social issues of its day: one that strongly influenced the results of three General Elections in 1880, 1885, and 1886 and, according to reformer Thomas Whittaker, threatened to split the nation in two— and one that at the same time led Stevenson continually to ponder his own, as well as his closest friends', "dipsomania." There are assuredly other momentous topical issues that surface in the novella, among those most pressing for the general public being the late-century dread of criminal degeneration — and, for Stevenson, a substantial anxiety over the power and claims of "high" and "low" literary marketplaces. On balance, however, if one looks as closely as we have done at the action, the characterization, the language, and the imagery of Stevenson's most influential text, there is little question that one dominant — and arguably *the* dominant — contextual theme is the social and moral impact of alcohol. Long a major concern both for the age and for the author, the "drink problem" was forced into particular prominence in the late summer and early fall of 1885, when *J&H* was taking imaginative and literal shape. On the public front, the General Election was about to turn in fair measure on Gladstone and Lawson's "Local Option"; August saw the clash of thousands between Salvation and Skeleton Armies in Derby; and in October the *Times* reported Lord Salisbury's admonitions on a possible reprise of the Hyde Park Sunday Trading Riots of '55 should alcohol reformers press their initiatives too hard. As for Stevenson (unlikely, of course, to have been oblivious to such salient topical developments), his long quest for a "vehicle" to carry his desired tale of "man's double being" was very possibly catalyzed by his August visit with Thomas Hardy, and consequently found its object amidst the famous dream images given to him mere weeks later.

As has been said all along, this argument makes no claim that every bit of the possibly "influential" material we have considered here is in fact embodied in the novella in any objectively verifiable way. Nor does it claim that everything we may be reasonably certain *should* be part of a valid exegesis of the tale's "allegory" is presented by Stevenson in a fully rationalized, self-consistent, or even a conscious way. "A Chapter on Dreams" makes a compelling case for the key role that the subconscious played in Stevenson's writing, and it contains the candid and useful acknowledgement that, even when the writer thought he was expanding in fully conscious and controlled ways upon the original dream inspiration, shadowy forces might still have been at work in selecting and presenting the text's specific matter. Recall his confession that "the part [of creativity] that is done while I am sleeping is the Brownie's part beyond contention; but that which is done when I am up and about is by no means necessarily mine, since all goes to show the Brownies have a hand in it even then" (207). One should add to this the letter to J. R. Vernon written the month after *J&H* appeared, in which Stevenson again suggests that more significant things find their way into texts than authors consciously put there: "others must look for what was meant; the allegorist is one, the commentator is another; I conceive they are two parts" (*Letters* 5.211). Nevertheless, the hard evidence of his textual revisions of *J&H* does suggest that the author was at times very consciously interested in alcohol and "dipsomania" in ways that go well beyond providing his audience with a widely-experienced analogue for the effects of Jekyll's drug. Especially if we hold that *J&H* was in part conceived as a vehicle for its author's deep contrition over the death of Walter Ferrier, a fair measure of its topically-suggestive concern with the dire effects of Jekyll's "transforming draught" must have been fully intended.

A number of Stevenson's emendations, then, reveal his determination to explore "man's double being" in the specific context in which he himself was best acquainted with it: strong drink. It was in Edinburgh that Stevenson first, and perhaps most closely, approximated the life of his main character, taking on along with Baxter the cloak of a pseudonym in order to live the night-life of a latter-day Deacon Brodie. As drink was calculatedly central to the statutory "liberties" of the "L. J. R. Society"—as indulged by Ferrier along with the others—so is it calculatedly central to *J&H*. It can be no accident that the first "transformation" of character in a novel that is *about* the transformation of character is effected by drink — by wine as a distinct literal foretaste to Jekyll's "blood-red liquor." Utterson, as the very first paragraph tells us, is a generally dreary fellow. But, "at friendly meetings, and when the wine was to his taste, something eminently human beaconed from his eye" (29). Stevenson went on to suggest that the lawyer is occasionally tempted to exercise that glimmering "humanity" as fully as his more abandoned acquaintances, "sometimes wondering, almost with envy, at the *pressure of high spirits* involved in their misdeeds" (Veeder, "Manuscript" 14; emphasis added). So, that is, in the Printer's Copy of the novella. But when Stevenson altered the italicized phrase to give us what we have in the final published edition — "wondering, almost with envy, at the *high pressure of spirits* involved in their misdeeds (29; italics added) — he more clearly signaled his subsequent and abiding interest in "misdeeds" driven by "spirits" of a physical (that is, of a literally "pressurize-able") sort. Similarly, as we have discussed, his moving Hyde's residence from the drafts' Holborn location — those "dreary and exiguous rooms off Gray's Inn Road" (Veeder, "Manuscript" 45) — to what is in the final text a Soho setting would seem to betray Stevenson's conscious decision to identify his villain directly with Thomas Whittaker's archetypal "Drunken Town," the notoriously gin-soaked section of London that Stevenson very explicitly and significantly recalled when he pondered the gin-soaked depravities of the Gilbert Islanders. The effective association between place and vice is driven home, of course, when Utterson and Inspector Newcomen pass the neighborhood "gin palaces" and encounter the sad crowd of women out for "a morning glass" (48) — and also when Hyde's rooms are found to be so well stocked with wine.

Other authorial changes were perhaps more over-determined — accomplishing effects that do more (or even other) than link Hyde to strong drink. Stevenson's adding that second explicit reference to the "Juggernaut which is Hyde" brings an established image of the Drink Traffic into the tale with all the more force; but it works so well as part of the literal description of Hyde's callous and relentless trampling of the little girl that Stevenson may not have given conscious thought to an emphatic doubling of temperance iconography. Emphasizing that Hyde and the girl collide at "the corner"—and that Utterson later dreams of myriad such collisions at myriad other "corners"—could, despite the marked topical suggestiveness, be a reflex of visual precision and nothing more. Similarly, Stevenson's substituting as the victim of Hyde's second street assault the "aged and beautiful" Sir Danvers Carew, Member of Parliament, for the shadowy Mr. Lemsome, the "incurable cad," opens up all of the rich, topical, *roman à clef* possibilities that we have explored. But it also fits so well with the anti-patriarchal drift of the rest of text that, even if *Punch*'s image of "Publican-Barrel and Pharisee-Pump" had been kicking around in his head just below the thresh-hold of awareness, Stevenson could well have made the change for no other overt reason than to give Hyde a solid father-figure to bump off. Still, if we grant that meaning (be it either "original" or "revised meaning") needn't always be intended in order to be present and significant, it seems very reasonable to read the author's long love affair with satirical drawings into an understanding of the text as so reworked. Once again, Stevenson contended, "my Brownies ... who do one-half my work for me while I am fast asleep, ... in all human likelihood, do the rest for me as well, when I am wide awake and fondly suppose I do it for myself" ("Dreams" 207). The most vociferous pundits on the drink question may, now and again, have been "the Little People"—be they drafters or revisers.

In the end, most hypotheses about Stevenson's reasons for making the changes he did must remain conjectural, even if we have hit on some convincing ones. We do know, however, that he completely re-wrote the original draft of the story in order to develop the "allegory" that Fanny complained he had originally missed. And if he was therefore "allegorizing" the same theme that he tells us he had originally set out to explore—"man's double being"—then the line of least resistance for the derivative narrative, in terms of any contemporary *topicality* (as opposed, say, to its exploring "good and evil" in a timeless, synchronic sense), would almost certainly have involved drink. This would hold, one might well argue, whether we consider the most broadly divisive social issue of the time or Stevenson's own most abiding sense of what could split him and members of his closest circle of friends into two separate natures. The way will only have been smoothed for him by the myriad dichotomizing stories and images he ran across and relished from his nursery encounters with *Cassell's Illustrated Family Paper* to his mature immersions in *Punch*, "William Wilson," and *The Mayor of Casterbridge*.

The shrewd reader who is leaning towards concluding that *Jekyll and Hyde*'s sub-text of strong drink was in *some* measure consciously constructed by the author might well be moved to ask why, then, Stevenson didn't simply make Hyde a literal alcoholic? The simplest and most convincing answer is that, for the story to work on the literal level, Hyde had to look like a *different man* than Jekyll — and thus his potion had to effect a physical transformation well beyond alcohol's routine capacity to flush the face or slacken the jaw or facilitate the disguise of the whole man, say, via a lampshade on the head. Nevertheless, for a number of readers steeped in temperance diatribes or simply the popular wisdom of the times, the fact that Jekyll's addictive drink should change him into an atavistic brute will have implied that the novella's sensational "letter" ought best be read with an eye to the well-known "spirit" of alcohol — *the* draught that commonly transformed the Teddy Henleys and Michael Henchards of the day into treacherous cads. The fable's literal Hyde might then stand in for the ultimately fleeting *illusions* of anonymity and non-responsibility that alcoholic excess so typically affords. One of the novella's compelling "psychological truths" for many readers is its nod to the way some drugs (and perhaps most commonly among them alcohol) reduce inhibitions and thus not only allow kinds of behavior that the individual would be ashamed to engage in when sober but also afford a convenient after-the-fact "excuse" for that behavior.[1] As Jekyll "cloaks" (86) his shameful pleasures in the alternate identity of "Hyde," so the binge drinker often seeks to escape responsibility for desires enacted under the influence. In Stevenson's day, one prime aim of the temperance movement was accordingly to abolish the "drunkenness defense," which appealed to British law's sometime willingness to see inebriation as a significant extenuating circumstance in the commission of crimes — as though the drunkard were largely "another person" than the sober man.[2] Such, it might reasonably be argued, are the psychological and moral issues that Stevenson is most intent on exploring in the novella, with Hyde's literal appearance as "another man" simply reflecting the semi-exculpatory notions discussed above. Of course, when all is said and done, the fact that Hyde is the behavioral result of what is clearly an addiction to an adulterated "blood red liquor" might, for some readers, be sufficient evidence that he *is* for all intents and purposes a *literal alcoholic* — albeit one for whom a secret cocktail ingredient adds a sensational physical component to the "normal" sense of exculpation that alcohol can afford. In any case, we needn't really argue that in order to appreciate the extent to which his story is a story of strong drink, as Stevenson could so fully appreciate it. And once again, if one assumes that a substantial measure of the text's concern with alcohol enters via some back door — via the Brownies in their "back garret" who were inventing only to the requirement that the tale deal with man's double being in a way that was inspiring for this particular author — then Hyde's potion needn't *literally* be alcohol for him to remain a de facto example of the sad lot of the addicted Walter Ferriers of the world.

If *J&H* is indeed an allegory of evil and of alcohol as well, then it also seems reasonable to ask what its moral might be. What is it finally arguing? *J&H* can certainly be read as one of the most potent and enduring warnings against substance abuse that exists in our language.[3] As a tale about the dangers of "unbalanced abandon," the novella would have served Stevenson well as he continued to wrestle with the Ferrier business. In addition, being in 1885 very much in want of a commercial success to match and surpass *Treasure Island*, he (along with his exacting in-house "editor" and "agent," Fanny) could have counted on the highly-charged political climate to move countless readers to embrace the story's trenchant message about addiction. Recall the lady in Bournemouth who went straight from the sermon to her bookseller for a copy of that story about "the doctor who took something, and came to a bad end." At the same time, however, the tale begins with the portrait of Utterson as a man who is distinctly humanized by his wine. It is impossible to read the accounts of Lanyon in his cups or Jekyll with his cronies or, especially, Utterson basking in vinous warmth with the aptly named Mr. Guest without acknowledging that the author who claimed that "wine is poetry in a bottle" had as much Disraeli or Lord Salisbury in him as he had Gladstone. While the novella may checker the age's faith in the restorative and vitalizing qualities of drink by associating them so strongly with the violent Hyde, its glimpses of the social and even rhetorical benefits of alcohol embody a Carnivalesque endorsement of Bacchus in the midst of a more apparently Lenten literary endeavor. In fact, if one views Jekyll's self-described moral "shipwreck" as resulting less from his secret indulgence in the "blood-red liquor" itself than from the suppressive moral intolerance which drove it underground in the first place, then the novella can be read as much as a warning against the over-avid forces of temperance as an exemplum of the dire impact of demon alcohol. Any moral, then, would seem to be "mixed."

In his *Academy* review of 27 February, 1886, Edward Purcell indeed remarked on the novella's "puzzling enigmatic ethics" (*Letters* 5.212). Stevenson responded that same day, allowing that "ethics are my veiled mistress; I love them, but I don't know what they are." This he associates in his character with "the dazzled incapacity to choose," a "morbid element," he claims, of "an age of transition" (*Letters* 5.213). One might in fact fault the author for a constitutional indecisiveness, for the kind of deliberative paralysis that leaves the eponymous hero of "Will o' the Mill" a kind of feckless prey to death. But we may finally do better to characterize him as "ambivalent" rather than "indecisive" and, taking our cue from the man himself, to set that attitude against the singular ambivalence of his Age and nation when it came to matters of drink.

If we think of late–Victorian Britain as a collective "Body Politic," it was one that didn't in the least know its mind. The cycling of Liberal and Conservative Ministries turned on far more than Irish Home Rule and Imperial policy, as the nation tried to decide what to do about the Drink Juggernaut, and the reformist fortunes of William Gladstone rose and fell accordingly. Benevolent prohibitionists and avid libertarians sorted themselves into Salvation and Skeleton Armies, exchanging words and blows across the land. Men and women of medicine argued with each other over the banes and blessings of drink — and often enough they all but argued with *themselves*: recall Kate Mitchell's teetotaling assault on alcohol as distinctly qualified by her own continuing faith in "medicinal spirits." Dickens was, at base, unable or unwilling to rise above the ambivalence of his time when it came to alcohol. Despite his eloquent public disdain for the teetotalers and his equally eloquent private encomia to the punch bowl, he reckoned drink to be the death of more Englishmen than he cared to number. It's no surprise, then, to find versions of the same ambivalence in Stevenson. One letter informs his father Thomas of his household's great progress filling wine bottles for the cellar in Hyères, and another confesses to Baxter that he couldn't allow himself to keep alcohol in his rooms in San Francisco. That same letter warns Baxter to dry himself out as well, while two more of them fondly recall their student ramblings in Edinburgh and solicit his old friend's help in finding some "dry, old" vintages for the crucial stock at Vailima. And while he mourns Ferrier and long laments the poor man's fatal "plunge," Stevenson can nonetheless affirm to Walter Simpson, "I am persuaded we gain nothing in the least comparable to what we lose, by holding back the hand from any provinces of life; the intrigue, the imbroglio, such as it is, was made for the *plunger* and not for the *teetotaler*" (*Letters* 5.21).

A life of course has many moments, and it may seem disingenuous to pull these last examples from a number of separate letters written over decades. A man's mind can change over time, and there's little doubt that Stevenson was more willing to compass prohibition after he'd seen the ruination caused by "perandi" in the Gilbert Islands than after he'd seen King Kalakaua manage a half dozen bottles of "fizz" on a single Honolulu afternoon with no ill effects whatsoever. But, on balance, Stevenson seems always to have had a healthy sense of both the banes and the benefits of alcohol, and his richest texts manage to reflect the complexity, if not the "indecisiveness," of his thought. Nowhere is his ambivalence towards drink more apparent than in *J&H*—because, one might argue, no work is more seriously or consistently about alcohol than this. Written in the lingering shadow of Ferrier's death and under the additional compunction to "get the allegory," the tale's most overt argument is restrictive. But, as we've repeatedly seen, there are permissive counter-arguments galore.

Stevenson's ambivalence is built into multiple contrasts in this text of contrasts. To give only one of the most striking examples, the marvelous scene with Utterson and Guest (in which a bottle of old wine is at the *heart* of domestic bliss and order, matched in the warmth of its bottled sunlight by the glowing hearth itself and thus well able to "disperse the fogs" of a foul London night; 54) is contrasted with the nightmarish Soho vision of slatternly women *deserting* home and hearth to quaff a pallid shot of gin in the thick of a lurid brown fog (48). It's crucial to note that this is *not* for Stevenson part of a simplistic class critique, as it might well be with Dickens: that is, for the great novelist, a contrast between professionals drinking wine responsibly in private and low-life prostitutes drinking gin shamefully in public. In the context of this novella, Stevenson goes out of his way to associate gin also with the stolid lawyer Utterson and wine with the murderous and effectively low-life Hyde. In the world at large, Stevenson knew all too well the awful things that the Walter Ferriers or the Teddy Henleys could do to themselves and others, despite their privileged upbringing. The author assured American journalist John Paul Bocock that Jekyll's profoundest flaw was his hypocrisy (*Letters* 6.56–57) and, as we've suggested, one of the reasons for turning the wine-drinking doctor Jekyll into the wine-drinking murderer Hyde was likely to expose the hypocritical "respectability" of the refined classes. So, these matched wine and gin scenes, in context, seem to evince two attitudes towards drink itself rather than towards class. One is cozy and congenial, the other chilly and alienated.

Stevenson's ambivalence towards alcohol is probably best and most simply evidenced — although again in what have been surprisingly unappreciated ways— by the rather illogical fact that one, single potion apparently turns Jekyll into Hyde and Hyde back into Jekyll. Throughout his narrative, Jekyll refers clearly to "*the* drug" (singular; emphasis added) and, while he admits that different days of experimentation required different dosages to effect the changes, there's never any mention of a second compound. Thus, he observes in the specific context of "the drug," "I was led to remark that whereas, in the beginning, the difficulty had been to throw off the body of Jekyll, it had of late gradually but decidedly transferred itself to the other side" (89). One drug begets two very "opposite" changes, albeit with altering effectiveness. In contrast, in the *Punch* parody of early '86, Trekyl swallows "acidulated drops" in order to become Mr. Hidanseek — who then requires what unfortunately turns out to be adulterated *sugar* in order to reverse the process. Similarly, in David Wickes' television film *Jekyll and Hyde* (1990), Michael Caine uses liquid from a phial labeled "Flux" to endue his monstrous alter-ego but then needs a dose of a discrete "*Re*-flux" to restore himself to normalcy. If we were somehow looking in the tale at a phenomenon of blood pressure, with Hyde's brutalities powered by an artificially-induced hypertension, then Jekyll would logically use one potion to raise his pressure and another, counteractive one to lower it. Or, if we were instead to indulge in a popular drinker's myth, if Jekyll were to drink too much alcohol, he might sober up with a hearty infusion of caffeine. Our Jekyll has but one drug.

Why? Stevenson contended that the majority of the errors and infelicities that F. W. H. Myers found in the novella were the unfortunate results of its hasty composition. One could accordingly argue that this illogical drug business is just the sloppiness bred of speed — although the central details of the plot (as opposed to the "touches" on which Myers generally comments) are otherwise worked out with remarkable care. Alternatively, a relatively facile explanation of the "theme of alcohol" sort might run this way: if Jekyll's drug stands for alcohol and if Hyde is a type of the violent drunk, then the drug/alcohol is also the "hair of the dog" that "steadies" the drunk the morning after and lets him get on with his normal day. The problem with this line of explanation, however, is that the return to Jekyll does not seem to involve any mild re-inebriation but rather a staunch and complete sobriety. Jekyll feels the most "himself" during the months when he's sworn off his addictive draught entirely (92).

A far more satisfactory explanation that also allows the drug to remain a figure for alcohol might simply concede the illogic of the drug situation in a realistic textual sense — but then argue that the problem is one of conflicting ideology *outside* of the text. Both Stevenson and his Age were demonstrably of two minds about drink. And just as *J&H* exposes the viciousness of drink in the character of Hyde and applauds its virtues in the character of Utterson, it also turns on the ingestion of a substance that, at one moment, makes a good man bad and, the next, renders that bad man good. Jekyll observes very revealingly at one point, "the drug had no discriminating action; it was neither diabolical nor divine" (85). Again, Stevenson is not writing as Dickens might; he's not claiming that drink can be "divine" for the middle- or upper-class social drinker and still be "diabolical" for the working-class drunk. *J&H* reflects alcohol's capacity to affect one man, of relatively gentle birth, in either of two ways. What might seem to be the writer's careless slip is, in fact, an extremely apt if subtle reflection of his own and his Age's conflicting ideas on the uses and effects of drink.

In many ways, *J&H* embodies artificially polarized answers to the drink question, as though an individual had but two choices when it came to alcohol: either to distance oneself from all forms of undignified abandon as Jekyll attempts to do (as "Jekyll") or to plunge headlong "into the sea of liberty" (as Hyde.) Just such an artificial polarization, however, was in some ways the fate of the nation, as reformers like Whittaker insisted that there was "no middle course" between perdition and prohibition (*Life's Battles* 203) and headlines consequently documented clashes between the teetotaling Salvationists and the drunken Skeletons. One good social extreme begot another, just as the overly-scrupulous Jekyll begot Hyde. Dickens, on the other hand, saw moderation as a middle way between abstinence and abandon, albeit one that it was necessary to cultivate in the political arena only for the sake of the plebes (as the patricians had already learned to take care of themselves). "If the lowest classes were bought with the influence of any wholesome example at all, which they are not now," he wrote in "Demoralisation and Total Abstinence," "is there no example in that quality of moderation which Tee-Total Societies so sorely need?" (166)

The idea of moderation was a congenial one for Stevenson as well, in general and in specifically applied ways. A letter to his father from December of 1883 notes "the great double danger of taking life too easily, and taking it too lightly, how hard it is to balance that" — but then it goes on to mention Hegel as an example of someone who could work past antinomies to the very kind of synthetic "balance" we see extolled in *J&H*. Writing to his mother ten days later, he tellingly asks her to remind Thomas to "beware of extremes" (*Letters* 242–43). A letter to Symonds from March 1886 lauds sticking to the "*via media*" as an imperative of life as well (*Letters* 5.221), while the genie's container in "The Bottle Imp" comes to Keawe with the equivalent caveat, "All you have to do is use the power of the imp in moderation" (580). Stevenson actually applies the concept to the specific matter of drink in a letter penned to cousin Bob Stevenson in March of 1875, observing that "Wine is not extry [sic] crooked ... as tips go, but requires to be used in moderation" (*Letters* 2.124). Similarly, the verses of his poem "Stormy Nights" imagine an ideal public house community with "dry sherry, / Good tobacco and clever talk with my fellows, / Free from *inordinate* cravings" (*Selected Poems* 25; emphasis added.) The letter to his father Thomas may well attest to the difficulty of achieving "balance" in the broad life, just as that moving letter to Baxter frankly acknowledges the dark days in San Francisco when Stevenson found moderation in matters of drink all but impossible to achieve. Yet, as a general standard of conduct, it was workable. All things in measure, nothing to excess. Thus, when the drink-wary loyalists take over the soon-to-be-besieged stockade in *Treasure Island* and must remain watchful in order to preserve their lives, Captain Smollett nonetheless orders Hunter to "serve out a round of brandy to all hands" (118). And when self-styled, sometime "temperance man" Frank Cassilis is equally up against the threat of a murderous siege in "The Pavilion on the Links," he too moderates his stance by uncorking a bottle of "good burgundy"; "it is useless," he explains, "to push principle to extremes" (51).

If there is a real exemplar in *J&H* of the moderate use of alcohol, it is probably Utterson — perhaps significantly the first drinker we meet.[4] His fondest taste seems to be for wine, but he is able to rein that in (to "mortify" it, we're told) with the odd glass of gin. And lest his use of spirits suggest more of an immoderate than a moderate nature, he is strongly established in the text as a man whose Sundays are given over to an all-but Sabbatarian sobriety. In a curious way, in fact, he is the human equivalent of Jekyll's potion, and thus an implicit example of balance. He is frequently invited to dine with his "cronies," all of whom are "judges of good wine" (43). And in the company of a professional like Mr. Guest and with a special bottle of his liking, he is the catalyst for an almost orgasmic "melting" into congenial fellowship (54). But at the same time, he is a kind of antidote to drink as well. "Hosts," we're told, "loved to detain the dry lawyer, when the light-hearted and the loose-tongued had already their foot upon the threshold; they liked to sit awhile in his unobtrusive company, practicing for solitude, *sobering their minds* in the man's rich silence, after the expense and strain of gaiety" (43; added emphasis). An inveterate drinker, he is also a kind of "anti-gaiety" (and thus anti–Hyde) tonic, as Stevenson's "allegory" again collapses the distinction between human being and material object. Yet the point to make is that, in a tale in which the main character loses himself to his "transforming draught," Utterson controls his own appetites and helps others do the same. If Ferrier was the most compelling model for Jekyll, perhaps *Utter*-son was at least partially based on the man *Steven*-son hoped he could be in setting other young men on a better path, as he told his father he so contritely wished to do.[5] Intriguingly, though not perhaps very consequentially, the character and his creator shared both legal credentials and a rangy physique, Utterson being "long, lean, [and] dusty" (29) and Stevenson "long, lean, and spidery" (McLynn 27).

The problem with Utterson is not any personal mismanagement of his drinking habit, as it is with Jekyll; it is his failure to save his friend. Despite his general solicitousness towards Jekyll and his extraordinary tolerance for "down-going men," he essentially turns his back on Jekyll's problems at least twice, once at the end of "Story of the Door" and again at the end of "Incident at the Window." He is assuredly a better friend to the troubled doctor than Lanyon is, and in that he ironically shows a closer kinship to Poole and the teetotalers than to any standard moderationist. But he is finally very unlike the Blakean narrator of "I am a hunchback, yellow faced," who manages to reach out both to the misshapen pariah of the title and to the "drunkard's lass" alike, in the kind of humble and all-but–Christian acceptance of the lowly that Jekyll tragically lacked:

> I am a man that God made at first,
>   And teachers tried to harm;
> Here, hunchback, take my friendly hand —
>   Good woman, take my arm [*Selected Poems* 27].

It is hard to come to this poem from *J&H* and not think, first, about Jekyll's disastrous refusal to embrace the "low" qualities of self that become Hyde or, second, about the universal revulsion that the novella's characters feel for the little man when they meet him. *J&H* is assuredly not a sentimental narrative, nor a soft-hearted one when it comes to Hyde's depravities. But we have established that the tale offers at least an implicit warning *against* intolerance and holier-than-thou moral disengagement. Appropriately, it is the least tolerant men, Jekyll and Lanyon, who suffer the most. But even Utterson is insufficiently engaged with Jekyll and his alter-ego to help them balance their foundering lives. On some level, if Jekyll represents the self-improving "march of civilization" which Dickens saw as leaving the lower elements of society behind, Utterson represents an attendant failure to re-engage with falling friend and fallen foe alike. It's both a bitter irony and a measure of the tale's darkness that the first words of the man who is in some ways the best person in the story should happen to be these: "I let my brother go to the devil in his own way" (29). Utterson may be admirably moderate, but he's also sadly disengaged.

If Ferrier was perhaps the dominant inspiration for Jekyll, there may also be something to be said for the Utterson-as-Stevenson formula outlined above. Both men knew how to reach out to tumbling comrades: Utterson to Jekyll in the matters of his will, Carew's murder, the doctor's self-claustration, and the troubles of "The Last Night"; Stevenson in his early letter to Ferrier about his being a "bug to frighten babes," his remonstrations with Baxter about his struggles with drink, and apparently with the alcoholic W. E. Henley into the bargain. Writing to Baxter in March of 1888, the author says somewhat cryptically of his old collaborator Henley, "I know the man, I loved him; I have shown it; even in the hardest trial, when I risked his anger on the drink business" (*Letters* 6.134). He must in some way at some time have confronted the "hard-drinking Falstaffian" with his concerns about him as well. But just as Utterson is finally no more than a witness to Jekyll's demise, Stevenson was unable to save Ferrier. Perhaps he thought it might have been different. "O if I had only written to him more," he lamented shortly after his death. But in the event, all he could do was write "Old Mortality" and *Strange Case of Dr Jekyll and Mr Hyde*. Perhaps one of the most poignant things about the novella is that Stevenson wrote into it a version of himself as a well-meaning but ultimately impotent friend to a self-destructive drinker.

Jekyll and Hyde is, in sum, the story of a need for balance. In the proto-psychological terms of "Henry Jekyll's Full Statement of the Case," it is about the need for the "upright twin" to continue to walk hand-in-hand with his "unjust" brother, to their mutual advantage and ultimate happiness. In the topical terms of the "drink question," it's about the need to affect a reasonable compromise between the physical, economic, and social vitality of Britain and the "liberties" of the drinker and of the Drink Traffic that served him. Jekyll's story becomes the tragedy of "imbalance" and excess, reflecting in that the fate of James Walter Ferrier and Michael Henchard alike. Stevenson's subtly-constructed "allegory" in turn mirrors that personal tragedy at the level of social movements and institutions, reflecting the dangerous polarization of the Realm into the extreme factions of Salvation and Skeleton Armies, wild extrapolations as they were of the opposed parliamentary ranks of Liberals and Conservatives. Despite the novella's dire outcome, however, the explicit optimism of "Old Mortality" is implicitly available in *J&H*, if we only know how to look for it.

Again, it's at the beginnings and the end of the text that some of its most significant matter can be found. That's "beginnings," plural, because, while the actual narrative starts with Utterson, the chronology of fictional events begins when Jekyll looks back at his youth. We've done well enough documenting the polemic "optimism" implicit in Utterson's moderate drinking habits, a reasonable model for anyone who cared to profit from them. They are there even in the novella's opening paragraph, with its depiction of a man who has a carefully "measured" taste for wine and who somehow balances an excruciatingly dry professional demeanor with a minor but winning modicum of convivial warmth. By Freud's measure of psychic health, he knows how to both work and love.

As for Jekyll's "early days," it's all but obvious that the young man should have embraced and nurtured the "impatient gaiety of disposition" that is the seed of Hyde, thereby securing the "happiness" that the reasoned, moderate indulgence of that very human trait would have brought to "many" (81). "There is no duty we so much underrate as the duty of being happy," Stevenson wrote in "An Apology for Idlers." "By being happy, we sow anonymous benefits upon the world" (Bell 227). If people approached life with the "affirmative" attitude of Christ rather than the "negatives" of the Ten Commandments, he wrote his mother, "you [could] begin to see some pleasure in it" (*Letters* 3.149.50). What accepting "Hyde" would have involved, in the specific terms of Victorian drinking practice, would have been Jekyll's dispensing with the nay-saying hypocritical standard of "respectability" and "carrying [one's] head high" and, instead, embracing the jocular communality that had characterized the public houses of pre–Victorian England and that continued to grace Stevenson's recollections of Edinburgh ramblings and texts such as "Stormy Nights" alike. In psychological terms, if Jekyll had been able to enjoy himself as

Jekyll, then his recreations would always have been balanced. In sociological terms, if the upper classes had been able to combine with their "march of civilization" a few tours of the park or a few rounds in the pub with their social inferiors, then Britain would have been in a better state. Unfortunately, at least in the first instance, the clock can't be turned back. The hope is merely for the future.

Which brings us to the other end of the tale, where Jekyll's and Utterson's stories both come to a close. As noted earlier, one of the subtle cruxes of the novella is deciding whether the creature cowering behind the "red baize door" when Utterson and Poole approach it with their ax is in fact totally depraved. Is it indeed a miracle that he hasn't destroyed Jekyll's revised will that names Utterson as his new beneficiary, as the lawyer claims; or did he instead compass or perhaps even write the new document? Is it similarly a function only of his "wonderful [and distracting] selfishness" that he doesn't destroy Jekyll's document left out for the lawyer to find, as the doctor contends he might (97); or might he see some value to himself or others in the account's surviving? Was it Jekyll who, in stereotypically civil fashion, put the tea-pot on the fire and laid out all the tea things in the scrupulously tidy room; or could it be Hyde who ultimately turns to comforting order and the quintessential temperance drink? These and other questions, one fears, can never be definitively answered. But, in ways we have touched on above, they all partake in one larger, over-arching question. Is Hyde as vile and unregenerate as Jekyll initially "sees" and subsequently makes him out to us to be — is he as the doctor says "wholly evil" (85) — or could there be any trace of good in him? And, more to the point for this study, if he is the type of the abandoned drinker, is he responsible for his own fate and therefore lost to the forces of redemption, or is he at least in part the victim of circumstances and still the worthy object of redemptive mercies?

Once again, Stevenson gives us in Poole the semblance of a teetotaler. He declines to drink the wine Utterson offers him and, at the door to Jekyll's laboratory, hints at the kind of sympathy for the Fallen that allowed the William Booths of the world to engage themselves in the salvation of the drunkard. "Once I heard it weeping," he confesses to Utterson. "Weeping like a woman or a lost soul.... I came away with that upon my heart, that I could have wept too" (69). Utterson the essential "moderationist," however, reacts to this news with "horror." And when Hyde cries out to him, "Utterson, ... for God's sake, have mercy," he responds, "That's not Jekyll's voice — it's Hyde's.... Down with the door, Poole!"

(69). On the simplest level of plot, of course, Utterson is right. And, not having read either of the revelatory accounts he will soon examine, either Lanyon's or Jekyll's, he can't yet know that Jekyll and Hyde are the same man. But in the context of a work as responsive as this one is to all the nuances of the temperance age, one can almost hear him agreeing with Lanyon that, whatever Jekyll has become, he is beyond help. Twice earlier, after all, he has along with Enfield virtually turned his back on Jekyll's problem, for all intents and purposes saying along with the conservative old doctor, "I am quite done with that person" (57).

This is admittedly a subtle reading; but if, in its fullest context, it is at all convincing, then out of the sad fact that the well-meaning Utterson is unable to save Jekyll comes the rather more hopeful possibility that a man more sensitive and more persevering and perhaps more courageous than this "dusty" old lawyer might be able to help the next Jekyll somewhere down the line. And if that's the case, then the tragic little "twelve-penny" thriller in which Stevenson mirrored not only the decline and fall of his old friend Walter Ferrier but also his own regrettable failure to help stem the tide that swept the man away, might just offer the hope for something better the next time around.

Strange Case of Dr Jekyll and Mr Hyde, then, manages not only to be the "crawler" on human duality that Stevenson originally intended it to be but also the more moral text that Fanny thought it had to be. Its morality, however, is neither reductive nor narrowly conservative but rather grows out of an extraordinarily balanced vision of the complicated choices faced by anyone who lives in an ideologically complex time. As much as it trades in the sensational excesses of vice, it also treats the attendant dangers of intolerant reactionary judgment. If I may be allowed to close in my own voice, I leave these pages convinced that what Stevenson called "the life of that unhappy Henry Jekyll" was, in many and significant ways, purposefully close to the far less fantastic lives of Stevenson and Ferrier and many other late Victorians besides. My readers will obviously decide for themselves how convincing the argument has been. Yet I hope at the very least to have shown that, in its manifold attention to the rhetoric and realities of the drink question, the novella is, in very substantial ways, an extraordinarily rich distillate of an author, an issue, and an age.

Appendix:
The Language of the Times

This study has taken Lowes' *Road to Xanadu* as a rough model for exploring many of the threads that Stevenson and his Brownies wove into *Jekyll and Hyde*. It has also presupposed that a novella might be read as carefully as a poem, its language as susceptible to a nuanced and "venturesome" close reading as any *Lyrical Ballad*. What follows might best be thought of as notes or glosses on a relatively narrow range of Stevenson's language that may spring especially to life in the context of an "alcoholic" reading — rather after the fashion of the word "spirit" as treated above. Having established, one hopes, the tale's sustained exploration of the psychology and politics of drink in late–Victorian Britain, we may now (and here) more convincingly treat the extent to which what could appear to be the least ideologically charged language in the text may in fact be meaningfully borrowed from the lexicon of temperance. Stevenson's most "quotidian" terminology may still advance his strong sub-textual agenda.

"Shipwreck" and the "Sea of Intemperance"

The "dreadful shipwreck" to which Jekyll feels doomed (82) — the "shipwreck of my reason" (75) as he decribes it to Lanyon — is of a piece not only with Ferrier's lamented alcoholic "wreck" (*Letters* 5.157) and the author's own anxieties about "making a shipwreck" should he too succumb to drink (*Letters* 6.207) but also with a dominant temperance image, which is in turn linked to a host of ancillary motifs. Thomas Whittaker thus uses a commonplace nautical metaphor to lament the fate of men who have all but triumphed in life, only in the end to lose everything through drink: "There is no more painful and distressing sight than to see a ship well manned and heavily laden, a ship that has braved many a storm and overcome tempestuous weather in many climes, nearing home, full of promise and hope, go to pieces within touch of land and sight of friends." "Brave men," he adds, "should haste to the rescue of wrecks on shore as well as at sea" (*Brighter England* 304, 317). Salvation Army founder William Booth works the same vein of imagery, arguing that missions charged with the drunkard's rescue needn't be glamorous or costly: "Here are millions of our fellow-creatures perishing amidst the breakers of the sea of life, dashed to pieces on sharp rocks, sucked under by eddying whirlpools, suffocated even when they think they have reached land.... An ugly old tub of a boat that will land a shipwrecked sailor safe on the beach is worth more to him than the finest yacht that ever left a slip-way incapable of effecting the same object" (*Darkest England* 271).[1] It would be wonderful, Booth claimed, if men could themselves "climb unaided to the rock of deliverance...," but the help of others is needed because "the general wreck has shattered and disorganized the whole man" (Preface n.p.). Poe's obituary accordingly mourned him as "a great man self-wrecked" (Pollin 137–8), while James Greenwood said of "a poor dejected slave to his passion for drink," "What a wreck was there!" (222). And David Lewis cited the memorable image of early temperance crusader F. R. Lees, who held that a government's licensing the sale of drink was like trying "to stop the leak of a sinking ship by employing some of the crew to bore experimental holes in the sides of the vessel" (*The Drink Problem* 175). Inventively but appropriately, then, when *The Ebb-Tide*'s "champagne ship" is nearly lost through the drunken negligence of its captain, Stevenson writes that "the *Farallone* drank deep of the encroaching seas" (223). And, to drive home the ship/drinker metaphor even more insistently, we're told of Davis that, once the adrenaline of crisis has sobered him up, "the captain was now the master of himself and of his ship" (223). Stevenson must have appreciated the singular irony of Michael Henchard carefully "steering off the rocks of the licensed liquor" when he and his family first arrive at the Casterbridge Fair, only to be wrecked on the hidden shoals of the furmity lady's unlicensed rum (6).

When Jekyll takes his potion, he "spring[s] headlong into the sea of liberty" (86) and it is quite logically there that he suffers his symbolic shipwreck. As these most recent quotations suggest, together with Frances Cobbe's aforementioned "Wife-Torture" and its maddening "seas of brandy and gin," to figure drink as a sea or an ocean was a commonplace of reformist rhetoric. A widely-circulated drawing showed a temperance lifeboat rescuing passengers on the "Ship of Moderation" as it foundered in the "Sea of Intemperance" (Shiman 18).[2] Charles Lamb recalled "losing [himself] in a sea of drink" as he washed in a "perilous flood" ("Confessions of a Drunkard" 175, 173), while the *Saturday Review* of 25 December 1858 claimed that for a reader to discover the temperance press was like finding "a little islet of primitive purity ... amid the guzzling, swilling ocean of unreformed humanity" (Harrison, "A World" 125).

Cruikshank wrote to Queen Victoria to ask if she might be willing to view and patronize his prodigious "Worship of Bacchus," in hopes that her endorsement might subsequently "assist in checking the tide of intemperance" (Jones 113), a typical phrase upon which David Lewis draws decades later when he too mentions the "tide of intemperance," the "tide of drinking and drunkenness," and the "tide of ruinous iniquity" that can "drown the voice of God" (*Drink Traffic* 78, 65–6, 8). Cruikshank's old, tippling friend Dickens similarly held that those who "have yielded to a depraved passion for strong liquor [have] fallen into a gulf of misery" ("Demoralisation" 169), echoing John Dunlop's use of the same term to specify a sub-oceanic basin of perdition (49). And a child's temperance alphabet, in which "B stands for Beer," likened beer's "frothy white head" to "the treacherous foam of the deep" (M. Booth 206). Thus, when Stevenson added the reference to this "sea of liberty" to the original phrasing of the Notebook Draft (Veeder, "Manuscript Drafts" 43), he strengthened the novella's alcoholic subtext in a way that many of his original readers could have recognized.

"The Plunge" into "The Torrent"

The same can be said for another of Stevenson's emendations. At the very beginning of his narrative, Jekyll epitomizes both the duality and, indeed, the whole course of his life when he says, "I was no more myself when I laid aside restraint and plunged in shame, than when I labored in the eye of day" (81). The word "wallowed" that he'd written in the Notebook Draft becomes "plunged" in the Printer's Copy. And although "wallowed" might have done very nicely with the drink-as-sea metaphor, "plunged" surely does a better job of capturing the willful abandon of Jekyll's project. Moreover, in addition to linking the tale's action to Ferrier's own "plunge" into alcoholism (*Letters* 4.159) and to Stevenson's once-declared and explicit preference for "plungers" as distinctly opposed to "teetotalers" (*Letters* 5.21), the change again brings the passage in line with contemporary temperance usage. Dickens' "The Drunkard's Death" treats the fate of one of the many who have "willfully, and with open eyes, plunged into the gulf from which the man who once enters it never rises more, but into which he sinks deeper and deeper down, until recovery is hopeless" (484). Kate Mitchell similarly cites the tragedy of countries "plunged" in the vice of intemperance, as they "sink into irretrievable degradation" (73–4). David Lewis, too, deprecates the extent to which the native population of India, especially the Bengalis, were reported to have "plunged into a depth of degradation" through their uncontrolled drinking (*The Drink Problem* 116–17).

Jekyll's "plunge" implies that he has immersed himself in "deep waters," as Utterson suggestively remarks once he's met Hyde (41)—arguably the same "yawning waters" that John Dunlop associated with drink (319). Several of Stevenson's metaphors, however, suggest waters that are dangerous not because they are deep but because they are fast and turbulent. When he first drinks his potion, Jekyll is "conscious of a heady recklessness, a current of disordered sensual images running like a mill race in my fancy" (83). If Stevenson's "heady" here could play on the public-house language of "B stands for Beer," as in "heady brew," "current" might conceivably evoke the same maritime associations as "tide." But "millrace" suggests a stream or river intentionally diverted by man and dangerous only if it is improperly used—more in line with the "floodgates of intemperance" that David Lewis claimed were opened by the Beer Act of 1830, leading to the subsequent "deluge" of "violence" (*Drink Problem* 151). Kate Mitchell speaks of the dire need to "stem the torrent of intemperance which has brought England to a perilous condition" (14), presumably seeing drink as a flooding river of some sort. Gladstone did the same when he complained in 1874 that the Liberals had been "borne down"—presumably "down-stream"—"in a torrent of gin and beer" (Gutzke 1). It's a metaphor that William Booth clearly has in mind as well when he suggests that England may in fact be "darker" than Africa, because his London has "many more public houses than the forest of the

Aruwimi has rivers" (24). It's evidently far more dangerous in Booth's mind to immerse oneself in the "streams" of the former than of the later, as Jekyll proves when his addiction to the life of Hyde involves the risk of his being "sucked down in the eddy of scandal" (53).

"License"

One of the terms Stevenson uses to express Hyde's lust for "liberty" takes on a very special resonance in the context of the temperance struggle. In the midst of the paragraph in which Jekyll declares his strongest determination to reform —"I resolved in my future conduct to redeem the past"— he allows that he was "still cursed with [his] duality of purpose; and as the first edge of [his] penitence wore off, the lower side of [him], so long indulged, so recently chained down, began to *growl for license*" (92; emphasis added). If we think of Hyde as the individual alcoholic, then the highlighted words suggest the stereotypical beastliness of the habitual drinker who craves his drug anew. If we also think of him as a type of the Drink Traffic, however, the word "license" *may* just evince the contemporary furor over the granting of vendor permits for the "licensed" selling of alcoholic drinks. The term had for obvious reasons been at the center of the temperance debate from 1830, when the Sale of Beer Act extended the right to sell malt beverages to anyone who could pay a two-guinea excise duty, without the need of a justice's license (Longmate 20). While not everyone necessarily agreed with David Lewis that the measure opened "floodgates of intemperance," the recorded number of vendors did increase exponentially and caused some substantial and widespread concern: in the first six months after the Act was implemented, 24,342 new establishments were selling beer, that number reaching 50,000 by 1860 (Levy 159). That same year, Gladstone's reduction of the excise on wine greatly stimulated the sale of another "moderate" beverage as well, allowing for the remarkably rapid expansion of firms like Victoria Wines.

Predictably, the liberties afforded to the drink industry by such free trade measures came to impress some reformers as counterproductive, foiling the very temperance ends that these pushes for alternatives to hard spirits had originally been meant to serve. Gladstone's government accordingly set out to revise the extant laws, imposing new restrictions on beerhouses in 1869 and proposing the Intoxicating Liquors Licensing Bill in 1871 to raise license duties, create a system of public house inspectors, shorten opening hours, and link the number of licenses directly to population in all locales throughout the country (Longmate 230; Harrison, *Drink* 264–5). The results were predictably in line with Thomas Whittaker's observation that "when we take [liquor from] the drinking adult, it is butter out of the dog's throat. It is difficult, and the dog barks, growls, bites" (*Life's Battles* 314). Faced, exactly like Hyde, with the prospect of being "chained down" after having been "so long indulged," the liquor trade "growled" in reactionary rage, claiming that the bill violated "every known principle of English freedom" (Longmate 230). The Liberals relented, their Intoxicating Liquor Licensing Act of 1872 being substantially less restrictive than the previous year's Bill. Nonetheless, in the General Election of 1874, what the drinkers and drink providers of the nation remembered was evidently what Home Secretary Henry Bruce had proposed in his original legislation, and the government was accordingly swept away in Gladstone's memorably-phrased "torrent of gin and beer."

The debate over licensing remained one of the prime catalysts of the "temperance fever" of the early 1880's. "Everybody has now a licensing Bill," Sir Wilfred Lawson complained in 1883. "A man is looked upon as rather an inferior sort of fellow if he has not a licensing scheme." Lawson's and the Alliance's goal, of course, was not reform but rather the complete abolition of all vending permits. Any license, Lawson claimed with his own pun on the word, was "the license of a man to do harm to his fellow subjects." Nonetheless, he granted, "every temperance reformer has to go through the license epidemic (like the distemper with dogs) before he becomes a vigorous and valiant soldier" (Longmate 234). Lawson anticipates Stevenson rather eerily when he associates the persistent popular craving for licensed drink with canine distemper (thereby echoing Whittaker and his "growling dog" as well). Anyone who resolves like Jekyll to "redeem the past," the Alliance leader claimed, is bound to be exposed to the threat of noxious beasts. Without claiming that Stevenson definitely and consciously endowed his language with the punning richness of a Palmerston when, in 1853, that Home Secretary claimed that "the words 'licensed to be drunk on the Premises' are by the Common People interpreted as applicable to the Customers as well as to the Liquor" (Spiller 11), it may be tempting to assume that the Wilfred Lawson the writer knew and so often referred to was the man who coined the canine metaphor that appears in Stevenson. Getting the image into the text might then have been the sub- or semi-conscious work of the Brownies. That said, the stereotypical rhetoric of the "beastly" drunk together with the marked resonance of a word that was every bit as topically current as "spirit" or "sober" could also have done the trick.

The "Slavery" of Drink

As early as 1839, John Dunlop remarked on the irony of citizens clamoring so passionately for the liberty to drink a substance that could, in turn, so easily deprive them of the fruits of their freedom. "The people of Great Britain and Ireland are slaves," he claimed, "as if in fetters, to drinking usage, and they know it not: they think themselves free, and do not even suspect their state of bondage" (256). *J&H* is about a man who, by plunging into that "sea of liberty," may pursue freedom from the disgrace and penitence that his undignified amusements entail — but he nonetheless finds himself increasingly under their sway. Stevenson's language accordingly echoes Dunlop's. Jekyll's first twinge of awareness as Hyde is to feel he is "sold a slave to [his] original evil" (84). As he aged, he tells us, he found he still regularly felt "merrily disposed," and he confesses that "it was on this side that my new power tempted me until I fell in slavery ... [to] the cup" (85). Utterson obsessively seeks the reason "for his friend's strange preference or *bondage* (call it which you please)" (38; emphasis added). When he goes by Jekyll's house but is refused admission, he is not unhappy; "perhaps, in his heart," we are told, "he preferred to speak with Poole upon the doorstep, and surrounded by the air and sounds of the open city, rather than to be admitted into that house of voluntary bondage" (59). This preference for the open spaces of temperance over the claustrophobia of alcoholic decay nicely anticipates the following "Incident at the Window," in which the lawyer and Enfield find Jekyll sitting "with an infinite sadness of mien, like some disconsolate *prisoner*" (60; emphasis added). So strong is Jekyll's thralldom that it is in fact effectively passed along to Utterson, who finds that, in addition to his intellect, his "imagination also was engaged, or rather enslaved," by the effects of his friend's addiction (37).

"Slavery" was a code word for Stevenson and his friends. "Poor Alan! He was drunk," muses the character John Nicholson, contemplating the lot of his Scots friend as he ironically mixes himself a "grog"; "and what a dreadful thing was drink, and what a slave to it poor Alan was, to drink in this unsociable, uncomfortable fashion" (*Complete Stories* 194). *The Ebb-Tide*'s Captain Davis, once he's broken into the cargo of champagne, equally spends his hours in "slavish self-indulgence or in hoggish slumber" (215). Henley writes to Baxter in 1884, describing Stevenson ("Johnson") in the very terms Stevenson used to judge others:

> Johnson, I regret to say, appears ... in short, tight. Ah! my dear Thomson, the Drink-Fiend is indeed a lion in the path. "Seeking whom he may devour" is, I believe, the beautiful language of Holy Writ. I never read the passage but I think of you and our M. F. ["Mutual Friend"] Johnson. Sad, sad indeed! That two so gifted and (I will say it, though perhaps I shouldn't) so honest as things go should be the slaves of so degrading a habit! [*Letters* 4.304].

As the quotation from Dunlop suggests, Stevenson and his cronies were only conforming to the usage of the age. Samuel Johnson deemed the drunken Richard Savage a "slave of every passion," while George Crabbe spoke of "Inebriety" and "her purple slaves" (Taylor 192, 29). Charles Lamb describes how drunkards "sell themselves for term of life" ("Confessions of a Drunkard" 170), while Kate Mitchell calls them "slaves of a pernicious custom" and claims that "the country wants as much to be freed from the slavery of drink as North America from the slavery of the negro" (33, 248). Thomas Whittaker accordingly mourns the drunk as "an ignorant and passion-bound slave" (*Brighter England* 319), and William Booth joins him in concern for "slaves of the bottle" (*Life's Battles* 347; *Darkest England* 47). Not to be left out, David Lewis seeks a remedy for those "enslaved by that terrible drink habit" (*Drink Traffic* 84), even as James Greenwood calls one of his "cursed" Londoners "a poor dejected slave to his passion for drink" (222). Meanwhile, Andrew Mearns claims that the slums which breed alcoholism "call to mind what we have heard of the middle passage of the slave ship" (58). And as with "slavery," so with "bondage" and "imprisonment." William Booth sets up to break "the bondage of strong drink" (185) fostered by publicans whom he likens to "ivory traders," while George Eliot re-invokes John Dunlop's "fetters" when she explains the sober Janet's lingering cravings by saying, "The prisoner feels where the iron has galled him, long after his fetters have been loosed" (*Janet's Repentance* 324).

"Drink and the Devil"

When Jekyll calls Hyde a "spirit of hell" (90), he nods very predictably to two other commonplace notions of temperance rhetoric: alcohol is Satan's drink; and men as a result become demons under its influence.

Thomas Whittaker called drink "the devil in solution" (*Brightest England* 98). Contradicting Dickens' assertion that drunkenness is the bane of the lower classes alone, Whittaker avers that "it is no less palpable that refined natures, nervous temperaments, acute intellects and cultivated minds, one and all, are not infrequently seized upon by the devil 'Drink,' and debased and destroyed" (*Life's Battles* 58). The illustration that accompanies the temperance alphabet poem, "B stands for beer," revealingly shows a serpent twining around a bottle of India Pale Ale, reflecting the same association between drink and forbidden knowledge that Stevenson exploits in the Hyde-Lanyon scene (M. Booth 206).

Devilish drink makes devilish men. George Eliot's Mrs. Linnet says of Janet's hard-drinking husband, "if iver Old Harry appeared in human form, it's that Dempster." Janet herself confesses to Tryon about her days of drinking, "It seemed as if there was a demon in me always making me rush to what I longed not to do" (*Janet's Repentance* 213, 286). An article published in the *Richmond Republican* after Poe's death cites the writer as saying he "felt as if his good angel had been grieved away, and a demon usurped its place"(Pollin 134) — like Jekyll, perhaps, overcome by the "insurgent" Hyde. And as with individuals, so with institutions. Just as Dunlop deprecated the "Satanic superstructure" that co-opted the children of Britain (317), so David Lewis cites Matthew Hill as evincing something like the Juggernaut metaphor in a specifically diabolical guise: "Whatever way we turn, and whatever we do for the welfare and elevation of the people, the drink-demon starts up before us and blocks the way" (*Drink Traffic* 53).

In Stevenson's early "Curate of Anstruther's Bottle," the doomed cleric literally meets up with Satan while staggering home in his cups. And in the late *Ebb-Tide*, the intemperate provocateur Huish breaks into the *Farallone*'s cargo of "fizz" and tempts Davis and Herrick to partake: "Try some; it's devilish good" (209). So, after Hyde has played the Gin Juggernaut, Enfield claims the little man looks frightened, but allows he was "carrying it off, sir, really like Satan" (32). Once Utterson has met Hyde, he sighs, "O my poor old Henry Jekyll, if ever I read Satan's signature upon a face, it is on that of your new friend" (40). Subsequently, Jekyll explains his violent outbreaks after a protracted bout of abstinence by saying, "My devil had been long caged, and he came out roaring" (90). And after the spontaneous reversion in Regent's Park, Hyde gnashes his teeth at the hansom driver "with a gust of devilish fury," and Jekyll goes on to allow that "that child of Hell had nothing human" in him (93–4), that he was made up instead "of something not only hellish but inorganic" (95). Hyde's association with devils and deviltry extends even to the level of puns, as Lanyon rather unwittingly signals both the villain's stature and his particular obsessions when he says about Jekyll to Utterson, "I have seen devilish little of the man" (36).

Once again, Stevenson's choices are clearly over-determined. There are plentiful reasons for associating Hyde with the devil that go well beyond signaling his ties with alcohol — reasons that may have to do with the stereotypical didactic cosmology that Fanny induced her husband to embrace; or with the more subtle reading of Stevenson's sub-text on gender that Katherine Linehan has recently advanced ("Closer Than A Wife"). But when in his very first paragraph Stevenson describes Utterson's fondness for both wine and gin, together with his envy for the way others can act under "the high pressure of spirits," it's hard to think that the lawyer's permitting his "downgoing" brother "go to the *devil* in his own way" wouldn't regularly have involved his brethren falling under the hellish sway of the strong drink that a preponderance of late Victorians associated with most cases of social and moral decline.

"Death in the Cup"

Of course drink was, for Stevenson's age, as frequently associated with physical as with moral death. Basil Montagu, friend to the Wordsworths, Coleridge, and Lamb, had in 1814 penned *Some Inquiries into the Effects of Fermented Liquors, By A Water-Drinker*, to warn "ingenuous youth" to "examine this gift of Circe and pause lest there be death in the cup" (Taylor 26). Cruikshank's "The Gin Shop" (1829) in turn set the tone for the temperance iconography of the 1830's. Three adults and three children are shown standing at a bar, all unwittingly poised in the jaws of an iron trap set on the floor as they are served by a skeleton disguised as a pretty bar-maid. The rows of spirit casks lining the walls are all of them shaped like coffins, and a posted notice alludes morbidly to one of those many and embroiling social roles that were actually played by the nineteenth-century drinking house: "Wanted, a few members to complete a burial society." Coming in the door is a night watchman, holding up his lantern; but he is yet another skeleton, punningly boasting, "I shall have them all dead drunk presently!" Below are printed the words of a "New Ballad":

> Now, oh dear, how shocking the thought is,
> They makes the gin from aqua fortis:
> They do it on purpose folks' lives to shorten
> And tickets it up at two-pence a quartern [Wardroper 128].

The Bottle and *The Drunkard's Children*, as well, figure disease, murder, and suicide as the inevitable consequences of strong drink. And as Dickens in 1837 catalogued the way drink "hurries its victims madly on to degradation and death" ("The Drunkard's Death" 48), so Kate Mitchell blamed alcohol not only for seventy percent of London hospital admissions in 1880 but also, more poignantly, for "this hideous mortality among the young" (114, 128). One of the most over-worked teetotaler jokes was in fact, very tellingly, based on the homonyms "beer" and "bier" (Longmate 200). Even the liquor trade itself rather grimly exploited the conceit from time to time. "Why is Burgess like an undertaker?" asked a riddle in Burgess's Wine and Spirit stores; "Because he does great business in the bier way" (Girouard 32).

Stevenson, as we have seen, was himself morbidly fond of invoking the ties between drink and mortal oblivion. Witness his telling Baxter, "I'm getting tired of this whole life business.... Let me get into a corner with a brandy bottle ... or as easily as may be, into a nice, wormy grave"; or Fanny Sitwell, "Opium and wine and everything that is death for soul and body, tempt me.... I often make up my mind that I shall begin to descend to the mouth of the pit"; or Henley, "Ferrier's grave gapes for us all"(*Letters* 1.271–2, 2.84, 4.262). "As he sat and talked to me," Stevenson wrote revealingly about the Samoan drunkard B. M. Haggard, "he smelt of the charnel house" (*Letters* 8.383). In "Will o' the Mill" (1878), Death literally comes to share a last bottle of wine with the eponymous hero, whisking him away soon after "a sort of cloud had settled over his wits ... [and] a dimness over his eyes" (*Complete Stories* 1.137). Stevenson later spoke of the *Hispaniola*'s tippling pirates in *Treasure Island* as having been done in by drinking an "artificially compounded death" (*Letters* 4.64), thereby fulfilling Dr. Livesey's early warning to Billy Bones: "The name of rum for you is death" (14). He subsequently and sensationally re-named the blind-drunk king whom he encountered in the Gilberts "Mr. Corpse" (*The South Seas* 251).

"Mr. Hyde" is arguably an earlier and more amplified version of "Mr. Corpse." "This was the shocking thing," says Jekyll; "that the slime of the pit seemed to utter cries and voices; that the amorphous dust gesticulated and sinned; that what was dead, and had no shape, should usurp the offices of life" (95). "Pit" is the very term Stevenson uses for the drug-taker's grave in the letter to Fanny Sitwell, the word perhaps conveying a bit more of the "hellishness" of the drunkard's fate than "grave" might do. "Slime" captures the odium of liquefying corruption in its later stages, but it also echoes the language of Frederic Farrar, the Dean of Canterbury, who in a series of essays written between 1885 and 1894 deprecated the drink trade that "everywhere leaves the slime of its overflow over devastated areas of society" (Gutzke 37). As literal an embodiment of Death, for Sir Danvers Carew, as the night-stalking skeleton of Cruikshank's "Gin Shop," Hyde's association with an "insurgent" mortality is perfectly in keeping with the temperance imagery that the text systematically exploits—and with the self-proclaimed threat of the "Skeleton Army" as well.

Lanyon, the novella's only practicing physician, is appropriately its most cogent commentator on the horrible risks that Jekyll is taking with his life. When Hyde has ingested the glass of restorative drugs in his presence, Lanyon is shocked to the core by what he sees: "pale and shaken, and half fainting, and groping before him with his hands, like a man restored from death—there stood Henry Jekyll!" (80). If alcohol is the "artificially compounded death" with which Hyde is associated, then for Jekyll to re-emerge from the dark body of Hyde—from the "slime of the pit"—is predictably and precisely for him to rise like a man restored from death. In fact, Stevenson obligingly makes just that point in "The Body Snatcher," when the wayward character Fettes is shocked from a literal alcoholic stupor into sudden sobriety, and the narrator accordingly confesses, "we were all startled by the transformation, as if a man had risen from the dead" (*Complete Stories* 1.420). Our author is working within exactly the same parameters as Charles Lamb, who claimed that freeing himself from the bondage of drink was akin to "resuscitation from a state of death almost as real as that from which Lazarus rose not but by a miracle" (169). Lanyon, however, evidently shares the skepticism of the Victorian upper classes regarding any addict's true and lasting ability to recover, for he subsequently tells Utterson, "I wish to see or hear no more of Dr. Jekyll.... I am quite done with that person; and I beg that you will spare me any allusion to one whom I regard as dead" (57). In the end, he's as right as Cruikshank about the ultimate outcome of his old friend's experiments with the fatal potion.

"The War among My Members"

Finally, Charles Lamb famously described himself as a drunkard who, as he wrestled with his terrible addiction, could scarcely bear "the anguish and pain of the strife within him" (169). Stevenson likewise confessed to Fanny Sitwell, "I have had a bad struggle with myself day by day and night by night. Opium and wine and everything that is death for soul and body, tempt me, one after the other" (*Letters* 2.84). Jekyll suffers equally from his "polar twins," the upright *versus* the unjust, "continuously struggling" "in the agonised womb of consciousness" (82)—as well as from feeling Hyde's alien being "caged in his flesh, where he heard it struggle to be born" (95). "Struggle," intriguingly the title of the reform journal in which that striking image of the anthropomorphized "English Juggernaut" appeared, is a key term for *J&H*. Probably the *most* memorable and significant phrase Stevenson uses to describe Jekyll's intellectual quest and psychomachic agony, however, is explicitly martial: "It chanced that the direction of my scientific studies," we're told early in the "Full Statement of the Case," "reacted and shed a strong light on [the] consciousness of the perennial war among my members" (81–2). That "damned old business of the war in the members" seems the quintessence of the novel as Stevenson describes it to Symonds: "This time it came out; I hope it will stay in, in future" (*Letters* 5.220–21). Once again, we're in the realm of the over-determined, as Stevenson's language must in substantial part be driven by the rhetoric of Scripture: James' "lusts that war in your members" (4:1), Peter's "lusts which war against the soul" (I.2:11), or Paul's rebellious "members" "warring against the law of my mind" (*Romans* 7:22–23), together with his sustained discourse on the Armor of God and the dire moral struggle that necessitates its use (*Ephesians* 6.11–17). The writer was unlikely to have grown up in the same house as Thomas Stevenson and his fiercely religious nanny, Alice Cunningham, without being well exposed to the tropes. But given the way he made the failing alcoholic Ferrier promise "for my sake as well as his own, to *continue the good fight*," the way he confessed to Henley after Ferrier died "I thank God he is out of the *battle*," and the way he later wrote to tell Baxter in the depths of his own struggles with drink "You have now before you one of the *hardest battles* possible, and I hope you will *fight it like a man* for the sake of your children," (*Letters* 3.64, 4. 154, 8.109; emphases added), it's reasonable to assume that—in this quintessential tale of chemical addiction—he had the lexicon of temperance in mind as well.

When *The Church of England Temperance Magazine* was founded in 1862, its first issue announced "a declaration of war on the pub" (Olsen 39). In the *Alliance News* of 18 December 1880, the Bishop of Reading's wife takes us even closer to Stevenson's vision of the human condition:

"It is such a sad pity that the world has been divided into teetotalism and anti-teetotalism, for that is what it has come to, as if it were war to the knife between the two" (Shiman 156). Nine years earlier, T. H. Barker had evinced the Pauline theological dimension with which *J&H* also toys, declaring that the struggle for prohibition was "part — and oh, how large a part!— of the great war between Heaven and Hell" (Harrison, *Drink* 372). David Lewis observes as well that "The struggle of the school, and the library, and the Church, all united against the beer-house and gin-palace, is but one development of the war between heaven and hell" (*The Drink Problem* 114–15). Elsewhere, Lewis cites the Reverend William Arnet of Edinburgh, who evinces a cavalier variant on the Hydian Juggernaut in asking, "Disciples of Christ, can you longer remain silent and inactive in this warfare, while this enemy of God and men rides rough-shod over the bodies and souls of your countrymen" (*The Drink Traffic* 109). And in *Brightest England and the Way to It*, Thomas Whittaker sounds another note that echoes Jekyll's when he proclaims that "temperance has ever been one development of the war going on between good and evil, heaven and hell, and there can be no question as to the side it is on" (269).

Other martial metaphors pepper the discourse of temperance as well, frequently re-evoking the traditional Pauline contexts. Whittaker's other book, published just the year before *J&H* was written, was aptly titled *Life's Battles in Temperance Armour*, incorporating the term that Stevenson used in his letter to Baxter. William and Catherine Booth's long campaign against intemperance found its fullest expression in The Salvation Army, established to combat the kind of Jekyllian collapse that Catherine had witnessed when her teetotal father fell back under the sway of alcohol and squandered the family fortunes (Shiman 131). The Salvation Army ironically begot its own dark twin, the "Skeleton Army," just as James Greenwood saw the many supporters of a sequence of "Permissive Bills" opposed by what he called "that other army of 150,000 publicans and beer-sellers encouraging the people to drinking habits" (225). And if the *British Temperance Advocate* declared itself in 1861 "a storehouse whence temperance reformers may draw their weapons both for attack and defence" (Harrison, "A World" 129), the implicit war was still raging sufficiently in 1885 for David Lewis to confess that "with 180,000 licensed liquor shops in full play, pouring as it were their shot and shell upon the doomed inhabitants [of Britain], we have had ample evidence to show that they are more than a match for the combined forces of temperance, philanthropy, and religion" (*The Drink Traffic* 96). Stevenson himself works a Caesarian variation on the same martial metaphors that he applied to Baxter and Ferrier when, in *The Ebb-Tide*, Davis succumbs almost instantaneously to Huish's temptation to "try some" of the "devilish good" champagne: "The Rubicon was crossed without another struggle. The captain filled a mug and drank" (209). A careful reading of *J&H* reveals just the same imagistic confluence of warfare and flowing waters and drink, all of them arguably laden with the ideological freight of the times. Saints Paul and Peter will have given Stevenson the term "war" in the context of moral psychomachia, but the lethal encounter between Hyde and Carew may well have taken some of its inspiration from the threat and reality of civil violence that was epitomized by the "full-scale neighborhood warfare" between Salvation and Skeleton Armies (Richter 74). That one ongoing campaign of the temperance war was fought in parliament may even have contributed to Hyde's original, wastrel victim being reconceived as an M.P.—and thus, perhaps, as a "warring Member" on a specifically political front.

Chapter Notes

Introduction

1. William Veeder, "Children of the Night: Stevenson and Patriarchy"; Elaine Showalter, "Dr. Jekyll's Closet"; and Wayne Koestenbaum, "The Shadow on the Bed: Dr. Jekyll, Mr. Hyde, and the Labouchère Amendment."

2. Patrick Brantlinger and Richard Boyle, "The Education of Edward Hyde: Stevenson's 'Gothic Gnome' and the Mass Readership of Late-Victorian England"; Stephen Arata, "The Sedulous Ape: Atavism, Professionalism, and Stevenson's *Jekyll and Hyde*," Ch. 2 in *Fictions of Loss in the Victorian Fin de Siècle*; and Robert Mighall, *A Geography of Victorian Gothic Fiction*, Ch. 4: "Atavism: A Darwinian Nightmare." For a discussion of atavistic language and imagery in the novella — in the specific and, until now, unexplored context of late–Victorian angst over the physical and social effects of alcohol, one of the prime "poisons" that Morel and Nordau saw as precipitating a degenerative plunge back down the Darwinian ladder — see Chapter 8 below.

3. Stevenson was never a "realist" in the sense that a Dickens or a Thackeray was. His long and friendly correspondence with Henry James, for example, was characterized by his staunch defense of a romantic latitude in invention and plot as over and against James's social realism. His customary mode of representation, however, was verisimilar and not referential, phenomenal and not noumenal.

Chapter One

1. The wide currency of the observation that alcohol affects the vocal cords is readily confirmed by a Google search for "drinker's voice." Such a search on 18 October, 2005, yielded twenty-one hits.

2. During their fatal last encounter, both Lanyon and Hyde himself attest to the latter's "impatience" as well (78).

3. Anya Taylor documents the impact of David Hume's novel theory of the human psyche on Romantic (and consequently Victorian) conceptions of inebriation in ways that shed light on Hartley Coleridge's and Jekyll's pronominal confusion. "But self or person is not any one impression," Hume argued in *A Treatise of Human Nature*, "but a bundle or collection of different perceptions, which succeed each other with an incredible rapidity and are in a perpetual flux and movement"(*Bacchus in Romantic England* 63). "Hume's witty pulverization of the coherence of the person," Taylor observes, "fragmented into moments, moods, forgetfulness and feelings, gave additional resonance to drunken self-loss, especially to the extent that it was self-willed or permitted. How stable was the human being if a

litre of liquid could transform him or her into an animal or a thing, and if that human being 'decided' out of some unfathomable depth of self-destructiveness to be so transformed" (2). It is tempting to assume that Stevenson was indeed somehow influenced by his fellow Scot in formulating his own conception of the self as an innately unstable, dualistic assembly of "faggots ... bound together ... [yet] continuously struggling," or perhaps as an even more multitudinous "polity of multifarious, incongruous and independent denizens" (*J&H* 82) — set to be tumbled into an ultimately self-destructive disarray by the imbibing of some transforming draught. It is especially intriguing that Hume likened the frequent effect of the chaotic "flux" of human perceptions, especially as exacerbated by drugs and alcohol, to a "shipwreck" (Taylor 63) — the very same metaphor that Jekyll uses to describe his own intellectual ruination (e.g. 75) and that we will discover to have been among the temperance movement's favorite tropes for alcoholic disaster. Stevenson certainly knew of Hume, and counted him along with Knox, Burns, and Scott as one of "Four Great Scotchmen." In February of 1874, he wrote to Fanny Sitwell describing Hume as, "of course, the urbane, cheerful, gentlemanly, letter-writing eighteenth century, full of niceness, and much that I don't yet know as to his work" (*Letters* 1.475). An earlier letter to Sitwell, however, strongly if rather cryptically suggests that Hume was well enough known to him as a religious skeptic — and furthermore that Stevenson felt a strong compulsion to "support his fame" despite realizing how much that support might offend his pious father (*Letters* 1.306).

4. Stevenson in fact added the reference to Hyde's "timidity and boldness" in the process of revising his manuscript, one of a number of textual emendations that we shall see make an alcoholic reading more attractive and plausible. See Veeder, *Texts* 6.

5. We shall subsequently explore the possibility that Jekyll's sense of "impunity" for Hyde's crimes reflects Stevenson's concern with the "drunkenness defense" variously admitted as a plea in British courts.

Chapter Two

1. "Port and Claret: The Politics of Wine in Trollope's Barsetshire Novels."

2. Stevenson may also be playfully (or perhaps unconsciously) re-literalizing a gustatory metaphor that lies curiously — like a kind of animalistic linguistic "Hyde" — at the heart of the spiritualized language of refinement: whatever heights it may attain, "taste" begins with whatever the self-indulgent appetites of the body lead us to put into our mouths to chew or swallow.

3. The author is familiar with Stephen Arata's insightful analysis of the ways Hyde is also rather paradoxically represented as a "gentleman" (e.g., on pages 31 [twice], 32 [twice], 33, 46, 68, 77); see *Fictions of Loss*, 33–43). As will shortly be seen, a careful examination of *J&H*'s allusions to alcohol leads one to roughly the same conclusion that is reached by Arata via a different path: that Stevenson's novella ultimately questions the clear delineations of class and moral worth to which its principal characters seem most deeply committed.

4. Arata is right that other of Myers' observations suggest that he felt Hyde, as an emanation of the gentleman Jekyll, should not be represented as too "low" — as in his remarks about the brutal clubbing of Sir Danvers Carew, a crucial and (indeed) sociologically-revealing scene to which we shall return. In both of the instances cited here, however, Myers' concern seems to be the opposite. True, his use of the word "unworthy" is curious. In isolation, it implies the solicitousness for a fellow man of "worth" that Arata reads into Myer's comments — but, in context, Myers is surely trying to say that Hyde wasn't in fact "worthy" of the refinements found in his rooms. One is inclined to leave a deconstructive reading of Myers' sociological commentary to others, contenting oneself with examining the ways in which *Stevenson's* text dismantles some of the staid assumptions on which it appears to be based.

5. Brian Harrison records a charming anecdote that attests to the strength of many a drinker's feelings for alcohol, as well as their conviction that drink was essential to physical vitality. When Richard Mee prepared to sign the first temperance pledge in 1834, his friend Peter Phillips thus expressed his solicitous alarm: "Thee mustn't, Richard, thee'll die!" (*Drink* 45).

6. If one may be allowed some venturesome close reading, it is at least interesting that a scoundrel whose literal urban neigh-

borhood is in substantial part defined by its "gin palace" should himself be described by Lanyon in terms of "the odd, subjective disturbance caused by his *neighborhood*" (77; emphasis added). While Lanyon goes on to detail the "sober fabric" of Hyde's apparel, he characterizes the effect of the man's touch in a rather suggestive way. When Hyde grasps his arm, says Lanyon, "I put him back conscious at his touch of a certain icy pang along my blood" (78). Poole has earlier remarked that there is something about Hyde "that you felt in your marrow—kind of cold and thin" (68). And, indeed, when Jekyll peers at himself as Hyde, he allows that "my blood was turned into something exquisitely thin and icy" (88). It is tempting to consider that, beyond describing the "chill" of horror, Stevenson may at least unconsciously be evincing the effect of strong spirits on the body physical as on (in terms of blighted neighborhoods) the body politic. The descriptions surely capture the shiver that a quick shot of gin flashes through the limbs and their vessels, and the "thinness" and "iciness" would catch gin's visual crystalline limpidness. Lanyon's somewhat curious phrasing, "I put him back," almost suggests that Hyde has temporarily become a thing, like perhaps a bottle, rather than a person. *If* the novella were a song about "John Barleycorn," such a reading would surely seem highly plausible. Whether it rises here above the level of an intriguing possibility is a matter for each reader to decide. (See Mighall, 190–91, for a more general exploration of this scene's interest in "morbidity [being] transferred from the 'patient' to the doctor.")

Chapter Three

1. Although Stevenson's own drug of choice was clearly alcohol, and wine especially, he was very much a creature of his age in having used laudanum (see his 1873 confession to Charles Baxter—*Letters* 1.271–2) and perhaps other forms of opium as well (*Letters* 2.84, writing to Frances "Fanny" Sitwell in 1874). On the extraordinarily widespread use of alcohol in the nineteenth century, even among children, see Chapter Four, below.

2. See the Appendix, below, for a discussion of "The 'Slavery' of Drink" as represented in late–Victorian Britain.

3. On the Darwinist, "degenerate" shadings of Stevenson's text, see for example Stephen Arata, *Fictions of Loss*, Chapters 1 and 2—and Chapter 8, below, in the present study.

4. F. M. L. Thompson notes that, "The police certainly had wide discretion in deciding whether to take no notice [of public drunkenness], to caution, or to charge. It was universally understood that gentlemanly drunks were not to be molested, although they might be helped home or into a cab" (*The Rise of Respectable Society* 330).

5. It is here that Arata's concerns with the text's little-noticed interest in the "degeneration" or "decadence" of the middle and upper classes begin to come into interesting and, one might say, very significant alignment with the present argument.

6. It is worth noting that Stevenson recycles in Lanyon's account a key verb from the earlier Utterson/Guest encounter—in a specific context that suggests that, while these two episodes are thematically related, the second is uniquely demonic. While we're told about Utterson in the presence of a close friend, a cozy fire, and a warming bottle of wine, "insensibly the lawyer *melted*" (54), Hyde conversely "seemed to swell—his face became suddenly black, and the features seemed to *melt and alter*" (80; emphasis added). Same "dissolution," very different valuation.

7. In light of the Wordsworth quotation—indeed of the general alcoholic resonance of *J&H*—even the version-book entry "double" which Dr. Lanyon finds written "perhaps six times" in Jekyll's notes and cites in his narrative just a few sentences after the "blood-red liquor" (76) *could* be seen to take on a new connotation. If Jekyll is referring to the quantity as opposed to the strength of the draught, "double" could appropriately designate the size of a serving of alcohol, as in the excerpt from "Benjamin" just cited. And if instead of volume it's a doubling of strength, then as early as 1555, English brewers had offered, along with their zestfully-monikered "mad-dog" and "dragon's milk," their "double beer" and even "double-double-double beer" (Longmate 4). Surviving advertisements of Victorian brewers and period photographs of Victorian pubs likewise regularly tout potent brews like "J. Drewry's 'Double Stout'" (Girouard 33; Spiller 26). One suspects that it's the volume

of Jekyll's draught that is at issue, but in either case, the discrete term "double"—appearing by itself in the context of a liquid that is being ingested—seems likely to have been borrowed by Stevenson from the established lexicon of drink.

8. As a subsequent chapter will explore, among the meanings of "spirit" also available to Stevenson was "a solution in alcohol of some essential or volatile principle" (*OED* 16.253). Given that Jekyll's potion involves the dissolving into Lanyon's "blood-red liquor" (deemed itself "to contain phosphorous and some volatile ether") of a "simple crystalline salt" (76) that alone "lent efficacy to the draught" (96), this would seem to be another definition on which Stevenson's word-play is solidly founded. Rather than moving us away from the lore of alcohol and back into the practice of the laboratory or chemist's shop, however, this concept of a "solution" is very much in keeping with our main argument. We'll return in Chapter Ten to the matter of volatile additives that intensified the effects of Victorian alcohol, in a section on temperance worries over the widespread commercial practice of "adulteration." For now let it be said that, when Jekyll attributes to his first taste of the potion a wicked "solution of the bonds of obligation" (83, and repeated on 92), or when he describes his the "racking torture" of transformation as involving the "pangs of dissolution" (85), his language is richly overdetermined. Given that Jekyll's quest is for the "dissociation" of mankind's "incongruous faggots" (82)—the "loosing" of "the bands that God decreed to bind" (as described in Stevenson's dedicatory poem "To Katherine de Mattos")—then for him to break the "bonds of obligation" is, on one hand, to affect a "solution" to (as in the "solving of") his overarching dilemma. But the passage also effectively describes the metaphorical "dissolving" of Jekyll's moral integrity into an alcoholic "sea of liberty" (86), and does so in a way that artfully if punningly evinces the literal concoction from both a liquid and a solid of the fatally "transforming draught."(See Note 6, above, for the parallel notion of a character's "melting" under the influence of alcohol.) Moreover, Stevenson may effectively be borrowing here from the admonitory lexicon of the temperance movement, as articulated in the very year of the novella's composition.

Prior to the inception of restrictive legislation, argued David Lewis in *The Drink Traffic in the Nineteenth Century*, "the country was fast sinking, and society threatened to be *dissolved* by the actions of alcohol" (76; emphasis added). To look at spirits and solvents from a slightly different but equally suggestive angle, Joseph Livesey had earlier anticipated Stevenson's "spirit of hell" or "idol in the glass" with his own observation that drink was "the devil in solution" (Longmate 59). In the novella, a potent drink leaves its mark on Hyde's visage (84). Then Utterson reads in Hyde's features "Satan's signature upon a face" (40). To complete the syllogism, drink must therefore on some level have been for Stevenson as for Lewis, "the devil [and his mark] in solution." For an exploration of a wonted association between "Drink and the Devil" in the rhetoric of the temperance movement, see the Appendix, below.

9. That Utterson's Sunday sobriety reflects in specific ways the reformist Sabbatarian movement is a possibility that will be considered below.

10. One might well note in this connection that the degenerate Felipe in "Olalla"—variously Hyde-like in his childishness, his swarthiness, his diminutive stature, his random cruelty, and his impetuous "gaiety" (428)—seems to the narrator "to drink in the world like a cordial" (428).

Chapter Four

1. Sidney Colvin vouched for Stevenson's successful application to London's relatively un-stuffy Savile Club in 1874 (McLynn 82). For an overview of the effects of the developing cult of "respectability" on social classes and drinking venues, see Thompson, *The Rise of Respectable Society*, 308–9, and Chapter 10, below.

2. It's particularly intriguing that Stevenson should have described the state of sobriety as being "shorn of grog," as though drink were some sort of hair. Recall that Hyde is represented in the novella as being darkly hirsute (88, 92) while Jekyll is "white" and smooth-faced (88, 43). When Jekyll describes his two natures as "polar twins ... continuously struggling" "in the agonized womb of consciousness" (82), Stevenson would seem to be recalling the pregnancy of

Rebekah, when the fraternal twins Jacob and Esau "struggled together within her" (Genesis 25.22). Hyde would then be Esau, "all over like an hairy garment" (25.25); and his "hair" would in turn be his addictive self (or drunkenness) as the "thick cloak" or "impenetrable mantle" in which Jekyll claims that his "safety was complete" (86). Stevenson's other possible scriptural reference, in the letter, may be to Samson, whose strength was in his hair. It would certainly be a clever way for the author to have registered his lingering belief in the empowering effects of alcohol despite his having to swear off his "grog." Intriguingly, one of Stevenson's letters recalls times when, as students in Edinburgh, Charles Baxter and he would drink "like Samson" and then quarrel till they cried (*Letters* 4.112).

3. For the alcohol reformers' persistent association of drunkenness with a form of death, see the Appendix, below — "Death in the Cup." In the novella, Lanyon says to Utterson about Jekyll after he has witnessed the horror of his drug-induced tranformation, "I beg that you will spare me any allusion to one whom I regard as dead" (57).

Chapter Five

1. The second half of Arata's chapter on *J&H* treats Stevenson's ambivalence about becoming a "professional" writer: *Fictions of Loss*, 43–53.

2. The author is greatly indebted here to Mairi McCormick's pioneering study of alcoholism in Victorian fiction, "First Representations of the Gamma Alcoholic in the English Novel" (1969); the tally of relevant works that follows is essentially hers. Unfortunately, McCormick's commendable lead has not been significantly followed by other critics; thus, for example, the virtual absence of attention to alcohol in Altick's *The Presence of the Present* (1991).

3. See T. J. Matheson, "Poe's 'The Black Cat' as a Critique of Temperance Literature"; David S. Reynolds, "Black Cats and Delirium Tremens"; and Domnhall Mitchell, "Drink and Disorder in *The Narrative of Arthur Gordon Pym*."

4. See Burton R. Pollin, "The Temperance Movement and Its Friends Look at Poe."

5. It is worth noting in passing that Stevenson's reference to "pouring forth" his story may hint at its deep thematic concern with drink.

Chapter Six

1. As the passage just cited may suggest, Stevenson could even have learned from Hogg his own puns on the word "spirits."

2. Elaine Showalter discusses the case of the unbalanced Frenchman, "Louis V.," who turned from an inoffensive streetwalker into a violent, heavy drinker and a political radical to boot. His history was known to F. W. H. Myers, although Myers mentions neither the man nor his alcoholism in his surviving letters to Stevenson ("Dr. Jekyll's Closet" 67).

3. Stevenson and Baxter actually spelled their pseudonyms very inconsistently, switching unpredictably between "Thomson" and "Thompson," on the one hand, and "Johnston," "Jonstone," and "Johnson," on the other. One of Stevenson's letters further allows that either man could go by either name (*Letters* 5.95–96). Whether this was mere whimsy or a semi-calculated acknowledgment that they were, after all, playing the game of slippery identities needn't be sorted out here.

4. I came across Claire Harman's brief commentary on the parallel fates of Ferrier and Jekyll only after this argument was fully drafted: see *Myself and the Other Fellow: A Life of Robert Louis Stevenson* (New York: Harper Collins, 2005), 257–8.

5. See the Appendix, below, for a brief discussion of alcohol reformers's partiality for nautical imagery, with "shipwrecked drunkards" foundering in "seas of drink" and saved by "temperance lifeboats": "'Shipwreck' and the 'Sea of Intemperance.'"

6. It is intriguing to note that, while the published edition of *J&H* drops the decades from annual dates (e.g., Jekyll's "I was born in the year 18 —"; p. 81), surviving draft fragments suggest that Stevenson had once conceived of the action as taking place very particularly between 1883 and 1885 (Linehan 21). Thus, the "whole story" as it first took shape in his mind covered precisely the years between Ferrier's death and the composition of the novella.

7. See, again, the Appendix on the commonplace temperance metaphor of "war" against strong drink: "'The War among My Members.'"

Chapter Seven

1. Historian F. M. L. Thompson contends that, after an initial flurry of debauchery

occasioned by the fiercely competitive price wars between the new marketers, beer consumption settled to reasonably moderate levels (*The Rise of Respectable Society* 312–13). Thompson observes as well that one of the temperance forces' prime motives behind the Beerhouses Act, along with the reduction in spirits consumption, was breaking what they took to be the dangerous monopoly of powerful breweries.

2. A. E. Dingle writes the history of the "U. K. Alliance" during the crucial later years of the century: *The Campaign for Prohibition in Victorian England: The United Kingdom Alliance 1872–1895.*

3. For a man of letters, Stevenson was remarkably devoted to visual images, especially those of a satirical nature. Two of his earliest letters attest to his fascination as a six-year-old with the drawings in *Punch* (*Letters* 1.91, 1.93), a particular taste that would stay with him for life. On reaching maturity, he himself contributed to Cassell's *Magazine of Art* under the editorship of his friend Henley (Nowell-Smith 132); relished long conversations with Colvin as Curator of Prints and Drawings at the British Museum (McLynn 70); confessed that his love for political cartoons earned him the title of a "Daumierist" (*Letters* 4.207); and reconfirmed his fondness for the pictures in *Cassell's Illustrated Family Paper* as one of the hallmarks of his infancy and youth (*Letters* 5.307). Even at Vailima, far removed from the dreary satirical world of Daumier into the florid and romantic realm of Gaugin, Stevenson featured among the decorations of his large reception hall "two reputed Hogarths" (*Letters* 8.2) and wrote to his erstwhile Old World purchasing agent Baxter that he harbored a "great need" to be sent two satirical "cuts" by Thomas Rowlandson — perhaps significantly adding that "they would really be of great use to me for a story that I have in hand" (*Letters* 8.20). His South Seas bedroom boasted "two or three favorite Piranesi etchings" (*Letters* 8.1).

4. On the derivation from the public house of the Victorian music hall, and on enduring parallels in their ethoi and social impact, see Thompson, *The Rise of Respectable Society*, 323–24.

Chapter Eight

1. The "scene at the window" is unlikely to have been the murder of Sir Danvers Carew, the only other extant option. Although the brutal crime is indeed witnessed by the "romantic maid" from the window of her Thameside house (46), her precise point of view is seemingly so insignificant that Stevenson is unlikely to have used it to name the scene. On the other hand, Utterson and Enfield's encounter with Jekyll, sitting disconsolately at the window of his house (60), makes up the whole of the chapter appropriately and revealingly entitled "Incident at the Window."

2. Some temperance reformers even went so far as to blame governmental authorities themselves for crimes that others committed under the influence, since they were ultimately responsible for giving criminals legal access to the drug (Harrison, *Drink* 327). In Stevenson's day, then, one predictable aim of the temperance movement was to abolish the "drunkenness defense" which saw inebriation as an extenuating circumstance; see Martin J. Wiener, "Judges v. Jurors: Courtroom Tensions in Murder Trials and the Law of Criminal Responsibility in Nineteenth-Century England," *Law and History Review* 17 (1999), <http://www.historycooperative.org/journals/lhr/17.3/wiener.html> (10 Mar. 2005). Of course what is essentially Jekyll's calculated and repeated exploitation of that "other person" excuse would effectively have invalidated this defense strategy had he ever been hauled into court. On judicial treatment of "artificially contracted madness by drunkenness," see Kerr, 359.

3. The term "missing link" in reference to a hypothetical creature that would establish the kinship of ape and man dates back at least to 1864 and the correspondence of the great British paleontologist Hugh Falconer. See *Ockham's Razor*, "The Missing Link," http://www.abc.net.au/rn/science/ockham/stories/s54.htm (14 January 2004).

4. On the commonplace association of alcoholism and degeneration, see Daniel Pick, *Faces of Degeneration*, 87 and 195; and William Greenslade, *Degeneration, Culture, and the Novel*, 190. That Hyde may for Stevenson have represented not only the retrograde behavior of a decadent individual but also the potential for the genetic decline of the human race under the influence of Nordau's "poisons," recall that Jekyll's relationship to Hyde is likened to that of a father to a ("dwarfish") son (89).

5. It is worth noting that the Metropoli-

tan Public Garden Association was especially well subscribed by London's middle-class professionals (Malchow 113), men precisely like Utterson, Enfield, Lanyon, and even Jekyll in his more humanitarian mode.

6. On Hyde as himself a kind of "spirit of spirits" who exerts a physically "evil influence," see Chapter 2, Note 6, above.

7. The chaos in Hyde's rooms strangely recalls the scene when Jim enters the abandoned ship's cabin and comes across the frightful disarray that's been left there by Silver's drunken men:

> It was such a scene of confusion as you can hardly fancy. All the lockfast places had been broken open in quest of the [treasure] chart. The floor was thick with mud where ruffians had sat down to drink or consult after wading in the marshes round their camp. The bulkheads, all painted in clear white and beaded round with gilt, bore a pattern of dirty hands. Dozens of empty bottles clinked together in corners to the rolling of the ship. One of the doctor's medical books lay open on the table, half of the leaves gutted out, I suppose, for pipelights. In the midst of all this the lamp cast a smoky glow, obscure and brown as umber [142].

The "domestic" disarray (another explicit violation of a "lockfast" place) and the muddy, murky atmospherics distinctly mirror Hyde's rooms in their fog-bound, "lurid brown" neighborhood — and thereby lend a further measure of plausibility to the theory that Hyde' "house-wrecking" is in a significant way inspired by stereotypical notions of a drunkard's blighting impact. It is also interesting to note that both Hyde and the pirates leave behind them altered and ruined books (see, as well, *J&H*, 71 and 96 on the "blasphemies" Hyde writes in Jekyll's "pious texts). Recall Stevenson's letter in which he clearly saw "taking to drink" as clearly antithetical to "writing books," leading instead to "shipwreck."

8. Once again, the temperance movement's commonplace likening of drink to a form of "bondage" or "slavery" is treated in the Appendix: "The 'Slavery' of Drink."

Chapter Nine

1. See *J&H*, 87, on Hyde's specific "act of cruelty to a child."

2. As we build the case for "Hyde the Juggernaut's" somehow standing for the pernicious effects of drink, it is worth noting that Utterson is unable to leave his nasty memory behind when he retires for the night, but repeatedly recalls the callous rogue moving "*the more swiftly and still the more swiftly, even to dizziness,* through wider labyrinths of lamp-lighted city." The content of the memory aside, the physiological effect is amusingly, and perhaps significantly, like the accelerating vertigo of the "whirlies" that can beset a bed-going drunkard.

3. To expand upon the association between drink and the power of a god, the classical model of Bacchus was naturally available for the reformers of the age, and they exploited it with some consistency. One of the Band of Hope's most widely-used textbooks was *The Worship of Bacchus, A Great Delusion*, published by Ebeneezer Clarke in 1876 and (a propos of Hyde's "victim") later re-issued in a two-penny abridgement for children (Longmate 127). George Cruikshank's monumental *Worship of Bacchus* (1863) shows the god of drink ruling in awesome and suggestive majesty over the streets and squares of London. Decades later, Thomas Whittaker cries out that alcohol "is the curse of Britain, it is the god of the nation; there is more money, there is more time, there is more health, there is more life sacrificed to the god Bacchus in this country than there is sacrificed to any heathen god in the known world" (*Brighter England* 153). Had Stevenson known either Cruikshank's *Bacchus* or Whittaker's or both, it would have been only a short imaginative step to Hyde as Juggernaut. The fact that both *Bacchus* and Cruikshank's *The Bottle* were reproduced as lantern slides for illustrated public lectures (Patten 2.418; 247) is especially intriguing if we note that Utterson, when he recalls Enfield's arguably polemic vignette, sees it passing "before his mind in a scroll of lighted pictures" (37). One wonders if Stevenson might possibly have either seen or heard about the works circulating in that technological medium, thus in part "paving the way" for Hyde as a latter-day exemplar of cataclysmic intemperance. Unfortunately, all we can do is speculate.

Other contemporary critics of drink brought it solidly into the Judaeo-Christian sphere. Most often they cast alcohol as "the other," the Enemy, Papism, apostasy. Whittaker recalls of 1830's momentous licensing decision, "the beer power was the Goliath of that day" (*Life's Battles* 284). David Lewis likens the "drinking system" to "the idol worship of the Israelites" (*Drink Problem* 232–3). A spirit shop could be called "the Gin-Vatican" (Spiller 51). A Bath vicar said of his flock, "The beer-shop is their church; they bow down before the beer barrel" (Longmate 32). More chilling, however, were visions of drink not as a demonic counter-religion to the Church of England but as a compromising, de facto protégé of the church hierarchy itself. Thus an 1867 editorial in *The Church of England Temperance Magazine* claims that clerics refused to sign the pledge for fear of losing the support of brewers in their dioceses: "Do not 'Our Bishops' and 'Our Clergy,' thus serve the great god that is made of beer-barrels and hopheads?" (Olsen 46).

4. As, for example, in the following *Punch* numbers: 30 July 1881, 4 February 1882, 11 March 1882, 28 October 1882, 20 October 1883, 12 April 1884, 18 October 1884, 3 October 1885, and 7 December 1885.

5. To see this crucial scene's vengeful females standing in for Mrs. Ferrier requires one to see a good bit of Ferrier in Hyde's *victim*, when we have to this point more readily seen him reflected in Hyde. Then again, when it came to Stevenson's recollections of his friend, he was a fellow possessed of two characters: "the good, true Ferrier" and "the lunatic brother." Having experienced the same duality in himself, Stevenson might readily have held his old friend in some ways accountable for his own doom: thus, the rash inebriated self, in essence, "crushing" the sweet innocent. But, as for Ferrier's mother, all the odium was evidently directed towards Stevenson and Stevenson alone. Given this whole dark episode in its author's life, there is likely nothing in *J&H* that was more wrenching for him to write than this scene. Thus, perhaps, Enfield's curious remark: "It sounds nothing to hear, but it was hellish to see" (31). A second-hand account simply doesn't cut the mustard, Enfield admits: "You had to be there." Stevenson most certainly had. Recall that Hyde's villainy in this scene is less a function of his colliding with the girl in the first place ("the two ran into each other naturally enough") but rather that he didn't, of his own volition, stop to look after her. In rather eerie parallel, and as he confessed to his father and to W. E. Henley, Stevenson faulted himself for not having done enough for his own toppled fellow night-traveller: "My dear friend, Walter Ferrier. O if I had only written to him more!"(*Letters* 4.159).

Chapter Ten

1. It was only after drafting this chapter that I came across Robert Mighall's reading of the way the topography of Stevenson's London replicates the schism between Jekyll and Hyde (*A Geography of Victorian Gothic Fiction*, 145–53). Predictably, Mighall's argument proceeds from many of the same textual details as my own. His prime interest, however, is in the way Stevenson's age charted criminal atavism in both physiological and geographical space, while my aim is to suggest that the novella reflects those Victorian programs of urban reform that were driven by the social depredations of alcohol.

2. For a social history of the period that focuses on the issue of social propriety, see F. M. L. Thompson, *The Rise of Respectable Society*. Despite his ultimately strong moral scruple — which contributed, among other things, to his marked disapproval of the abandoned life-style of his fellow Scots writer Robert Burns — Stevenson's correspondence regularly evinces his *disdain* for the unrealistic obsession with respectability that fueled the hypocrisy he saw everywhere around him. The frequency and forcefulness of his comments strengthens any reading of *J&H* that faults Jekyll for his disingenuous propriety.

3. Whether he's a barrister or merely a solicitor, the lawyer Utterson is fittingly seen to drink wine only behind the closed doors of a private home, and gin solely in the complete privacy of domestic solitude. Similarly, despite his love of the theater, he hasn't even been to a play for twenty years (29). In some ways, then, he's as wed to the idea of respectability as his client Jekyll — although, as we've seen, his tolerance for the follies of "down-going men" clearly sets him apart from the doctor.

4. Although we know of no evidence that Utterson's partiality for gin ever drives him to any of the personal "iniquities" he seems to dread (42), Stevenson's sketch of Utter-

son's drinking habits hints at the dangers of private drinking that the author himself (although he was in every important way a "gentleman") experienced in San Francisco and later confessed to Baxter (as treated above). Here again, Arata's sense that the text concerns itself with the "decadence" of the upper classes as well as with the "degeneration" of the lower is very much a propos.

5. On the general phenomenon of Victorian suburbs, see F. M. L. Thompson, *The Rise of Suburbia*.

6. Once again, for further discussion of the temperance rhetoric that may lie behind Stevenson's metaphors, see the Appendix: "'The Plunge' into 'The Torrent.'"

7. Given that the novella literally involves the depraved recreations of a *professional* man, one might initially assume that the present argument on the new-found (and uncontrolled) leisure of the industrial *working* class is somewhat irrelevant. Nevertheless, although Hyde is sometimes constructed as the decadent side of a gentleman (as in his stock of fine wines or his heightened rhetoric with Lanyon to which Myers took such exception), he is elsewhere very much associated with the working classes (as in his short stature, his swarthy and hirsute skin, his Soho residence, and his being generally the kind of man whom Poole says would never "dine" with Jekyll). Moreover, if his name indeed owes anything to the Hyde Park Riots of 1855, he is directly associated with the fractious leisure of the drinking masses. In a text as richly suggestive as Stevenson's, it would be a mistake to allow Hyde's literal class origins to limit one's sense of what he might represent, by way of widely shared social anxieties. If drink in general is the novella's prime concerns, Hyde may as well stand for the drunken masses as for (or in addition to) drunken gentlemen like Ferrier or Teddy Henley. It is interesting in this regard that Utterson should first hear Hyde's ominous footsteps "spring out distinct from the vast hum and clatter of the city" (38). Elsewhere associated with the polluting smog of Soho, Hyde can at times almost seem to be the threatening personification of the industrialized city itself. The "Juggernaut" imagery discussed above is very much in line with Hyde's urban associations.

8. On the worrisome potential for rural youths drawn to expanding urban labor markets to suffer the fate of an English Pinocchio, Forster Crozier wrote in March of 1885: "If in the country, they were kept to the school, the Sanctuary, and a profession of religion by their associations, companionships, parental oversight, and the good opinions of others: they find that all these are now cut off; each youth is cast upon his own responsibility. His time, his money, his character are in his own keeping; if he will have a backbone of religious principle and moral strength, he will connect himself forthwith with his own Church, and get interested in Christian work, and thus he will be saved. But if he lack within himself the elements of strength, he must inevitably sink, and may sink even lower than the grave.... The Methodist youth will often find himself a considerable distance from a Methodist chapel, but near enough to a music hall or a dancing saloon; his fellow-students or fellow-journeymen are already well-versed in town life. They are smart in appearance, gentlemanly in manner, with money always in their pockets; by these he is led on, first innocently to see London sights, perhaps to hear its great preachers, then in a short time, if he be not wary, to taste its forbidden pleasures; and often, when it is too late, he finds himself dismissed from his situation, and bankrupt both in cash and in character. Now, what is to be done to save this class of youth?" asks Crozier: "Providing a house of prayer as convenient ... as the public house is now" ("Methodism and 'The Bitter Cry'" 102–04). As we'll see, others saw alternatives to Church and chapel as effective and necessary countermeasures to the alcoholic ruin of industrialized Britain.

9. In *The Ebb-Tide*, the university-educated Herrick, himself a moderate drinker, evinces the same disdainful attitude as Lanyon when Davis promises to amend his drunken ways: "Excuse me, I desire to see no more of you" (224).

10. See the Appendix on "Death in the Cup."

11. There is, on the surface, a certain moral propriety to Hyde's behavioral "impurities" being enabled by a chemical that is equally tainted. The "lesson" might thus be that "he who lives (or is brought to life) by impurity shall die by impurity." On the other hand, because Jekyll's consummate crisis is precipitated by his inability to find more of the "impure salt" in order to *restore* his

"good" self," one could argue that Stevenson is subtly exploring the ways "impurity" may be central to the full functioning of the human psyche, for worse and for better. A Freudian reading might assert that, just as the "impure" salt is necessary for the only version of a "full" life of which Jekyll happens to be capable, the action of the id as an "impure" but nonetheless as an "efficacious," energy-providing component of the psyche is crucial to any balanced existence. We'll return somewhat later to the curious fact that Jekyll uses *one* drug to effect two very different transformations—from "good" to "evil" and then back again. Do we assume for now that the salt's "impurity" is always ultimately and self-evidently evil because it allows for the whole, ultimately damning process? Or do we allow for its doing some "good" work as well? As we'll see, Stevenson's "single" but "dual-functioning" potion may reveal something very significant about his ultimate attitudes towards alcohol.

12. One of the most favored and inexpensive strategies to make drinkers "like their liquor more" was actually to introduce quantities of simple salt into commercial beverages (Mitchell 86–7). That Jekyll's "secret ingredient" is itself a "salt" may constitute an equally simple nod to that common practice, not specifically in terms of the effects of impurity but rather in terms of stimulating the "excess consumption" that we associate with Hyde. For a recent and engaging treatment of the way another late–Victorian literary text responds to the problem of impure comestibles, see Rebecca Stern's "Adulterations Detected: Food and Fraud in Christina Rossetti's 'Goblin Market.'"

13. The incongruity of Hyde's apparently being a tea-drinker in cozy settings opens up another largely untapped line of critical analysis on the novella—one beyond the scope of this study, but one which would focus on the ways in which Hyde isn't always quite as vile and destructive a creature as Jekyll and others make him out to be. While Utterson expects that Hyde would naturally destroy any copy of a will in which he is replaced as Jekyll's beneficiary by the lawyer himself (72) and while Jekyll expresses his fears that Hyde will destroy the "Full Statement" that he leaves out in the open for Utterson to discover (97), Hyde in fact does neither. The practical necessity of Jekyll's written confession reaching Utterson and, through him, the *reader* does suggest that, however implausible Hyde's restraint with (or obliviousness to) the manuscript may seem to be in a realistic sense, he *must* not destroy the statement. The same, however, cannot be said for the will. A portion of a burned paper could have sufficed to give Utterson any information he needs to document Jekyll's change of testamentary heart. Instead, Hyde leaves (or, given that he shares Jekyll's "hand," possibly even *writes*) an entirely valid legal document conducive to the welfare of a man "he had no cause to like" (72). One might be appropriately reluctant to claim that Hyde should be forgiven his crimes, but the fact that he effectively preserves both the will and Jekyll's salutary moral narrative suggests that Stevenson wrote the story of a "man" who was made, and made out to be, worse than he initially and really was. The same damaging bias which originally led Jekyll to inhibit an innocuous "impatient gaiety of disposition" to the point that it finally burst out with a murderous "roaring" is very much there in Jekyll to the end (as he predicts Hyde's response) and in his friend Utterson as well (as he wonders why Hyde hasn't destroyed or altered the will). Nevertheless, if we look at the things that Hyde is expected to do to crucially important manuscripts but never actually does, that bias is never quite justified. Even Utterson, the most tolerant character in the novel, never rises above demonizing Hyde, the man whose face he claims bears Satan's autograph. It's finally intriguing to think that, in re-writing his "allegory" under Fanny's exacting eye, Stevenson crafted a "perfect" "allegorical" villain who, nonetheless, looks slightly less purely villainous the more closely one examines him. If we consider Lanyon to be one of his essential victims, it's well to remember that the doctor was clearly warned by Hyde himself not to watch the transformation scene that fatally unhinges him (79). See 1877's "A Lodging for the Night" for what may be a parallel example of Stevenson's interest in the ways that the morally righteous may be tempted, unjustly, to write off all virtue in criminals: that story's Lord of Brisetout considers Villon to be completely without "honour" despite the hard-drinking rogue-hero's pointed refusal to kill the hospitable man and steal his gold plate.

14. That Stevenson meant to attribute the

order in the room to Hyde and not Jekyll is confirmed in a letter to Myers, who had objected that this detail too was "unworthy" of the villain: "The tidiness of the room, I thought ... was due to the dread weariness and horror of the imprisonment. Something has to be done; he would tidy the room" (Linehan 85). While the author went on to concede that the effect was "false," it's clear he was tempted to credit Hyde with some more or less civilized reflexes. Cf. the preceding note, and Arata, *Fictions of Loss*, on Hyde as a decadent gentleman.

Chapter Eleven

1. This is the definition that reviewer Julia Wedgwood evidently had in mind when she hailed the "profound allegory" of a tale that "investigate[s] the meaning of the word *self*" (April 1886; Maixner 223). Somewhat ambiguously, Andrew Lang had pronounced in a review three months earlier that, "[*J&H*] is not a moral allegory of course; but you cannot help reading the moral into it, and recognizing that, just as every one of us, according to Mr. Stevenson, travels through life with a donkey (as he himself did in the Cevennes), so every Jekyll among us is haunted by his own Hyde" (Linehan, *Strange Case* 94).

2. Another passage describes the way Utterson comes to "know" Hyde as involving a kind of ontological solidification of Word into Thing that mirrors the imaginative process of personification allegory. The more Utterson learns the man's particulars, the more distressed he becomes: "It was already bad enough when the name was but a name of which he could learn no more. It was worse when it began to be clothed upon with detestable attributes; and out of the shifting, insubstantial mists that had so long baffled his eye, there leaped up the sudden, definite presentment of a fiend" (35–6).

3. On the presence of any calculated and consistent referentiality in the text, Cyndy Hendershot asserts that "Jekyll and Hyde [sic] may be read as an allegory, but only if allegory is understood as an overdetermined and indeterminate mode" ("Overdetermined Allegory" 37); "Simplistic moral allegory is Jekyll's conception of his story, not the novella's" (36).

4. The chapter in which the "Black Mail House" and "Queer Street" references appear may strike one as fairly remarkable in the matter of narrative self-awareness. Enfield confesses that "it's a *bad story*" — not least because "a man does not, *in real life*, walk into a cellar door at four in the morning and come out of it with another man's cheque for close to a hundred pounds" (32; added emphasis). These details suggest Stevenson may have known he was "pushing the envelope" not only of credibility but also of narrative realism.

5. Gillian Cookson complicates any hypothesis that a number of the novella's names could have been simply "invented' for their allegorical resonance. Arguing that, as early as July of 1885, Stevenson's work on the never-finished biography of Fleeming Jenkin would have put him in touch with the names of Jenkin's fellow engineers, she traces to actual, historical Victorian professionals the names "Hastie" and "Guest" — as well, incidentally, as "Lanyon," "Danvers," "Newcomen," "Poole," and, indeed "Jekyll" and "Hyde" ("Engineering Influences" 118–19). The timing of the Jenkin project and the striking number of nominal parallels makes Cookson's case quite convincing. Nonetheless, Stevenson is unlikely have "culled" any such names with no regard at all to their function and resonance within the particular text he was creating. Thus, Lanyon may indeed be too "Hastie" first to judge Jekyll and, second, to agree to watch Hyde take his potion. "Guest" may still suggest a stereotypical recipient of the warm hospitality with which wine was so predictably associated. And "Hyde" might have leapt out of Stevenson's biographical working papers as the perfect name to coalesce notions of hidden-ness, bestial-ness, and popular revolt against the restraints of temperance.

6. The novella's susceptibility to allegorical understanding may be quickly — if subtly — signaled in the description of the relationship between the two first characters we meet. When the narrator admits of the cousins Utterson and Enfield, "It was a nut to crack for many, what these two could see in each other" (29–30), he intriguingly uses a commonplace metaphor for literary exegesis to explain the way "many" try to make sense of the cousins; crack the shell or flay the husk of the literal and you get to the nut or grain of allegorical meaning. Conrad, for example, works a variation on the motif in *Heart of Darkness* (1899) when the narrator

confides that, unlike Marlow's "inconclusive" narratives (5), "the yarns of seamen have a direct simplicity, the whole meaning of which lies within the shell of a cracked nut" (3). And at the heart of the "many's" attempts to unpack the cousins' motives in *J&H* is the inner question of "what these two could *see in each other*," which suggests there's even more hermeneutic work to be done, for characters and readers alike.

7. Once again, a portion of the conclusion, below, seeks to explain that curious fact in a way that attends to Stevenson's inconsistent attitudes towards alcohol.

8. See "'Shipwreck' and the 'Sea of Intemperance'" in the Appendix.

Chapter Twelve

1. This social and ethical phenomenon has been a remarkable constant in class discussions at Dickinson College during the ten or so years I have taught the novella. While I haven't implemented a scientific survey, more often than not, students immediately recognize Jekyll's psychic "ploy" as being to this day extremely useful, both for facilitating and for excusing "youthful indiscretions" of one sort or another.

2. See Martin J. Wiener, "Judges v. Jurors," cited in Chapter 8, Note 2—and the various references to Norman Kerr's discussion of the issue in *Inebriety* (1882)—above.

3. A fairly recent animated version intended for children, for example, turns the tale into an explicit warning against recreational drug use: Marcia Hatfield, *Jekyll and Hyde* (1986).

4. Granted, Utterson is not exactly "moderate" in his theater-going; despite his having once loved plays, we're told on the novella's opening page that he hasn't been to one in twenty years.

5. Of course, just as Utterson's solicitousness for Jekyll flies in the face of his earlier willingness to "let [his] brother go to the devil in his own way," so did Stevenson's concern and solicitousness for Ferrier (and indeed for Baxter) develop only after the early "devil-may-carelessness" of the L. J. R Society.

Appendix

1. One thinks, perhaps, of the humble Poole's solicitousness for his addicted employer vs. Lanyon's (and even Utterson's and Enfield's relative) indifference.

2. Temperance forces on either side of the Atlantic dearly relished the "lifeboat" metaphor. A popular British play was accordingly entitled *The Temperance Lifeboat* (Longmate 199), while the reformist journal of one Massachusetts municipality was called *The Taunton Lifeboat* (Pollin 120). The trope was sufficiently powerful that "actual" temperance lifeboat "crews" were founded as early as 1861, with tee-totaling activists donning appropriate nautical uniforms and parading through the streets with model boats (Longmate 215). Dickens himself comments on the "infusion of allegory" into political commentary as he describes such a crew, albeit following a flag that touted "The Peckham Lifeboat" rather than an actual craft ("A Plea for Total Abstinence" 360).

Bibliography

Primary Texts

Booth, Charles. *Charles Booth's London: A Portrait of the Poor at the Turn on the Century, Drawn from His* Life and Labour of the People in London. Edited by Albert Fried and Richard M. Elman. New York: Pantheon, 1968.
Booth, General [William]. *In Darkest England and the Way Out*. London: International Headquarters of the Salvation Army, n.d. [1900].
Brontë, Anne. *The Tenant of Wildfell Hall*. Oxford: Clarendon, 1992.
Brontë, Emily. *Wuthering Heights*. London: Collins, 1952.
Bunyan, John. *The Pilgrim's Progress from this World to That which is to Come*. Oxford: Clarendon, 1960.
Chant, Mrs. Ormiston. *Why We Attacked the Empire*. Sel. in Ledger and Luckhurst, *The Fin de Siècle*, 69–72.
Conrad, Joseph. *Heart of Darkness*. New York: Dover, 1990.
Crozier, Forster. "Methodism and 'The Bitter Cry of Outcast London.' [1885]" In Mearns, *The Bitter Cry of Outcast London*. 91–109.
Dickens, Charles. "The Big Baby." In *Dickens' Journalism*, 3.310–18.
_____. "Demoralisation and Total Abstinence." In *Dicken's Journalism* 2.159–69.
_____. *Dickens' Journalism*. Edited by Michael Slater. 3 vols. London: Dent, 1994–98.
_____. "The Drunkard's Death." In *Dickens' Journalism*, 1.463–72.
_____. "Frauds upon the Fairies." In *Dickens' Journalism*, 3.166–74.
_____. "Gin Shops." In *Dickens' Journalism*, 1.180–85.
_____. *Hard Times*. London: Oxford U. P., 1966.
_____. *The Letters of Charles Dickens*. Volume 7: 1853–55. Edited by Graham Storey, Kathleen Tillotson, and Angus Easson. Oxford: Clarendon, 1993.
_____. *Oliver Twist*. Oxford: Oxford U. P., 1982.
_____. *Selected Journalism, 1850–1870*. Edited by. David Pascoe. Harmondsworth: Penguin, 1997.
_____. *Sketches by Boz Illustrative of Every-day Life and Every-day People*. London: Oxford U. P., 1957.
_____. "Sunday under Three Heads." In *Dickens' Journalism*. 1.475–99.

_____. *The Uncommercial Traveller and Reprinted Pieces*. London: Oxford U. P., 1958.
_____. "Whole Hogs." In *Dickens' Journalism*. 3.18–25.
Disraeli, Isaac. *Curiosities of Literature*. 2 vols. New York: Olms Verlag, 1969.
Doré, Gustave and Blanchard Jerrol. *London*. Newton Abbot: David & Charles, 1971.
Doyle, Sir Arthur Conan. *The Hound of the Baskervilles*. In *Sherlock Holmes: The Complete Novels and Stories, Vol. II.*, 1–146. New York: Bantam, 1986.
Dunlop, John. *The Philosophy of Artificial and Compulsory Drinking Usage in Great Britain and Ireland*. London: Houlston and Stoneman, 1839.
Eliot, George. *Janet's Repentance*. In *Scenes of Clerical Life*, 189–335. Oxford, Clarendon, 1985.
Geduld, Harry M. *The Definitive Dr. Jekyll and Mr. Hyde Companion*. New York: Garland, 1983.
Greenwood, James. *The Seven Curses of London*. Oxford: Blackwell, 1981.
Hardy, Thomas. *The Mayor of Casterbridge*. New York: Norton, 1977.
Hatfield, Marcia. S.P. *Dr. Jekyll and Mr. Hyde*. DVD. Burbank Films Australia, 1986.
Hazlitt, William. "On the Spirit of Obligations." In *The Complete Works of William Hazlitt*, 12.78–87. London: Dent, 1931.
Hogg, James. *The Private Memoirs and Confessions of a Justified Sinner*. Edinburgh: Edinburgh U. P., 2001.
Keats, John. "Hyperion." In *English Romantic Poetry, Vol. 2*. Ed. Harold Bloom. Garden City: Anchor, 1963. 415–39.
Kerr, Norman. *Inebriety, Its Etiology, Pathology, Treatment and Jurisprudence*. (London: 1882) Philadelphia: Blakiston, 1888.
Lamb, Charles. "Confessions of a Drunkard." In *The Works in Prose and Verse of Charles and Mary Lamb*, 1.168–77. London: Oxford U. P., n.d. [1908?].
Lawson, Wilfrid. "The Drink Difficulty." *Nineteenth Century* 5 (1879), 405–17.
Ledger, Sally and Roger Luckhurst, eds. *The Fin de Siècle: A Reader in Cultural History c. 1880–1900*. Oxford: Oxford U. P., 2000.
Lewis, David. *The Drink Problem and Its Solution*. London: National Temperance Publication Depot, 1881.
_____. *The Drink Traffic in the Nineteenth Century: Its Growth and Influence*. National Temperance Publication Depot, 1885.
Maixner, Paul, ed. *Robert Louis Stevenson: The Critical Heritage*. London: Routledge, 1981.
Mayhew, Henry. *The Illustrated Mayhew's London*. Ed. John Canning. London: Weidenfield & Nicholson, 1986.
_____. *Mayhew's London*. London: Pilot, 1949.
Mearns, Andrew. "The Bitter Cry of Outcast London: An Inquiry into the Condition of the Abject Poor." In *The Bitter Cry of Outcast London*. Ed. Anthony S. Wohl. New York: Leicester U. P., 1970. 53–90.
Mill, John Stuart. *On Liberty*. New York: Norton, 1975.
Milton, John. *Paradise Lost*. In *John Milton: Complete Poems and Major Prose*. Ed. Merritt Y. Hughes. New York: Odyssey, 1957. 207–469.
Mitchell, Dr. Kate. *The Drink Question: Its Social and Medical Aspects*. London: Swan Sonnenschein, 1889.
Nashe, Thomas. "Pierce Penilesse His Supplication to the Divell." In *The Works of Thomas Nashe*, 137–245. London: Sidgwick & Jackson, 1910.
Sala, George Augustus. *Twice Round the Clock or the Hours of the Day and Night in London*. New York: Leicester U. P., 1971.
Stead, W. T. "The Maiden Tribute of Modern Babylon." Sel. in Luckhurst & Ledger, *The Fin de Siècle*, 32–38
Stevenson, Robert Louis. "The Beach of Falesá." In *South Sea Tales*, 3–71.
_____. "The Body Snatcher." In *The Complete Short Stories*, 1.419–35.
_____. "The Bottle Imp." In *The Complete Stories of Robert Louis Stevenson*, 577–605.

———. "Books Which Have Influenced Me." In *The Works of Robert Louis Stevenson*, 16.272–78.
———. "A Chapter on Dreams." In *The Strange Case of Dr. Jekyll and Mr. Hyde*. Ed. Emma Letley. London: Oxford U. P., 1987, 198–209.
———. "The Coast of Fife." In *The Scottish Stories and Essays*, 260–68.
———. *Collected Poems*. 2nd ed. London: Rupert Hart-Davis, 1971.
———. *The Complete Short Stories*. 2 vols. New York: Holt, 1994.
———. *The Complete Stories of Robert Louis Stevenson*. New York: Modern Library, 2002.
———. *In the South Seas*. In *The Works of Robert Louis Stevenson*, 18.5–347.
———. *Kidnapped*. London: Penguin, 1994.
———. *The Letters of Robert Louis Stevenson*. Ed. Bradford A. Booth and Ernest Mehew. 8 vols. New Haven: Yale U. P., 1994–95.
———. "Olalla." In *The Complete Stories of Robert Louis Stevenson*, 420–57.
———. *The Master of Ballantrae*. New York: Current, 1913.
———. "Old Mortality." In *Memories and Portraits*, 38–56. London: Chatto & Windus, 1887.
———. "The Merry Men." In *The Scottish Stories and Essays*, 99–141.
———. "A Note on Realism." In *The Works of Robert Louis Stevenson*, 16.234–40.
———. "A Plea for Gas Lamps." In *The Works of Robert Louis Stevenson*, 2.420–23.
———. *The Scottish Stories and Essays*. Ed. Kenneth Gelder. Edinburgh: Edinburgh U. P., 1982.
———. *Selected Letters of Robert Louis Stevenson*. New Haven: Yale U. P., 2001.
———. *Selected Poems*. Ed. Angus Calder. Harmondsworth: Penguin, 1998.
———. *The Silverado Squatters*. In *The Works of Robert Louis Stevenson*, 2.173–275.
———. "Something in It." In *South Sea Tales*, 255–57.
———. *South Sea Tales*. Ed. Roslyn Jolly. Oxford: Oxford U. P., 1996.
———. *The Strange Case of Dr. Jekyll and Mr. Hyde and Other Stories*. Harmondsworth: Penguin, 1979.
———. "The Suicide Club." In *The Complete Stories of Robert Louis Stevenson*, 3–69.
———. *Travels with a Donkey in the Cevennes*. Köln: Könemann, 1997.
———. *Treasure Island*. New York: Signet, 1998.
———. "Walt Whitman." In *The Works of Robert Louis Stevenson*, 3.74–100.
———. *The Works of Robert Louis Stevenson*. 25 vols. London: Chatto & Windus, 1911–12.
Robert Louis Stevenson and W. E. Henley. *Deacon Brodie: or The Double Life*. In *The Works of Robert Louis Stevenson*, 15.1–89.
Robert Louis Stevenson and Lloyd Osborne. *The Ebb-Tide*. In *The Strange Case of Dr. Jekyll and Mr Hyde and Other Stories*, ed. Calder, 171–301.
Stead, W. T. Selections from "The Maiden Tribute of Modern Babylon." In Ledger and Luckhurst, *The Fin de Siècle*, 32–38.
Stoker, Bram. *The Essential Dracula: The Definitive Annotated Edition of Bram Stoker's Classic Novel*. New York: Plume, 1993.
Stowe, Harriet Beecher. *Temperance Tales*. London: J. Cassell, 1853.
"The Untold Sequel of the Strange Case of Dr. Jekyll and Mr. Hyde." In Harry M. Geduld, *The Definitive Dr. Jekyll and Mr. Hyde Companion*, 129–36. New York: Garland, 1983.
Whittaker, Thomas. *Brighter England and the Way to It*. London: Hodder & Stoughton, 1891.
———. *Life's Battles in Temperance Armour*. London: Hodder & Stoughton, 1884.
Wickes, David, dir. and script. *Jekyll and Hyde*. Videocassette. Vidmark, 1990.

Secondary Sources

Altick, Richard D. *The Presence of the Present: Topics of the Day in the Victorian Novel*. Columbus: Ohio State U. P., 1991.

Arata, Stephen. *Fictions of Loss in the Victorian Fin de Siècle*. Cambridge: Cambridge U. P., 1996.
Ausubel, Herman. *John Bright: Victorian Reformer*. New York: Wiley, 1966.
Bailey, Peter. *Leisure and Class in Victorian England: Rational Recreation and the Contest for Control, 1830–1855*. London: Methuen, 1987.
Booth, Michael R. "The Drunkard's Progress: Nineteenth-Century Temperance Drama." *Dalhousie Review* 44 (1964): 205–12.
Brantlinger, Patrick. *The Spirit of Reform: British Literature and Politics, 1832–1867*. Cambridge: Harvard U. P., 1977.
Brantlinger, Patrick and Richard Boyle. "The Education of Edward Hyde: Stevenson's 'Gothic Gnome' and the Mass Readership of Late-Victorian England." In Veeder and Hirsch, *Dr Jekyll and Mr Hyde after One Hundred Years*, 265–82.
Briggs, Asa. *Wine for Sale: Victoria Wine and the Liquor Trade 1860–1984*. London: Batsford, 1985.
Bristow, Edward J. *Vice and Vigilance: Purity Movements in Britain since 1700*. Dublin: Gill and Macmillan, 1977.
Bryant, Marie, ed. *The Comic Cruikshank*. London: Bellew, 1992.
Burnett, John. *Plenty and Want: A Social History of Food in England from 1815 to the Present Day*. 3rd. ed. London: Routledge, 1989.
Calder, Jenni. *R.L.S.—A Life Study*. London: Hamilton, 1980.
Calder, Jenni, ed. *Stevenson and Victorian Scotland*. Edinburgh: Edinburgh U. P., 1981.
Chesterton, G. K. *Robert Louis Stevenson*. New York: Dodd, Mead, 1928.
Clark, Peter. *The English Alehouse: A Social History 1200–1830*. London: Longman, 1983.
Cookson, Gillian. "Engineering Influences on *Jekyll and Hyde*." In Jones, *Robert Louis Stevenson Reconsidered*, 117–23.
Craik, W. H. *The Brontë Novels*. London: Methuen, 1968.
Crouch, Robin N. "Samuel Johnson on Drinking." *Dionysos* 5 (1993): 19–27.
Crowley, John W. "'Alcoholism' and the Modern Temper." In Reynolds and Rosenthal, eds. *The Serpent in the Cup*, 165–79.
Cunningham, Hugh. *Leisure in the Industrial Revolution c. 1780–1880*. London: C. Helm, 1980.
Danahay, Martin A., ed. *The Strange Case of Dr Jekyll and Mr Hyde*. Peterborough, Ont.; Broadview, 1999.
Dingle, A. E. *The Campaign for Prohibition in Victorian England: The United Kingdom Alliance 1872–1895*. New Brunswick, NJ; Rutgers U. P., 1980.
Dollar, Gerald J. "Addiction and the 'Other Self' in Three Late Victorian Novels." In Vice, Campbell, and Armstrong, eds. *Beyond the Pleasure Dome*, 268–74.
Driscoll, Lawrence. "Something strange but not unpleasant': Freud on Cocaine." In Lilienfeld and Oxford, eds. *The Languages of Addiction*, 70–90.
Dudley, Edward and Maximilian E. Novak. *The Wild Man Within: Thought from the Renaissance to Romanticism*. Pittsburgh: U. of Pittsburgh P., 1972.
Dury, Richard. "The Hand of Hyde." In Jones, *Robert Louis Stevenson Reconsidered*, 101–16.
Dyos, H. J. and Michael Wolff. *The Victorian City: Images and Realities*. 2 vols. London: Routledge, 1973.
Feaver, William. *George Cruikshank*. London: Arts Council of Great Britain, 1974.
Federico, Annette. "'I Must Have Drink': Addiction, Angst, and Victorian Realism." *Dionysos* 2 (1990): 11–25.
Girouard, Mark. *Victorian Pubs*. London: Studio Vista, 1975.
Goodwin, Donald W. "Alcohol as Muse." *Dionysos* 5 (1993): 3–14.
Greenslade, William. *Degeneration, Culture, and the Novel 1880–1940*. Cambridge: Cambridge U. P., 1994.
Gutzke, David W. *Protecting the Pub: Brewers and Publicans Against Temperance*. Woodbridge, Suffolk: Royal Historical Society, 1989.

Gwynn, Stephen. *Robert Louis Stevenson*. London: Macmillan, 1939.
Haley, Bruce. *The Healthy Body and Victorian Culture*. Cambridge: Harvard U. P., 1978.
Hammond, J. R. *A Robert Louis Stevenson Companion*. London: Macmillan, 1984.
Harrison, Brian. *Drink and Victorians: The Temperance Question in England, 1815–1872*. Pittsburgh: U. of Pittsburgh P., 1971.
_____. "The Power of Drink." *The Listener*. 13 February 1969. 204–06.
_____. "Pubs." In Dyos and Wolff, *The Victorian City*, 161–90.
_____. "The Sunday Trading Riots of 1855." *Historical Journal* 8 (1965): 219–45.
_____. "A World of Which We Had No Conception: Liberalism and the Temperance Press, 1830–1872." *Victorian Studies* 13 (1968): 125–58.
Harvie, Christopher. "The Politics of Stevenson." In Calder, *Stevenson and Victorian Scotland*, 107–25.
Hendershot, Cyndy. "Overdetermined Allegory in Jekyll and Hyde." *Victorian Newsletter* 84 (1993): 35–38.
Hewett, Edward and W. F. Acton. *Convivial Dickens: The Drinks of Dickens and His Times*. Athens, OH: Ohio U. P., 1983.
Hibbert, Christopher. *London: The Biography of a City*. Harmondsworth: Penguin, 1969.
Hinz, Evelyn J., ed. *Diet and Discourse: Eating, Drinking and Literature*. Winnipeg: U. of Manitoba P., 1991.
Hurley, Kelly. *The Gothic Body*. Cambridge: Cambridge U. P., 1996.
Inglis, K. S. *Churches and the Working Classes in Victorian England*. London: Routledge, 1963.
Jefford, Andrew. "Dr. Jekyll and Professor Nabokov: Reading a Reading." In Noble, ed. *Robert Louis Stevenson*, 47–72.
Jellinek, E. M. *The Disease Concept of Alcoholism*. New Haven: Hillhouse, 1960.
Jones, Michael Wynn. *George Cruikshank: His Life and London*. London: Macmillan, 1978.
Jones, William B. *Robert Louis Stevenson Reconsidered: New Critical Perspectives*. Jefferson, NC: McFarland, 2003.
Koestenbaum, Wayne. "The Shadow on the Bed: Dr. Jekyll, Mr. Hyde, and the Labouchère Amendment." *Critical Matrix* 1 (1988): 31–55.
Levin, David Jerome. *Introduction to Alcohol Counseling: A Bio-Psycho-Social Approach*. 2nd. ed. New York: Taylor and Francis, 1995.
Levy, Hermann. *Drink: An Economic and Social Study*. London: Routledge, 1951.
Lilienfeld, Jane. "'I Could Drink a Quarter-barrel to the Pitching': *The Mayor of Casterbridge* Viewed as an Alcoholic." In Lilienfeld and Oxford, eds., *The Languages of Addiction*, 225–44.
Lilienfeld, Jane and Jeffrey Oxford, eds. *The Languages of Addiction*. New York: St. Martin's, 1999.
Linehan, Katherine. ""Closer Than a Wife": The Strange Case of Dr. Jekyll's Significant Other." In Jones, *Robert Louis Stevenson Reconsidered*, 85–100.
Linehan, Katherine, ed. *Strange Case of Dr. Jekyll and Mr. Hyde*. New York: Norton, 2003.
Longmate, Norman. *The Waterdrinkers: A History of Temperance*. London: Hamish Hamilton, 1968.
Lucia, S. B. *Alcoholism and Civilization*. New York: McGraw-Hill, 1963.
Malchow, H. L. "Public Gardens and Social Action in Late Victorian London." *Victorian Studies* 29 (1985): 97–124.
Malcolmson, Robert W. *Popular Recreations in English Society, 1700–1850*. Cambridge: Cambridge U. P., 1973.
Manlove, Colin. "'Closer Than an Eye': The Interconnection of Stevenson's Dr. Jekyll and Mr. Hyde." *Studies in Scottish Literature* 23 (1988): 87–103.
Matheson, T. J. "Poe's 'The Black Cat' as a Critique of Temperance Literature." *Mosaic* 19 (1986): 69–81.

Mattingly, Carol. *Well Tempered Women: Nineteenth-Century Temperance Rhetoric.* Carbondale: Southern Illinois U. P., 1998.
McCandless, Peter. "'Curses of Civilization': Insanity and Drunkenness in Victorian Britain." *British Journal of Addiction* 79 (1984): 49–58.
McCormack, Kathleen. *George Eliot and Intoxication: Dangerous Drugs for the Condition of England.* Houndmills, England: Macmillan, 2000.
McCormick, Mairi. "First Representations of the Gamma Alcoholic in the English Novel." *Quarterly Journal of Studies on Alcohol* 30 (1969): 957–80.
McLynn, Frank. *Robert Louis Stevenson.* London: Hutchinson, 1993.
McNally, Raymond T. and Radu R. Florescu. *In Search of Dr. Jekyll and Mr. Hyde.* Los Angeles: Renaissance, 2000.
Merrett, Robert J. "Port and Claret: The Politics of Wine in Trollope's Barsetshire Novels." In Hinz, *Diet and Discourse*, 107–25.
Mighall, Robert. *A Geography of Victorian Gothic Fiction: Mapping History's Nightmares.* Oxford: Oxford U. P., 1999.
Millgate, Michael. *Thomas Hardy: A Biography.* New York: Random House, 1982.
Miller, Karl. *Doubles: Studies in Literary History.* New York: Oxford U. P., 1985.
Mills, Ken. "Alcoholism and the Apocalypse" Reflections on a Norm in Nineteenth-Century Literature." In Brian Keith-Smith, ed. *Bristol Austrian Studies.* Bristol: U. of Bristol P., 1990, 117–37.
Mitchell, Domnhall. "Drink and Disorder in *The Narrative of Arthur Gordon Pym.*" In Vice, Campbell, and Armstrong, *Beyond the Pleasure Dome*, 101–08.
Miyoshi, Masao. *The Divided Self" A Perspective on the Literature of the Victorians.* New York: New York U. P., 1969.
Nabokov, Vladimir. "Robert Louis Stevenson: 'The Strange Case of Dr. Jekyll and Mr. Hyde.'" In *Vladimir Nabokov: Lectures on Literature.* New York: Harcourt, Brace, Jovanovich, 1980, 179–205.
Navarette, Susan J. *The Shape of Fear: Horror and the Fin de Siècle Culture of Decadence.* Lexington: U. P. of Kentucky, 1998.
Neuberg, Victor E. "The Literature of the Streets." In Dyos and Wolff, *The Victorian City*, 1.191–209.
Noble, Andrew, ed. *Robert Louis Stevenson.* London: Vision Press, 1983.
Nordau, Max. *Degeneration.* Trans. Anonymous. 3rd ed. New York: Appleton, 1895.
Nowell-Smith, Simon. *The House of Cassell 1848–1958.* London: Cassell, 1958.
Olsen, Gerald W. "The Church of England Temperance Magazine." *Victorian Periodicals Newsletter* 11 (1978): 38–49.
Patten, Robert L. *George Cruikshank's Life, Times, and Art.* 2 vols. New Brunswick, NJ: Rutgers U. P., 1992–96.
Pick, Daniel. *Faces of Degeneration: A European Disorder, c. 1848–c.1918.* Cambridge: Cambridge U. P., 1989.
Pittock, Murray G. H. "The Naming of Characters in Scott and Stevenson." *Notes & Queries* 42 (1995): 174–75.
Pollin, Burton R. "The Temperance Movement and Its Friends Look at Poe." *Costerus* 2 (1972): 119–44.
Purdy, Richard Little. *Thomas Hardy: A Bibliographical Study.* London: Oxford U. P., 1954.
Rather, L. J. "Mr. Hyde and the 'Damned Juggernaut.'" *Synthesis* 14 (1987): 49–54.
Reynolds, David S. "Black Cats and Delirium Tremens." In Reynolds and Rosenthal, *The Serpent in the Cup*, 22–59.
Reynolds, David S. and Debra J. Rosenthal. *The Serpent in the Cup: Temperance in American Literature.* Amherst: U. of Massachusetts 1997.
Richter, Donald C. *Riotous Victorians.* Athens, OH: Ohio U. P., 1981.
Sandison, Alan. *Robert Louis Stevenson and the Appearance of Modernism: A Future Feeling.* Houndmills: Macmillan, 1996.

Shields, David S. "The Demonization of the Tavern." In Reynolds and Rosenthal, *The Serpent in the Cup*, 10–21.
Shiman, Lilian Lewis. *Crusade against Drink in Victorian England*. New York: St. Martin's, 1988.
Showalter, Elains. "Dr. Jekyll's Closet." In Smith and Haas, *The Haunted Mind*, 67–88.
Smith, Elton E. and Robert Haas, eds. *The Haunted Mind: The Supernatural in Victorian Literature*. Lanham, MD: Scarecrow, 1999.
Smith, Michael A. "Social Usages of the Public Drinking House: Changing Aspects of Class and Leisure." *British Journal of Sociology* 34 (1983): 367–85.
Sournia, Jean Charles. *A History of Alcoholism*. Trans. Nick Hindley and Gareth Stanton. London: Blackwell, 1990.
Spiller, Brian. *Victorian Public Houses*. Newton Abbot: David and Charles, 1972.
Stern, Rebecca. "Adulterations Detected: Food and Fraud in Christina Rossetti's 'Goblin Market.'" *Nineteenth-Century Literature* 57 (2003): 477–511.
Swearingen, Roger C. *The Prose Writings of Robert Louis Stevenson: A Guide*. Hamden, CT.: Archon, 1980.
Taylor, Anya. *Bacchus in Romantic England: Writers and Drink, 1780–1830*. New York: St. Martins, 1999.
_____. "Coleridge and Alcohol." *Texas Studies in Literature and Language* 33 (1991): 355–72.
Thompson, F. M. L. *The Rise of Respectable Society: A Social History of Victorian Britain, 1830–1900*. Cambridge: Harvard U. P., 1988.
_____. ed. *The Rise of Suburbia*. New York: St. Martins, 1982
Vaillant, George. *The Natural History of Alcoholism: Causes, Patterns, and Paths to Recovery*. Cambridge: Harvard U. P., 1983.
Veeder, William. "Children of the Night: Stevenson and Patriarchy." In Veeder and Hirsch, *Dr Jekyll and Mr Hyde after One Hundred Years*, 107–60.
_____. "Collated Fractions of the Manuscript Drafts of *Strange Case of Dr Jekyll and Mr Hyde*." In Veeder and Hirsch, *Dr Jekyll and Mr Hyde after One Hundred Years*, 14–56.
Veeder, William and Gordon Hirsch. *Dr Jekyll and Mr Hyde after One Hundred Years*. Chicago: U. of Chicago P., 1988.
Vice, Sue, Matthew Campbell, and Tim Armstrong, eds. *Beyond the Pleasure Dome: Writing and Addiction from the Romantics*. Sheffield: Sheffield Academic Press, 1994.
Wardropper, John. *The Caricatures of George Cruikshank*. London: Gordon Fraser, 1977.
Warner, Nicholas O. "The Drunken Wife in Defoe's *Colonel Jack*: An Early Description of Alcohol Addiction." *Dionysos* 1 (1989): 3–9.
_____. "God's Wine and Devil's Wine: The Idea of Intoxication in Emerson." *Mosaic* 19 (1986): 55–68.
Webb, S. and B. *The History of Liquor Licensing in England*. London: Cass, 1963.
Wigley, John. *The Rise and Fall of the Victorian Sunday*. Manchester: Manchester U. P., 1980.
Wolf, Leonard, ed. *The Essential Dr. Jekyll & Mr. Hyde*. New York: Plume, 1995.
Daniel L. Wright. "'The Prisonhouse of My Disposition': A Study of the Psychology of Addiction in *Dr. Jekyll and Mr. Hyde*." *Studies in the Novel* 26 (1994): 254–67.

Index

The Academy 65, 67, 191, 203–4
Accum, Friedrich Christian (*Treatise on Adulterations of Food*) 179, 180
Act for Preventing the Adulteration of Food and Drink 179
Adam, Henry Brooks 54
Adam, John (clerk of Edinburgh courts) 59
Addiction, as represented in *J&H* 4, 9–18, 46 and *passim*
Adulteration 5, 178–82, 193, 196, 234
Agnew, Sir Andrew, M. P.: as possible model for Sir Danvers Carew 148, 151; as temperance reformer 121, 135–36, 162, 183
Alcohol: as "death" 177–78, 224–26; as detrimental to housing 124–130; as hygienic 32, 48; licensing of sale of 219–21; as medicine 1, 49–50; as physically beneficial 20–21, 26, 31, 35–36, 48–50, 203; and prostitution 29, 156–58; sea as a metaphor for 217; and violence 117–19, 129, 143–45, 153–54
Alcoholism: as restricted to the lower classes 33–35, 162–63; and Satan/the Devil 222–24, 234; shipwreck as a metaphor for 203, 215–16; slavery as a metaphor for 221–22; symptoms of in *J&H* 14–18
Allegory: in *J&H* 1, 2, 3, 5–6, 199–201, 203, 205, 211, 241–42; Stevenson and 186–90
The Alliance News 227–28

Altick, Richard 6, 179, 196, 235
"Angel of the House" 164
Arata, Stephen 3, 231, 232, 233, 235, 239, 241
Arnet, Rev. William 228
Axton, W. F. 196

Baildon, H. B. 85
Bailey, John 148
Bailey, Nat (reformed drunkard) 155–56
Bailey, Peter 170, 171, 172
Balfour, Clara 158
Balfour, David 81
Balfour, George (RLS's uncle and physician) 1, 21, 83–84, 100
Balfour, Graham 63, 186
Balfour, Jane 64
Band of Hope 101, 158, 159; *The Worship of Bacchus, a Grand Delusion* 237
Barker, T. H. 228
Barrie, J. M. 83, 88
Bass, Sir Arthur 139, 141
Battersea Park 123
Baudelaire, Charles 58
Baxter, Charles 54–56, 61, 71, 76, 91, 100, 101, 104–5, 146, 184, 188, 204, 208, 210, 222, 225, 229, 233, 235, 236, 238; as an alcoholic 58, 95, 141, 242; as pseudonymous fellow carouser with RLS 82–83, 86, 199–200, 235; as RLS's "wine agent" 54–56; as university chum 53, 59
Bedford, Duke of 165, 166, 167

251

Bedford Park 167
Beerhouses Act of 1830 (Sale of Beer Act) 47, 49, 97, 144, 172, 177, 179, 218, 219, 236
Belgravia 150
Bell, Ian (RLS biographer) 14
Bengalis and alcohol 218
Bergman, Ingrid 165
Bessbrook (Ireland) 167
"Bill W." 178
Birmingham Daily Mail 134
Birmingham Daily Post 182
Birstall (Yorkshire) 167
Bishop of London: on nutritional role of beer 49
Bloomsbury 165, 166, 167
"Blue Ribbon Army" 100
Bocock, John Paul 205
Booth, Catherine 228
Booth, Charles 15, 16, 115; *Life and Labour of the People of London* 142, 155
Booth, Richard 100
Booth, William 16, 41, 52, 153, 154, 173, 212, 216, 218, 222, 228; *In Darkest England* 15, 117, 142
Boswell, James: on beneficial effects of alcohol 37
Boyle, Richard 3, 25, 231
Bramwell, Lord 22
Brantlinger, Patrick 3, 25, 231
Brash, Thomas (Edinburgh spirit merchant) 59–60, 72, 79, 82, 87, 188
Brewer's Guardian 97
Bright, John 148
British and Foreign Temperance Intelligencer: "Which Way Shall I Turn Me?" 108
The British Critic 21, 35–35
British Temperance Advocate 228
British Women's Association 184
Broad Walk 169
Brodie, William "Deacon" 80–81 82, 95, 200
Brontë, Anne 66; *The Tenant of Wildfell Hall* 66
Brontë, Branwell (alcoholic brother) 66, 118
Brontë, Charlotte 196; *Jane Eyre* 66
Brookfield, C. H. E. 81
Bruce, Henry (Home Secretary) 220
Buckingham, James Silk 99, 122
The Building News 143
Bunner, Henry 195
Bunyan, John 186, 188, 190, 192; *The Pilgrim's Progress* 82, 188
Burgess's Wine and Spirits shops 225

Burns, Robert 57, 63, 232; criticized by RLS 238; praise of alcohol 36, 40
Butaritari (Gilbert Islands): drunkenness in 61–62 118

Caine, Michael 165, 206
Canterbury Committee on Intemperance 157
Carlile, Anne 158
Carnes, Patrick 10, 11
Cassel, John (publisher) 64, 65, 99, 105, 152
Cassell's Illustrated Family Paper 64, 97, 102–3, 113, 201, 236
Cavendish Square 167, 169, 189
Charrington, Frederick 110, 140–41, 155, 187
Chatterton, Thomas 63
Chesterton, G. K. 88
Children: as abused owing to alcohol 28 29, 133–34, 141; as drinkers 133–34
Cholera 47–48, 124
Church of England 98, 124, 238
Church of England Temperance Magazine 71, 158, 227, 238
Churchill, Lord Randolph 36
Clark, Sir Andrew: on beneficial effects of alcohol 49
Cobbe, Frances Power: "Wife Torture in England" 155 180–81, 217
Cocaine 12
Coffee: as a temperance drink 184
Coffee Public House: How to Establish and Manage It 184
Coleridge, Hartley (son of S. T. Coleridge) 16, 231
Coleridge, Samuel Taylor 16, 32, 37, 84, 118, 224
Colvin, Sidney 1, 3, 55, 57, 60, 64, 69, 84–5, 86, 87, 89–90, 100, 103, 139, 164, 188, 234, 236
Conrad, Joseph: *Heart of Darkness* 241–42
Conservative Party 96–97, 99, 204, 211
The Contemporary Review 194
Cooke, Ebeneezer 171
Cookson, Gillian 241
Cornhill (magazine) 187
Coutts, Mrs. Burdett 150, 154
Covent Garden 167
Crabbe, George 222
Creggan, Samuel 81–82
Cross, R. A. (Home Secretary) 100, 149, 151
Crozier, Forster 239
Cruikshank, George 16, 34, 48, 50, 98, 127,

136, 138, 139, 141, 186, 195; as an alcoholic 34, 164
Cruikshank, George, Works of: *The Bottle* 34 48, 64, 124–25, 144, 155, 156, 225, 237; *The Drunkard's Children* 125, 133, 156, 225; "The Gin Juggarnath" 43; "The Gin Shop" 224, 226; "London Going out of Town" 122; "Salus populi suprema lex" 48; "The Worship of Bacchus" 217, 237
Cunningham, Alice ("Cummy") 64, 80, 103, 113, 139, 188, 227

Darwin, Charles 3, 117, 233; *The Descent of Man* 116; *The Expression of the Emotions in Man and Animals* 116; *The Origin of Species* 116
Daumier, Honoré 236
Davos 3, 57
Delirium tremens 168
de Mattos, Katharine (RLS's cousin) 1, 87, 234
Deptford 159
De Quincey. Thomas 32, 117
Dickens, Charles 20, 21, 30, 35, 42, 49, 127, 135, 136, 154, 159, 164, 175, 177, 196, 204, 210, 231, 242; associates alcohol with the lower classes 34, 50, 98, 163, 205, 207; and medicinal value of alcohol 49; on need of affluent to set example for poor 172–73; on poor housing driving alcoholism 125
Dickens, Charles, Works of: *Barnaby Rudge* 37; *Bleak House* 65; "Demoralisation and Total Abstinence" 118 207; "The Drunkard's Children" 125; "The Drunkard's Death" 125–26, 218, 225; "Gin Shops" 138; "The Great Baby" 118, 149–50; *Hard Times* 65, 117–18, 158; *The Old Curiosity Shop* 65; *Oliver Twist* 29, 49; *Our Mutual Friend* 179; *The Pickwick Papers* 38; "A Plea for Total Abstinence" 98, 152; "Sunday under Three Heads" 98, 148; *A Tale of Two Cities* 65–66; "Whole Hogs" 98
Dickinson College 242
Dingle, A. E. 6, 236
Disraeli, Benjamin (Conservative P. M.) 48, 203
Disraeli family 20
Dollar, Gerald 12, 196
Druitt, Dr. Robert 56
"Drunkenness defense" (in British law) 202, 236
Dunlop, John 27, 29, 39, 43, 50, 52, 66, 108, 140, 144, 170, 217, 221, 222, 223; *The Philosophy of Artificial and Compulsory Drinking Usage in Great Britain and Ireland* 51
Dury, Richard 84

Edgar, John: *Female Virtue — Its Enemies and Friends* 157
Edinburgh 1, 53, 56, 57, 59, 80, 85, 86, 87, 89, 188, 199–200, 204, 211, 228, 235; "New Town" 169; "Old Town" 82–83, 169
Einfurer, Paul (drunken cook in Samoa) 60–61
Eliot, George 118, 196; *Janet's Repentance* 15–16, 39, 43, 66, 155, 222, 223
The Embankment 123
Eton: boys drinking beer with meals 48

Fabian Society 22
Falconer, Hugh 236
Farrar, Fredric (Dean of Canterbury) 226
Federico, Annette 196
Fergusson, Robert (Scots poet) 57
Ferrier, Elizabeth ("Coggie") 90–91, 93, 94
Ferrier, James Walter 5, 14, 101–2, 104, 141, 200, 203, 210, 211, 229, 242; death by alcohol 88–90, 113, 199, 204, 205, 215, 225, 227; as model for Jekyll 88–95, 148, 209, 213, 239; mother blames RLS for son's death 90–91, 159–60, 238
Fielding, Henry: decries social effects of gin 29 34, 35, 42, 115
Florescu, Radu 80
Forbes-Mackenzie Act 121–22
Frank, Joseph 37
Fraser, James (Bishop of Manchester) 37
Fraustino, Daniel 14, 196
Freud, Sigmund 3, 211, 240
Frost, Thomas 150

Gale, Henry 152
Gaskell, Elizabeth 66, 196; *Mary Barton* 66, 196; *North and South* 66
Gaugin, Paul 236
Gautier, Theophile: *Le Chevalier Double* 67
Gin 28–31, 43, 62, 136–38, 165; associated with crime 29, 35; associated with lower classes 28–31
Gladstone, William: and alcohol reform 21–22 25, 56, 96–97, 99, 113, 140, 180, 184, 198, 203, 204, 218, 219; use of alcohol before speeches 37
Glasgow 39
Gosse, Edmund 65, 69
Gough, James B. 98

The Graphic (magazine) 69
Gray's Inn Road 23, 200
Great Portland Street 169
Greenslade, William 236
Greenwood, James 16, 50, 146–47, 158, 216, 222, 228; *Seven Curses of London* 118, 125, 180
Grosvenor, Lord (Sunday Trading Bill) 99, 149–50, 154
Guinness 48, 140
Gwynn, Stephen 13, 196

Haggard, B. M. (brother of H. Rider Haggard) 60, 101, 184, 225
Haggard, H. Rider 60
Hamerton, P. G. 84
Hardy, Thomas 20, 139; RLS and wife visit 68–69, 96, 153, 199; *The Mayor of Casterbridge* as a possible influence on *J&H* 12, 15, 19, 46, 69–71, 79–80, 155, 180, 184, 185, 201, 202, 211, 216
Harman, Claire (RLS biographer) 235
Harper's Weekly 69
Harris, Thomas: *The Silence of the Lambs* 25
Harrison, Brian 140, 163, 165, 171, 177, 232
"Harvest beer" 49
Hatfield, Marcia 242
Hegel, G. W. F. 208
Hendershot, Cyndy 241
Henley, Teddy (brother of W. E. Henley) 34, 61, 79, 144, 202, 205, 239
Henley, W. E. 34, 80, 83–84, 85, 90, 91, 92, 94, 100, 210, 222, 225, 227, 236, 238; as heavy drinker 61, 210; as a model for Long John Silver 61
Hess, Magnus 57
Hewett, Edward 196
Hill, Matthew 223
Hill, Octavia 122, 168; Open Space Movement 123
Hogarth, William 139, 236; "Beer Street" 108; "Gin Lane" 28, 108, 155
Hogg, James 41; *Private Memoirs and Confessions of a Justified Sinner* 5, 80
Holborn 23, 200
Home Office 153
Home Rule (Irish) 204
Homo economicus 170
Homo ludens 170
Howitt, Mary 158
Howitt, William 179
Hughes, William 140
Hume, David: *A Treatise of Human Nature* 231–32

Hyde Park 99–100, 154, 165, 168, 170, 199, 239; as source for Hyde's name 148–52

Ingram, John 67
Intoxicating Liquors Licensing Bill and Act 219–20

Jacob and Esau 234–35
James, Henry 54, 58, 101, 184; gives RLS a case of champagne 54
James, W. Bosville 25
Jefford, Andrew 13
Jellinek, E. M. 16, 58, 70
Jenkin, Fleeming 241
Jevons, Stanley 175
"John Barleycorn" 187 233
Johnson, Samuel 15, 115, 118, 222
"Johnston and Thomson" (pseudonyms for RLS and Charles Baxter) 82–83, 86, 89, 101, 155, 220
Juggernaut: Hyde as 131–33 141–42, 158, 187, 237; as symbol of the drink trade 135–43

Kalakaua (King of Hawaii) 61, 205
Keats, John: associates alcohol with the Fall 40; *Endymion* 41
Keppler, Joseph 195
Kerr, Norman 13, 16, 17–18, 20, 32, 115, 134–35, 236, 242; *Inebriety, Its Etiology, Pathology, Treatment and Jurisprudence* 12, 144
Kingsley, Charles: *Alton Lock* 66; *Yeast* 66
Kingsley, Mary 75
Kirton, J. W.: *Four Pillars of Temperance* 108 142
Knox, John 232
Koestenbaum, Wayne 3, 148–49, 231

L. J. R. ("Liberty, Justice and Reverence") Club 89, 200, 242
Labouchère Amendment 149
Lamb, Charles 106, 217, 222, 224, 226–27
Lang, Andrew 67, 241
Lawson, Sir Wilfrid, M. P. 100, 102, 183, 220; "The Drink Difficulty" 100; as possible model for Sir Danvers Carew 145–48, 151–52; as temperance reformer 96–97, 99, 113, 140, 195, 198
Lecter, Hannibal 25
Lees, F. R. 98, 216
Leisure 51, 170–75
Letterman, David 105
Lewis, David 34, 96, 106, 117, 121–22, 124, 126, 127–28, 135, 140, 141–42, 144, 159, 216, 218, 219, 222, 223, 228, 234, 238

Liberal Party 25, 99, 196, 204, 211, 218, 220; and alcohol reform 22, 37
Licensed Victualler's Gazette 163, 164
Licensed Victualler's Guardian 153
Linehan, Katherine 12, 224
Little Portland Street 169
Livesey, Joseph 50, 72, 97–98, 99, 121, 122, 124, 127, 128, 177, 234; "Malt Lecture" 49
Local Option (on licensing sale of alcohol) 22, 96–97, 99, 100, 146, 151, 195, 198
Lombroso, Cesare 3, 117
London 42 82, 99, 110, 122, 123, 140, 141, 143, 149, 156, 158, 163, 165, 166, 167, 168, 169, 190, 195, 205, 218, 237, 238, 239
London Congregational Union 125
London, J.: *The People of the Abyss* 69
Longman, Charles 69
Longman's (publisher of *J&H*) 67
Lord's Day Observance Society 121
"Louis V." (French alienist patient) 235
Low, William (American painter) 2, 64, 84, 87
Lowes, John Livingston: *The Road to Xanadu* 3 215
Lyceum (theater) 195
Lyrical Ballads 215

Madden, Dr. Moore 133–34
Magazine of Art (Cassell's) 236
Maine, State of (and 1851 prohibition law) 76, 98, 101, 158
Malchow, H. L. 174
Malcolmson, Robert 39
Malietoa (King of Samoa) 62
Manchester Guardian 150
Mansfield, Richard 195
Martin, Valerie: *Mary Reilly* 133, 183, 197
Marx, Karl 99, 150, 165
Matheson, T. J. 235
Mathew, Father 99, 152, 159
Mattingly, Carol 159
Mayfair 165, 167, 168, 169, 173, 190
McCormack, Kathleen 196
McCormick, Mairi 196, 235
McLynn, Frank (RLS biographer) 82
McNally, Raymond 80
Mearns, Andrew 125, 133, 222
Medical Temperance Journal 49
Mee, Richard 232
Mehew, Ernest 151
Menton 1, 57
Meredith, George: "Love in the Valley" 54
Merrett, Robert J. 21
Methodists 37
Methuen's "English Classics" 188
Metropolitan Commons Act 123

Metropolitan Police Act (London) 122
Metropolitan Public Gardens Association 124, 174, 236–37
Mighall, Robert 3, 231, 233, 238
Mill, John Stuart 98, 136, 144
Miller, J.: *Prostitution, Considered in Relation to Its Causes and Cures* 157
Milton, John: associates alcohol with the Fall 40
Mitchell, Domnhall 235
Mitchell, John: *Treatise on the Falsification of Food* 179
Mitchell, Dr. Kate (temperance physician) 18, 35, 36, 37, 50, 105, 108, 117, 118, 133, 142, 144, 153, 156, 180, 204, 218, 222, 225
Montagu, Basil: *Some Inquiries into the Effects of Fermented Liquors, By a Water-Drinker* 224
Montesquieu, Baron de 122
Moors, Henry 86
Morel, B. A. 3, 116, 231
Mortimer Street 169
Mozart 160
Music Halls 106–08, 236
Myers, F. W. H. 24, 36, 39, 88, 191–92, 196, 206, 232, 235, 241

Nabokov, Vladimir 13, 19, 20, 87, 196
Nash, John 166–67, 168
National Temperance Association 159
National Temperance League 158
"New Ballad" (on gin) 224–25
New York Herald 114, 116
Noble, James Ashcroft 65, 191
Noel Park 167
Nordau, Max 3, 116, 117, 231, 236
Nottingham 37

Open Space Movement *see* Hill, Octavia
Opium 12, 225, 227, 233
Osborne, Lloyd (RLS's stepson) 76, 81, 86

Palmerston, Lord (Home Secretary) 220
Park Crescent 169
Park Square 169
Pasteur, Louis: on beneficial effects of alcohol 49
Paul, C. Kegan (publisher) 81–82
Peacock, Thomas Love 20
"The Peckham Lifeboat" 242
Permissive Bill 22, 99, 152, 228
Phillips, Peter 232
Phiz (Dickens' illustrator) 38; "Effects of Tea" 110; "John Bull Recovering from His Watery Humour" 110
Phylloxera 56.

Piccadilly Circus 169
Pick, Daniel 236
Pinocchio 239
Piranesi, Giovanni Battista 236
Pledges (of abstinence): "long pledge" 50; "short pledge" 50
Poe, Edgar Allan 3, 191; as an alcoholic 41, 58, 216; "The Black Cat" 68; "The Cask of Amontillado" 68; "King Pest" 68; *The Narrative of A. Gordon Pym* 68; "William Wilson" and influence on *J&H* 67–68, 79–80, 201
Pollin, Barton R. 235
The Popular Educator: "The Influence of Morality or Immorality on the Countenance" 103–5
Porter, G. R. 163
Portland Place 169
"Portland Street" 169
Preston Pledge (of total abstinence) 50, 98
Primrose Hill 123
Prostitution 153–54, 167; associated with alcohol 156–58
Prudentius (*Psychomaciha*) 186
Public Houses 122, 123, 158, 163, 165, 167, 171, 218; as located on corners 142–43; roles in Victorian life 51–53; as seldom frequented by Victorian gentlemen 34; Stevenson and 53, 73
Puck (magazine): "An Explanatory Failure" (drawing) 195
Punch (drawings): "An Afterthought" 37; "Beer and Water: An Election Eclogue" 110; "Dark Monday vs. Bright Monday" 110 121; "Mistaking Cause for Effect" 47–48; "Neat and Tidy vs. Tight and Needy" 110; "Our Once Facetious Contemporary . . ." 148; "Pot and Kettle" 110–113, 145–46; "Publican Barrel and Pharisee-Pump" 113, 146, 151, 187, 201; "A Seasonable Song" 181–82; "Sunday Equality: The Reunion of Champagne and Porter" 22, 110; "What will he become?" 105
Punch (magazine) 35–36, 43, 44, 56, 99, 139, 141, 183, 201, 236, 238; parody of *J&H* ("The Strange Case of Dr. T. and Mr. H.") 182, 185, 192–93, 206
Punch-making, rituals of 38–41
Purcell, Edward 203–4

Queen's Park 167

"Railroad to Hell" 64
"Railway milk" 48
Read, Charles: *Drink* 64

Reagan, Nancy 105
Redding, Cyrus: *History and Description of Modern Wines* 180
Regent Street 71, 128, 166–67, 169
Regent's Park 122, 124, 166, 167, 174, 175, 223
Respectability 1, 9–10, 31, 33, 34, 53, 71, 98, 123, 162–67, 190–91, 233, 234, 238
Restaurants 163–64
Reynolds, David S. 235
Reynold's Newspaper 150–51
Rhodes, Cecil 75
Richmond Republican 223
Roche, Valentine (RLS's maid) 54
The Rock (magazine) 191, 193–94
Roebuck, J. A. 34
Rossetti, Christina: "Goblin Market" 240
Rowlandson, Thomas 139, 236
Rowntree, B. Seebohm 157
Royal Commission on Liquor Licensing 151
Royal Commission on the Housing of the Working Classes 125
Royal Institution 179
Ruskin, John 122

Sabbatarianism 45, 119–23, 208
St. James 227
St. Paul 227, 228, 229
St. Peter 227, 229
Sale of Beer Act of 1830 *see* Beerhouses Act
Salisbury, Lord 97, 151, 199, 203
Saltaire (Yorkshire) 167
Salvation Army 41, 52, 153, 196, 198–99, 204, 207, 211, 216, 228, 229
Saturday Review 217
Savage, Richard 222
Savile Club 164, 234
Schweppes (bottled drinks) 48
Scott, Dr. Thomas 64
Scott, Sir Walter 232
Scribner's Magazine 88
Select Committee on Drunkenness 122
Self-Help 31, 98, 172
Serpent: alcohol associated with 40
The Serpentine 123, 150
Shaftesbury, Lord: on unhealthy drinking water 48
Shaftesbury Park 167
Shakespeare (Prince Hal) 30
Sharpe, Dr. William 40
Sherlock Holmes 11, 12, 35
Shiman, Lillian 37, 96, 167
Showalter, Elaine 3, 27, 231, 235
Sideways (motion picture) 26

Simpson, Walter 100–01, 204
Sitwell, Frances ("Fanny") 56–57, 187–88, 225–26, 227, 232, 233
"Skeleton Army" 153 196, 198–99, 204, 207, 211, 226, 228, 229
Slaney, Robert, M. P. 123, 174
Slavery: as a metaphor for alcoholism 221–22
Smith, Goodwin 171
Smollett, Tobias: *History of England* 29
"Snob screen" 123 163–64
Soho 13, 16, 22–23, 24, 25, 29, 30, 41, 43, 62, 71, 85, 104, 108, 119, 125, 128, 133, 136, 141, 155, 157, 165, 166, i67, 168, 175, 189, 190, 200, 205, 239
Somerset, Lady Henry 158
Sophocles 143
Stead, W. T. 87; "Confessions of a Brothel Keeper" 156–57; "Maiden Tribute of Modern Babylon" 29
Stephen, Leslie 187
Stern, Rebecca 240
Stevenson, Fanny (RLS's wife) 1 36, 49, 54, 58, 64, 69, 81, 82, 83, 85, 87, 92, 95, 203, 224; requires RLS to re-write *J&H* 186, 187, 189, 201
Stevenson, Louisa (wife of Robert Alan Mowbray Stevenson) 57
Stevenson, Margaret Balfour (RLS's mother) 85, 211
Stevenson, Robert Alan Mowbray (RLS's "Cousin Bob") 37, 57, 63, 76, 81, 86, 90, 208
Stevenson, Robert Louis: as an addict 1 4, 58; and anger 85; and "Brownies" (creative imagination) 3, 5, 70, 79, 87, 88, 114–15, 120, 129–30, 135, 188–89, 192, 199, 201, 203, 215, 220; on moderation 6, 58, 178, 207–10; as possible model for Jekyll 83–88; as possible model for Utterson 209–10; and wine 20, 53–57
Stevenson, Robert Louis, Drafts and Copies of *J&H* 199–201; "Notebook Draft" 23, 134, 144–45, 217–18; "Printers's Copy" 43, 132, 143, 200, 218
Stevenson, Robert Louis, Fiction of: *The Beach of Falesá* 59 74–75, 143, 144, 156, 181; *The Black Arrow* 64; "The Body Snatcher" 226; "The Bottle Imp" 41, 208; *Catriona* (*David Balfour* in U.S.) 81; "The Coast of Fife" 72; "The Curate of Anstruther's Bottle" 71–72, 223; *The Ebb-Tide* 18, 36, 41, 75–76, 101, 119, 196, 216, 221, 223, 229, 239; *Kidnapped* 50, 64, 81, 134, 144; "A Lodging for the Night" 240; "Markheim" 80, 81; *The Master of Ballantrae* 41, 73–74, 181, 196; "The Merry Men" 72; "The Misadventures of John Nicholson" 53, 73, 82, 224; "Olalla" 234; "An Old Song" 72; "The Pavilion on the Links" 101, 143, 208; *Prince Otto* 81; "Something in It" 102; "The Suicide Club" 37–38; *Treasure Island* 15, 19, 23–24, 37, 64, 72–73, 75, 81, 101, 129, 132–33, 134, 135, 143, 144, 153, 163, 181, 203, 208, 225, 237; "The Treasure of Franchard" 53, 181; "When the Devil Was Well" 41; "Will o' the Mill" 187, 204, 225
Stevenson, Robert Louis, Non-fiction of: "An Apology for Idlers" 211; "Books Which Have Influenced Me" 64 188–89; "A Chapter on Dreams" 88, 114–15, 188, 201; "Crabbed Age and Youth" 187; "Gospel According to Walt Whitman" 64; "Lay Morals" 92–93; "Old Mortality" 92–95, 103, 210, 211; "A Plea for Gas Lamps" 138; "Popular Authors" 103; *The Silverado Squatters* 20; *The South Seas* 61, 117, 119, 128, 144; *Travels with a Donkey* 188
Stevenson, Robert Louis, Poetry of: "Alcaics to H. F. Brown" 76; "Brasheanna" 59–60 77, 83; *A Child's Garden of Verses* 1; "The Cruel Mistress" 76; "Epistle to Charles Baxter" 115; "Heather Ale" 77–78; "I am a hunchback, yellow-faced" 76, 209–10; "Not I" 77; "On Himself" 57, 126; "Stormy Nights" 208, 211; "When I was young and drouthy" 100
Stevenson, Robert Louis, et al.: *The Dynamiter* 81; *An Object of Pity, or The Man Haggard* 60
Stevenson, Robert Louis, and W. E. Henley: *The Deacon Brodie, or Double Life* 61 80–81
Stevenson, Thomas (RLS's Father) 54, 91, 95, 187–88, 204, 207–8, 238
Stoker, Bram: *Dracula* 35
The Stranger Case of Dr. Hide and Mr. Crushall: A Rum-antic Story 194
Strong, Joe 61
The Struggle 138, 139, 141
Strutt, Joseph 122
The Subtle Spell (American Temperance novel) 159
Sullivan, Thomas Russell 195
Sunday Closing Act (Wales) 122
Sunday Trading Bill 99–100, 122, 149, 151, 154
Sunday Trading Riots of 1855 (Hyde Park)

99–100, 122–23, 148–52, 165, 168, 170, 195, 199, 239
The Surprise (Lloyd Osborne's juvenile paper) 77
Symonds, John Addington 2–3, 24, 87, 190, 208; *Wine, Women and Song* 2, 54

Taine, Hippolyte 122
The Taunton Lifeboat 242
Taylor, Anya 196, 231
Taylor, Sir Henry and Lady 85
Tea 182–85; as temperance drink 183–84, 212, 240
Teare, James 152
The Temperance Intelligencer: "Temperance and Intemperance" (cover drawings) 125
The Temperance Lifeboat 242
Temple, Frederick (Bishop of Exeter) 152
Thackeray, William Makepeace 188, 231; "On the Genius of George Cruikshank" 136, 138, 141, 186
Thompson, F. M. L. 233, 235, 236, 238, 239
Thomson, Robert (Edinburgh schoolmaster) 85
Thomson, William (Archbishop of York) 173
"Thomson and Johnston" *see* "Johnston and Thomson"
Thornton, Cyril (punch master of Glasgow) 39
Times of London 56, 63, 106–8, 151; on youthful drinking 47
Toasts 38–39; as prods to drunkenness 50–1
Toxteth Park (Liverpool) 167
Tracy, Spencer 165
Traquair, Willie (RLS's cousin) 81
The Trial of John and Jane Temperance 187
The Trial of John Barleycorn Alias Strong Drink 187
Trollope, Anthony: on taste in wine and political party 21; *Can You Forgive Her?* 179–80

United Kingdom Alliance for the Suppression of the Traffic in All Intoxicating Liquors (U.K. Alliance) 99, 135, 146, 148, 158, 220, 236

Veeder, William 3, 145, 154–55, 190, 231
Vernon, J. R. 193, 199

Victoria, Queen, of England 51, 217
Victoria Park 123, 174–75
Victoria Wine Company 140, 219
Wedgwood, Julia 192, 241
Weir, R. M. 61
Wesley Chapel (London) 158
Westminster Review (J. S. Mill) 136
Whitaker, Thomas 1, 37, 52, 99, 106, 117, 119, 126, 128, 135, 167, 173, 177, 189, 198, 200, 216, 220, 222, 223, 237, 238; *Brightest England and the Way to It* 228; *Life's Battles in Temperance Armour* 142, 147, 152–53, 187, 207, 228
Whitechapel 22, 52; "Ripper" murders in 195
Whitman, Walt: *Franklin Evans; or The Inebriate* 64
Whitmore, B. W. 164
Wickes, David 206
Wiener, Martin J. 236, 242
Wight, John 136, 139, 141
Wightman, Julia 158
Wigley, John 148
Wilde, Oscar: *The Picture of Dorian Gray* 12
Willard, Frances 158
Wilson, George (Westminster grocer) 163
Wilson, H. J. 152
Wilson-Patten Act 99, 149
Winchester College: boys drinking beer with meals 48
Wine 19, 33, 40; in *J&H* 20–28 and *passim*; association with upper classes 21–25, 33, 50, 98
The Wine Spectator 26, 182
Wollstonecraft, Mary 118; *Maria*, 118; *Vindication of the Rights of Women* 118
Women: as campaigners for alcohol reform 158–60; as victims of drink 155–57
Women's Christian Temperance Union 158
Wordsworth, William 224, 233; "Benjamin the Waggoner" 42–43
Wright, Daniel 11–12, 196
Wuthering Heights (Emily Brontë) 66, 134

Yeats, William Butler 54

Zola, Emile: *L'Assommoir* 64

www.ingramcontent.com/pod-product-compliance
Lightning Source LLC
Chambersburg PA
CBHW051215300426
44116CB00006B/579